PITTSBURGH SERIES
IN
SOCIAL AND LABOR HISTORY

THE STEEL WORKERS

By

JOHN A. FITCH

With a new introduction by Roy Lubove

UNIVERSITY OF PITTSBURGH PRESS

Published by the University of Pittsburgh Press, Pittsburgh, Pa., 15260
Copyright © 1989, University of Pittsburgh Press
All rights reserved
Feffer and Simons, Inc., London
Manufactured in the United States of America

.

Library of Congress Cataloging in Publication Data

Fitch, John A. (John Andrews), 1881–1959
    The steel workers / by John A. Fitch, with a new introduction by
Roy Lubove.
        p.   cm. — (Pittsburgh series in social and labor history)
    Reprint. Originally published: Russell Sage Foundation, 1910.
    Bibliography: p.
    ISBN 0–8229–1153–1.   ISBN 0–8229–6091–5 (pbk.)
    1. Iron and steel workers—Pennsylvania—Pittsburgh.   I. Title.
II. Title: Steelworkers.   III. Series.
HD8039.I52U54   1989
331.7′669142′097—dc19   88 –19813
                                                                             CIP

CONTENTS

JOHN A. FITCH,
THE STEEL WORKERS,
AND THE CRISIS OF DEMOCRACY

ROY LUBOVE

THE LIFE work of John Andrews Fitch (1881–1959) was determined by a single, dramatic event. He accompanied his University of Wisconsin mentor, Professor John R. Commons, to Pittsburgh in the fall of 1907 when the Pittsburgh Survey was getting under way. Fitch remained in the field for nearly a year, and in 1910 his classic, *The Steel Workers,* was published by the Russell Sage Foundation. The Pittsburgh experience resulted in a lifetime commitment to the field of industrial relations, and the book insured his immortality.

Born in South Dakota, Fitch graduated in 1904 from Yankton College, taught history and civics at Weeping Water Academy, Nebraska, and entered the University of Wisconsin for graduate studies in political economy in 1906. After the Survey investigations, Fitch returned to Wisconsin for a year, but left without a degree to join the New York State Department of Labor (1909–10). He then served for nearly a decade (1911–19) as an editor and writer for the industrial department of *Survey,* the leading magazine of social work and social reform, edited by Paul U. Kellogg. He taught classes at the New York School of Social Work, beginning around 1917, and after accepting a full-time appointment, taught industrial relations until his retirement in 1946.[1]

During the *Survey* years, Fitch investigated and reported extensively on labor conditions in the mines and mills of the Colorado Fuel and Iron Company, a Rockefeller fiefdom, covering the violent strike of 1913–14. He wrote extensively about the testimony before the U.S. Commission on Industrial Relations, appointed by President Wilson in 1914. Fitch returned to Pittsburgh in 1919 to report on the steel strike. Although he is identified almost exclusively with a single book on the steel industry in Allegheny County, he prepared a broader study of the steel industry for *Survey* in 1911–12: "The Human Side of Large Outputs: Steel and Steel Workers in Six American States."[2]

Fitch's *Steel Workers* exemplified the aims of the Pittsburgh Survey as a whole. Its brilliant editor, Paul U. Kellogg, described the Survey as an attempt to consider "both civic and industrial conditions, and to consider them for the most part in their bearings upon the wage-earning population." Equally important, the Survey aspired to "reduce conditions to terms of household experience and human life."[3] And like the broader Survey, Fitch's work combined unprecedented scope and depth, the research skills of the social investigator, and the communication skills of the journalist.

Fitch examined, in exhaustive detail, the history and organization of the steel industry: labor force and unionism, machinery and technology, management. Employing seventy to eighty thousand men in Allegheny County, it was the master industry and thus a controlling influence in the social and civic life of the region. In a sense, the Pittsburgh Survey was an extended indictment of that influence. Edward Devine, secretary of the New York Charity Organization Society, condemned an industry in which the "mass of the workers . . . are driven as large numbers of laborers whether slave or free have scarcely before in human history been driven." In the years following the Survey, Fitch became the nation's most outspoken critic of the twelve-hour day, seven-day week—the basis of the industry's great productivity according to steel management, but the basis for the destruction of family life and citizenship, according to its critics. Everything, Devine pointed out, was "keyed up to it. Foremen and superintendents, and ultimately directors and financiers, are subject to its law."[4]

Fitch vividly portrayed the steel workers and their relation to each element in the technology of production: the blast furnace crews; the puddlers and rollers; the crucible, Bessemer, and open-hearth processes of steel making; the rolling mills. He examined the health and accident problems which inevitably flowed from the pressure of long hours and hazardous machinery, not to mention the speed-ups resulting from cuts in tonnage rates (a key management technique to control labor costs). Fitch provided a detailed history of unionization in the steel industry, and the uncompromising opposition on the part of the recently organized United States Steel Corporation (1901). But the steel industry's labor control policies were not limited to outright repression of union sentiment. Fitch deals with alternate techniques to manage the heterogeneous labor force. These were the experiments in welfare capitalism: accident prevention and compensation, pensions, stock ownership and bonuses (for supervisors).

The Steel Workers will always remain a valuable resource for understanding the structure of the steel industry in the first decade of the twentieth century. Yet I would contend that Fitch's vivid portrayal of steelmaking and steel labor was essentially the documentation for his real concern: the relationship between work and industrial relations, on the one hand, democracy, self-determination, and personal freedom, on the other. In this respect, also, Fitch captured the essence of the broader Pittsburgh Survey.

The harshest labor policies of the steel industry were embodied in the twelve-hour day, seven-day week, the speed-up, and above all, "in a system of repression that stifles initiative and destroys healthy citizenship." The latter, particularly, shocked Fitch when he first arrived in the Pittsburgh district in the fall of 1907. Having grown up on a farm in the Midwest, he was conscious of similarities between the farmers he knew and the skilled steelworkers he met for the first time: "there were the same shrewd common sense, the homespun wisdom, the evidence of character that made me feel comfortable among them."[5] The big difference was not in hardships experienced, but in personal freedom. The farmers were unafraid and outspoken. The steelworker, however, could not bargain over working conditions, could not publicly criticize his employer, and could not evade an atmosphere of intimidation and fear. All this was exceedingly strange and wrong for Fitch, a betrayal of the progressivism and populism of the Midwest, a denial of the spirit of democracy. Fitch's encounter with the Pittsburgh steel worker was a shock and a revelation, an event, he said, which "impressed me and roused me as nothing else in my life ever had." The spirit of midwestern agrarian progressivism could never reconcile itself to the regimentation and repression of the worker in the steel mills of America. Upon returning to the University of Wisconsin after his field work, he attended labor bill hearings at the state capital, and when he heard manufacturers oppose all labor legislation, he "raged inwardly" in his youthful zeal.[6]

The rage was accompanied by frustration. He had experienced a revelation, but the average, complacent, comfortably situated American understood nothing of the working people or their hardships. What did they know, for example, of life in the remote company towns belonging to the Colorado Fuel and Iron Company? The miner, even more than the steelworker, was a kind of latter-day serf. Fitch encountered, during his first visit to Colorado in 1911, the camp marshalls, company paid, deputized by the sheriff, who kept the mining towns closed to the outside world and arrested or beat union organizers. Were the fear, repression, and violence which characterized labor relations in Pittsburgh, Colorado, and elsewhere, the uncompromising bitterness on both sides, a vision of America's future as an industrial nation?

Fitch's perception that freedom, autonomy, and self-determination—the essential attributes of citizenship and democracy—were disintegrating in the context of contemporary industrial relations helps explain his relentless criticism of the twelve-hour day. The issue involved more than economics or health: for Fitch (and the Pittsburgh Survey) the issue was the survival of democracy. What could men whose work consumed their total existence contribute to their communities? How could they possibly fulfill the civic and family obligations necessary for a democratic society to function?

Industrial relations in the steel industry did not improve much between 1907 and 1919, when Fitch returned to the Pittsburgh district to report on the great steel strike. He visited mill towns, spoke to strikers, officials, police, ordinary citizens. Corporation spokesmen, newspapers, politicians all insisted the strike was inspired by the recent Russian Revolution and had to be repressed. Fitch dismissed these views as self-serving nonsense. The strike was about the right to organize and a reduction in working hours. As always, this was heresy to the steel companies, determined that the men would remain unorganized, silent, weak, with no channel for redress of grievances. The strike of 1919 dramatized the central issue—the logic of production and management in the steel industry clashed with the logic of citizenship in a democratic society. Unless hours were reduced to permit the leisure for self-cultivation and the time to socialize with family and friends, "there can be no opportunity for the development of good citizenship in the mill towns."[7] Any industry which required half its work force to toil twelve hours a day, seven days a week, was destroying the future of America.

There was only one resolution to the conflict between industrial organization and democracy. This was trade unionism which, in the industrial context, would satisfy the democratic imperative of self-determination. Self-determination, in turn, would put an end to the working conditions which adversely affected family life and civic obligation. As things stood, the absence of organization and collective bargaining on the part of the worker led, inexorably, to a "despotism of capital." A police state existed in Allegheny County, based on company espionage, spies, and the support of elected officials and police in the unrelenting campaign to repress unionism. Fitch found the workers of the United States Steel Corporation to be suspicious of each other, friends, neighbors. He was suspected of being a company agent.[8]

Fitch, in *The Steel Workers*, explored in considerable detail the other dimension of labor force control—the welfare programs of the steel industry. As early as 1883, the Carnegie Company decided to sell coal below market price to employees at its Edgar Thomson works in Braddock. It established a savings department and loaned money to employees for home building. Andrew Carnegie's gift of four million dollars led to the establishment of an accident and old age pension plan in 1902. This

was reorganized in 1910 following a United States Steel dona-
tion of eight million dollars. Relief and safety programs, along
with a stock subscription scheme instituted in 1903, were consolidated in 1911 in a Bureau of Safety, Relief, Sanitation, and
Welfare.

These welfare programs were desirable, but in Fitch's view
they were no substitute for unions and the self-determination
they would permit. Fitch did not idealize unionization, but there
was no alternative if American industrial relations were to be
made compatible with democratic ideals. The major institutions
of American society had failed the worker, especially the unskilled and foreign born. The employer regarded him as little
more than a factor of production. The church was reluctant to
criticize the steel companies in the mill and mining towns. Public
officials and police usually supported the employer in any conflict with labor. The courts were hostile and quick to issue
injunctions. And welfare capitalism was surely not the solution
to a system of industrial relations incompatible with citizenship
and democracy. It was fatally flawed by virtue of being unilateral
and conditional; it conferred no rights and stifled independence.
In Fitch's view, welfarism was "a policy that begins in a spirit of
apparent benevolence and ends in a spirit that is in sinister
opposition to democracy." It was feudalism in modern dress, a
denial rather than a fulfillment of rights. Despite the welfare
work, "sociological departments" and Sunday Schools, the true
spirit of the steel companies was expressed in "arrogance and
contempt for the rights both of their employees and of the
public."[9] The supreme irony of industrial relations in early
twentieth century America was that the steel companies, not the
labor organizers, threatened the welfare of American society:
"The only dangerous agitators are those who attempt to build an
industry on a foundation of wages too low to admit of decent
standards of family life, of hours too long to admit of proper rest
or relaxation, and of silence and acquiescence as the price of a
job."[10]

The Pittsburgh Survey was a masterpiece of social investigation which studied the relationship among work, worker, and
community life. Fitch's *Steel Workers* explored that theme in a

single industry, bringing into sharp focus the key concern of the Survey: worker, family, community, democracy in conflict with the prevailing system of industrial relations. The resolution of the conflict depended upon abolition of the twelve-hour day and other improvements in working conditions. These changes, in turn, necessitated the right to organize. The worker had to have an organized base of power in order to negotiate with powerful corporations. It was a prerequisite to democracy in an industrial age. A man who lacked any voice in something so vital as the conditions under which he worked was not a free man in a free country.

Fitch gave the steelworker a voice. He consciously and explicitly viewed his mission in this light. Fitch would have preferred that the worker speak for himself and control his own destiny, but American society was not yet prepared for this. Consider the views of L. M. Bowers, chairman of the board, Colorado Fuel and Iron Company, during the labor strife of 1913–14: "The main question, and in fact the only matter up between the United Mine Workers of America, and the Colorado Fuel and Iron Company, is recognition of the union, which we flatly refuse to do, or even meet with these agitators." Union labor meant inferior work, obstructions to the discharge of incompetents, and "numerous requirements that practically take away the mines from the control of the owners and operators and place them in the hands of . . . disreputable agitators, socialists and anarchists." If labor agitators and politicians "together with the cheap college professors and still cheaper writers in muckraking magazines . . . are permitted to assault the business men who have built up the great industries . . . it is time that vigorous measures are taken to put a stop to these vicious teachings."[11] Unionism, for Fitch, was the alternative to the cycles of repression and violence that characterized American industrial relationships, but as long as the employer and the community refused to acknowledge this, and as long as the worker had no voice in his destiny, Fitch did not have to apologize for his role. If, like the broader progressive reform movement, this role embodied a degree of paternalism, it could not be helped at this point in American industrial history.

xiii

NOTES

1. Biographical material about Fitch is scarce. Helpful for this purpose are William Graebner, "John Andrews Fitch," in *Biographical Dictionary of Social Welfare in America*, ed. Walter I. Trattner (New York, 1986), pp. 288–90; Steven Roy Cohen, "Reconciling Industrial Conflict and Democracy: The 'Pittsburgh Survey' and the Growth of Social Research in the United States," Ph.D. diss., Columbia University, 1981.

2. The six articles in this study are: "Lackawanna—Swamp, Mill, and Town," *Survey* 27 (Oct. 7, 1911): 929–45; "Illinois: Boosting for Safety," *Survey* 27 (Nov. 4, 1911): 1145–60; "Bethlehem: The Church and the Steel Workers," *Survey* 27 (Dec. 2, 1911): 1285–98; "Birmingham District: Labor Conservation," *Survey* 27 (Jan. 6, 1912): 1527–40; "The Steel Industry and the People in Colorado," *Survey* 27 (Feb. 3, 1912): 1706–20; "The Labor Policies of Unrestricted Capital," *Survey* 28 (April 6, 1912): 17–27.

Besides *The Steel Workers* and dozens of articles, mostly in *Survey*, Fitch published four other books: *The Causes of Industrial Unrest* (New York, 1924); *Capital and Labor* (Chicago, 1929); *Vocational Guidance in Action* (New York, 1935); *Social Responsibilities of Organized Labor* (New York, 1957).

3. Paul U. Kellogg, "The Spread of the Survey Idea," New York Academy of Political Science, *Proceedings* (1911–12), p. 476.

4. Edward T. Devine, "Results of the Pittsburgh Survey," *American Journal of Sociology* 14 (March 1909): 664, 663.

5. John A. Fitch, "Old Age at Forty," *American Magazine* 71 (March 1911): 655; Fitch, *Social Responsibilities of Organized Labor*, p. xii.

6. Letter from Fitch to Cara Cook, Nov. 5, 1924, quoted in Cohen, "Reconciling Industrial Conflict and Democracy," p. 67.

7. John A. Fitch, "The Closed Shop and Other Industrial Issues of the Steel Srike," *Survey* 43 (Nov. 8, 1919): 86.

8. See *The Steel Workers*, chap. 16.

9. Fitch, "The Labor Policies of Unrestricted Capital," p. 27.

10. Ibid.

11. Quoted in John A. Fitch, "What Rockefeller Knew and What He Did," *Survey* 34 (Aug. 21, 1915): 462–64.

THE STEEL WORKERS

The Twelve-hour Day

THE STEEL WORKERS

By

JOHN A. FITCH

FELLOW, UNIVERSITY OF WISCONSIN, 1908–09; EXPERT, NEW
YORK STATE DEPARTMENT OF LABOR, 1909–10

THE PITTSBURGH SURVEY
FINDINGS IN SIX VOLUMES

EDITED BY
PAUL UNDERWOOD KELLOGG

NEW YORK
CHARITIES PUBLICATION
COMMITTEE . . . . . MCMX

PRESS OF WM. F. FELL CO.,
PHILADELPHIA

EDITOR'S FOREWORD

BOUND by a hundred ties to the dramatic story of the Pittsburgh people, this inquiry is, nevertheless, of more than local significance. Steel is a basic industry in America. It has been a beneficiary of the most fiercely contested governmental policies since Civil War times. Its products enter into every tool and structure and means of traffic in civilization. By the side of half a hundred mill sites along the Ohio and its tributaries, at our newest lake ports and above the old mineral beds of the Superior Basin; in the sun-baked Southwest, in the mountain valleys of the New South, and, by anticipation, in the ore regions of Alaska, what men may earn by digging, reducing, rolling, and fabricating this master metal, what leisure and resource they may gain in the process of it all, set the standards of life for hundreds of communities. A constructive statesmanship demands that Americans look well to what those standards tend to become for so numerous and vital an element in the population.

Moreover, the largest employer of steel workers in Pittsburgh is the largest employer of steel workers in the country as a whole; and the largest employer of labor in America today. That employer is in the saddle. So far as the mills and the shifts that man them go, the steel operators possess what many another manager and industrial president has hankered after and has been denied—untrammeled control. What has this exceptional employer done with this exceptional control over the human forces of production? Here our findings state concretely the problems of an industrial democracy in ways which cannot be lightly thrust aside.

Such a social interpretation of steel making could not but bulk large in the scheme of the Pittsburgh Survey. It depicts the industry which gives wealth and business preëminence to the region, which directly determines the well-being of a great company of wage-earners and their families, and which influences all other lines of employment in and about Pittsburgh. Mr. Fitch deals with the work-relationships of the steel men. The family end of their wages problem is the subject of Miss Byington's "Homestead: The Households of a Mill Town." Of the series of six books in which the Pittsburgh Survey is published, these two, therefore, are companion volumes. Mr. Fitch entered upon his commission without any promptings other than the general instincts toward an independent, resourceful citizenship inbred by the spirit of the Northwestern prairies and that quickening sense of economic justice which stirs the University of Wisconsin. To Professor John R. Commons of that University, both for his initial field work and for his consecutive suggestions and advice, author and editor are indebted. For information and insight, acknowledgment is due to steel workers of the greater city and the neighboring mill towns, Braddock, Duquesne, Homestead, McKeesport, to engineers, foremen, superintendents and higher corporation officials, many of whom are facing in their every-day work problems which are beyond the power of isolated men to solve.

Underlying the initial reasons for such a portrayal of labor conditions in the steel industry, is another reason which developed in the course of the inquiry, and which, as with the Mariner's tale, leaves no choice open as to the telling. The issues which Mr. Fitch takes up are of a sort which are not publicly discussed in the mill towns of the Pittsburgh district. Old employes do not dare petition their employers to consider them. Men have been discharged for calling meetings to discuss them. It would mean instant dismissal for large numbers of men should they act together to affect these things in the way that farmers would take up freight rates or the price of apples at a grange hall; and dismissal would mean the entire dislocation of life. An old resident is quoted by Miss Byington as saying, "If you want to talk in Homestead, you must talk to yourself."

It is fully time to bring these issues out into the open, where a man will not risk his livelihood by discussing it. That is the manner of America.

As the author points out, the steel industry could be interpreted from other points of view,—from that of its tremendous administrative burdens, of its fierce commercial competition in the past, of its wonderful technical progress. For these there are many spokesmen. Mr. Fitch makes articulate what the steel industry means to the men who are employed in it—for whom it makes up the matter of life, and who have no voice.

PAUL U. KELLOGG
Director Pittsburgh Survey

TABLE OF CONTENTS

xxiii

LIST OF TABLES

THE STEEL WORKERS

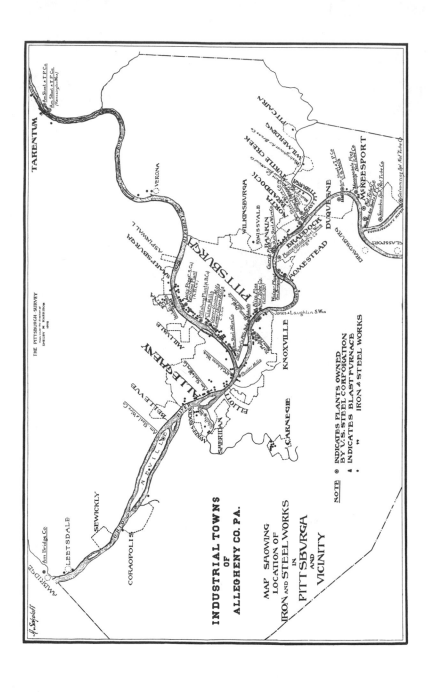

J. Sololoff

THE PITTSBURGH SURVEY
Directed under the direction of
SHELBY M. HARRISON
1908

INDUSTRIAL TOWNS
OF
ALLEGHENY CO. PA.

MAP SHOWING
LOCATION OF
IRON AND STEEL WORKS
IN
PITTSBURGH
AND
VICINITY

NOTE ⊚ INDICATES PLANTS OWNED
BY U.S. STEEL CORPORATION
▲ INDICATES BLAST FURNACE
" • IRON & STEEL WORKS

CHAPTER I

INTRODUCTORY

THERE is a glamor about the making of steel. The very size of things—the immensity of the tools, the scale of production—grips the mind with an overwhelming sense of power. Blast furnaces, eighty, ninety, one hundred feet tall, gaunt and insatiable, are continually gaping to admit ton after ton of ore, fuel, and stone. Bessemer converters dazzle the eye with their leaping flames. Steel ingots at white heat, weighing thousands of pounds, are carried from place to place and tossed about like toys. Electric cranes pick up steel rails or fifty-foot girders as jauntily as if their tons were ounces. These are the things that cast a spell over the visitor in these workshops of Vulcan. The display of power on every hand, majestic and illimitable, is overwhelming; you must go again and yet again before it is borne in upon you that there is a human problem in steel production.

The purpose of this study is other than to paint word pictures of steel making, or to describe processes for engineer or metallurgist; the purpose is rather to discuss iron and steel, not in terms of ore, and tonnage, and machinery, but in terms of the working life. However ponderous the machinery, somewhere men are controlling its movements. However automatic a process, it is under the guidance of human intelligence. The glare of the fires, the tumult of the converters, the throb of the engines are less wonderful, less difficult of comprehension than the lives of the men who control and guide.

The human problem in the iron and steel industry is more than a labor problem, for it reaches beyond the questions of hours and wages, and beyond the relations of employer with employe, and touches vitally the principles of democracy itself.

It is a problem modified and complicated by many separate and more or less unrelated forces. The nineteenth century was one of constant development in the metal trades. In the later seventies and early eighties came the substitution of steel for iron; in the past fifteen years, the steel industry itself has been practically revolutionized, and so rapid and continuous is this movement that today is in advance of yesterday and tomorrow will see today's record eclipsed. Yet there were forces at work half a century ago that have a bearing upon the present situation; the rise of trade unionism in the iron industry, its rise and fall in the steel industry, the policies of the union, its successes and its failures,—all have contributed their part. Moreover, the cut-throat competition between the leading steel companies and the consolidation of their interests in the greatest employing corporation of the times, contributed directly to making conditions what they are.

The labor problem in the steel industry is not a new one therefore; it is rather a developing one. Each of these three great organic changes, involving in turn the machinery, the men, and the management, has affected it.

Through the revolutionary changes in method, machinery has displaced men to a remarkable extent. The proportion of skilled steel workers needed for the operation of a plant has decreased. At the same time, the large companies have so increased their capacity that they are employing more men than ever before, until today 60 per cent of the men employed in the steel industry are unskilled, and that 60 per cent is greater in numbers than was the total working force twenty years ago. The demand for unskilled labor in the steel industry has made Pittsburgh, during the last dozen years especially, a veritable Mecca to the immigrant. Steel manufacturers have not been at all averse to the rush of foreigners to the mills, for southeastern Europeans are well adapted to the necessities of the industry. For example, of the nearly 7000 men employed at Homestead, more than half are Slavs, and two-thirds are foreign born. Thus a race problem has been added to the labor problem, complicating it.

There were labor troubles in the late forties in the Pittsburgh iron mills. In 1858 a few puddlers of unusual temerity met and formed a labor union which by the end of the sixties had a national organization with some thousands of members, and occupied a

4

position of strength. Later, other trades of iron workers were organized, and in 1876 four separate organizations in Pittsburgh came together to form the Amalgamated Association of Iron and Steel Workers. Prior to 1860 the employers, practically untrammeled by any trade-union restrictions, had been free to bring their best efforts to the adjustment of conditions. That the men were not satisfied with the conditions thus adjusted is evidenced by the steady growth of the unions from that time to 1892, when the Amalgamated Association reported a membership of over 24,000. During this period of thirty years the employes made definite and conscious efforts to control working conditions. In 1892 came the famous Homestead strike, and with the failure of that strike the power of the union was broken. By 1901 the Amalgamated Association had been driven from every important steel mill in the country. Since that time the employers have again been free to work out their own policies.

But unionism and non-unionism are bound up with a third and larger movement. The formation of the United States Steel Corporation has brought more than 50 per cent of the steel workers of the country under one employer, with a resulting promotion of uniformity of conditions of labor. Administrative decisions from a single head affect, without chance of protest, vast masses of men.

These are the facts historically considered. They give us the bearings of work which in America offers a livelihood to a quarter of a million men. This book deals with conditions in 1907 and 1908 in Allegheny County, Pennsylvania, which for forty years has been the producing center of the iron and steel industry in the United States. In the course of stupendous changes in processes and in corporate organization, unionism has been driven out from the mills of this Pittsburgh District. With its elimination has come an increase in hours until the eight-hour day has practically disappeared. A majority of the employes engaged in processes of making steel work twelve hours. Many work seven days in the week, either without a full day of rest or with a free Sunday one week and twenty-four hours of continuous duty the next. Speeding-up methods have augmented production in every department. Even where no new processes or machines have been introduced, the output has increased and in many cases is double

5

what it was fifteen years ago. The stress inevitable under such a system of work is heightened by the heat and dangers of accident which are to be found in handling a great tonnage of molten metal. There are positions commonly spoken of as "hot jobs," where men work close to ladles of fluid iron or steel, or where heat radiates from ingots and from furnaces. Such positions are uncomfortable, to say the least, at any season of the year; but when a July sun is blazing upon the roof they are wellnigh intolerable. These physical conditions, coupled with the prolonged tension, result at many points in the working life of the mills in human overstrain.

Entering into the relations between the Steel Corporation and its employes are two co-operative factors: a restricted scheme of stock-ownership by employes, and, more recently, the development of a system of preventing accidents in which committees of the men are enlisted. These in no wise affect or limit the underlying labor policy in both Corporation and independent mills. That is a determination to control, in pursuance of which object the employers inflexibly exclude the men from any voice in the conditions of their employment. Consistent with this policy, repressive measures have been introduced designed to enable the companies to retain the advantages which they gained for themselves when they eliminated the unions. These measures are doubtless intended to preserve industrial efficiency, but they have resulted in a thorough-going and far-reaching censorship that curtails free speech and the free activity of citizens. The effect of these measures is seen in every department of community life wherever, in Allegheny County, steel is made.

There is one issue the strands of which run unbroken through all the complicated forces mentioned, indistinct at first because uncertainly defined, but standing out finally clear and unmistakable,—responsibility. However divided this responsibility may have been at different periods in the history of the industry, control is today in the hands of the employers. They can change or continue conditions at their will. And beside this issue is another and mightier one,—that of democracy. Through all the following pages of this book it is hoped that these issues will not for one moment be forgotten. With them in mind, the facts presented become a question and a challenge.

6

PART I
THE MEN AND THE TOOLS

A Group of Skilled Men—Americans

CHAPTER II

THE WORKMEN

IT is estimated that between 70,000 and 80,000 men are employed in the manufacture of steel in Allegheny County. Their homes are clustered about the mills along the rivers, they are clinging to the bluffs of the South Side, and they are scattered over Greater Pittsburgh from Woods Run to the East End. Up the Monongahela valley are the mill towns—Homestead of Pinkerton fame, Braddock with its record-breaking mills and furnaces, Duquesne, where the unit of weight is a hundred tons, and McKeesport, home of the "biggest tube works on earth." Here are countrymen of Kossuth and Kosciusko, still seeking the blessings of liberty, but through a different channel,—high wages and steady employment. Here are British, German and Scandinavian workmen, full of faith in the new world democracy; and here are Americans, great-grandsons of Washington's troopers, and sons of men who fought at Gettysburg.

Fully 60 per cent of these men are unskilled; but the remaining 40 per cent, the skilled and semi-skilled, are the men who give character to the industry. This is the class from which foremen and superintendents and even the steel presidents have been recruited, and it is the class that furnishes the brains of the working force. It is of them, chiefly, that this book is written.

In a ten months' residence in the Pittsburgh District—eight months in the city of Pittsburgh and two months in the town of Homestead—I visited once every large mill in Allegheny County, and most of them I entered repeatedly in company with the regular mill guides, with officials of the steel companies, and with men well acquainted with steel manufacture but now in no way connected with the industry. Skilled workmen also volunteered their services and I owe much to the painstaking care with which they explained the part performed by labor in the process of iron and

9

steel manufacture, from the blast furnaces to the piling beds. I watched the men at work under all sorts of conditions and in all sorts of positions, and often I talked with them as they rested between heats or during a "spell."

To understand these men you must first of all see them thus at their work; you must stand beside the open-hearth helper as he taps fifty tons of molten steel from his furnace; you must feel the heat of the Bessemer converter as you watch the vesselmen and the steel pourer; and above the crash and roar of the blooming mills you must talk with rollers and hookers, while five- and ten-ton steel ingots plunge madly back and forth between the rolls. You must see the men working in hoop mills and guide mills, where the heat is intense and the work laborious; you must see them amid ladles of molten steel, among piles of red hot bars, or bending over the straightening presses at the rail mills.

But the visitor in a steel mill may see only faces reddened by the glare of fire and hot steel, muscles standing out in knots and bands on bare arms, clothing frayed with usage and begrimed by machinery. The men do not differ materially from other workmen, and the visitor passes on and forgets them. The world is full of men in greasy overalls.

To really know them you must see them at home. There the muscular feats of the heater's helper and the rough orders of the furnace boss are alike forgotten, and you find them kindly, open-hearted, human. You grow into an understanding of them as they tell of hopes and plans or mistakes and failures, and understanding becomes sympathy as it comes home to you how close some half-spoken ambition or disappointment presses in upon them. Through the courtesy of friends, I obtained introductions to leading steel workers and these in turn gave me the names of others, paving the way for visits at their homes and long talks at the end of a "turn." In this way I got close to the lives and experience of typical skilled and semi-skilled men.

The skilled workers are generally of Anglo-Saxon, German or Celtic origin, the largest proportion being American born. They are not educated so far as school and university training are concerned, but they are graduates in the school of experience. By way of opening up a view of the general situation, I shall introduce some of these men and let them talk as they talked to me. Of course, the things they speak of could be taken up from another point of view,—that of the employer. These are the issues of life as seen by the men themselves. And we shall be in better position to disentangle these issues and study each one, if we see at the outset how, not singly but in combination, they enter into the work-experience of the individual man.

John Griswold is a Scotch-Irish furnace boss who came to America and got a laborer's position at a Pittsburgh blast furnace when the common labor force was largely Irish. Those were the days before the advent of the "furriners." I sat in Griswold's sitting room in his four-room cottage one evening and he told me about the men who work at the furnaces, and about the "long turn."*

"Mighty few men have stood what I have, I can tell you. I've been twenty years at the furnaces and been workin' a twelve-hour day all that time, seven days in the week. We go to work at seven in the mornin' and we get through at night at six. We work that way for two weeks and then we work the long turn and change to the night shift of thirteen hours. The long turn is when we go on at seven Sunday mornin' and work through the whole twenty-four hours up to Monday mornin'. That puts us onto the night turn for the next two weeks, and the other crew onto the day. The next time they get the long turn and we get twenty-four hours off, but it don't do us much good. I get home at about half past seven Sunday mornin' and go to bed as soon as I've had breakfast. I get up about noon so as to get a bit o' Sunday to enjoy, but I'm tired and sleepy all the afternoon. Now, if we had eight hours it would be different. I'd start to work, say, at six and I'd be done at two and I'd come home, and after dinner me and the missus could go to the park if we wanted to, or I could take the childer to the country where there ain't any saloons. That's the danger,—the childer runnin' on the streets and me with no time to take them any place else. That's what's driven the Irish out of the industry. It ain't the Hunkies,—they couldn't do it,—but the Irish don't have to work this way. There was

* See Chapter XIII.

fifty of them here with me sixteen years ago and now where are
they? I meet 'em sometimes around the city, ridin' in carriages
and all of them wearin' white shirts, and here I am with these
Hunkies. They don't seem like men to me hardly. They can't
talk United States. You tell them something and they just look
and say 'Me no fustay, me no fustay,' that's all you can get out
of 'em. And I'm here with them all the time, twelve hours a day
and every day and I'm all alone,—not a mother's son of 'em that
I can talk to. Everybody says I'm a fool to stay here, —I dunno,
mebbe I am. It don't make so much difference though. I'm
gettin' along, but I don't want the kids ever to work this way.
I'm goin' to educate them so they won't have to work twelve
hours."

There is a considerable difference between a blast furnace
foreman and a Bessemer steel pourer. The furnace man gets rather
low wages for a twelve-hour day and seven-day working week,
while the steel pourer is well paid and works eight hours a day
for six days in the week. It was Jerry Flinn who told me how
he had worked up from his first job as laborer to a position as steel
pourer. I met him just as he got home from the mill one day,
and I asked how he managed to work only an eight-hour shift
when other men had to work twelve. He told me that attempts
have been made to introduce a twelve-hour day in the Bessemer department but without success. Two Pittsburgh mills have
tried it and both went back to the eight-hour day because the
heat is so great as to make it impossible for the men to work
longer.

"It must be hard," said Flinn, "for the twelve-hour men to
have to work alongside of us eight-hour men. During the twelve
hours of their day they work with all three crews of the eight-
hour men. One crew gets through and goes home soon after the
twelve-hour men come out, the next crew works its eight hours
and goes home, and the third crew comes out before those twelve-
hour fellows can quit. The eight-hour men get a lot more pleasure
out of life than the twelve-hour men do. We can go to enter-
tainments and social affairs as we couldn't if we had to get up
next morning and go to work at six o'clock."

12

Flinn is fifty-two years old, and he tells you that his strength is not up to what it was, say, fifteen years ago. The men who went to work with him as young men are nearly all dead, and today he is one of the oldest men in his mill. He speaks lightly of the danger of accidents,* and says that he has encountered only the minor ones. Once when they were changing stoppers, the crane dropped the old one just as it swung clear of the edge of the ladle. It fell on him, burning him and breaking his leg. At another time he failed to lower the stopper in time, and the stream of molten steel struck the edge of a mold as the train was shifted; it splashed onto the platform, burning his legs so severely that for six weeks afterwards he was unable to turn over in bed. It is a common thing for metal to fly that way; the sparks strike his face, they lodge in his nose or his ears, and once he nearly lost the sight of an eye. He refers to these things as trifles.

What I said of the half concealed disappointments which are real and tragic in the life of a steel worker, would have been clear to you had you heard the story of Robert Smith, as he told it himself. As a boy he went to work in the coal mines of eastern Pennsylvania and did not get into the mills until he was about thirty years old. Then he came to Pittsburgh, took a laborer's position, and began to work up slowly year after year until he occupied a place of some importance, though not in the first class of skilled men. After he had been there a few years, a labor difficulty occurred in this mill and he left and went to another plant where he took a position similar to his last one. As a new man he could not advance as rapidly as he might have done in the old mill, and before he could get into the best of standing he was thrown out of work by further labor troubles. He secured a position in another mill where he remained for two years till forced by a strike to seek work in a fourth mill. Here he remained for ten years in a subordinate position. At the end of that time he was promoted and became, for the first time in his life, the first man in the crew. Then, in some way, he incurred the dislike of the superintendent, and the man on the opposite shift worked against him because he wanted Smith's job for a friend.

* See Chapter VII.

So, after working for three years in a position for which, as he said, he had served a ten years' apprenticeship, Smith again lost his place and was obliged to apply for work in still another mill. He had been a leader in the union, and a feeling almost religious in its devotion bound him to it. To get into this new mill he had to agree to give up his union card. Today he says that he is a strong union man at heart, but his connection with the union is over. Now, at nearly sixty years of age, he is working in a semi-skilled position, although fitted to take his place among men of the best skill and to handle a crew.

Smith is a man of more than ordinary intelligence. He is a man of religious inclinations and a church member. He regrets the twelve-hour day now chiefly on the ground that it keeps the young men away from church. If he had not become a church member when he had an eight-hour day, he doesn't see how he ever could have become interested in religious matters. He lives in a comfortable home which he owns and where he spends most of his time when not in the mill. After supper he sits down to read for a short time before going to bed, but he told me with considerable regret that he was unable to do any systematic reading. A few years ago he read several of Shakespeare's plays, but he had to force himself to do it, he gets sleepy so soon after supper. Since that time he has not attempted anything more serious than the daily paper.

Jim Barr is a man thirty-five years old who came from England when he was a small boy. It has been only during the last ten years or so that Barr has worked in a steel mill, but he has lived in the steel district longer than that. He occupies a skilled position in one of the mills, where at the time I visited him he was working an eleven-hour day one week, and the next, a thirteen-hour night. On alternate Sundays he had the long turn of twenty-four hours. This Sunday work, he told me, came in after the union had been driven out, and the twelve-hour day is more general now than it was under unionism.

"Tell me, how can a man get any pleasure out of life working that way?"—Barr asked me this almost with a challenge. We were sitting before the grate in his comfortable and tastefully furnished parlor. There were pictures on the wall, a carpet on the floor, and the piano in the corner spoke of other things than endless drudgery. He seemed to interpret my swift glance about the room, for he went on, "I've got as good a home here as a man could want. It's comfortable and I enjoy my family. But I only have these things to think about. I'm at work most of the day, and I'm so tired at night that I just go to bed as soon as I've eaten supper. I have ideas of what a home ought to be, all right, but the way things are now I just eat and sleep here."

Barr works in a position where he encounters considerable heat, and he says that alone is very exhausting even when a man does not do hard physical labor. There is great danger, too, in the sweat that keeps a man's clothing wet all the time. If he gets into a draught he is likely to contract a cold or pneumonia. Working under such conditions shortens a man's life, to Barr's mind, and although he is only thirty-five years old he tells you he feels a decline in his strength. The men find that it costs more to live, too, when working in the mills, for they need the best of food and the warmest clothing in order to keep going. The little chance for recreation leads them to the saloons as the natural place for relaxation. They go there much oftener, in his opinion, than they would if they had more time for social enjoyment; and of course a good deal of money is spent there that is needed for other things. He says that men frequently spend twenty dollars in a single night after pay day. But the thing on which Barr seems to have the strongest conviction is the plan of the United States Steel Corporation of issuing stock to employes.* It's a scheme, he claims, to keep out unionism and prevent the men from protesting against bad conditions.

Now, just by way of contrast, listen to the story of George Hudson, who occupies a position similar to that of Barr, and has been in mill work about the same length of time. After having tried another line and found it unsatisfactory, Hudson came to the mills when about thirty years of age. He did what American young men dislike very much to do,—he took a common laborer's position along with the "Hunkies." Being a man of perseverance

* See Chapter XVI; also Appendix V, p. 306.

15

and some education, he worked up very rapidly until he now occupies a skilled position.

"The Steel Corporation is a fine one to work for," said Hudson to me with enthusiasm. "It gives every man a chance for promotion, and listens to every workman who has a plan for improvement. All the intelligent men are satisfied. If you can find any dissatisfied men, you will find that they are men who would be discontented anywhere you put them. Take the way they loan money to men who want to build homes. A good many men have their own cottages now just because the company helped them. The company has a savings department, too, and it pays 5 per cent on all deposits, and that is more than the savings banks pay. Then, on the other hand, it charges only 5 per cent interest on the money loaned, and that is a lower rate than you can get anywhere else. The company owns houses which it rents to employes at 30 per cent or more below what other people charge. I pay twenty-five dollars rent, and I've got a friend in a company house which is better than mine, and he pays only eighteen."

Hudson is ambitious, and he was very proud that his department during recent months had succeeded in beating all previous records known.

To turn to the question of church attendance raised by Smith in our talk before his fire,—if number of organizations were any criterion, the churches in the mill towns would be strong. I found a considerable number of loyal church members among the steel workers. Such of them as have to work on Sunday chafe under the necessity that drives them to disregard the Sabbath. Especially does this bear heavily on the wife who must attend church alone, while her husband is in the mill or at the furnaces. A Scotch Presbyterian mother at whose home I called one afternoon, just as the man was preparing to go to the mill for the night, spoke regretfully of having left Scotland. They might not have been able to live so well there, but "Oh, man, we could have brought up the childer in the fear o' God and in a land where men reverence the Sabbath." There are, too, men like Smith who fear the effect of twelve-hour work on the morality of the boys.

In spite of this religious sentiment which exists among the

ONE OF THE TWENTY-SIX PER CENT AMERICAN BORN

In the Light of a Five-ton Ingot

workers, there is, on the other hand, a good deal of feeling that the churches do not understand the needs of the workingmen.* Frank Robinson, for instance, believes that they are not interested in some problems which are very real to him.

"There are a good many churches in this borough," he said to me one day, "and they are supported generally by the women. The preachers don't have any influence in securing better conditions for the men,—they don't try to have. They never visit the mills, and they don't know anything about the conditions the men have to face. They think the men ought to go to church after working twelve hours Saturday night. The preachers could accomplish a lot if they would try to use their influence in the right direction; let them quit temperance reform until they get better conditions for the men. It's no time to preach to a man when he's hungry; feed him first, then preach to him. The same thing with a workingman; get a decent working day with decent conditions, then ask him to stop drinking. Let the preachers go into the mills and see the men at work in the heat, and outside the mills let them notice the men with crushed hands or broken arms or with a leg missing. If they would stop their preaching long enough to look around a little they could do something for us, if they wanted to try."

Unionism is not entirely dead in the mill towns; at least the spirit of it is to be found among the men, though the form is absent. Some of them expect to see again an organization in the mills. Others have given up hope of gaining shorter hours or higher wages through collective bargaining, and are looking for government interference and a legal eight-hour day. There is considerable variety of opinion as to how this is to be brought about. Pittsburgh steel workers are traditionally republican in politics; Speaker Cannon himself does not fear "tinkering" with the tariff more than they. The majority of them have been hoping that their representatives would after a while consider and pass the labor legislation that the workingmen desire. However, there has been much loss of faith in the last few years.

A good many men in the mills are socialists at heart, and

* See Chapter XVII.

though they still vote the republican ticket, they would vote with the socialists if that party were to manifest strength enough to give it a chance of carrying an election. A considerable number of others have gone the whole way and are active working socialists. One of these is Ed Jones, a skilled steel worker. He was left an orphan, came to Pittsburgh from New York as a boy of eighteen years, and worked for a short time as a laborer in one of the mills. After trying his hand at several unskilled trades he went back to a small mill in New York, where his wages were $1.25 a day. He was determined to work up in the industry, and after a year or so as a laborer he found himself in a semi-skilled position with wages correspondingly better. A year or two later he returned to Pittsburgh and at length secured a skilled position at $5.00 a day. Since then, in spite of reverses, he has worked up slowly until now he holds one of the most important positions in his mill. Jones has never been a union man. He says that he does not believe in unions, because they accomplish things only in prosperous times and go to pieces in a panic. "It is no use for them to try to regulate wages, anyhow," he says, "for labor is a commodity and its price is regulated by supply and demand. The only way out for the laboring men is to get together in a labor party,"—and this to him means the socialist party.

"We must go back to the condition when workmen owned their own tools," declares Jones. "We must own the instruments of production. Labor is now the helpless victim of capital, and capital must be overthrown. The workman is given enough to buy food and clothes for himself, and no more if the capitalist can help himself. They keep these workmen employed twelve hours a day at some work, while if every man in the country would work two hours a day, all the labor that would be necessary to support the population of the country could be performed. Now all of this excess, this ten hours over the necessary amount, goes to the employer in profits, and many people throughout the country are living in idleness because other people are working overtime for them." Jones himself is in comfortable circumstances; he owns his house and he owns some United States Steel stock, but he says he is one out of thirty-eight men in his whole plant who could have done as well.

One of the near-socialists who hopes for both unionism and

governmental relief, gave me a statement of his belief one Sunday afternoon as I sat in a comfortable chair in his little parlor. "I think there will be a labor organization in the mills again," he said. "It may not come in our day, but it is bound to come; the men will be driven to it. There would be a union now but for the foolishness of the men. They begin to talk as soon as a movement is started, and of course the news reaches the ears of the bosses before the organization is really on its feet. Then the men, who are not in a position to resist, are threatened with discharge. That has happened in this very mill. It may be that political action will be necessary before a union will be possible. There are two things that we've got to have,—an eight-hour day and restriction of immigration. I think that we will have to get together in a labor party. I'm not a socialist myself, though quite a good many of the mill men are, and there are a good many things about socialism that I like, all right. I would vote with them if I thought they were going to win and there are others who feel the same way. I used to vote the republican ticket, but I'm tired of it. They haven't done much for the workingmen when you consider the length of time they've been in power. I'm disgusted with the whole thing and I haven't voted at all for several years."

Several of the men had said to me: "Go to see Joe Reed; he can tell you more about the mills than anyone else." So one day I climbed the hill to his home, and found him. I had been led to expect a good deal and was not disappointed, though he was just recovering from an illness and was unable to talk as much as I had hoped. Reed is just the man that one would pick as a leader,—six feet tall, broad shouldered, with strong, intelligent features,—and he was in truth a leader of the Amalgamated Association years ago, before the steel mills became non-union. He took a prominent part in a strike that was of considerable importance in the steel district. He is a skilled man, and if he had cast his lot with the company in the dispute, it is quite likely that he would have best served his personal interests. But he stood by the men, and when the strike was lost Reed left the steel district. He might have had his former position again, but he was too proud to ask for it and lived away from Pittsburgh until the bitterness engendered by the struggle had begun to die out. After several years he came back and got a job again in a Pittsburgh steel mill. It is a non-union mill and of course Reed is a non-union man.

Reed told me how during the strike he had received letters of encouragement from all over the country, from men prominent in many walks of life. I asked him what he had done with them. He shook his head. "I burned them," he said, "when I came back to the mills. I have nothing in my possession now which would suggest in any way that I ever had connection with the union. When I came back here, I knew I was coming to a non-union mill and I took a job in good faith as a non-union man. That is a chapter in the history of my life that is ended. The whole matter of unionism is a thing of the past, and as an employe in this mill, I have no part in it." This fine sense of honor in conforming to the new régime is not so unusual among men of his sort as some people would expect.

These are the steel workers. I have not chosen extreme cases; on the contrary, it has been my aim to select men who are typical of a class,—the serious, clear-headed men, rather than the irresponsibles,—and with one exception, each case is fairly representative of a large group. The exception is the man whom I called Hudson. Not over three men out of the hundred and more with whom I talked at length indicated like sentiments, and he is the only one who gave them such full expression. It should be understood that these are the skilled men,—it is only among the skilled that opinions are so intelligently put forth. The number of positions requiring skill is not large, relatively speaking, and competition for them is keen. The consequence is that the skilled workers are a picked body of men. Through a course of natural selection the unfit have been eliminated and the survivors are exceptionally capable and alert of mind, their wits sharpened by meeting and solving difficulties. Through this disciplinary process have risen men like John Jarrett, consul at Birmingham during Harrison's administration; Miles Humphreys, now chief of the fire department of the Smoky City; M. M. Garland, collector of customs for Pittsburgh; A. R. Hunt, general superintendent at Homestead; Taylor Alderdice, vice-president of the National Tube Company; A. C. Dinkey, president of the Carnegie Steel Company; and W. B. Dickson, vice-president of the United States Steel Corporation.

In telling about their fellows who are numbered today among the rank and file, I have tried to introduce the leading types,—the twelve-hour man, the eight-hour man, the church member, the man who is at outs with the church, the union man and the socialist. There are many others who talk and think as Flinn and Smith and Robinson do, and I could furnish examples of much more radical thought and speech. These are typical cases representing different degrees of skill and different shades of opinion. It is highly significant that there are such men as these in the Pittsburgh mills. In a discussion of the labor problem in the steel industry, it must be borne in mind that these men are more than workers; they are thinkers, and must be reckoned with.

That representative workmen in one of the great groups of American manufactures regard their employment in such light, that there are more than 70,000 men so employed in a single county, means that the issues of life and labor as they see them may become formidable matters both in industry and in popular sovereignty. These opinions have in part been molded by the conditions in which the men have spent their lives. With such men in mind, the elemental forces, the heat, the speed, the hugeness of the appliances for reducing, melting, lifting and rolling out the tonnage of steel and iron, to be described in the next chapters, will be of more than technical interest. They react powerfully on human nature. To arrive at an understanding of the labor issues in their broader bearings, we must thus familiarize ourselves with the work processes; we must also have a knowledge of the unsuccessful struggle of the workers throughout a generation to control the terms of their employment, and of the actual conditions of hire and labor under the employers' régime now in full sway. These factors are taken up in turn in the three main divisions of this book. They will lead us to final chapters which will discuss the policies by which the employers seek to retain control, and the spirit of the workers toward the existing situation.

CHAPTER III

THE BLAST FURNACE CREWS

WHEN you consider the Allegheny County of today, with its acres of steel plants, its rows of blast furnaces, its quadruple railroad tracks with their unceasing traffic, its smoking, vibrant, roaring industry, it is hard to realize that the iron and steel plants have grown from comparative insignificance to their present stature within the memory of men not yet past middle life.

The bituminous coal field which stretches in all directions from Pittsburgh, and the rivers which furnish cheap transportation, combine to make this one of the great workshops of America. The Great Lakes bring the iron mines of Northern Michigan and Minnesota to Pittsburgh's back door; and a railroad haul of a trifle over one hundred miles is sufficient to carry the ore from the docks on Lake Erie to the furnaces in the Monongahela Valley. So great has been the development, that today there is no other area of equal size in the world where so large a tonnage of pig iron is annually produced as in this county of Western Pennsylvania.

To understand this development, we must understand each of the great stages in which the metal is handled. Raw ore from the mines is put through the blast furnace and reduced to what is called "pig iron," a crude product, full of impurities. Some pig iron is used in making car wheels and for certain other purposes, but the vast bulk of it is refined either by puddling, the product of which is wrought iron, or by the crucible, Bessemer or open-hearth processes, the product of which is steel. After this, iron bars or steel ingots, softened with heat, are passed between rolls which press them out to the size or shape desired.

In 1908, 44 blast furnaces, employing about 180 men to the stack, were operating in Allegheny County. There were, then, some 8,000 blast furnace workmen, a considerable army;

22

and when it is realized that more than half of these men are heads of families, we catch a first glimpse of the human problem in pig iron, which a half century has called into being in the neighborhood of Pittsburgh.

The first permanent blast furnace to be constructed in this section was built in 1859.* A furnace was built at Shadyside in 1792 and was operated a part of the time until 1794, when it was abandoned for lack of ore. During the sixty-five years following, not a ton of pig iron was produced in Allegheny County. When the Clinton furnace was built in 1859 on the South Side of Pittsburgh, it demonstrated that Connellsville coke was adapted for pig iron production. Other furnaces were soon built and in less than twenty years the Pittsburgh District had surpassed all other iron-producing districts in the country.

This growth in production has been due partly to the natural development of the region. As it became demonstrated that iron could be produced here economically, furnaces were built in increasing numbers. Of more importance than the construction of additional furnaces, however, has been the growth in the science of furnace building and operation. The average tonnage of a single day now is often more than could be produced in a week under the best of conditions fifty years ago.

A typical Pittsburgh blast furnace is a barrel-shaped structure of masonry and steel plates somewhere between 85 and 100 feet in height and about 20 feet in diameter at the bulge, or, technically speaking, the "bosh." In order to extract the iron from the ore, two things are of especial importance: a heat intense enough to melt every part of the charge, acting as a reducing agent and separating the metallic from the non-metallic constituents in the ore; and a substance which will act as a flux, attracting to itself and making more readily fusible the non-metallic constituents. The first end is gained by driving superheated air at a high pressure into the lower part of the furnace, causing the coke, which is used as fuel, to burn at an intense heat; the second is accomplished by introducing limestone into the furnace along with the ore and the fuel. Ore, coke and limestone are charged

* Swank, James M.: History of the Manufacture of Iron in all Ages, pp. 225–231. Phila., James M. Swank, 1892.

alternately into the furnace top until it is filled with a succession of layers of material. As the molten iron is taken out at a tap hole at the bottom, the stock, which always fills the furnace nearly to the top, slowly sinks downward. The hot blast forces its way through, igniting the coke as the stock descends and causing it to burn with great heat, so that at a point just above where the blast is admitted, at the "zone of fusion" as it is called, the whole mass becomes liquid.

Every blast furnace is accompanied by a row of "stoves." There are usually four to a furnace, and they are so prominent by reason of their number and size that the uninitiated often mistake them for furnaces. The stoves are 75 to 100 feet in height and about 20 feet in diameter. It is here that the air blast is heated before it enters the furnace. These stoves are lined with fire brick, and the interior is an open checker work which forms a series of communicating chambers. Gas is admitted at the bottom of a stove, and burned. The resulting hot gases and air rise and pass through the brick checker work, thus permeating and heating every part of the interior of the stove. When a stove is hot enough, the gas is cut off and the air blast, driven by the blowing engines, is turned on. It rushes through, absorbing the heat from the red hot chambers, and passes from the stove at a temperature of 1000 degrees Fahrenheit. Connecting pipes, or tuyeres ("tweers"), to the number of a dozen or sixteen, penetrate the circumference of the furnace at points about seven feet above the hearth, and through these the hot air from the stove enters the furnace under a pressure of about fifteen pounds to the square inch. When the air blast begins to cool down a little, it is changed to the stove that has been longest subjected to the flame and is, consequently, the hottest one, and the gas is turned on again in the cooled stove. In this way each stove is used in turn, and the blast is kept at a uniformly high temperature. The tuyeres are encased in jackets, and cold water is kept circulating around them to prevent their melting.

Below the melting point or zone of fusion in the body of the blast furnace all is molten, the iron settling, while the non-metallic elements and the residue from the limestone and the coke float above it in the form of slag. The tapping hole for the iron is therefore at the bottom, while the slag or cinder is tapped out through the "cinder notch," a second hole a little above the other. The iron is tapped, or, as the men say, a "cast" is made, about once in four hours; the men breaking out the tapping hole, which is closed with fire clay, by drilling part way and knocking a rod through to the metal. The molten iron, with some four or five hundred tons of stock weighing down upon it from above, bursts out with a rush and a roar of flame, and the man who fails to jump quickly gets burned. The iron pours down a runner to the ladle cars, sparkling fire all the while, its course directed from one car to another as they become filled.

When a cast is made, practically all of the melted iron is taken out; that is, the furnace is emptied up as far as the tuyeres. The tapping hole is stopped up again by driving fire clay into it with a steam ramrod. The stock above presses down, and the pasty but unmelted mass just above the zone of fusion drops into the hearth. The melting process continues above the tuyeres, and as the molten iron trickles downward the mass in the hearth is raised again to the tuyere level and is speedily reduced to liquid.

This in simple, non-technical terms, describes the method employed in the manufacture of pig iron. It affords no explanation, however, of the truly marvelous expansion in the capacity of single furnaces which, as indicated above, has taken place in the last half century. A comparison between the fifties and the present in the matter of tonnage furnishes remarkable figures. In 1858 the greatest achievement on record for blast furnace production was 319 tons in one week.* Today the average furnace of Allegheny County produces from 400 to 600 tons every twenty-four hours.

It is for engineers to state the factors involved in this marvelous development, but it is interesting, even for the layman, to examine some important changes that time has worked in the industry. The most important ones may be grouped under three heads: fuel, method and construction.

A good blast furnace fuel should be porous and firm, so that the weight of the stock will not crush it, and at the same time the blast may find a passage through. It is necessary also that

* Swank: Iron in all Ages, p. 455.

it should burn with great heat, leaving little ash. In the early history of the industry in this country, charcoal was used exclusively. Then anthracite coal came into use early in the nineteenth century and, requiring no preparation, it was preferred to charcoal. The output of the anthracite furnaces surpassed the charcoal product in 1855. Meanwhile bituminous coal began to be used both in the raw state and as coke. The latter has been found to be the fuel most nearly ideal. By 1875 the tonnage produced by bituminous coal and coke was greater than the anthracite tonnage, and today it is far in the lead. Anthracite is still used to a considerable extent in eastern Pennsylvania, and there are still a few charcoal furnaces, which supply a special demand for charcoal iron.* In the Pittsburgh District coke is used exclusively; indeed, one of the great reasons for the wonderful development of the industry in this district is the proximity of the Connellsville coal fields. This coal makes a better blast furnace coke than any other grade of coal mined in the United States.

Prior to 1835, a cold blast was used in this country.† The hot blast came into general use between 1835 and 1840. Since then the tendency has been to increase the blast temperature, though there are wide variations in present-day practice. The highest temperature used is about 1700 degrees Fahrenheit, the average being much lower, probably between 900 and 1200 degrees. With the iron stoves used at first, it was impossible to get a higher temperature than 1000 degrees on account of the danger of melting. The use of fire brick stoves dates back to 1875.‡

Another important change is the building of furnaces in groups. The labor force can by this means be used more economically. It is also an economy to build them in connection with a steel plant, as the metal can be converted directly into steel without cooling. Far the larger number in Allegheny County are so built today. The isolated furnaces illustrate in the present the prevailing method of thirty years ago. In the older style furnaces an extensive bed of sand, carefully arranged with channels and molds, is found at the front. Into these molds the

---

* Charcoal iron is very tough and is used mostly by car wheel manufacturers. —Campbell, Harry Huse: The Manufacture and Properties of Iron and Steel, p. 42. Published by the *Eng. and Mining Journal*, 1903.

† Swank: Iron in all Ages, p. 453.   ‡ Ibid., p. 453.

molten iron is run from the furnace and allowed to cool. Each mold is so shaped as to make a piece of pig iron, two or three feet long and four to six inches thick. When cooled, the pigs in the molds are still attached at one end to a strip of iron remaining in the channel alongside, from which the iron has run into the mold; the whole section is called a "sow and pigs." When the casting bed is sufficiently cool, laborers go upon it with hammers and break apart the pigs and the sow, and cart them in wheelbarrows to a car.

The sand bed has been superseded in many furnaces by the pig casting machine, consisting of a series of cast iron molds arranged on a long endless chain. The iron is poured from a ladle at the end where the molds emerge from the under side; the chain moves on as each mold is filled, just far enough to bring the next mold under the ladle. By the time the filled molds reach the far end where they dip down over a sprocket to begin the return trip, the iron is cooled sufficiently to hold its shape and the pigs drop from the molds into a car. Most of the furnaces that serve as adjuncts to steel works are equipped with these machines, so that the iron may be handled when for any reason the steel works are not in operation.

A further step in advance is the direct process, by which molten iron is converted at once into steel. This has been coming into use during the last twenty-five years. No time or labor is used up in connection with casting bed or machine. Instead, a main runner extends down from the furnace, and from it branch runners lead down and terminate above a depressed railroad track. Large, brick-lined ladles, on four-wheel trucks, are brought alongside by a dinkey engine, and one is stationed at the terminus of each runner. The iron is then allowed to course down the main runner, and is deflected from one runner to another as the ladles are successively filled. When the cast is over, the locomotive couples on to the train of ladles, and hauls them with their seething contents to the steel works. There the iron is poured into a huge "mixer" or hot-tank, whence it is drawn as required by the Bessemer converters or open-hearth furnaces.

The changes in construction have not been as numerous as they have been important. One of the most important improve-

27

ments was made about the time the industry began to develop west of the Allegheny Mountains. Prior to this time, the furnaces were left open at the top and a column of flame was constantly issuing forth. It was recognized that this was a great loss of energy. Accordingly a cap was put on the furnace top, closing it tightly between periods of charging the stock; and a pipe, known today as the "down-comer," was fixed so as to conduct the gas from the top down to where it could be utilized. There was still a loss, however, which is evident today in the occasional old style furnaces. The hopper at the furnace top is closed by a cone-shaped wedge known as a "bell." The charge is deposited upon this bell, which is then lowered to allow the material to slide down into the furnace. Every time this is done there is an escape of gas, which at once catches fire. These furnaces are readily distinguishable by the rush of flame which leaps up perhaps twenty feet at periodical intervals and is as suddenly extinguished. This defect was finally obviated, in the more important plants, by the use of a double bell and hopper. The load is deposited in the first hopper and the upper bell descends, letting the charge slide down around it into the second hopper. The bell then returns to position, completely closing the aperture. The second bell is then lowered and the charge drops into the furnace itself, sliding down on all sides and spreading out rather evenly. The gas is thus practically all conserved, and it not only furnishes power to operate the powerful blowing engines, and heat for the stoves, but in some plants an excess remains which is piped over to the steel works and used there to generate power.

With other changes, the size of the furnaces has been increased. It has resulted in an economy of fuel to increase the height of the stack. The furnace that made the record run in 1858 measured 55 feet in height and 20 feet in diameter.* Forty years ago the prevailing height was 50 to 60 feet. Today a majority of the furnaces are 80 to 100 feet in height and about 20 feet in diameter.

Another important change in recent years is in the manner of elevating and charging the stock. There are two furnaces in Pittsburgh where the old equipment is still in use. Men at the foot

* Swank: Iron in all Ages, p. 455.

of the furnace fill push carts with the raw material and shove them onto an elevator. The carts are raised to the furnace top, and other men, known as "top fillers," draw them to the edge of the hopper and dump them. All the more modern furnaces are equipped with an automatic hoist which carries the little cars, or "skips," up an inclined track to the furnace top. A skip is filled and is sent upward to be dumped automatically into the hopper. The bells and the automatic hoist are operated by a man on the ground. Two skips operate together; as the filled one goes up, the empty one comes down. Thus the work is carried on uninterruptedly.

Simultaneously with changes in method and construction have come changes in labor. The labor directly employed about the Pittsburgh blast furnaces is divided between the "front" and the "back." Those working at the front of the furnace take care of the molten iron and slag. The men at the back, the stock yard men, fill the skips with ore, fuel and limestone, all of which is piled at the rear. The method here varies greatly, ranging from the practice at the Clinton furnace on the South Side, to that of the Edgar Thomson plant. At the Clinton furnace the men fill carts with the raw material, and push them around to the foot of the hoist where they dump them into the skip. At the Edgar Thomson furnaces there are chutes arranged with the stock ready to slide down. The men push a steel bucket, suspended from a trolley, under a chute and release a portion of the stock by pulling a rod. The bucket is then rolled back until it is suspended above the skip, and the movable bottom is adjusted so as to drop the load. The men at the front have opportunities to rest between their periods of activity in making the casts; but whatever the method employed at the back, the work is hard, for it is uninterrupted. The furnace is charged continuously twenty-four hours every day, so there is little opportunity to rest from the beginning of the twelve-hour shift to the end.

The foreman, or "head blower," is the responsible head of a large blast furnace plant. He has supervision over all of the furnaces, making the rounds to see that everything is working right and directing the work if necessary. A sub-foreman, or

"blower," is in charge of two or three furnaces and directly super-
vises the work. The "keeper," who is the head man on each furnace, regulates the blast and directs the work of making a cast. The
"hot blast man" has charge of the stoves and of changing the gas
from one to another. He is responsible for the condition of the
stoves and for the temperature of the blast. A number of laborers,
two of whom are helpers to the keeper, and a large force of yard
laborers, complete the crew.

Not only have the improvements in furnace construction
and practice mentioned above reduced the labor force and eliminated some of the heaviest labor, but they have also decreased the
danger of accidents. The automatic hoist and dump has done
away with the top fillers. These men were in great danger from
the gas, which can hardly be prevented from escaping to some
extent from the furnace top. In case of an explosion the position
was most perilous. Today it is not necessary for anyone to work
at the top. Ten years ago nearly all the important furnaces had
been equipped with the automatic hoist. It was still necessary,
however, for one man to be on the top to measure the height of the
stock in the furnace. Now this is unnecessary, for a device has
been perfected by which the measuring can be done from the
ground, yet there are still a number of furnaces which have a
man at the top for this purpose. The introduction of the direct
process and of the casting machine has eliminated the necessity for
the heavy physical labor of breaking the pigs and loading them
on cars.

Although these changes and improvements have reduced the
labor cost and increased tonnage, they have not improved working
conditions in proportion. Modern furnaces, for technical reasons,
are held to require continuous operation and all the men are
worked an average schedule of twelve hours a day, seven days a
week,—and, unless there is an accident or a financial panic, 365
days in a year. The variations from this schedule and the need-
lessness of the seven days' routine for the men are set forth in a
later chapter.

Blast furnaces require little skilled labor. There is no deli-
cate machinery—it is simply a question of feeding the furnace
with the raw material, and tapping out the molten product.

Fifteen or twenty years ago, the labor force was largely Irish. Now it is made up almost entirely of Hungarians and Slavs, an interesting example of the shifting of races that is going on to a greater or less degree in all departments of the iron and steel industry. Irishmen still hold the better positions, such as those of blower and foreman. In other departments of the industry the shifting has not gone so far; yet it seems to be only a question of time when in all but the most highly skilled positions the Anglo-Saxon, Teuton and Celt will be displaced by the Slav; nor have we any reason to think it will stop short there. Reasons for this change will be discussed later. It is sufficient to note it now as one of the important elements in the labor situation in the iron and steel industry.

CHAPTER IV

PUDDLERS AND IRON ROLLERS

P IG IRON, the product of the blast furnace, contains so large an amount of carbon as to be weak and brittle for purposes involving tensile strain. A further process of manufacture is necessary before it can meet the demands of industry.* As already noted, most of the pig iron produced in this country is refined in puddling furnaces, crucibles, Bessemer converters or open-hearth furnaces, the product of the puddling furnace being wrought iron, while that of the crucibles, Bessemer converters, and open-hearth furnaces is steel.

There is not, however, so clear a line of division between iron and steel as the last statement might indicate. The difference is one over which even scientific men have had some difficulty, and a Committee on Uniform Nomenclature† had to be appointed to straighten out this and other confusions of terms. The difference seems to be mainly a difference in the per cent of carbon (the iron containing the greater amount).

* Stoughton, Bradley: Metallurgy of Iron and Steel, p. 51. N. Y., Hill Publishing Co., 1907.

† "The following definitions are selected with slight changes from the report of March 31, 1906, of the Committee on the Uniform Nomenclature of Iron and Steel of the International Association for Testing Materials:

" 'Cast Iron:—Generically, iron containing so much carbon or its equivalent that it is not malleable at any temperature. . . The Committee recommends drawing the line between cast iron and steel at 2.20 per cent carbon. . .'

" 'Wrought Iron:—Slag-bearing malleable iron, which does not harden materially when suddenly cooled.'

" 'Steel:—Iron which is malleable at least in some one range of temperature, and in addition is either (a) cast into an initially malleable mass; or (b) is capable of hardening greatly by sudden cooling; or (c) is both so cast and so capable of hardening.'

" In the definition of steel the first sentence 'is malleable at least in some one range of temperature' distinguishes steel from cast iron and pig iron, the second sentence 'is cast into an initially malleable mass' distinguishes it from malleable cast iron, and the third sentence 'is capable of hardening greatly by sudden cooling' distinguishes it from wrought iron. At the best, however, the definition of steel is in a shockingly bad condition."—Stoughton, Bradley: Metallurgy of Iron and Steel, pp. 6, 7.

There were about 400 puddling furnaces in Allegheny County in 1907–08.* With two puddlers to a furnace and two shifts to the twenty-four hours, this would mean 1,600 puddlers in the county. But two plants with a total of at least 60 furnaces were operated with three shifts, bringing up the number of puddlers, roughly, to 2,000. These men represent the oldest, the most picturesque and most self-assertive of the crafts of the iron trades.

A puddling or boiling furnace is a brick structure, like an oven, about seven feet high and six or seven square, with two compartments, one a receptacle into which pig iron is thrown, the other a fuel chamber beside it where the melting heat is generated. The drafts are so arranged that the flame sweeps from the fuel chamber directly upon the surface of the iron. From five hundred to six hundred pounds of pig iron is put into the furnace at one time, after which the furnace is closed, and sufficient heat is applied to melt down the iron. Then the puddler begins to work it with an iron rod through a hole in the furnace door, so as to stir up the liquid and bring as much as possible in contact with the air. As the impurities become separated from the iron they rise to the top as slag and are tapped out through the cinder notch. A constantly higher temperature is required to keep the iron in a liquid condition as it becomes freer from impurities, and gradually it begins to solidify in granules, much as butter is formed after sufficient churning of the cream. These granules tend to come together and the iron becomes a spongy mass composed of many particles of iron with liquid slag in the interstices. After the iron begins to solidify, or "come to nature," the puddler generally works the mass into three balls, for convenience in handling and in removing through the furnace door.

When the iron has been finally worked into balls, the furnace door is opened and one by one the balls, each alone the size of a bushel basket, are taken out with iron tongs suspended from a trolley and shoved along to the "squeezer." This is a revolving cylinder with a roughened or corrugated surface, nearly surrounded by a cylindrically shaped case having a simi-

* The Iron and Steel Works Directory for 1908 names fourteen plants in Allegheny County having 362 single and 28 double furnaces. One firm refused to give its equipment.

larly roughened interior. The outer case is so placed that at the opening, where the inner cylinder is exposed, the crevice between the case and the cylinder is greater at one side of the opening than at the other; that is, the cylinder and case are placed eccentrically with respect to each other. The ball is introduced into the wider crevice. The inner cylinder, as it revolves, carries the ball around with it so that an increasing pressure is exerted upon it as it progresses. The principle is the same in a coffee mill, except that the berries go in at the top instead of at the side and are ground instead of squeezed. The pressure serves to squeeze out the slag and to shape the iron so that it can be rolled. It emerges after making the circuit, a bar three or four feet long, called a "bloom."

The working of one charge is called a "heat" and requires about two hours. Five heats constitute a day's work in a "two-turn" mill, and the men accomplish it in from eight to ten hours according to the nature of the iron that is being worked. In the two mills in Allegheny County operating in 1908 on the "three-turn" system, the puddlers never got over four heats to a turn, and sometimes not over three. These men received no more per ton than the men who worked in the two-turn mills, and their earnings per day were correspondingly less.

There have been few essential changes in puddling furnaces within fifty years. Inventions have been made with a view to eliminating labor and making the process mechanical. Some have met with a degree of success; but as yet, nothing has been discovered that will do the work as satisfactorily as human labor.

Puddling is very hard, hot work. It is conceded by mill workers that few other positions in either an iron or a steel mill are so taxing, physically. There are always two men and sometimes three to a single furnace, and they take turn about at working the metal. No man could stand before the furnace and perform that back-breaking toil continually. Even when working by "spells," a man is often nearly exhausted at the end of his "spell." The puddler stands in the full heat of the furnace and works his rod through a hole in the door. The intensity of the heat may be alleviated by shielding the furnace with water-cooled plates. This arrangement is in use in some, but by no means all, of the mills of Allegheny County.

34

THE PUDDLER

Iron Mill Showing Crews at Hammer and Furnace

After a ball has gone through the squeezer, it is ready for the "muck" or "roughing" rolls. The bloom is not compact and solid in spite of the squeezing process. The pressure has not as yet been sufficient to give much firmness to the bar, and at this stage it is in danger of falling to pieces. The reason for the further working of the iron is to increase its strength by giving it greater compactness and to press out the slag left by the squeezer. The roughing rolls are two horizontal rollers in a "two-high" mill, or three in a "three-high," set firmly in housings and revolving in opposite directions after the manner of a clothes wringer. Most of the muck mills are three rollers high so that the iron can be worked back and forth; in a two-high mill it can receive pressure only on every other pass. Grooves on the rolls so correspond as to form a number of rectangular openings, decreasing in size from one end of the rolls to the other. As the bloom falls from the squeezer, the "rougher" seizes it with his tongs and shoves one end into the largest gap in the rolls. There is a crash and a shower of sparks and the bloom emerges on the other side of the rolls, slightly longer and more compact. The "catcher" stands waiting, and as the last end of the bloom comes through the rolls, he catches it with his tongs and in a three-high mill returns it through the next and smaller opening. So the bar passes back and forth until it has gone through the last opening. It is then "muck bar," and is still in an unfinished state.

The next step is to cut up the muck bars into convenient lengths, pile several sections together, and charge them into a heating furnace. This is like a large oven, with the flame sweeping fiercely across, and it brings them to a welding temperature. They are then rolled again in the finishing rolls, and the particles of slag left are forced into a texture which binds and strengthens the whole. The sections weld perfectly and a bar of merchant iron is the result. This is the finished iron of commerce.

In an iron mill the length of the working day for the muck roll hands cannot vary much from the puddler's hours, for they handle the puddler's product. In the Pittsburgh mills the day shift of puddlers begin work very early in the morning—anywhere from two to four o'clock. Eight to ten hours is needed for the five heats required by both custom and union rules in the two-

35

turn mills, and then the so-called night shift comes out—finishing between six p. m. and eleven p. m. The muck roll hands come to work about an hour and a half later than the puddlers of the same shifts, so as to be ready to roll the first heat, and they finish when the last heat is rolled. The "finishers" are independent of the puddlers and muck rollers because they take the product cold, and re-heat it; but they, too, work by heats, eight heats constituting a day's work, and this requires from eight to ten hours.

The men actually work less than the number of hours they are on duty. The puddlers, as has been pointed out, change about with the heavy work. On the muck rolls the same custom obtains. There are two roughers and two catchers, four men for the two positions. On the front of the rolls the "roller," who is the boss of the rolling crew, takes his turn occasionally, so the roughers work less steadily than the catchers. The reasons for this arrangement are obvious to any one who has observed the men at work. A bloom weighs from 180 to 200 pounds. To stand for eight or ten hours, with an intermission only at lunch time, lifting and shoving about a commodity weighing 200 pounds, would be hard labor under any circumstances. But when that commodity is a red hot iron bar, it is even more difficult. The men stand close to the hot iron all the time, where the temperature is always high. They are subjected to a constant bombardment of sparks, and must wear masks to protect their faces. They are obliged also to stand on steel plates, hot from the iron that is always passing over them. The roll hands wear shoes with heavy wooden soles, but in spite of these their feet are always hot.

Where an old style furnace is used the men on the finishing rolls get a chance to rest between heats. The "heater" fills the furnace with piles of muck bar and each pile is taken out and rolled when it arrives at the right heat, the whole charge being rolled before any cold iron can take its place. It is a fine piece of work to get a pile of iron at the right welding heat, and if cold iron were charged alongside, the whole furnace might be chilled. But this is true of heating furnaces where the flame is admitted from one side only. With a modern reversible furnace, the heater begins to draw the piles from the side of the furnace where the flame is admitted. When he has the furnace half cleared out, he reverses the gas, the opposite side becomes the point of greatest heat, and the helper begins charging cold iron into the side that has just been cleared out. With a furnace of this sort the operation may be continuous.

Curiously enough, it is the prevailing opinion that work in the iron mills is very healthful. The air is usually smoky and filled with dust from the various operations. Practically all of the men work in great heat; they grow accustomed to it after a time, but that fact only makes adjustment to normal conditions more difficult. In winter the change from the mill atmosphere to the chill of the out-of-door air must be a shock to the system of the average mill man. That iron mill workers are for the most part healthy is undoubtedly due to the precautions that they take against the weather and to the comparatively short working day interspersed with rests, rather than to the nature of their work.

CHAPTER V

THE STEEL MAKERS

THIRTY years ago, iron began to lose its hold upon the market. Making steel by the Bessemer process was so much cheaper than puddling iron that in spite of prejudice against it steel won its way, until today it takes the place of iron and wood in every conceivable form and in nearly all kinds of manufacture and construction. But for some purposes, steel has not yet been able satisfactorily to take the place of iron. For this reason, and because of the capital already invested, the puddling furnace persists, and seems likely to retain a place, subordinate though it be, for a long time to come.

There are three distinct methods in use today for converting cast iron into steel: the crucible, the Bessemer and the open-hearth processes. By the oldest, which has been in use for over a century, steel is made by putting a mixture of wrought iron and some substance high in carbon into a covered crucible and heating it until it is thoroughly melted. A very high grade of steel is made in this way, and it is used wherever an especially hard metal is required, as for armor-piercing projectiles, automobile parts, razor blades, and edged tools generally.

There are eight mills in Allegheny County making crucible steel. So far as tonnage goes, their output is insignificant compared with that of the Bessemer and open-hearth steel plants. Their method is distinct, and for the purpose of this study it seemed best to confine the presentation to the mills of greater tonnage which produce the main staples of the industry.*

There were sixteen separate plants, including foundries, where open-hearth steel was made in 1907–08 in Allegheny County,

* The tonnage of crucible steel produced in the United States in 1905 was six-tenths of one per cent of the total steel production. Of the total steel production in Pennsylvania in 1905, eight-tenths of one per cent was crucible steel. Census Bulletin No. 78, pp. 70, 71.

and five plants making Bessemer steel. These are in most cases departments of rolling mills, and for this reason I cannot give the total number of employes with accuracy because my most authentic figures, with few exceptions, are for entire plants, not for departments. A conservative estimate would be that 4000 or 5000 men are employed in these departments in Allegheny County. All open-hearth employes have a work-day of twelve hours, and most of them in 1907 had work on Sunday each alternate week. A small proportion of the men employed in the Bessemer departments have an eight-hour day, but the majority work double shift, twelve hours each, as in the open-hearth departments.

The Bessemer process has not been changed in essential details since Sir Henry Bessemer perfected it in 1858. Air is blown directly through a vessel of molten iron and by an oxidizing process burns out practically all the silicon and carbon. At the end of a "blow" there is added an alloy of iron and manganese containing the carbon necessary to give the desired hardness to the steel. The method is a very rapid one, and because it made steel a cheap commodity, it is directly responsible for the rapidity with which other building materials have been supplanted by steel within the last forty years. The first Bessemer steel made in the United States was manufactured at Wyandotte, Michigan, in 1864.*

It is the present custom, as already explained, to bring the molten iron directly from the blast furnaces to the converting works, and pour the product of different furnaces together into a large heated tank called a " mixer." Before the introduction of this direct process, all of the iron used in the converting department was melted down in "cupolas," which are built somewhat on the plan of a blast furnace. Although the direct process has been in use in Sweden since 1857,† cupolas were used generally in this country until late in the nineteenth century, because of the irregularity of blast-furnace products. They are still used to some extent, their merit being that the quality of iron used may be absolutely determined. Pig iron and coke are charged into the cupola and a low blast of air is kept on to assist combustion. By charging the grade or combination of grades of pig iron desired, the quality of the product may be controlled. With a mixer the grade of iron used in the converters may be determined as absolutely as in the cupola process, and the saving of labor, time and fuel is important.

A Bessemer converter is like an immense egg-shaped barrel hung on axles. It is constructed of steel plates and lined with some material that will withstand the fierce heat of molten iron. The bottom end is made with a deep layer of the same refractory material, in which are set a number of cylinders of fire clay about eighteen inches long, five or six inches in diameter and extending clear through the bottom. These cylinders, pierced through with ten or a dozen holes about half an inch in diameter, are the tuyeres. Below this bottom is a second one, with a space left between, making an air-tight chamber. The air blast, at an initial pressure of 30 pounds to the inch, is forced into this chamber and thence through the tuyeres.

A dinkey engine crew brings the iron in a ladle car from the mixer, the mouth of the converter is turned down to a horizontal position, the converter men tip the ladle, and the iron is poured from the one to the other. The bulge in the walls of the converter is so great that a charge of ten to fifteen tons of molten iron, poured in when the vessel is in a nearly horizontal position, will lie in the barrel-like curve of the wall without touching any of the tuyeres in the bottom. The blower turns on the blast and moves a lever which allows the converter to return to a vertical position, while the air roars up through the molten contents. It takes from eight to twelve minutes to make a "blow," the time varying with the size of the converter and the quality of the iron. When the charge is ready to be poured, a pot-shaped ladle six feet deep and six or seven feet across is swung around by a hydraulic crane responsive to a lever in the hands of a regulator man. The converter is tipped to the horizontal above it and what was once liquid iron empties from its mouth as liquid steel. The alloy of iron and manganese is thrown in at the same time. No sooner has the converter been relieved of the blown metal than it receives another charge from a new ladle of iron and is tipped up for another blow. No time is lost.

Meanwhile the ladle of steel is raised by the crane and swung around to the opposite side of the enclosure where a row of cast iron molds stand on trucks, or "buggies," on a narrow gauge track. These molds are six feet high and 18 to 24 inches square. They are open at the top and the ladle is suspended just above them so that the steel may run out through a bung in its bottom directly into the molds. A stopper, thrust down through the metal and as long as the ladle is deep, regulates this outlet.

The pouring of the steel into the molds is attended to by men who stand on a platform about on a level with the tops of the molds. As a mold is filled, the "steel pourer" lowers the stopper into the tap-hole by means of a lever, and the train of buggies is shoved along until the next mold is in position. When the ladle is emptied of steel, the slag which floats on the metal has sunk to the bottom and is dumped into a car which is waiting on a narrow gauge track beneath.

Over in one corner, or along one side, is a raised platform called a "pulpit." Here are the "blower" and the "regulator" men. The blower is in direct charge of the work. Next to the foreman he is the most important man in the department. He watches the flame intently, for it is by the eye alone that he determines the time to turn down the converter and shut off the blast. There is a considerable strain on the blower, for he owes a responsibility not only to his employers, but also to the men below him. If he turns down too soon, the metal will not run well from the ladle and trouble will be made for the steel pourer. If he does not turn down soon enough, the heat may be completely spoiled—a serious loss to the company, and to the men who are paid by the ton. The regulator men have a row of levers before them and by pulling these they tip the converter, work the cranes, and operate the hydraulic machine that shoves the buggies and molds.

A corps of "bottom-makers" and "ladle-liners" are kept at work, for the action of the metal on the linings is such that a converter must be relined once a week, and the ladles oftener. The converter bottoms are attacked most fiercely of all, and these have to be rebuilt at least once in two days. The stopper in the ladles, a steel rod covered with fire clay, also has to be rebuilt frequently.

The vesselmen and the steel pourers constitute the small group of eight-hour men referred to at the opening of the chapter. The vesselmen are a sort of "first aid" contingent. They work on the platform close beside the converter, on the ground, or in the bottom-makers' shop as occasion demands. In pouring out a heat of steel, some is constantly solidifying on the lip of the converter. The vesselmen must knock this off. While the converter is in a horizontal position pouring out a heat, the boss vesselman steps in front and inspects the bottom, peering through holes in a shield of sheet steel with which he protects himself from the intense heat. Occasionally he makes a more careful examination by removing the lower part of the air chamber at the bottom of the converter and with a rod measuring the length of the tuyeres. If a tuyere has been burned down to a point where it might burn through and fill the air chamber with molten metal, his helpers simply stop it up with clay and fasten a plate over it. In this way a bottom may be kept in service with safety several hours longer than would be the case if no attempt were made to check the destructive action of the metal.

The third method employed in the manufacture of steel, the open-hearth process, came into use later than the Bessemer, and despite certain advantages made slower headway, as relatively it took longer to produce the same tonnage and the expense was greater. The method consists in exposing molten pig iron, steel scrap, and certain chemical agents to the heat of a gas flame and to the action of air as it passes over the surface of a containing tank. An open-hearth furnace is arranged with brick checker work chambers at either end of the hearth, or reservoir, of the furnace. These are connected with the flues, and as the gas is admitted from one end through the checker work the flame sweeps across, and the resulting heated gases and air pass through the checker work at the other end, heating the contents of the hearth to a high temperature. By occasionally reversing the gas, that is, admitting it from the opposite end, the chambers are kept heated and the gas and air always enter the hearth at a high temperature.

As in the Bessemer process, it is quite generally the custom now to charge molten iron directly from the mixer, although cold pig iron is sometimes used. Molten iron is poured from the ladle cars which run on a track in front of the furnaces. A chain from an electric crane above is attached, and as the ladle is drawn up it tips, pouring its charge into the hearth. For charging cold pig iron, scrap, ore and dolomite, electrical charging machines are used. The essential feature of the machine is a horizontal bar, like a great arm, moving forward or backward, up or down. Charging boxes about four feet long, with a socket at one end to fit this bar, are filled with the charge. The operator, who sits in the rear of the machine and manipulates the levers, moves the bar in such a way as to pick up a box. He then runs the machine before a furnace door, thrusts the bar with its load through into the hearth, and gives it a half revolution; the box turns turtle, releasing its contents. The bar is drawn back, the empty box is quickly set aside, a filled one picked up, and the operation repeated.

At the back of an ordinary open-hearth furnace there is a pit about eight feet deep and perhaps ten feet in diameter. Into this pit a ladle is lowered which is large enough to hold all of the steel in the furnace. When a tap is made, about eight hours after the furnace has been charged, a hole in the back of the furnace is knocked out, just as in tapping a blast furnace. The steel pours out into the ladle and fills it to the brim so that the slag, which always floats on the surface of the metal, runs over the lips of the ladle into the pit below. At this point an alloy of iron and manganese is introduced, as in the Bessemer process. The ladle is raised by a crane and a pouring crew fills the molds. The slag is left in the pit to cool. Steel hooks are placed in the bottom of the pit before the heat is poured, and when the slag has solidified around these hooks, it is easily removed by a crane.

There are three men regularly employed at an open-hearth furnace,—"first helper," "second helper" and "cinder-pit man." The first helper was formerly called a "melter," but now, with a different organization, a melter has charge of several furnaces. In an open-hearth plant there are usually a superintendent and an assistant superintendent in control, a foreman or boss melter in active charge of from three to five furnaces, and a first helper on each furnace. The superintendent gets the orders from the office specifying the quality of steel desired. He delivers them to the melters and they, in turn, to the first helpers. A first helper is supposed to know how to get the desired result and he sees that

43

the necessary steps are taken. Each furnace crew works together when tapping the furnace, and in fixing bottom between heats, but there is much of the time when the first helper is idle except for watching the heat. The second helper and cinder-pit man are busy between tapping periods throwing lime or other material into the furnace to change the quality of the steel when that is necessary, but they too have periods of rest. There are in addition laborers who get stock ready, wheel in limestone and dolomite, and assist the furnace men when necessary.

In spite of the greater expense of manufacture, the future appears to be much brighter for open-hearth than for Bessemer steel. Railroads are beginning to call for open-hearth steel in their rail orders, and other consumers favor open-hearth steel for withstanding heavy pressure. This demand is due largely to the fact that the Bessemer process is not quite as accurate as is the open-hearth. When the Bessemer blower thinks his steel is in condition, he turns down the converter. He usually gets a product closely approximating that desired, but he cannot produce absolutely accurate results, for he cannot interrupt a blow to take tests. The open-hearth melter may know the condition of his furnace at any time. Tests are frequently taken and analyses made at the laboratory, and the metal can be kept in the furnace until it is brought to the exact point desired. In addition, the open-hearth method has an advantage over the Bessemer in that it can convert any quality of iron into steel, while a special grade of iron is required by the Bessemer process.

This introduces another factor more influential even than the growing demand for open-hearth steel,—the diminishing supply of ores suitable for the Bessemer process. The outcome is that steel companies everywhere are enlarging their open-hearth plants. The Homestead plant, which made far more Bessemer than open-hearth steel fifteen years ago, operates today sixty open-hearth furnaces, while its two Bessemer converters are idle half the time. At Duquesne, the same company has torn out its converters and built more open-hearth furnaces. The Jones and Laughlin Company in its new plant at Woodlawn, Pennsylvania, and the United States Steel Corporation at Gary, Indiana, are prepared to manufacture open-hearth steel exclusively.

MOUNTAINS OF ORE AT BLAST FURNACES

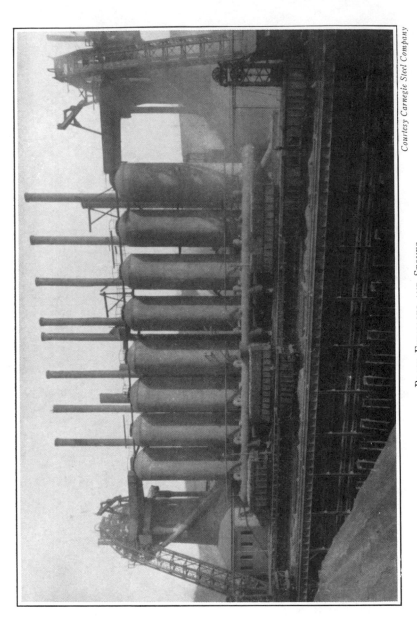

BLAST FURNACES AND STOVES

The Eight Cylindrical Structures in Center of Picture are Stoves, Heating the Air Blast for the Two Furnaces, Located at Either End

CHARGING MACHINE ABOUT TO DUMP A BOX OF PIG IRON INTO AN OPEN-HEARTH FURNACE

AT THE BACK OF THE OPEN-HEARTH FURNACES—TAPPING OUT A HEAT OF STEEL

Courtesy Carnegie Steel Company

THE STEEL POURER'S PLATFORM

An Ingot on Its Way from Soaking Pit to Blooming Mill

CHAPTER VI

THE MEN OF THE ROLLING MILLS

BESSEMER men and open-hearth operatives, no less than the blast furnace workers, are craftsmen in heat. They deal with molten metal. The iron which the blast furnace men turn over to them in ladles or hardened into pigs becomes, in their hands, "ingots" of steel—the units with which the steel mills begin their work. From now on, not heat, but pressure, with heat as its ally, is the chief agent of production; for the ingot as it leaves the mold is not in condition to make a good finished article, on account of its lack of homogeneity and the presence of blow holes. The steel needs to be "worked" in order to give it a firmer quality and a greater strength. This is accomplished in the rolling process, during which the pressure is such that the blow holes are practically eliminated by welding. At the same time, the ingot is broken down and shaped into forms for the market— rails, beams, plates, tubes, etc.—which give name and character to the plants producing them.

Altogether, rolling mills handling steel exclusively were to be found in 36 plants in Allegheny County in 1907–08. Some of these are special mills, not typical of the steel industry, and are not considered in this study. The facts here presented are based, chiefly, upon the practice in the mills owned by the companies subsidiary to the United States Steel Corporation, and by the Jones and Laughlin Steel Company, the largest of the independents in the Pittsburgh District. Of the 60,000 men engaged in all departments of these plants a majority are employed in the rolling mills.

In the last chapter we left the molds full of molten steel at the pouring platform. From there a dinkey engine crew takes them into the mill yard to cool down. As soon as the ingots are cool enough to stand alone, the molds are taken to the "stripper." An ingot mold has no bottom and is made with a projection or lug on either side near the top like the handles of a jug. The stripper is a crane arrangement with a pair of huge links or clamps which fit over the lugs and lift them, and an iron plunger between the two clamps which presses down on the ingot. The molds slip up and off easily once they are loosened, and the crane sets them over one at a time on empty buggies drawn up alongside, thus leaving on one track a train of empty molds ready to be filled again, and on the other, the red hot steel ingots standing upright on the buggies. An ingot made in a mold of ordinary size weighs more than three tons.

When the molds are removed the outside has solidified to a depth of a few inches but the interior is still in a molten condition.* At this stage the outside is in condition to roll, but by the time the center has been reduced to a temperature fit for rolling, the surface is black and comparatively cold. It is necessary to adopt some means of equalizing the temperature. Various methods have been tried. Burying the ingot in sand so as to hold the temperature of the exterior was at one time the custom in Europe. In this country twenty-five years ago the ingots were shoved horizontally into heating furnaces. The general practice now is to use a "soaking pit." Brick-lined pits are sunk below the floor level of the mill, each pit usually large enough to accommodate four ingots at one time. A crane grips the ingot with a pair of tongs not unlike those that the ice man uses, carries it over and lowers it into a pit. The pit is at once covered and the ingots are submitted to a comparatively low gas heat, calculated to equalize the temperature throughout, or to "soak" the ingot.

The man in charge of the soaking pits is the "heater." His work involves judgment rather than physical labor. He decides which ingot is sufficiently soaked for the crane man to draw. To do this he comes in contact with considerable heat. A crew of bottom-makers repair the pit bottoms whenever these are in danger of burning through, placing a shield with a small hole in it over the pit, and working with a bar or rod through this hole. This work is difficult and taxing to the physical strength on

---

* As an ingot cools, the metal contracts, leaving a cavity at the top called the "pipe." This is done away with by cutting off the "crop end," after the ingot has been rolled down.

46

account of the heat. The foreman bottom-maker occupies the position next to the heater, and is next in line of promotion.

In the chapter on iron mills, the rolls were compared to those of a clothes wringer. This is a homely description that will apply, in a general way, to all rolling mills,* but there are, nevertheless, wide variations in their shape and size. Steel is usually rolled in at least two different kinds of mills, with an interval of re-heating between. The "blooming" and "slabbing" rolls "break down" the ingot; that is, they reduce it to a more convenient size, and at the same time, by working it, increase its strength. This is the first stage in the process, and the product varies according to the ultimate purpose the steel is intended to fill after going through the second, the finishing mills. If the ingot is to be rolled out to rails, it is broken down to about one-half or one-third its initial thickness and the product is called a "bloom." If something smaller is to be made, the ingot is rolled down to billets of lesser sizes. If plates are to be made, the ingots are first broken into slabs.

When the ingot has soaked long enough, the overhead crane seizes it and sets it on end in a sort of dump cart, which carries it to the proper point, tips over and deposits it on a "roll-table." This is a succession of steel rollers ranged on each side of the blooming rolls and so geared that they must revolve and carry the ingot forward or backward at the will of the man operating a lever.

There are few more interesting or spectacular sights in a steel plant than a blooming mill. The roll-table extends for 75 feet or more on either side of the rolls, and to one side at the far end rests the ingot, glowing and inert. Then a man, high up on a raised platform, moves a lever and the three-ton block rumbles forward. At the same moment, the roll engine is set in motion, the clank and sweep of the connecting-rod suggesting a power relentless and irresistible. The heavy blooming rolls seize the ingot with seeming fury and it passes through with a bang that sounds like an explosion, heard even above the roar of the mill. Sparks and red fragments of scale fly in a shower. The engine is suddenly reversed, the rolls revolve in the opposite direction, and the partially flattened ingot comes back on a second pass. Then,

* Each set of rolls is technically called a mill, though the term is usually applied also to the entire train, consisting of several sets of rolls.

47

from beneath the roll-table, a row of great steel fingers push up; they tip the ingot, now twice its original length, one-quarter way over, and toss it about as if it were a plaything. Again it goes through the rolls, and soon is pressed square again, as in the beginning, while its thickness lessens and its length as steadily increases.

The slabbing or "universal" mill differs from a blooming mill, in that it has vertical as well as horizontal rolls, making it unnecessary to tip the ingot. Pressure is exerted on all four sides, and the ingot is rolled down four to six inches thick and cut into rectangular slabs about 30 inches square instead of to the billet size.

The labor involved is about the same in slabbing as in blooming mills, and in either it seems absurdly small, considering the tons of steel handled. A blooming mill requires a roller, an engineer and a "tableman." Three men supervise the rolling of 600 to 1000 tons of steel in twelve hours. They stand in an elevated box where they can obtain a direct view of the rolls. A gauge shows the roller just what the space is between the rolls, and each time after an ingot has passed through, he moves his lever and narrows the gap a little more. On one side stands the tableman grasping levers that operate the roll tables and the manipulators; and on the other side the engineer, controlling the engine, stopping it, starting, or reversing, as may be necessary. The work about a slabbing mill is similar. Here the roller reverses the engine and adjusts both the vertical and the horizontal rolls; so he has three levers before him. A tableman stands with the roller in the pulpit, and performs the same duties as in the blooming mill.

After an ingot is brought down to a bloom, it is usually passed on to another mill where small work can be done more advantageously. In some plants what is termed the continuous process is used. A series of mills are placed in line, and after a few passes through the blooming mill the bloom passes, without again being reversed, straight down through the mills. These are set at such distances apart and their relative speed is so finely adjusted that, as the bloom gets drawn out, it will at the last stage of its journey be passing through as many as three mills at the same time, with the forward end traveling about twice as fast as the rear. Attempts have been made to roll out finished products in this way, and the method is regularly employed in some mills for rolling rails. It is conceded, however, that the best results cannot be attained without re-heating and a more thorough working of the steel, so the continuous process is used principally for making billets.

We have now arrived at the point where differentiation and specialization begin. Practically every form in which steel is found today is a further transformation after the soaking pits and blooming mills have done their work. Every process up to this point is preparatory. Now come what are called the "finishing" mills, of which there are as many distinct kinds as there are forms of product. One variety shapes the girders and beams of bridges and skyscrapers. Another rolls out the pathway for our "Limited" express trains; a mile or more an hour, for twenty-four hours in the day and twenty-five days in the month. There are plate mills of massive proportions; tube mills where pipe is made from a quarter inch to two feet in diameter; hoop mills and rod mills whirling out their product with amazing velocity; and merchant mills of all sizes, the last to succumb to automatic processes.

But before slabs and blooms pass through these finishing rolls, they go through the re-heating furnaces which are a part of every variety of mill. The size and manner of operation of these furnaces vary greatly, but the principle involved in the heating process is everywhere the same. The most noticeable variations are in the manner of charging and drawing. As in the re-heating furnaces at the iron mills, the billets or blooms lie in the furnace side by side and a gas flame sweeps over them from one end of the furnace to the other.

The billets used in the smaller merchant mills are charged by hand, and are drawn with a pair of tongs. A welding heat is not desired in the case of steel, and consequently the process is not so difficult as in the iron mills. In the larger mills using blooms or slabs a mechanical device is necessary for drawing and charging. At Homestead the heating furnaces for the 84-inch plate mill are arranged in a semicircle and the charging and drawing are done by an electric crane which swings about in the air. The slabs are

49

brought in on buggies, and are picked up one at a time by the crane by means of an arrangement like a thumb and forefinger. A heavy steel bar with a hook-shaped projection at the end is extended over a slab. The hook is brought down over the edge in front, a clamp grips from behind, and the slab is thus held firmly as it is lifted into the furnace. In the same way, the slabs are drawn when heated and are placed on the roll table. At the. rail mills of the Edgar Thomson works in Braddock, the blooms are brought to the rear of the furnace three or four at a time on an electrically driven buggy or car, and a bar, so extended from a movable electric machine as to strike them on the end, simply shoves them in. The furnaces have doors opening both in the front and in the back. When a bloom is sufficiently heated a door at the front is opened, and electrically operated tongs are thrust in to drag it out onto a second buggy. An endless cable carries it to the rolls.

An example of modern ideas in furnaces is to be observed in mills Number 15 and 16, together referred to as the "Double storage" mill, in the plant of the Jones and Laughlin Steel Company. These are automatic bar mills, and the process is a continuous mechanical operation. The furnace at the Number 15 mill uses 5 x 5 billets about seven feet long. A billet is laid down by a crane at the door of the furnace, and an electric machine forces it in. The furnace is about twenty feet long, and the billets push each other along each time a new one is admitted. By the time a billet has crossed the furnace it is heated and ready to roll. At the opposite end, a great pair of hooks reaches in and drags it out into a steel channel where rollers carry it at once to the rolls. The Number 16 mill has a furnace almost equally automatic.

Classified by product, finishing mills fall into four general groups. In the first class are included the mills turning out the smaller material, such as guide mills, bar mills, rod mills, wire mills and mills rolling hoops and cotton ties. Guide mills and bar or merchant mills roll rounds, squares, hexagons, angles, and flats, all to be used in some subsequent process in the production of a finished article; the main distinction is that bar mills roll larger sizes than do the guide mills. The product of rod mills may be cut up for rivets or chain links or it may be drawn out into wire.

Various mills in the Pittsburgh District carry on these specialized processes. Hoop mills roll out flat strips for barrel hoops and a smaller size used to bind up bales of cotton.

These mills give you a better idea than any others of what the steel industry used to be, for in most plants the man and the tongs are still essentials. Yet it is but a suggestion of the older days; for you have only the little rods, after all, to help you to imagine how the great ingots used to be handled by human labor at the blooming rolls.

They are the younger men who work at these mills. Here where agility is at a premium and where a false step may possibly mean death, there is no room for the man whose joints are stiff or whose eye is not keen. I remember one such mill especially, where I watched the heater's helper before the furnace, pulling out billet after billet and throwing them along the steel floor to the "rougher." Dressed only in trousers and a flannel shirt with sleeves cut off at the shoulder, the sweat was pouring from his body and his muscles stood out in knots. The rougher was leaping at his work, thrusting the red billets almost in a stream through the first pair of rolls, and yet before he could turn back there was always another billet on the floor behind him. The rolls were built in a train side by side in line; the billets went through one pair and the "catcher" shoved them back through the next; back and forth, back and forth, they went at an ever increasing speed and with ever increasing length, until the catcher at the last pair of rolls, seizing the end of the rod as it came through, described with it a fiery circle high in the air as the snake-like band leaped against the restraining force which bent it back and through again.

Automatic processes are beginning to take the place of human labor in guide, rod, bar, and hoop mills. In a continuous furnace for a bar mill in the Jones and Laughlin plant, as has been described, the hot billet falls from the furnace into a channel fitted with rollers. This channel leads to the first set of rolls, then on to the next. After passing through two or three sets of rolls, the billet is so drawn out that it bends readily and the channel which carries it winds about from one set of rolls to another. Rollers are no longer needed to drive it down the channel, for the next set of rolls seizes it before its tail has left the last one. From the final set of rolls, a channel with rollers leads to the cooling beds, far down the mill. During all of this process the bar is scarcely touched with a pair of tongs. Similar methods are coming into vogue in other mills of this character, and apparently it will not be long before the process in all becomes largely automatic.

Where such speed is maintained, and such heat encountered as in the finishing mills described, it is conceded that the men cannot stand up to their work twelve hours without rest. Consequently, as in the iron-rolling mills which belong in this group, "spell hands" are provided, and the men in the most difficult positions rest about a third of the time.

These are the mills where the greatest amount of human exertion is employed. Regardless of product, whether flats or hoops or rods, the work is much the same. It is unnecessary for the purposes of this book to attempt a detailed description of each.

The second class of mills includes those rolling sheet and plate. The meaning of the terms "plate" and "sheet" is doubtless plain enough. The main distinction is with respect to thickness, plate steel being the thicker.

The sheet mills require as much human labor as the bar mills, but there has been no tendency to introduce automatic processes such as we found in the latter. Two heating furnaces are required with every sheet mill,—the "pair" furnace and the "sheet" furnace. Into the pair furnace are charged bars or plates of steel about six inches thick and eight by twenty inches square, a size that can be conveniently handled with tongs. When heated, two bars are drawn, and they are rolled, one after the other, in a small mill with even but roughened rolls. After two or three passes, which flatten them out, one is placed on top of the other and they are put through together. Singly they would be too thin for the rolls to take hold, and also would lose their heat too quickly. From the roughing rolls the steel is taken, without re-heating, to the finishing or "chill" rolls, and rolled out to a sheet three to four feet in length and two or two and a half feet wide. Three or four sheets are then placed on top of each other, or "matched," and put into the sheet furnace. After being re-heated they are again rolled, this time to a length of eight or nine feet. The sheets are next peeled apart; each one is folded over, heated a third time and rolled to the length desired. After being sheared to proper size, put through the cold rolls—that is, rolled without being heated—and heated once more in the annealing furnace, the sheets are ready for shipment.

To understand plate rolling we must go back to the slabbing mill, which, it will be remembered, starts like the blooming mill with the ingot from the soaking pits. The ingot is rolled down to a thickness of about six inches and then cut up into slabs which vary in size according to the size of the plate that is to be rolled, for each slab must make one plate. The slabs are re-heated and then they are rolled down in the ponderous plate mills with their big, smooth rolls, built three-high so that they do not have to be reversed. A section of the roll table on either side of the rolls is movable, and after the slab has gone over the lower roll, the table on the far side is raised to the level of the upper surface of the middle roll, and the slab comes back on the upper pass.

The labor required about the plate mill appears quite similar to that about the blooming mill, but the work is really much more difficult, for the finished plate must not vary far from the standard gauge. Accordingly the plate roller stands down near the rolls, where he can keep careful watch. He carries a micrometer and measures the thickness of every plate. The man who stands in the pulpit and does the work required of a roller in a blooming mill is called a "screw-down." There are in addition two men called "hookers," who stand beside the rolls and with hooks or levers suspended from above turn the slab around as may be required.

Structural and rail mills belong in a class fairly distinct from the mills described. Their product is more nearly finished than are rods, bars or plates, because it does not require any further manufacturing process. Moreover, the shapes to be rolled are more intricate and the process is more difficult. It is a simple thing as far as the construction of a mill is concerned, to roll a round bar or rod, and comparatively so to roll an angle, but it is evident that a more difficult technique is involved in rolling a bar for a T-rail or an I-beam so that it shall be thinner in the middle than at the edges.

The Edgar Thomson plant, at Braddock, is equipped for rolling rails exclusively. Each ingot, after it has gone through the blooming mill, is cut into three thick bars not a quarter the length of a rail, and square or rectangular in the cross-section. Each of these blooms, re-heated and sent through a series or train of rolls, will make a rail. The first pair of rolls are so shaped as to indent the bar as it passes through. A "collar" on the rolls presses in on the soft steel in the same way that a wagon wheel makes a rut in a muddy road. In the next pair the indentation is made more distinct, and so on with a half dozen sets of rolls, until in a very few minutes the standard shape emerges.

The principle of the structural mill is similar, but to produce the many different shapes demanded there is greater variety in the sizes and surfaces of rolls, and more time and labor are consumed in changing them.

Tube mills stand in a class altogether by themselves, and to the uninitiated they seem the most ingenious in the trade, for not only must the steel be rolled, but it must be curved at the same time, so that a flat strip may become a smooth, symmetrical pipe. The National Tube Works at McKeesport makes all sizes of pipe up to two feet in diameter. For this purpose plate mills roll out strips of plate, called "skelp," in widths which will roll lengthwise into tubes of the diameters desired. A pamphlet issued by the National Tube Company affords a very lucid description of tube making, from which I can do no better than quote:

> Wrought pipe is made by the butt-weld or lap-weld process. Butt-welding consists in heating the plate in a long furnace to a welding heat throughout and then drawing through a bell-shaped ring whereby the edges of the plate are forced together and welded. The pipe is now passed through suitable rolls which give the correct outside diameter and is finished by cross-rolling. The latter straightens the pipe, and at the same time gives the surface a clean finish. Leaving the cross-rolls the pipes pass on to an inclined cooling table, up which they are rolled to the conveyors, thus preventing unequal cooling.
>
> When cold the ends of the pipe are cut off and threaded if desired, after which it is tested. An hydraulic testing machine is provided for each pair of threading machines, so

arranged that the pipe can be adjusted between two water-tight heads connecting with the hydraulic line. An hydro-static pressure of 600 pounds per square inch is applied to each piece unless a higher test is required. The pipe is now bundled and tagged, or in case of sizes two inches or over is stenciled with the tester's mark and the length.

The butt-weld process has been greatly improved of late years in respect to the uniformity of the weld, due to improvements in pipe steel and the machinery in use. A number of tests have shown butt-weld steel pipe to stand 3,000 to 6,000 pounds per square inch hydrostatic pressure, according to the size, frequently not bursting at the higher pressure.

The lap-weld process consists of two operations, bending and welding. The plate is brought to a red heat in a suitable furnace, and then passed through a set of rolls which bevel the edges, so that when overlapped and welded the seam will be neat and smooth. It now passes immediately to the bending machine where it takes roughly the cylindrical shape of a pipe with the two edges overlapping. In this form it is again heated in another furnace similar in general construction to that used in the butt-weld department. When sufficiently heated the skelp is pushed out of the opposite end to which it was charged, into the welding rolls. Each of these rolls has a semi-circular groove corresponding to the size of pipe being made. A cast iron ball, or mandrel, held in position between the welding rolls by a stout rod serves to support the inside of the pipe as it is carried through. This "ball" is shaped like a projectile and the pipe slides over it on being drawn through the rolls. Thus every portion of the lapped edge is subjected to a compression between the ball on the inside and the rolls on the outside, which reduces the lap to the same thickness as the rest of the pipe, and welds the overlapping portions solidly together. Following the welding rolls are the sizing rolls, straightening rolls and cooling tables. As the width of overlap of the edges is three or four times the thickness of the material, the weld is as strong as any other part of the pipe, if not stronger.

In no part of steel manufacture have inventions and improvements had such an effect upon working conditions as in the rolling mills. Twenty years ago these mills were alive with men. To-day you will find large numbers of men in the guide and merchant mills, but at the blooming mills, the plate mills and the structural and rail mills you have to look sharply not to miss them entirely. These mills have become largely automatic.

The two improvements that have contributed most to the cutting down of the labor force are the electric crane and the movable roll tables. Hydraulic cranes were in use before electric cranes, but they are useful only within a limited range. The electric crane operates over the whole length of a mill. Heavy material that formerly a dozen men moved with difficulty, is now picked up and moved easily by two men, working with a crane. Roll changing has become an easier and swifter process through the aid of the crane, and practically all of the heavy lifting and carrying within the mill is thus accomplished by electric power.

The advantage of the roll table is obvious. At the structural mills, for example, where men formerly struggled with the heavy beams, the tables are made to move laterally so that one table serves in succession the different sets in a train of rolls.

Not only have these and other inventions greatly reduced the number of men necessary to a process, but they have occasioned more or less friction between employer and employe. They have made possible a greatly increased tonnage, with consequently increased returns to industry, the equitable division of which is a point of controversy.

As in the case of blast furnace improvements, the effect has been to reduce the number of men employed, rather than the length of the working day. The standard length is twelve hours, and the rolling mills stop only from Saturday night to Sunday night.

BLOOMING MILL AS THE INGOT ENTERS THE ROLLS

RAIL STRAIGHTENER

CUTTING STEEL PLATE WITH HYDRAULIC SHEARS

TYPICAL SHIPPING YARD

CHAPTER VII

HEALTH AND ACCIDENTS IN STEEL MAKING

THE foregoing chapters have put in simple terms how iron and steel are treated in the mills of Pittsburgh. The story is only partly told, however, if we say nothing of the effect of the processes upon the men who control them. Yet in the labor conflicts that are to be discussed in the succeeding chapters, it will be seen that the points of controversy have been usually wages, hours, or the right to organize. Until recently, little attention has been paid by those most directly concerned to two other fundamental subjects,—health and accidents in steel making.

What I have to say about health is very largely the result of impressions gathered during my ten months' stay among the steel workers. Medical opinion and other data support these impressions, and show the need for a thorough inquiry by experts in hygiene into the subject of health conditions in the steel mills.

I began my study of the industry with no preconceived ideas as to health. I did not know what effect the work might have, and in fact, I ignored that side of the subject for some time. As time went on, however, and I repeatedly visited the mills, certain facts began to thrust themselves upon my attention.

I discovered that there is always a fine dust in the air of a steel mill. It was not very noticeable at first, but after being in a mill or around the furnaces for a time, I always found my coat covered with minute, shining grains. A visitor experiences no ill effect after a few hours in a mill, but the steel workers notice it and they declare that it gives rise to throat trouble. There is ore dust around the blast furnaces, and wherever saws are used for cutting the finished product into lengths there is steel dust. Many a workman justifies his daily glass of whiskey on the ground that it "takes the dust out of my throat." The irritation of the throat and air passages caused by this mineral dust may lead to catarrh or even to tuberculosis.*

I began to notice after a time that the men with whom I talked were often a little hard of hearing. It was some time before I connected this fact with the noise of the mill. The rolling mills are all noisy, the blooming mills and the plate mills especially so, while the cold saw bites into the steel with a screech that is fairly maddening. When I finally began to make inquiries I found that among the men I met, partial or slight deafness was quite common, and that they all attributed it to the noise. This noise has an effect also on the nerves, which is intensified by the constant vibration of the machinery; a strain more wearing on some of the men than the work itself.

The prevalence of nervous strain is a matter not to be lightly turned aside. Physical labor has without doubt been greatly lightened by the improved processes that have so changed the character of the steel industry within the last fifteen or twenty years. But where the strain upon the body has been lessened, responsibility has in most cases grown more tense, with a consequent increased demand on the nervous energy. This is true also in some work where the physical activity is not less than formerly. Improved processes frequently reduce the total amount of human toil by throwing part of a gang out of employment, only to leave the few who remain with as hard physical labor as before. Rollers, particularly, work as hard today as they did twenty years ago, and under an added strain due to the more complicated machinery under their control, and the greater speed of operation, which increases the danger of accident.

---

* "The particles of mineral dust produce an irritation of the mucous membranes of the nose, throat, respiratory organs and eyes. . . According to Arnold, the dust which is inhaled lodges on the mucous membrane of the air passages and vesicles of the lungs, there to be coughed up. . . If not expectorated, they will cause harm by clogging up the air vesicles and interfere with respiration. In the meantime not infrequently an irritation is set up, causing catarrhal conditions of the mucous membranes, or a more serious chronic inflammation of the respiratory organs, so common among persons engaged in dusty occupations. The chronic inflammatory conditions thus produced favor infection with the tubercle bacillus." Kober: Industrial Hygiene, U. S. Labor Bulletin No. 75, p. 476.

Photo by *Hine*

READY FOR A HOT JOB

Photo by *Hine*

BETWEEN SPELLS

WASHING AT THE BOSH

One of the hard conditions which the working force must face in iron or steel manufacture is heat. It is difficult to convey to the understanding of one who has never visited a mill, or who has visited one only in winter, the intensity of the heat in certain departments during the summer months. Lofty and specially designed roofs have added greatly to the comfort of the men in the more recently constructed plants; but in rolling mills the sheds can never be made so large nor the ventilation so good that much discomfort will not be occasioned by radiation from the red hot steel. In the blooming mill a glowing ingot weighing from two to ten tons is being worked all the time.

It is possible to afford relief to the men by means of air tubes, such as are in operation in the rod mill of the American Steel and Wire Company at Rankin. Here the heat is very great and the work requires considerable strength and activity. A revolving fan sucks air from the outside of the mill and forces it into a main that runs over the heads of the men at work. From this main smaller tubes run down and terminate with a flaring mouth just above each workman, supplying him steadily with air comparatively pure and much cooler than that of the mill. A similar system is in operation in the rod mill of the Schoenberger works of the American Steel and Wire Company. At the welding furnaces of the National Tube Company at McKeesport, large-sized electric fans play on the men in the hot positions, who are further protected by water-cooled shields.

It would be difficult to make such a system of service to those whose work requires considerable moving about, as in the Bessemer and open-hearth departments, where the greatest heat is encountered; but it could be adapted to any rolling mill and would be a boon to the employes.

The puddler's position is the hottest one in an iron works. While such an air tube system would seem entirely feasible, I know of no puddling furnace where it is in use. The old, independent plants in Pittsburgh are not equipped with any device for protecting the puddler from the heat of his furnace. Water-cooled shields are effectively employed in other places for this purpose and I understand that they are employed by the National Tube Company, which is the only one of the subsidiary companies of the United States Steel Corporation that has a puddling department in its Pittsburgh mills.

In open-hearth steel making the labor is not continuous, long periods of rest elapsing between the tapping of heats. But the temperature is high in the summer months; it could not be otherwise with a row of a dozen or more great ovens, containing each of them from 30 to 75 tons of molten steel. In the Bessemer department the situation is, if that were possible, more trying, for the work is continuous. There is not usually as much hot steel on hand at one time to radiate its heat, but the men work closer to the metal. The vesselman and his assistants, the "manganese" man and others, must stand frequently on the platform close beside the converter itself, while the steel pourer and his helpers work constantly close beside a ladle brimming with from ten to fifteen tons of liquid steel. There are other departments where the general atmosphere may be at a lower temperature than those just described, but where contact with the heat is equally trying, if not more so. I refer especially to places where the men stand on a heated floor. In sheet mills, small guide mills, muck and bar mills, and all mills of that class, the floor plates become heated by the hot steel continually passing over them. I have seen men standing on floors so hot that a drop of water spilled would hiss like a drop on a stove. The shoes with thick wooden soles that they wear, act as some protection, yet their feet are heated to a point of great discomfort; and this is a thing that they must encounter every day and for from eight to twelve hours, practically without relief.

The effects of working in the heat are noticeable. On a street car the men who are employed where the heat strikes their faces can often be singled out because of their peculiar complexion. Sometimes their faces are red, sometimes covered with pimples, and the skin is nearly always rough. Many people, including steel workers themselves, believe that copious perspiration is healthful under such conditions of temperature. The mill men drink great draughts of water and sweat freely. This may be healthful within certain limits, but beyond these limits it is weakening to the whole system.* Yet without this perspira-

* "One of the bad effects of profuse perspiration is that the blood is deprived of some of its constituents. The blood is taken away too long from the internal

tion I am told that the blood would not keep at a normal temperature permitting work; consequently steel workers drink a great deal. During working hours they drink water and after work they drink beer and whiskey. It would seem that the round of heat, perspiration, copious water drinking, and the use of alcoholic stimulants could not fail in time to weaken considerably a man's vital energy.

The abnormal heat of the mills may lead directly or indirectly to other ailments, some of which could be avoided by precaution on the part of the men, and some of which are inevitable. It should be remembered that there is great heat even in the winter months; as much physical exertion is required then as at any other time, and the men perspire freely in the coldest weather. No man, with his work clothes in such condition, can go from the atmosphere of the mill out into the cold winter air without incurring great risk. To be safe, every man ought to take a bath and make a complete change of clothing before leaving the mill. This, however, is impossible because of the lack of bathing facilities and privacy in most of the Pittsburgh mills.

In view of the difficulties, a surprising amount of precautionary action is taken by the men. In most mills each man is provided with a locker in which he may keep extra clothing. Most of them carry an extra shirt so that they may put on a dry garment before leaving the mill, and most of them bathe at least their arms and faces in the "bosh," a trough of water in which tools are placed to cool after use. What convenient shower baths and clean towels would mean to mill men may be readily imagined.* With but a single exception, the men to whom I mentioned bathing facilities agreed that they would be generally used and appreciated. Because of the lack of such facilities it is human nature for some men to leave the mills without preparing for the

organs; the proper distribution of the blood supply is interfered with, and in consequence the tone and nutrition of the stomach, lungs, heart and other internal organs is lowered. There is loss of appetite and indigestion ensues; the red corpuscles are decreased; languor and general enervation is experienced, and the system in consequence is rendered more susceptible to disease." Kober: Industrial Hygiene, U. S. Labor Bulletin, No. 75, March 1908, pp. 541–542.

* At the National Tube Company works in McKeesport there are stationary bowls with running water, and recently shower baths have been installed in some of the departments.

shock of the cold air beyond putting on an overcoat. Many others make a preparation that is wholly inadequate. I chanced to meet several men and was told of a number of others, who were affected, or had been, with throat, bronchial and pulmonary troubles which they attributed to the conditions just described. Rheumatism also seems to be a common trouble in the steel districts.

The Amalgamated Association of Iron and Steel and Tin Workers established a death benefit fund in 1904, and since then they have kept a record of the number and causes of deaths. This record is not a complete list even for the members of that organization, for deaths of members not in good standing, and so ineligible to the benefits, are not reported. The reports indicate, however, that the diseases causing the most deaths among iron, steel and tin workers are of a sort likely to be induced by dust, heat conditions, and sudden changes in temperature. Among these tuberculosis leads and pneumonia stands second. Accidents claim a larger percentage than any other one cause; stomach and bowel troubles, especially typhoid, are common. Oliver states * that English iron and steel workers have a mortality figure 37 per cent above that of the standard of occupied males, and the same writer ascribes to iron workers greater suffering than that endured by others "from influenza and from diseases of the nervous, circulatory, respiratory, digestive and urinary systems." Their mortality figure from lung diseases he says is "more than double the standard figure."

As long as the twelve-hour day prevails, attempts to improve health conditions in the mills will be largely nullified. If the best of bathing facilities were installed, although the men to-day feel their lack, it would probably be the unusual man who would avail himself of them. At the end of twelve hours in the mill most men want the shortest cut out to what remains of the day.

When the mills are running full the men are chronically tired. The upsetting of all the natural customs of life every second week when the men change to the night shift, is in itself inimical to health. It takes until the end of the week, the men say, to grow sufficiently accustomed to the change to be able to

* Oliver, Thomas: Dangerous Trades, p. 141. London, J. Murray, 1902.

sleep more than four or five hours during the day. And then they change back.* The alternation of day and night shifts every fortnight is desired by the men; it gives each man 26 weeks a year of day employment. But the seven-day week and the twelve-hour shifts accentuate the evils inherent in all night work.

By far the greatest menace to health in the steel industry is, in my belief, this twelve-hour day. Beside this, heat and even speeding are unimportant. If the other conditions that I have mentioned are at all unhygienic in their nature, the effect of every one is intensified by the abnormal work-day. Who can doubt that toward the end of a twelve-hour shift a man's vital energy is sub-normal, and his power of resistance to disease materially lowered? If this is true, it must be trebly so at the end of the twenty-four hour shift, which is experienced fortnightly in Allegheny County by nearly 6,000 blast furnace men.

Turning now to the subject of work-accidents, every workman in an iron or steel mill is in danger, because he is working with forces which are, seemingly, always watching for a chance to get beyond human control. The steel companies recognize the element of danger when they admit visitors to their mills, and before one may enter a mill of the United States Steel Corporation, he must sign an agreement freeing the company from liability for any injury to his person while on the company's premises.† In twelve months the records of the coroner of Allegheny County showed 195 deaths from work-accidents in blast furnaces and in iron and steel mills, but this was no indication of the number of men whose earning power was cut down by injuries which threw them out of work for longer or shorter periods, or who were so crippled as to be put into the dependent classes.

The results of a systematic study of accidents in the trade are presented in the chapter on The Steel Workers in Miss East-

* On this subject see Homestead: The Households of a Mill Town, by Margaret F. Byington, pp. 36–37. Pittsburgh Survey series.

† On the face of the passes used by the Carnegie Steel Company there is this statement: "The person or persons, accepting this pass, in consideration therefor, agree that the Carnegie Steel Company shall not be liable, under any circumstances, whether of negligence of employes, or otherwise, for any injury to the person, or for any loss or damage suffered while on the company's premises." The visitor must sign an acceptance of these conditions on the back of the pass. A form similar to this is used by the other companies of the Steel Corporation.

man's book, Work Accidents and the Law, a companion volume of the Pittsburgh Survey. She shows that as far as number of casualties are concerned, "railroads in the yards, dinkey trains throughout the mills, and traveling cranes overhead, as destroyers of life, are much more to be feared than blast furnaces, converters, and rolling mills."

TABLE I.—195 FATALITIES IN STEEL PLANTS OF THE PITTSBURGH DISTRICT, JULY 1, 1906–JUNE 30, 1907.—BY CAUSES

Cause		Number of Fatalities
Hot metal explosions	22	
Asphyxiation by furnace gas	5	
Operation of rolls	10	
Total		37 (19 per cent)
Operation of broad gauge railroad . . .	18	
" " narrow gauge railroad . . .	13	
" " cranes	42	
Total		73 (37 per cent)
Falling from height or into pit	24	57%
Electric shock	7	
Loading and piling of steel and iron products	8	
		39 (20 per cent)
Due to miscellaneous causes		46 (24 per cent)
Total number killed in steel making .	195	

Over half the accidents in the steel mills thus are due to causes common to all heavy mechanical work, and I must refer the reader to Miss Eastman's book for an adequate discussion of them. Here I may set down some observations on the special hazards in the processes of iron and steel making. Blast furnaces have a bad record for accidents, fewer in number than in the steel mills, but often marked by ghastly consequences. In January, 1907, Number 2 furnace of the Eliza group, owned by the Jones and Laughlin Steel Company, exploded without warning, blowing out the whole side of the furnace and burning to death fourteen men. In February, March and May, accidents occurred in these same furnaces, resulting in injuries and loss of life. On November 15, 1907, nine men were badly burned by an outburst of flame and stock, while doing repair work at the top of one of the Lucy furnaces, owned by the Carnegie Steel Company. On February 12, 1908, at McKeesport, an explosion occurred at the

Monongahela Furnaces of the National Tube Company, causing the death of two men and seriously burning three others.

One of the chief causes of what are commonly called blast furnace explosions is a "slip." When a furnace is working properly, there is constant settling down of the stock, as the material at the zone of fusion is melted away, but sometimes the whole mass is checked in its movement by adhering to the walls of the furnace. The melting process goes on and the result is that a gap occurs between the molten iron and the unmelted stock above, which tends to form an arch, and thus remain more securely in place. As the melting continues, this gap becomes wider. When a furnace keeper finds the stock is hanging, he orders the blast reduced or taken off, and this will usually let the mass slip down. This is a thing that occurs every day and usually there is no trouble; but occasionally there is a bad hang,—a large amount of material is melted away, widening the gap, so that when the slip finally does occur the upward rush of the blast may be strong enough to lift the top of the furnace and blow out several tons of stock with it. In most furnaces the workmen are protected from the falling mass after a slip, by a heavy iron roof over their heads. In a few of the old independent plants there is no protection. If the slip is excessive, or the furnace defective, the sides may give way and the molten metal burst out at the bottom, bringing death to the crew at the base of the stack. Another fruitful cause of explosions is the burning through of pipes or plates, letting water come in contact with the molten iron. But there are other causes; blast furnaces are inclined to be erratic; they often behave badly when the best furnace experts cannot detect the cause,* and every furnace employe is always in the presence of danger.

It is noticeable that the men on the pouring platform and the vesselmen in the Bessemer departments have their clothes burned full of little holes. Sometimes the molds will be shifted at the wrong time and the stream of metal, instead of pouring into the mold, strikes the edge and is thrown in a shower on all sides.

---

* Many engineers from all parts of the country came to Pittsburgh in January, 1907, to examine the Jones and Laughlin furnace after the explosion referred to. All agreed that the accident could not have been foreseen and that the furnace was constructed according to the best known model.

Molds have been known to explode when the hot steel struck them because a little moisture had in some way found its way into them. The men who work on the converter platform are in danger from the "spittings" which collect above. During a blow, considerable spray is thrown up which adheres to cross beams or to the mill wall. Unless removed, an increasing mass forms which ultimately falls of its own weight, greatly endangering the men below. On the first day of January, 1908, two or more men were killed and fifteen badly injured by an explosion of a fifteen-ton converter in the Edgar Thomson Works of the Carnegie Steel Company. The men on the floor below the converter were caught without warning or chance to escape.

The open-hearth department is equally dangerous. I talked with a man who had been burned when the fluid steel broke out sooner than he had expected as he was knocking out the tapping hole. The steel came with a rush and his face and body were badly seared. This man had been a first helper, the man in charge of a furnace, but he gave up the job because, as he said, he lost his nerve over another accident in which a man under him was killed. A furnace had just been tapped. The crane lifted the huge ladle of molten steel out of the pit and was about to swing it around, when something gave way and the whole load dropped eight or ten feet, with an explosion as it struck the ground. Some of the metal flew completely over the furnace and striking the ground on the opposite side, rebounded and splashed over a workman standing some distance away. This man was horribly burned and died almost instantly. He had been standing where anyone would have thought him safe—on the far side of the furnace. Men standing near were severely burned, but recovered from their injuries.

So long as steel is made there will be accidents. Before their occurrence can be absolutely prevented, it will be necessary to change human nature, and in some way to make sure and unchanging man's control over inanimate things. But allowing in the fullest measure for all reasonable lapses, and for everything unexpected, the list of accidents in iron and steel works is shockingly long. Many accidents occur because an employe is negligent or careless. Some employers would have us believe that most of them occur because of such negligence. It is usually impossible to tell, in any accident case, just how much the negligence of the employe contributed to the occurrence. Here again the long work day enters as a factor. Even if the extent of the employe's negligence could be ascertained, inquiry should be made as to whether he had been continuously on duty one hour or twenty-four, and whether his work had been more or less than one man might reasonably be expected to perform. It is a rare man who can keep his mental faculties keenly alert and centered on one object for twelve consecutive hours. In blaming their employes for lapses of attention which have resulted in accidents, manufacturers may often be demanding a self-control and mental alertness such as few men can sustain throughout practically their entire waking hours.

Granting, however, that employes should be held up to the highest standard of efficiency, the companies can never reasonably disclaim responsibility unless they have taken every possible precaution known to promote safety. Let me cite two illustrations from conditions the year of my investigation. In the South Side plant of the Jones and Laughlin Steel Company, along the side of one of the long roll tables leading to a blooming mill there is a line of cogged wheels, the gearing that operates the rollers. This gearing was, when I visited the plant in the spring of 1908, absolutely unguarded, although it was common knowledge that workmen had been caught in just such places and badly injured. Not only that, but the factory law of Pennsylvania requires that such gears be protected. I do not know that any one had ever been injured on this particular roll table in the Jones and Laughlin plant, but if an employe had been injured, could the company have pleaded the negligence of the injured man and on that basis have escaped liability? They could, according to traditional court decisions, but not in common reason before the bar of public opinion. In many places in this plant I found unguarded fly wheels and belting, especially in the cold rolled shafting department and in the spike and bolt factory.

Soaking pits are usually sunk below the level of the mill floor. At the plant of the National Tube Company at McKeesport, the pits were built of solid brick work so as to stand some ten feet above the floor level of the mill and escape the water in times of flood on the Monongahela River. Along one side, down below, was run the narrow gauge track to bring the ingots on from the stripper. It was the practice for a "tongsman," who assisted the craneman, to walk along on the edge of the brick work of the raised furnaces, just above this narrow gauge track, steadying the ingot on its way to the pits or to the rolls. A sudden jerk of the crane, and he was bound to have hard work keeping his footing on that parapet. In February, 1908, the heater fell from the edge and fractured his skull on the rail. Later, in his weakened condition resulting from the accident, he contracted pneumonia and died. The danger at this point has since been removed by a change in method. Tongsmen are no longer required, and it is unnecessary for anyone to walk near the edge above the tracks. And had there been no such change in equipment, it is improbable that such an obvious hazard would have continued under the present efficient system of safety inspection developed by the Tube Company.

Hook-ons, the brakemen on the dinkey trains, frequently have hands or fingers smashed between cars. I noted very few cars equipped with automatic coupling devices. A dinkey engineer who had been running an engine for twenty-five years, told me that he has killed two men in that time and smashed fingers or hands for so many hook-ons that he has no idea as to the number.

It is often asserted, and probably with some truth, that the foreign element in the mills has much to do with the frequency of accidents, and in proof of this it is claimed that the majority of the injured men are foreigners. This proves little, when it is remembered that practically two-thirds of the men employed in the large steel plants are foreign born. In blast furnaces, aside from the Irish foreman, there are seldom any but Slavs or Hungarians employed. In the converter explosion at the Edgar Thomson plant on January 1, 1908, the men in the pit below the converter were naturally the ones caught, and the men who work in the pit are generally immigrant day laborers. It is undoubtedly true, however, that many accidents are attributable to the ignorance of what is going forward in the mill on the part of "greeners" who are put to work before they have a knowledge of English or of the processes in which they are to take a part. If the foreigner is a menace to the skilled worker's pocketbook, he is probably a greater menace to both their lives. Unacquainted with the machinery, and with an exasperated boss shouting unintelligible orders, the Slav workman is as likely to run into danger as out of it, and may throw the lives of all his fellows into jeopardy.

Some of the steel companies are making efforts to grapple with the situation. With the appointment of a central Committee of Safety, in April, 1908, the United States Steel Corporation entered upon an energetic campaign to bring the safety standards of all its subsidiary companies not only up to the levels set by the most progressive plants among them, but to overhaul all plants from the standpoint of protective machinery, to define safety specifications for all new equipment, and to work out new methods of prevention. Experts employed by the constituent companies are devoting their whole time to studying the problem. A system of inspection has been introduced, and the inspectors in each plant make regular reports with recommendations to those in authority. In some of the mills committees of workmen co-operate.*

Much is being accomplished in these directions, but it is too soon to pass judgment. On my last visits to the mills I found much raggedness in the standards installed in some plants as against others. Old machinery and cramped floor space cannot be changed over night; the experts are not always able to secure at once the installation of safety devices needed, because of the expense or inconvenience. The inertia of superintendents and foremen who chafe at precautions which are troublesome or which interfere with output, must be overcome. Workmen must be educated to a change of habit and sentiment with respect to everyday risks.

No large corporation is manifesting a more intelligent determination in regard to accidents than the United States Steel Corporation. Its safety men have a big work before them; one which is rendered trebly difficult by the nature of the industry, by the

---

* For a description of this work of prevention see "Safety Provisions in the United States Steel Corporation," by David S. Beyer, chief safety inspector, American Steel and Wire Company, published as Appendix III in Eastman's Work-Accidents and the Law.

speeding up and the twelve-hour day, and by the years of inexcusable negligence and downright disregard of human life which have characterized the steel industry in the past. To quote from Miss Eastman's conclusions:

> At least 57 per cent of the steel mill fatalities are simple, and altogether within the understanding of the ordinary man. One does not need the training of an engineer nor the experience of a mechanic to see how the side of a steel car may slip from crane chains and fall on a man below, or how a machinist walking a greasy beam sixty feet in the air may lose his balance, or how a pile of iron pipe may fall and crush a man or two if something gives out at the bottom of the pile. The large steel companies have long defended a policy of silence with regard to the number and character of their accidents, largely on the ground that any other policy would result in unintelligent hysterical outcry and clamor on the part of the public. If accidents in steel mills were altogether a result of processes which only experts can understand, there might be some reason in such a policy. But finding that at least 57 per cent of the fatal accidents studied were due to ordinary understandable causes, we can maintain not only that the public has a right to know the facts but that its possession of this knowledge is an important factor in the prevention of accidents.
>
> If legislation is in view, there is a second significance in this 57 per cent of "simple" accidents. They serve to unite the steel industry with other industries in regard to its commonest accidents. Industrial railroads and traveling cranes are common in all large construction companies; in almost all factories there is repair work, cleaning, oiling, etc., to be done at a dangerous height; it would be hard to find a mill which does not use electricity. Therefore, legislation looking to the prevention of the commonest accidents of the steel mills need not be special legislation for one industry. It can be an extension of the present factory law. . . .
>
> There can be no doubt that the unrelaxing tension and speed in the American steel mill makes for danger. To go slower would be to go backward in industry, and that is more than can be expected of America. But by shortening hours of work the dangers of speed can be lessened; the minds and bodies of the men can be kept up to the pace of the mill. Greater intensity of work necessitates longer periods of relaxation. If the strain of the work cannot be lessened the duration must be. Think of the crane man, upon whose

alertness and care depend the lives of several others. His is a hot, unpleasant, lonely job. There is no one to spell him. He cannot get down from his cab for any reason. And he works twelve hours every day in the year except Christmas and Fourth of July. No steel company can maintain that it has done everything to prevent accidents until it has reduced the working hours of men in such responsible positions.

Another observation which one cannot fail to make is not only that some companies maintain higher standards of safety than others, but that different plants of the same company, different parts of the same plant, are not kept up to equal standards of safety. The reason is obvious. "This isn't one of our best plants," an inspector will say. "You see, we're very much crowded here and that makes things more dangerous. Eventually, I suppose, we'll have to abandon this plant." Or, "This part of the mill is old. We haven't put safety devices in here. It would hardly pay. We are going to tear all this down in a few years."—Ordinary business economy, to be sure. But meanwhile men go on working in the crowded plant where things are not safe; men go on working in the old, badly lighted part of the mill where it "isn't worth while" to put in guards.

This sort of economy is of a piece with that of the miner who wants to finish loading his car and takes his chance of a fall of slate by failing to put up needed posts. It is human nature, but taking chances with other men's lives ought not to be so easy.

If during the past twenty years the factory inspection laws of Pennsylvania had been adequately enforced in Pittsburgh, if every death and serious injury had by law carried with it a sure and considerable compensation to the family of the men injured, taking such chances would not have been so easy nor so cheap; nor the toll of suffering so large. Pennsylvania is without such state factory inspection or such compensation laws.

PART II
THE STRUGGLE FOR CONTROL

CHAPTER VIII

UNIONISM AND THE UNION MOVEMENT

THE labor problem in the iron and steel industry is typical, in its most fundamental aspects, of the labor problem everywhere, and all of the remaining chapters of this book are devoted to its discussion. As in all industries, the underlying cause of friction has been the essential difference in the objectives of employer and employe. To the employe, the objective is high wages and a short working day; however interested he may be in the success of the establishment in which he is engaged, that is not his primary consideration. To the employer, output and profits are the things of first importance. Both may believe in a theoretically equitable division of proceeds; but in practice the workingman endeavors to get the highest possible wage, while the employer regards labor as a cost to be reduced to the minimum, like any other cost. There are many individual cases where this statement would not be exactly true. Human and fraternal relations enter in, especially when an industry is small and managers and men are thrown close to each other. It expresses, nevertheless, the economic conflict underlying all dealings between capital and labor. As such, it is tempered by the fact that at bottom what the employer is after is low labor cost, rather than low wages; and that what the employe is after is high wages rather than high labor cost. Production may be increased, the earnings of labor raised, and labor cost decreased, all at the same time; and while a recognition of this fact does not do away with the inherent conflict of interests, it has become a basis in some industries for more reasonable and far-sighted relations.

The controversy over the length of the working day is similar in its nature to the wage problem, and it becomes more acute in an industry like iron and steel manufacture, where the process is carried on continuously through the twenty-four hours of the day.

In such employment there can be no ten-hour compromise. The vast majority of the employes must work either eight hours or twelve, and an eight-hour system means 50 per cent more employes than a twelve-hour system, because it requires three shifts instead of two.

Restriction of output and "speeding-up" methods are fruitful causes of controversy, in adjusting the terms of employment. The "soldierer"—the man who gives niggardly of his effort, all would condemn; and everyone would concede, also, theoretically at least, that a workman should not be required to injure his health by overwork. Where to strike the balance between these two extremes is a question upon which honest men may differ. With the lack of medical surveillance of industry in America, it is usually impossible to say with assurance that there is injury to health until that injury has actually been done. But the question is not one of determining just where the danger line is. It would be an atrocious system that required every man to work up to that point. It is rather a question of how much energy an employer has a right to demand. If he should demand all, there would be nothing left for family or society; with manhood and citizenship both taken away, only a brute would remain.

These are issues over which employer and employe are still in dispute. Each has tried to control them in accordance with his own theories. Consequently, trade unions have arisen on the one hand, employers' associations on the other, and controversies have been waged between organizations instead of between individuals. Trade union has been arrayed against association or trust, until a new setting has been given to the whole problem by the successful attempts of the employers, in these later days, to weaken the employes' organizations in their fight for a control of the conditions of work or to destroy those organizations utterly. So the further question arises whether workingmen should be protected in their undoubted right to organize themselves in unions, or whether some substitute for unionism and collective bargaining should be sought.

The Pittsburgh puddlers were the leaders in the labor movement in the iron industry. As early as 1849, before there is any record of union activity in the iron trade, they conducted a prolonged strike which lasted from December 20 of that year until May 12, 1850.* The workmen lost, but it may be that in this strike they learned the necessity of organization. The first union movement in the industry grew out of the panic of 1857. That panic threatened the iron trade with disaster, and the manufacturers, as one measure of safety, reduced wages of puddlers to $3.50 per ton at the beginning of 1858, and later in the same year to $3.25.

A little company of puddlers in the city of Pittsburgh was in the habit of meeting on Saturday evenings at an old hotel on Diamond Street; and here, over their beer, they used to discuss all sorts of questions, political, social and economic. In 1858, spurred on by the low wages then prevailing, this group organized itself into a union, the members calling themselves "Sons of Vulcan."† This was a dangerous thing to do, for trade unions were looked upon as revolutionary bodies and their members classed with anarchists and similar "undesirable citizens." The legal right of workmen to organize is no longer questioned; the moral right is seldom disputed; the country and the world have since moved on so far that it is hard to realize that it would be even more hazardous today for the Pittsburgh steel workers to join a union than it was for that little band of puddlers to start the movement in 1858. Yet such is the fact.

The organization was launched with great caution; only a few tried men, who could keep their own counsel, were invited to join. Little was attempted for over two years, the organization merely keeping together and biding its time. In 1861, with the outbreak of the Civil War and the passage of a favorable tariff bill, the iron trade began to revive and the Sons of Vulcan, in August of that year, effected a reorganization, with Miles Humphreys, now chief of the fire department of Pittsburgh, as "Grand Vulcan." The next year was spent in vigorously extending the organization and on September 8, 1862, secrecy was abandoned, a constitution was adopted, and a national organization was effected in Pittsburgh called the "National Forge." Miles Humphreys was elected president, Patrick Graham vice-president, M. Grogan secretary, and H. Thompson treasurer. The organization was extended east

* Pittsburgh *Commercial-Gazette*, May 30, 1882.
† *National Labor Tribune*, August 1, 1874.

77

and west, and local "forges" were organized in other states. Growth was slow at first, but in 1865 became more rapid. The convention which met August 5, 7 and 8 of that year issued an "Address to Boilers and Puddlers of the United States,"* in which the statement was made that a greater number of locals had been established in the four months preceding than in all the seven years before, and that within that time the membership had trebled. The delegates at this convention were from five different states. The next year a more determined effort was made at extending the membership, and Miles Humphreys and Patrick Graham were appointed traveling organizers.† They traveled throughout the iron manufacturing districts of the country, from Boston to St. Louis, visiting nearly every iron mill on their journey and organizing a large number of local forges. Yet President Mc-Laughlin, in his address to the convention in 1873, stated that when he first became a member in 1868, there were less than 600 members.‡ This shows how slow and painful was the growth of unionism in its early years in the iron industry. From this time, however, it would appear, from the fragmentary data to which I have access, that the advance was more rapid. In 1872, the president reported the existence of 55 lodges§ and every journeyman puddler in Chicago was said to be in the organization.‖ In 1873, the secretary reported a total of 3,331 taxable members in 83 lodges, located in 12 states,¶ and in 1876, the year of the amalgamation of the organizations in the iron and steel trade, the Sons of Vulcan was regarded as one of the strongest unions in the United States.

The first few years of the existence of the Grand Forge showed few results as far as recognition from employers was concerned, though the trade was so enlivened by the war that wages rose steadily from $3.56 per ton in October, 1861, to $9.00 in the latter part of 1864. In 1865 the war ended and the future of the iron market did not look particularly promising. The manufacturers

---

* *Fincher's Trade's Review*, September 16, 1865.   † Ibid., August 16, 1866.
‡ *Vulcan Record*, Vol. I, No. 12, 1873, p. 23.
§ *Workingman's Advocate*, March 30, 1872.   ‖ Ibid., April 13, 1872.
¶ *Vulcan Record*, 1873, Vol. I, No. 12, pp. 18–19.   There seems to have been a slight falling off in 1874.   At any rate, only 74 lodges were represented in the convention.   (*National Labor Tribune*, Aug. 15, 1874.)   I have no data as to membership for 1875 or 1876, but in any event the decline was only temporary.

Drawn by Joseph Stella

A BREATHING SPELL

Photo by *Chautauqua Photograph Co.*

GROUP OF MILL WORKERS

[This picture was long since popularized in Pittsburgh by its use on colored postal cards. The group presented is a thoroughly characteristic one]

then came in direct contact with the union for the first time in an attempt to reduce wages. The strike which followed was a contest over the principle of unionism as well as over wages. The question was whether the manufacturers would sign a scale with the Sons of Vulcan, and it is probable that the puddlers understood that this strike was to settle the question whether they had a right to a union. The contest lasted eight months and was a victory for the men on both points, for the Pittsburgh employers—the battle was fought out in the Pittsburgh mills—recognized the union and signed a scale of wages based on the selling price of bar iron.* As the price continued at a high point, the puddlers' wages remained around $8.00 or $9.00 a ton until 1867. This sliding scale system, devised by Miles Humphreys and his associates, is a plan by which wages are made to fluctuate with the condition of the market. When the price of bar iron advances, puddlers' wages go up a certain per cent, and when it falls, wages drop correspondingly down to the base—a sum arbitrarily fixed, below which it is mutually agreed wages shall not go, however low the price of bar iron may fall. Bi-monthly adjustments are made and the wages fixed for the next two months in accordance with the selling price prevailing during the period just past. Thus, if there is a fall in prices wages do not follow it immediately, and the workingmen, who watch closely the market quotations, know a month or two in advance that their wages are to be reduced, and so can be prepared for it. This system, inaugurated by the Sons of Vulcan in 1865, is still in force in the iron trade without substantial modification.

The national officers at first devoted only a part of their time to the affairs of the organization. None of them were paid salaries and they worked over union business, many a time, far into the night, after a day's work in the mill. The first money paid out for salaries was in 1866, to organizers. These were paid puddlers' daily wages, and were furnished with traveling expenses. Later the officers were put on salary.†

* See Appendix IV, p. 300.   First Sliding Scale in Iron Industry.

† The first remuneration ever given to the national president was provided for at the convention which met in Chicago, August 1, 1871. It was voted to assess each member fifty cents in order to provide a fund to remunerate the incoming president for his services for the next year. (*Workingman's Advocate,*

The dominant position of the Pittsburgh District in the union was unquestioned from the beginning of the movement down to the Homestead strike in 1892. This position was made plain in the 1874 convention, when a committee was appointed to revise the constitution. A resolution directed that the committee be chosen from the Pittsburgh forges, and the chair, in appointing them, instructed them to obtain, if possible, the assistance of the "best talent" of the subordinate forges of Pittsburgh and vicinity.

It is difficult to locate the date of the beginnings of unionism in the other branches of the iron industry. In the labor papers published in 1860 to 1870 there are just enough references to unionism among iron workers to show that there was a distinct movement in the finishing trades, but the omissions are too important to enable me to get a connected history. A New York correspondent of the Boston *Weekly Voice*, in a communication dated August 12, 1867, announced the "seventh annual" convention of "Nail Makers of the United States and Canada," which had just been held in that city. The correspondent referred to it as "one of the strongest and most permanent organizations of mechanics in this country."* If this correspondent was correct the union may have been in existence from 1860, thus antedating the active organization of the Sons of Vulcan. But this is the only reference I have found to such a union, and when the unions of the various iron trades were amalgamated in 1876, the "United Nailers" were

August 5, 1871.) In 1872 the president's salary was fixed at $500. The secretary was still serving without pay. At the convention of 1873, held August 5 to 8, in Troy, New York, the secretary reported that he had found it impossible to work in the mill and attend to his official duties at the same time, so he decided to stop mill work, and he had drawn on the treasury for a salary of $500. At this convention the Committee on Ways and Means brought in a report of which Section 4 was as follows:

"On account of the spread and growth of our organization, we recommend that our next president receive the sum of twelve hundred dollars per annum, clear of all traveling expenses, and that he shall devote all his attention to the welfare and workings of our craft."

The convention, after voting an amendment changing "twelve hundred dollars" to "fifteen hundred dollars," adopted the section (*Vulcan Record*, Vol. I, No. 12, 1873, pp. 17, 46). At the convention of 1874, held in Youngstown, Ohio, the president's salary was continued at fifteen hundred dollars, although there was some agitation in favor of reducing it, and the duties of secretary were added to those of president, the office being designated "president and secretary." (*National Labor Tribune*, August 15, 1874.)

* Boston *Weekly Voice*, August 22, 1867, p. 1.

represented by one delegate, and the organization comprised a few local lodges with no formal national organization.

It seems quite clear that the first union of roll hands in this country was organized August 6, 1864, in Troy, New York. A Troy correspondent of a labor paper described the organization as a union of "all rollers, roughers and catchers who have a practical understanding of the business." The name of this organization was "Troy Iron Rollers Association." M. Maran was the president and Dennis Lynch corresponding secretary.* Early in 1865 the iron rollers of Elmira, New York, organized as the "Iron Mill Rollers Union and Benevolent Association."

The heaters of Cleveland, Ohio, formed a union as early as 1865. *Fincher's Trade's Review* published in its trade union directory a card of a "Heaters' Union" of Cleveland, Ohio, in that year.† In 1866 cards of Heaters' Union Number 2 of Troy, New York, and Heaters' Union Number 8 of Pittsburgh,‡ were published. July 6, 1865, a convention was held at Cleveland, "pursuant to call," with delegates of heaters' unions present from various states for the purpose of "organizing a national union, or more properly, of effecting a more complete national organization." They remained in session two days and adjourned to meet at the same place July 5, 1865.§ It would appear that this movement was rather widespread, for the officers elected were from different sections of the country, including Buffalo and Troy, New York; Cleveland and Newburg, Ohio; Indianapolis, Indiana; and Chicago, Illinois. In spite of such promising beginnings, I have found no record of these organizations after the middle sixties.

It would appear that the first permanent organizations in the finishing trades were started in Chicago mills. In 1861, a local lodge of heaters was organized in Chicago and the name "Associated Brotherhood of Iron and Steel Rail Heaters" adopted. During the next few years, other similar locals were organized, and in 1872 a national convention was held in Springfield, Illinois, with nine lodges represented. In this convention the word "rail" was dropped from the name and the organization was opened to

---

* *Fincher's Trade's Review*, September 17, 1864, p. 63.
† Ibid., August 19, 1865, p. 94.　　‡ Ibid., May 12, 1866, p. 190.
§ Ibid., July 22, 1865, p. 64.

bar, plate and guide mill heaters also.*   In 1873, the second annual convention was held in Allegheny City, Pennsylvania, May 6 to 9 inclusive.   Thomas P. Jones of Chicago was elected worthy grand sire, and James D. Kelly of Joliet, Illinois, grand recording secretary.†   The committee on the state of the order reported a membership of 480 with lodges in seven states,—Missouri, Illinois, Michigan, Kentucky, Ohio, Pennsylvania and New Jersey.‡ Seventeen lodges were represented and six were unrepresented, making a total of 23 lodges,—a substantial increase over the nine lodges reported in 1872.§   The constitution was amended so as to make rollers and roughers eligible to membership, and the name of the organization was changed to "Associated Brotherhood of Iron and Steel Heaters, Rollers and Roughers."‖

At the convention of 1874, held in Covington, Kentucky, the address of the president indicated that the organization had made substantial progress, the committee on the state of the order reporting 28 lodges, with a membership of 700.   Eight states were represented, Maryland having been added to the list.¶

Up to this time there had been no local of the Heaters' Union in Pittsburgh, though there had been one across the river in

* Pennsylvania Bureau of Industrial Statistics, Report for 1887, p. G. 2.

† *Workingman's Advocate*, June 7, 1873, p. 4.   ‡ Ibid., June 14, 1873, p. 4.

§ The finances of the young organization evidently did not permit the payment of salaries, for the committee on the president's address recommended that some means be adopted to remunerate the worthy grand sire for his "outlay of money and fidelity to our Cause."   The convention voted to levy a semi-annual tax of one dollar per member on all lodges to defray the expenses of this session of the Grand Lodge, and when all expenses were paid, the remainder, if any were left, to be paid to the worthy grand sire for his labor during the past year.

‖ *Workingman's Advocate*, July 14, 1873.

¶ The convention met June 7, and was in session three days.   Eighteen lodges were represented, with a total membership of 476.   Adam Schada, of Bethlehem, Pennsylvania, was elected worthy grand sire, Benjamin F. Spangler of Springfield, Illinois, grand recording secretary, and Isaac Williams of Philadelphia, treasurer. (*Workingman's Advocate*, July 11 and 18, 1874.)   The question of compensation of officers came up again and it was decided to allow the recording secretary to keep the $37 already in his possession and $50 more was voted to him by the convention.   The worthy grand sire was tendered $200 in payment for his services for the year ending July 7, 1874.

Except as otherwise noted, the account of the 1874 convention is taken from a manuscript copy of the minutes of the convention, and other subsequent statements regarding the Heaters and Rollers' Union from a manuscript record of the grand recording secretary's correspondence, 1874–1876, both of which were furnished by G. R. S. Benjamin F. Spangler, and are on file in the library of the Wisconsin State Historical Society, Madison.

Woods Run, Allegheny City. A resolution passed the Covington convention that the "brethren in going back through Pittsburgh be asked to find out by spending a few hours there if it is possible to organize the heaters and rollers, and, if so, devise some means of doing it." It would appear that these efforts were effective, for Pittsburgh Central Lodge No. 10 was organized January 23, 1875. A membership of 65 was reported March 10, and June 26, 1876, there were 93 members to report.

The third organization of iron and steel workers to reach beyond the confines of a single mill or locality was the "Iron and Steel Roll Hands of the United States." That there was a local union of roll hands in Troy, New York, in 1864, has already been noted, but the movement which culminated in a national organization was organized in a Chicago mill in 1870.* At this time there was no other organization open to the full crews who worked at the rolls. The Heaters' Union admitted rollers and roughers in 1873, and to that extent there was an overlapping of jurisdiction; but the Roll Hands' Union admitted all men who worked around the rolls,—catchers, hookers, straighteners and buggymen, as well as the rollers and roughers. Thus the Heaters' Union was less democratic and admitted only the highly paid men.† The Roll Hands formed a national lodge at Springfield, Illinois, June 2, 1873,‡ with 15 lodges and 473 members.§ The Roll Hands' Union was never very important numerically. The local lodges were scattered from Chicago to Johnstown, Pennsylvania, chiefly in the rail mills. Perhaps the chief claim that this union had to distinction is the part it played in bringing about the amalgamation of the three organizations in the iron and steel industry in 1876.

After a number of years of experience it became evident to the different trades in the iron and steel mills that their purposes

* Report Pennsylvania Bureau of Statistics, 1887, p. G. 3.

† In the 1875 convention held at Covington, Ky., it was decided to permit a certain local lodge to use its own discretion about admitting night rollers.—Manuscript of Convention Proceedings.

‡ Martin, Wm.: Brief History of the Amalgamated Association. Souvenir pamphlet. Privately printed by the Association.

§ Alfred Sowers of Springfield, Illinois, was elected president, and William Houston of Springfield was elected treasurer. The second convention of the Roll Hands was held in Columbus, Ohio, in April, 1874. David A. Plant of Columbus was elected president and William Martin of the same place was chosen secretary. These officers continued to serve until the amalgamation of the Unions in 1876.

were common and that they were merely dissipating their strength by maintaining separate organizations, without co-operation or mutual understanding. In times of trouble it was found a source of weakness that the various trades were not in position to act together. If the puddlers went on strike in a mill, muck iron would be purchased in the market and the heaters and rollers would work on unconcerned about the troubles of the puddlers. And so it was with the other trades, with the result that wages were reduced or strikes lost when a united effort on the part of all trades might have meant victory.

The Heaters' Union conventions in 1873 and 1874 appointed committees for the purpose of conferring with the Sons of Vulcan on the subject of amalgamation. The matter was discussed in the columns of the *National Labor Tribune,* a labor paper published in Pittsburgh, devoted chiefly to the iron, steel and mining industries, and both communications and editorial opinion served to create sentiment in favor of the movement. One of the strongest arguments for amalgamation was put forth by the mill men of Louisville, Kentucky, and New Albany, Indiana, who met in Louisville, December 10, 1874, and framed an appeal to mill men all over the country.*

The first effective move taken in this direction was due to the agitation of the Roll Hands. In the fall of 1873, locals representing the three national unions, in the Columbus Rolling Mill, Columbus, Ohio, led by the Roll Hands, formed a local Amalgamated Association, and thereafter acted in unison, although maintaining their separate organizations.† This action was approved by the national officers of the Heaters' Union and seems to have been a force in crystallizing sentiment on the subject. In April, 1874, the Roll Hands in their convention in Columbus, Ohio, voted by a large majority in favor of joining with the Sons of Vulcan and the Heaters and Rollers' Union. President David A. Plant was appointed to present the matter to the Heaters and Rollers' convention in the following July, at Covington, Kentucky. The Covington convention discussed the question and appointed a committee of three to confer with committees from the Roll

---

* See Appendix I, p. 247.
† Martin, Wm.: Brief History of the Amalgamated Association.

Hands and the Sons of Vulcan. It was hoped that the latter would take favorable action at their convention in August in Youngstown, since it was known that President David Harris was in sympathy with the movement; but for some reason nothing definite was done.

Both Heaters and Roll Hands, however, proceeded with their agitation for amalgamation, determined to carry out their plans without the puddlers if need be. After considerable correspondence between the two committees, a joint circular,* signed by the national officers and addressed to all the subordinate lodges of the two organizations, was issued April 20, 1875. In this circular it was suggested that the national conventions for that year be omitted, and instead arrangements be made for amalgamation by the committees appointed for the purpose. The lodges took favorable action and on August 3, 1875, the two committees on amalgamation met in Indianapolis and drew up a constitution for the proposed union. The committees had adjourned and the constitution was about to be sent to press when word was received from the Sons of Vulcan, in session in Philadelphia, that they were ready to meet committees from the other organizations and had appointed a committee for that purpose. Accordingly all plans made at Indianapolis were set aside and arrangements made for another conference where the puddlers should be represented.

On December 7, representatives of the three organizations met in Pittsburgh and spent six days discussing plans for amalgamation and drawing up a constitution. It was agreed that this constitution should be submitted to the various subordinate lodges, and that the three organizations should hold their conventions at the same time and place. Accordingly the constitution and all the issues involved were discussed by the rank and file and when the conventions met they were ready for action. August 1, 1876, the three organizations convened in different centers in Pittsburgh. Two days later the Heaters and Rollers and the Roll Hands adjourned to the hall where the Sons of Vulcan were in session. In addition to the representatives of the three national organizations, there was one representative of the "United Nailers."† This joint

---

* See Appendix I, p. 249.

† Report Pennsylvania Bureau of Industrial Statistics, 1887, p. G. 3.

convention adopted practically without change, the constitution that had been agreed upon by the amalgamation committees in December, 1875. Then by a rising vote the convention declared that the various bodies were united to form the "National Amalgamated Association of Iron and Steel Workers." The officers elected for the new organization were: president and secretary, Joseph Bishop of Pittsburgh, formerly president of the Sons of Vulcan; treasurer, Ed. McGinniss of the Sons of Vulcan, of Youngstown, Ohio; trustees, David Plant and William Martin of Columbus, Ohio, formerly president and secretary respectively of the Roll Hands' Union, and John Jarrett of the Sons of Vulcan, of Sharon, Pennsylvania. Of the vice-presidents, two were from the Heaters and Rollers' Union, while five and probably six were from the Sons of Vulcan. The convention adjourned August 5, 1876.

Of the several bodies that formed the Amalgamated Association, the Sons of Vulcan was much the largest as well as the oldest. In 1873 that body had reported a membership of over 3000 and in 1877, one year after the new organization was formed, we find but 755 members added to this number. During the next five years there was rapid growth and the combined organizations enrolled 16,000 members. In the summer of 1882 there was a long and costly strike, which showed its effects upon the ranks of the union down to 1885 when the tide turned again and there was steady increase until 1891, when 24,068 members were reported. This was the high water mark of membership. The next year the organization encountered the most disastrous strike in its history, that at the Homestead Steel Works, and received a setback from which it has never recovered. The membership fell to 13,613 in 1893, and fluctuated between 15,000 and 10,000 until 1907; it fell to 6,295 in 1909, rising again in 1910 to 8,257.

In order to understand the development of the policies of the Amalgamated Association it is necessary to give due weight to the fact that the organizations that met in Pittsburgh in 1876 and formed a joint national body were organizations of iron workers. Pittsburgh was in fact as well as in name the "Iron City." It was before the day of the great steel plants and there was but one important steel mill in the district. The Edgar Thomson works had just been built and the first Bessemer steel

86

produced in Allegheny County was blown there in 1875. Homestead was not in existence as a steel town. The National Tube Works at McKeesport made nothing but iron; Jones and Laughlin were the largest producers of iron in the lower Monongahela Valley, and Carnegie Brothers and Company were operating only the Upper and Lower Union mills, where iron alone was handled. The policies and acts of the Amalgamated Association have been modified from the beginning by the fact that it has been and is largely an iron workers' union. The name "Iron and Steel Workers" was almost a misnomer, for the steel workers who participated at the organization meeting were so few in numbers as to be almost negligible. The Sons of Vulcan, composed of iron workers exclusively, contributed, as we have seen, over 85 per cent of the original membership, and formed the backbone of the new organization. The members of the Heaters and Rollers' and of the Roll Hands' unions were largely iron workers also. The first three presidents of the association were puddlers, the fourth was a puddler and heater of iron, and it was not until 1898 that a steel worker was elected to that position.

Through the decade from 1880 to 1890, practically all of the iron mills in Allegheny County were unionized. The list of manufacturers who signed the scale was practically a list of those engaged in the business. There were difficulties and strikes occasionally; there was a long and determined strike in the summer of 1882, and now and then there was a lockout. But upon the whole this decade was the period of most effective agreement between the employers and the men that the association ever experienced. Each knew and respected the strength of the other and, while hard blows were dealt on both sides, there was much mutual confidence and good will.* There are instances where Pittsburgh

---

*The lodges of Western Pennsylvania, Eastern Ohio and Northern West Virginia used to hold a reunion and picnic every summer in some centrally located spot, and thousands of workingmen with their families would gather for a day of pleasure. In the issue of January 7, 1884, of the *National Labor Tribune*, there is an account of a wage conference just held between representatives of the employers and of the Amalgamated Association. At the close of the conference, after the scale had been signed, the *Tribune* says, "President Weihe (of the Amalgamated Association) suggested that as the annual reunion of the association was to take place June 7, he would feel obliged to the employers if they would shut down the mills in the Pittsburgh, Wheeling, Youngstown and Sharon districts on that day. The manufacturers cordially consented and promised to suggest the same to those

employers requested the privilege of appearing before the convention of the association so that they might explain their position directly to the delegates.

With the rise of the steel industry, the organization spread into the new mills, carrying its policies with it; but with the great strike which broke the unions' hold in the steel mills in 1892, the iron workers lost their grip on their own trade. After 1892 the iron mills in Pittsburgh began to leave off making agreements with the union, until now hardly a third of the iron worked in Allegheny County is handled by union labor.

Unionism in the steel industry was never so general as in the iron mills. In Illinois, the steel mills became fairly generally organized, but this was never true of the Pittsburgh District. There are but four large steel mills in Allegheny County that were built for the purpose of manufacturing steel; all the others were originally iron mills and have been built over. The four are the Homestead, Edgar Thomson, Duquesne and Clairton plants, all owned now by the Carnegie Steel Company. The oldest of these, the Edgar Thomson, was built at Braddock by Carnegie, Brothers and Company in 1874, and began to roll rails in 1875. This was a non-union mill down to 1882, when a lodge of the Amalgamated Association was formed.* The lodge was short-lived, however; as was a second one formed there in 1890. The Duquesne mill, completed in 1889 by the Allegheny Bes-

not present." Again, in the issue of the same paper for May 22, 1886, there is a letter signed by President Weihe and Secretary Martin of the Amalgamated Association, which had been sent to the employers, asking them to shut down the mills on June 5, so that the employes and the manufacturers themselves could attend the picnic at Beaver Falls, Pennsylvania. Favorable replies had been received from Jones and Laughlin, Oliver Brothers, Carnegie Brothers and Company, and Shoenberger and Company. These events show the relations existing at the time.

*An incident told in connection with this first lodge at Braddock would seem to show the standing of the Association with at least one employer at that time. Captain "Bill" Jones, general superintendent at the Edgar Thomson plant, resigned his position when he heard that the men were organizing, thinking that trouble was inevitable. Mr. Carnegie, not wishing to lose the services of Captain Jones, who was one of the most capable mill engineers of his time, sent for William Martin, secretary of the Amalgamated Association, asking him to come to the Carnegie offices to meet and reassure Mr. Jones. Mr. Carnegie told Mr. Martin that he had assured Mr. Jones that the Amalgamated Association was a fair and reasonable body, but he wanted him to meet an officer of the organization, and learn more about its purposes. After the interview with Mr. Martin, Captain Jones withdrew his resignation. (*National Labor Tribune*, April 28, 1888.)

semer Company, was purchased by the Carnegie Steel Company in 1890. This was never a union mill. There were a few attempts to organize the men, coupled with one or two embryonic strikes, but there never was any successful unionism. Clairton, which is a new mill, has been non-union from the beginning.

The only one of the four mills ever to be successfully unionized is Homestead, where the union was driven out in 1892. The Homestead works, built in 1881 by the Pittsburgh Bessemer Steel Company, were purchased about a year later by Carnegie, Phipps and Company. Two lodges of the Amalgamated Association were organized here as early as October, 1881. This continued a union mill during the 11 years succeeding, though the union strength remained by no means uniform. After the middle of the decade, the union membership began to grow, and in 1889 there were six lodges at Homestead. These were all disbanded at the close of the "big strike," and Homestead has since been non-union.

Of the other steel mills in Allegheny County, those which began as iron works, a majority had by 1890 become union mills; but the succeeding decade saw the falling away of the men's organizations in all of them. Jones and Laughlin, originally an iron company and thoroughly unionized, continued to deal with the organization down to 1897, when the plant became non-union. The Shoenberger plant of the American Steel and Wire Company was a union mill down to 1892 and a number of the smaller steel mills dealt with the union for a half dozen years longer. The works of the National Tube Company at McKeesport have been pretty steadily non-union from the beginning.

It is doubtful whether the Amalgamated Association at the height of its strength in 1891 numbered 50 per cent of the steel workers of Allegheny County among its members; it is certain that such a proportion were never effectively organized. Since 1901 all of the steel mills in Allegheny County, large and small, have been non-union.

CHAPTER IX

POLICIES OF THE AMALGAMATED ASSOCIATION

THE policies of the Amalgamated Association of Iron and Steel Workers that have most definitely marked its history may be divided into two classes: external, those designed to secure benefits, and internal, those relating to the character of the membership and the relations of members to one another. Under the first head are included those aims that are common to all labor unions,—the regulation of wages, hours and what may be vaguely denominated "general labor conditions." Under the second are certain policies which, specifically, may be peculiar to this organization, but which are types of policies to be found quite generally among unions, varying according to a trade's characteristics and development.

In the Amalgamated Association, after the recognition of the union and of the principle of collective bargaining,* the possession most carefully guarded has always been the existing scale of wages, and an advance in the scale the object most eagerly sought. In every important strike from the sixties down to and including the Homestead strike of 1892, the wage question was an issue and usually it was uppermost.†

It was doubtless natural that the Amalgamated Association should give first and most insistent attention to wages. But events have shown that it was a mistake to emphasize this aim

---

* In its earlier years, before the steel mills had grown to large proportions, the Amalgamated Association maintained rigidly the "closed shop." With the advent of the steel mills, which they had more difficulty in organizing, and with the dissipation of the strength of the union which came with the loss of the strikes of 1892 and 1901, the closed shop has become less of an issue.

† In 1884 Secretary Martin, in the convention of the association, declared the "main object" of the organization to be the "keeping up of wages." (Journal of Proceedings, 1884.) In 1889 a committee of the convention brought in a resolution condemning strikes for any purpose but in relation to wages. (Journal of Proceedings, 1889, p. 2786.)

to the practical exclusion of other matters. While the Association has never been strong in the steel mills, it was very strong in the iron industry before steel supplanted iron, and had it exercised its power in such a direction, it might have made some progress toward an eight-hour day. But since the method of wage payment was a piece-wage system, a reduction in hours would have been bound to lessen daily earnings at first,—a fact of special concern in the iron industry, owing to the fixed custom in vogue for determining what was a day's work. If such a movement had been carried on with any degree of success wages would doubtless, after a time, have adjusted themselves to the new conditions; as, indeed, was the case with the sheet workers, who changed during the eighties to an eight-hour day without a loss in earnings.

From the beginning of the industry in the Pittsburgh District, five heats have been a day's work for a puddler. The length of time required for getting them out depends upon the quality of pig iron used, the condition of the furnace, and the skill of the workman. Ordinarily five heats of 550 pounds each require about ten hours of work, but if conditions are as favorable as possible they may be finished in eight hours. Conditions do not usually permit such rapid work, however, so the men look with suspicion upon the three-turn system. In 1908 there were two iron mills in Pittsburgh that had the three-turn system in operation in their puddling departments. The men were extremely dissatisfied and claimed they could not do a full day's work and so did not draw a full day's wage. They usually succeeded in getting out four heats in eight hours, but often they could not make over three.

With tonnage rates based on five heats as a day's work, it can readily be seen that a time limit, making it impossible for a man to do the full five heats in a turn, would be bound to seriously affect his daily earnings. The highest price for puddling since March, 1880, was paid in September and October, 1907—$6.62½ per ton. Five heats of 550 pounds each would total 2750 pounds as a day's work, or $1\frac{510}{2240}$ tons, since the long ton is used in reckoning earnings. The price paid at the rate named would be about $8.14. This would be divided between the two men at the furnace, thus allowing each puddler on a two-turn mill about $4.07 per day. If on a three-turn mill a puddler got out only four heats he would at the same rate receive $3.26 for his day's work, and if he got out only three heats, he would receive $2.44.* But the tonnage rate named is above the average. The following table shows the daily earnings of a puddler working 550 pounds to a heat, for five, four or three heats, when the price of puddling is $6.62½ per ton as it was October, 1907, $6.12½ as it was in June, 1908, and $5.50, which is about the usual average.

TABLE 2.—DAILY EARNINGS OF A PUDDLER AT VARYING TONNAGE RATES.—BY NUMBER OF HEATS

Number of Heats	Daily Earnings at $6.625 per Ton	Daily Earnings at $6.125 per Ton	Daily Earnings at $5.50 per Ton
5	$4.07	$3.75	$3.38
4	3.26	3.00	2.70
3	2.44	2.25	2.03

Iron mills, like puddling furnaces, are operated on the two-shift, five-heat system almost everywhere. According to the union rule, the time for each of the five heats is one hour and forty-five minutes, and no heats are to be charged after eight hours and thirty minutes, from time of commencing to charge. The working time of the muck roller crew who handle the puddler's product is thus determined by the puddler's day. The scale agreement makes no provision for a limit on the finishing mills, but custom has one, and in all departments of the iron mills an average working day is ten hours long. In some mills the turn's work can be done in eight hours; seldom more than ten are required. In some iron mills the so-called "night crew" go to work at noon, or soon after, and finish their work before ten in the evening.

It can readily be seen that the "heat system" of working grew up very naturally. In puddling, one charge has to be melted, worked, and taken out before the next can go in. Thus the work progresses in heats. In an old style heating furnace, which served the men who rolled the iron, it was necessary also as we have seen, to work by heats, for the flame was admitted from one side of the furnace only. In the mills rolling sheet iron, too, the working day

* In the summer months three men instead of two are often employed at a furnace. This would, of course, reduce daily earnings still further.

was determined by the number of heats. Further, in both puddling and sheet rolling there was a restriction on the number of pounds of iron to be worked.

When the iron business was young in this country, and the number of heats in a working day was first set at five, it took about twelve hours for the day's work and the two shifts practically covered twenty-four hours. As improvements were made in furnace construction and better methods were discovered, it became possible to finish a turn in a shorter time and the prevailing day gradually shrunk to one of ten hours or less. Thus the union discovered that a rule that had at first merely limited output to such an extent as to prevent speeding and overstrain, was coming, without reducing the conventional number of heats, and without reducing output or earnings, to operate in the direction of a shorter work day.

All this was a very different process, however, from a conscious movement for reduction of hours. The only clear eight-hour movement in the iron industry that ever became important was in the sheet mills, under circumstances so peculiar that it may well be recorded. It is interesting both in its relation to the movement for a shorter work day, and as throwing light upon the psychology of the members of the Amalgamated Association at that time.

As improvements in sheet mill construction made it possible to finish a turn's work in a shorter time than twelve hours, there came to be periods of idleness between shifts. This is undesirable in a mill of this character, for sheet iron is rolled so thin that good results can be obtained only when the rolls are expanded by the heat. The rolls are so shaped that when cold they cannot turn out a sheet of uniform thickness; consequently after a period of idleness hot scrap is sent through them until they reach the correct expansion. To avoid these periods of idleness, the manufacturers tried to introduce an eight-hour day. This was resisted by the union. In 1883, it was reported in the convention of the Amalgamated Association that Moorhead, McCleane and Company of Pittsburgh were about to force the eight-hour day upon their men. This was cited as an example of the "encroachments of aggressive and designing capital," and the executive committee ruled that under no circumstances should a mill go on three turns.* The reason for this seemingly inexplicable attitude lies in the fact already indicated that the men feared a reduction in earnings. It took longer than eight hours to get out the tonnage which was considered a full turn's work. If they changed to the eight-hour system a crew could not do a full day's work, judged by the old standard, and this would mean less pay, since they were paid by the ton.

Notwithstanding the resolution of the executive committee, some mills went on three turns, and two lodges in 1884 had their charters revoked† by the national lodge in consequence. The report of President Weihe to the convention in 1885 is very interesting. The eight-hour controversy was a troublesome dilemma, for while realizing the benefits of an eight-hour day, he was confronted by a law of the Association which he was supposed to enforce. In his report he pointed out that on three turns the rolls were always warm, while on two turns time was lost in warming them up after they have been "standing idle six or seven hours." Furthermore, the three-turn system would call for a third more men and the Amalgamated Association by enforcing the double turn rule was keeping some of its own members in idleness by preventing an increase in the number of available positions. In spite of these considerations, after "hesitating and pondering for some time," he had finally decided "to carry out the law." There were at that time seven mills running on the three-turn system, and the president had revoked the charters of the lodges in those mills.‡ The convention of that year, however, moved by the president's reasoning, voted to permit eight hours in sheet mills. From this time the sheet mills began to go on three turns, with the consent but not with the co-operation of the Amalgamated Association, until at the present time all sheet and tin mills are operating under that system. In 1904 the limit on output was removed, but the eight-hour system was not abandoned. The output has so increased and the speed of the mills is so great that a twelve-hour day is now considered an impossibility, for sheet mills, unlike other

* Journal of Proceedings, A. A. of I. and S. W., 1883, p. 171.
† Financial Statement, A. A. of I. and S. W., quarter ending March 31, 1884, p. 3.
‡ Journal of Proceedings, 1885, p. 1547.

branches of mill work, require as much manual labor as they ever did.

In other rolling mills, both iron and steel, the Amalgamated Association was slow to favor the eight-hour day. The Association did not oppose it, but seemed indifferent. During the decade preceding 1890, manufacturers put their mills on three turns and changed them again to double turn, seemingly without so much as exciting the interest of the Association. In 1887 the rail mill at Homestead went on three turns and in 1888 it was changed back to double turn. In 1889 the men in the pipe mill of Spang, Chalfant and Company at Etna, were changed from three turns to double turn, and the *National Labor Tribune* remarked that "none of the men care about working the eight-hour shift."* In 1888, when the Carnegie Company reduced the wages of its employes in the Edgar Thomson plant, and at the same time changed their hours from eight to twelve, Secretary William Martin of the Amalgamated Association said that he considered the twelve-hour provision the "least objectionable point."† In 1887 the rolling mill men at the Edgar Thomson plant went on eight hours through the efforts of the Knights of Labor, but in 1888 they were defeated and the twelve-hour day was instituted again. A prominent labor paper, commenting on the probable failure of the strike then in progress at the Edgar Thomson plant, remarked:

> It is a commentary that requires no elaboration to impress this incapacity, that in a few years plants that were on the up-grade as to hours and wages have fallen away, until of them all, the Edgar Thomson is the only one left—and it is threatened with a retrograde movement—except alone the Cambria, which, as we understand it, has the three turns in the converting department, so that a non-union mill remains as the last of the eight-hour mills, and of course it must follow the others. This comparison between union and non-union men is quite too palpable to be pleasant. ‡

It should be noted, however, that the officers of the Association favored the eight-hour day when the rank and file did not. In 1890 President Weihe said in his report§ to the convention:

* *National Labor Tribune*, August 3, 1889.
† Ibid., April 14, 1888.   ‡ Ibid.
§ Amalgamated Association, Journal of Proceedings, 1890, p. 3029.

"While the iron workers are not in a general way ready to go into a movement for the eight-hour system, the steel workers have a better opportunity and should not lose sight of a chance when it presents itself, to take the advantage and adopt it." The convention passed a resolution to the effect that the eight-hour system should be adopted wherever practicable, and permitting it in all departments. As a result of this policy, three departments at Homestead had secured an eight-hour day by 1892. This marks the height of the eight-hour movement in steel mills. In that year the union strength began to decline. The resolution of 1890 was amended the following year* so as to except the boiling department, but evidently this did not satisfy the iron workers, for a petition was presented to the Amalgamated Association convention in 1892, signed by "a large number of heaters, rollers, roughers, catchers, etc.," which complained that their connection with the American Federation of Labor placed them in a false light in appearing to favor the eight-hour movement, which "was not practicable for them as iron workers." They suggested, therefore, that the Association sever its connection with the American Federation of Labor.† The petition was tabled without action.

M. M. Garland, who took the presidency in 1892, was favorable to the eight-hour system in iron mills, and at this period, also, it began to be favored by some of the manufacturers. During the depression of 1893, when the mills were running on part time, a number of iron manufacturers wished to divide up the work by making up a crew of men from the idle furnaces and introducing the three-turn system on the furnaces working. The executive board decided to permit it‡ and President Garland did all he could to extend the idea. He showed the manufacturers how they could economize heat by building their boilers above the puddling furnaces and using the surplus heat to generate steam. When this was done, continuous firing became necessary and so continuous puddling was also desirable. The three-turn system grew in popularity with the employers, and although it was opposed considerably by the rank and file of the organization, Garland was

* Journal of Proceedings, Amalgamated Association, 1891, p. 3643.
† Ibid., 1892, p. 3761.
‡ Ibid., 1894, p. 4561.

able to report in 1898 that three-fourths of the members were working under the eight-hour system,* a proportion due mainly. however, to the large number of sheet mill men in the Association,

For the majority of the puddlers have always worked double turn and as a body the iron workers today are as much opposed to the three-shift system as they were twenty-five years ago.   In 1907, Vice-President B. F. Jones of the Amalgamated Association, with the co-operation of the employers, tried to introduce the three-shift system in an iron mill in Cleveland, Ohio.   The men not only refused to go on eight hours, but denounced Mr. Jones for his activity and threatened to prefer charges against him before the national lodge for dereliction of duty.

The opposition to an eight-hour day in the iron mills, where the heat system was so firmly entrenched, is easier to understand than the failure to demand an eight-hour day in the steel mills, where the heat system had only a partial foothold.   But it is to be noted that at no time were the majority of the Pittsburgh steel workers unionized; consequently they lacked bargaining strength to secure a shorter day and at the same time obtain such an increase in rates as would keep their daily earnings up to the old figure.   This was doubtless the chief factor in their acquiescence in the twelve-hour day.

Wages and hours are always the important issues from the labor standpoint, but there are numberless others of greater or less importance that continually present themselves and frequently provoke much controversy.   With regard to these, the policy of the Amalgamated Association has been similar to that of other labor organizations; it has secured whatever bargaining strength and strategy were able to command.   And like other democratic bodies, it has been hampered by conflicts of interest among its own members.

The internal policies of the Amalgamated Association have been not less important than those for which it has been known to the outside world.   The Association has always been an organization of skilled workers and has centered its efforts on securing better conditions for that class of labor alone.   Since 1889, to be sure, the constitution has permitted the admission of all men ex-

* Journal of Proceedings, 1898, p. 5418.

97

cept common laborers, but this has not affected to any great extent the top-heavy character of the organization. Its usefulness has been impaired and its power less than if it had included in its membership all of the workmen in every union mill. Out of 3,800 men at Homestead when the strike began in 1892, only 752 were members in good standing of the Amalgamated Association.* It must be remembered, however, that while the Amalgamated had a more or less secure footing in pressing the demands of the skilled workmen, indispensable to the trade, they would have been shouldering an immensely heavier load in attempting to secure higher pay for day laborers in the steel mills than such labor could be secured for in the general market.

Limited as the membership of the Amalgamated Association has been, much internal dissension has existed throughout its history. This has apparently been due to two main causes. One is the clannishness of the races making up its original membership. These included Scotch, Irish, Welsh, English and Americans, and there seems to have been a good deal of race antagonism. The other source of trouble has been jealousy among the different trades, a factor still making for trouble within the union. At first the puddlers were in control and ran the union to suit themselves. Afterward the finishers got into the saddle, and now for twenty-five years have been able—most of the time—to dictate policies. When the puddlers ruled, the finishers sulked, and when the finishers got control the puddlers were disgruntled. Hence there have been various dissensions and secessions. In 1882 the finishers complained that they were outnumbered by the puddlers and not fairly represented in meetings, and there was some discussion of a reorganization or of a new union. In 1885 the nailers seceded and formed a separate union, returning to the Association the following year. At different times in the nineties the puddlers manifested a rebellious disposition, though no positive step was taken. In 1893 the rollers and roll hands in a number of mills left the Amalgamated Association and formed a short-lived union called the

* This is no measure of the real union strength, for in 1890 there had been 1,123 members at Homestead. The potential strength of a union consists in the number of men that it can control in an emergency, and at Homestead all of the 3,800 men went out on strike, although the majority were not eligible to membership.

"National Union of Iron and Steel Workers." So it has gone. The most extensive revolt since the organization of the Association occurred in 1907, when a considerable number of puddlers in the Pittsburgh mills left the organization and formed a separate union, calling themselves by the old name of the sixties—"Sons of Vulcan." The president, John Weigant, was a member of the original organization, before 1876. This new craft-union seems to have had some success in extending its membership.

Because of these various and warring elements the Amalgamated Association has always been weak in discipline. The national lodge has experienced difficulty in enforcing its laws upon the subordinate lodges and their members. It has shown a spirit of compromise that, however necessary, has been destructive of real control. For example, it was years before the Association was able to root out one common practice from the mills. This was a method of hiring labor which prevailed in the early eighties and which still exists in some of the independent mills—the contract system. Its existence was a constant menace to the wages of all but the boss of a crew.

A man would contract with the company to run a single mill, from the furnaces to the piling beds or the shears, and like any other contractor, he derived his profit from the margin between what the company paid him for the tonnage turned out and what he paid the men for it. The contractor, while usually known as the roller, frequently did no work at all, having two practical rollers employed on the mill. At the same time he secured a considerable income for himself by paying the men as low wages as possible, and steel workers got a reputation for being very highly paid workmen on account of the large earnings of these contractors.* A statement from the proprietor of one of the "largest rolling mills in the District," regarding wages paid in his mill in 1881–1882, was to the effect that under the contract system one steel worker had made $25,000 in a year. A sheet shearer made $12 per day and paid his helper $2.00. A hammerman in charge of both turns made $17 per day and paid his helper $2.50.† This gouging was combatted by the "one job" rule of the Amal-

* *National Labor Tribune*, August 6, 1887.
† Pittsburgh *Commercial-Gazette*, June 26, 1882.

gamated Association. This rule defined what a "job" was and prohibited any member from holding two or more. In the later seventies, a single job was defined as meaning "one furnace, one train of rolls, one steel smelting gas furnace, both turns, or two steel smelting gas furnaces one turn."* Note the wording of this rule. It so defined a "job" as to permit one man to control a furnace or a train of rolls during both turns and control the crews on both shifts. This illustrated the extreme wariness with which the system was attacked at the start. A further evidence of this conservatism appears in the next clause, which declared that the rule should be enforced "when practicable."

The latter clause was dropped and the rule was strengthened and made more explicit in 1882; "one furnace single turn and one train of rolls double turn" was declared to be a job. † But it was some five years later before the Association found itself able to take a positive stand against the system. In 1887 the convention stigmatized as a "black sheep" any man who received pay for more than one job and made the introduction or continuance of the contracting system a sufficient cause for a strike without action on the part of the executive committee.‡ The effect of this move was to drive out the contracting system, though it was not entirely eliminated and continued to cause difficulty for some time.§

An evidence of the same spirit today is the Association's failure to put a stop to the custom through which one man draws pay for a crew. This is an abuse allied to the old contracting system and is productive of much evil. A puddling furnace is no longer worked by a puddler and a helper, but by two puddlers who divide equally the pay for the work done. Yet one man gets the money at the office and the other receives his share from his fellow puddler. A puddler who is about to migrate, as a good many of them are constantly doing, sometimes forgets to give over to his

* Constitution of A. A. of I. and S. W., 1879, Article 14, Section 7.

† Ibid., 1882, Article 16, Section 5.

‡ *National Labor Tribune*, August 6, 1887.

§ There was a case in 1887 where a roller in Youngstown, Ohio, disagreed with his roughers over the amount due them. The executive committee of the district sustained the roughers, but the roller still refused to pay the price demanded so the men struck and the mill was closed down for a week. A meeting was then held and a scale was made for roughers and signed by "roll hands of the first part and muck roller of the second part." (Journal of Proceedings, 1887, p. 1948.)

"mate" his share of the last pay. On all iron rolling mills the rollers are retained steadily on the same turn, while the crews change about each week. The day roller has charge of both crews, draws the money at the office, and pays the men. An iron worker in a Pittsburgh mill, sixty years of age, who has been night roller for thirty years, told me that he liked the system. Most of the responsibility was taken by his day roller, and furthermore, this particular man was a "good boss." He paid the night roller more than the scale required. How well the latter would like it had he got no more than the scale, or what his redress would have been if the day roller paid him less, would have been another story.

Both national and local officers have often acknowledged their inability to control their members and have sometimes seemed to feel that this relieved them of responsibility. During the 1892 strike at Homestead the advisory committee sent word to the Carnegie Steel Company that the smoke issuing from one of the stacks in the mill was exciting the men, and that if it were not stopped they would not be responsible for what the men might do.*

How far such internal causes have contributed to the decline in membership and strength of the Amalgamated is best known to the members and former members themselves. Unquestionably, some have had a far-reaching effect upon the outcome of the struggle between the union and the corporations. Of these I have emphasized the exclusive character of the membership, the consequent failure to utilize the effective bargaining strength of the full working force, and the internal dissensions, due to racial and trade jealousies and to the subordination of the interests of the rank and file to the uses of the few. The decline in membership since the Homestead strike has not been uniform or constant, but the official figures for 1909 revealed the smallest membership of the whole period—but little over 25 per cent of the number in 1892.

The causes of this decline have unquestionably included powerful assaults upon the Association's strength from the outside, that bear no relation to the policies that have been described. On the other hand, much of this hostility on the part of the employers has been engendered or intensified by certain of the union tactics.

*Homestead Strike Investigation, Mis. Doc. No. 335, 52nd Cong., 1st Sess., p. 35.

It is not to be doubted that what would be regarded by a non-partisan as legitimate and proper activities on the part of the union were so irksome to certain employers that they were anxious to rid themselves of it. A union that never protested and never made demands would probably excite no opposition from employers. The Amalgamated Association demanded many things that in decency should have been granted, but it had to fight to get most of them, nevertheless. There were in addition practices either of the union or of union men that would have been irritating to any employer and these egged on the millowners in a desire to exterminate the union.

Such, on the one hand, were controversies over points that did not concern the real interests of labor, and on the other, the abuse of power by the lodges once they had a hold on a situation. A prominent official of the Carnegie Steel Company told me that before the strike of 1892, when the union was firmly entrenched at Homestead, the men ran the mill and the foreman had little authority. There were innumerable vexations. Incompetent men had to be retained in the employ of the company, and changes for the improvement of the mill could not be made without the consent of the mill committee. I had opportunity to talk with a considerable number of men employed at Homestead before 1892, among them several of the prominent leaders of the strike. From these conversations I gathered little that would contradict the statement of the official and much that would corroborate it. Some of these strikers are still working at Homestead; some are in other mills in the Pittsburgh District. All that I talked with were still loyal to the union, but after sixteen years they had a clear view of its defects and they did not hesitate to mention them. Men prominent in the strike freely admit today that the union was arbitrary. "We kept men employed who ought to have been fired," said one, "and that wasn't right. But what could we do? There are many men in any mill or factory who are ignorant, unreasonable and irresponsible. There is no way of keeping such men out of the union and their votes count for just as much as those of the better sort. It was no more than natural that these men should, to some extent, have dictated the policy of the union." Members of this type frequently brought embarrassment upon their more conservative fellows. Mill committees sometimes were obliged to go to the office to secure the adjustment of grievances which were largely imaginary and which the members of the committee knew were unworthy of consideration. A member of the mill committee at Homestead in 1892 said to me, "I was in the office with the committee one day, with a grievance, and Superintendent Potter said to me, 'John, there have been a good many times since you've been on the committee, that you have come into this office with a grievance, when you were ashamed to state your case.' I didn't tell him so, but, by George, he was right."

One of the things that made the membership careless of discipline and inclined to abuse of power was the fact that throughout most of the history of the Association there have been important rules that the national lodge made no effort to enforce. The "one man, one job" rule that remained unenforced for years is a case in point. If that rule could be disregarded, why not the rule respecting grievances? Once, in the union days at Homestead, a foreman told a workman to leave his job on one furnace and take an identical job on another furnace. The workman refused and the foreman discharged him. A meeting of all the union men was called and it was voted to strike in order to force the company to retain the man. After the vote had been taken, a conservative member succeeded in getting the floor and pointed out that the man had had no grievance in the first instance; and that even if he had one, he had lost the right of appeal according to the rules of the union because he had left the mill without first reporting his trouble to the mill committee. The speaker succeeded in putting the case so plainly that the action was reconsidered and the man with the grievance voluntarily withdrew his complaint. No doubt wise counsel often prevailed as in this case, but the incident illustrates the readiness of the rank and file to take unpremeditated and arbitrary action.* The evidence gathered from steel workers and from manufacturers in Pittsburgh seems to indicate that repeatedly, when a lodge of the Association was strongly entrenched,

* In the 1884 convention Secretary Martin in his report condemned those who were concerning themselves in "petty disputes," and a vice-president deprecated threats to strike for trifling causes and other "attempts at intimidation." (Journal of Proceedings, 1884.) In 1889 a committee of the convention reported as follows: "It is high time in order to preserve the Association, that some method be adopted whereby a stop can be put to the putting of a mill on strike for little frivolous purposes." (Journal of Proceedings, 1889, p. 2786.)

a sufficient number of its members misused and abused their power to discredit, to a certain extent, the whole organization.

More disruptive than the petty disputes in the mills was the attitude sometimes taken by the union when it came to the practical application of the external policies already described as vitally concerning the interests of labor. For example, the men were justified in many of their demands as to the wage scale; but where new machinery increased output, they often demanded all the benefit of that increase, and would not accept a reduction in the tonnage rate. As a result, a roller would sometimes earn more money in a year than his superintendent.

Another point of controversy had to do with the length of the working day in its bearing upon mechanical changes. When steel began to take the place of iron, the heat system was not a desirable or reasonable arrangement, for the steel mills require continuous operation, as iron mills do not; yet to a certain extent an attempt was made to foist the heat system on the steel mills.* In the sheet mills this was general. How far it went in other steel mills I have no means of knowing, but there was some effort in this direction in plate mills at least.† The union membership could not foresee the supplanting of iron by steel and the introduction of continuous processes; they could not believe it even after it was an accomplished fact; and hence, while they in some cases interrupted the continuous operations of the steel rolling mills, they did not work concertedly for an eight-hour day as the only effective check against overwork in the new processes. When they finally did recognize the trend of the change they were not strong enough for an eight-hour conflict.

One policy further should be mentioned. The attitude of certain union leaders with regard to the obligation to keep their contracts has probably been a factor if not in the decline in the or-

* A steel worker who was employed at Homestead before the strike of 1892 told me that it was customary in those days, at Homestead, on a double-shift mill, to stop half an hour after every two hours of work; so in the twelve hours there were only ten hours of actual work.

† The 119-inch plate mill at Homestead was changed to the three-turn system in 1891. Before that time it had been operated with two crews working a specified number of heats. One turn was eleven hours long and the other ten hours, leaving three hours in which the mill was idle. (Homestead Strike Investigation, Mis. Doc. No. 335, 52nd Cong., 1st Sess., p. 187.)

ganization's strength, at least in its failure to rehabilitate itself. The leaders of the Amalgamated Association have been, for the most part, firm in maintaining the honor of the organization. Contracts have been regarded by most of them as sacred obligations. On one occasion, when the members of the Association in a certain mill in Pittsburgh went on an illegal strike and refused to return to work when ordered to do so by the executive committee of the district, Secretary Martin advertised in the name of the Association for men to take the strikers' places and got them. In 1887, Joseph D. Weeks, secretary of the Western Association of Iron Manufacturers, was quoted as saying that in twenty-one years the iron workers had not once broken a contract.* President Garland, who held office from 1892 to 1898, was active in maintaining the principle that contracts are made to keep. In the fierce conflicts of 1892 President Weihe, on the other hand, countenanced the breaking of contracts when the lodges in mills where the scale had been signed for another year came out on strike in sympathy with the men at Homestead. This was, as far as I am able to ascertain, the first instance of that sort. But in 1901, Shaffer, who was then president of the Amalgamated Association, repudiated all contracts that had been signed with companies which had later become merged in the United States Steel Corporation.†

The purpose of this chapter has been to discuss those policies of the Amalgamated Association that have affected most deeply its history as an organization. A study of union policies, as such, was not intended. Accordingly, this presentation is by no means exhaustive, but is confined to those union tactics which directly affected the share which the men won and lost for their organization in determining the conditions of their employment. Mistakes of leaders and men alike contributed to this decline, but we must recognize that they were made in a period of contest, during which the unions never mustered half the men employed in the iron and steel trades in Allegheny County, nor controlled more than a small proportion of the plants. We may believe that fair minded employers no less than honest labor leaders bore a

* Report of Pennsylvania Bureau of Industrial Statistics, 1887.
† For a discussion of the different factors entering into this incident see pages 133–134.

part in not a few of the adjustments of these years when, more than has since been the case, the two parties to the bargain of employment were on something like an equal footing. But the known methods of warfare employed by different manufacturers with respect to each other during this period of fierce competition for the steel trade, can but suggest the lengths to which, conceivably, the same companies went in combating and weakening the union's strength in that period. Those methods which to my knowledge are resorted to today to keep unionism out of the steel industry, afford further clues as to the external forces with which leaders and members were confronted in those years. These they were confronted with, not merely in higgling over the points discussed, but in securing substantially better terms for the men in the trade and holding them for a period of years.

In spite of its decline in strength, there have been many strong and able men in the Amalgamated Association. The national officers especially have been men of intelligence and force. Most of them have displayed ability of an order which has won considerable recognition from both the public and the adroit political leaders of Pennsylvania. Miles Humphreys, who first presided over a national union of iron workers, served in the legislature of Pennsylvania for two years. In 1881 he was nominated by the republicans for mayor of the city of Pittsburgh, and later he was for two years chief of the Bureau of Industrial Statistics of the state. For a number of years he has been chief of Pittsburgh's fire department. Joseph Bishop, who was the president of the Sons of Vulcan in 1876, was elected as the first president of the Amalgamated Association. He held office until 1880, when he resigned in the middle of his term. Bishop is now secretary of the state board of arbitration of Ohio. John Jarrett, a puddler from Sharon, Pennsylvania, was elected to fill the vacancy caused by Bishop's resignation and held office until 1884. During this period Jarrett did much to strengthen the Association. One of the plans that he tried to have his fellow members adopt was the building or purchase of an iron mill to be managed for profit by the Association. It was not a co-operative scheme; no one was to make a profit as an individual; all was to go into the Association treasury. The merit of the plan, according to Jarrett, consisted in the fact that the Association, by definitely embarking in the iron business, could know the market and so could understand the position of the employer as well as that of the wage-earner; consequently he held it would go into wage conferences better prepared to negotiate intelligently. This interesting experiment was never made. After his retirement in 1884, Jarrett was, for a time, secretary of the American Tin Plate Company. During Harrison's administration he was consul at Birmingham, England, and at present he is engaged in business in Pittsburgh.

From 1884 to 1892, William Weihe, of the South Side, Pittsburgh, served as president of the Amalgamated Association. "Honest Bill Weihe" and the "Giant Puddler" are the affectionate terms which unionism used to apply to him. During his administration the Association enjoyed its greatest season of prosperity and received its most staggering blow. From 1892 he was in the service of the government in connection with the immigration station at New York, until his death in the autumn of 1908. M. M. Garland, an iron worker, a puddler and a heater, followed Weihe as president. A man of fine presence, and a natural leader, he won the widespread regard of the iron and steel workers. Taking the office just as the panic of 1893 was beginning to show its teeth and at the close of the Homestead strike, it was a hard task that he had to face, and it is not surprising that the membership did not increase during his incumbency. In 1898 Garland resigned, to accept an appointment from President McKinley as collector of customs for Pittsburgh. Appointed a second time by McKinley and again by Roosevelt, he still occupies that position. Theodore J. Shaffer followed Garland in 1898 and continued in office to 1906. Shaffer was, in addition to being a sheet roller, a man of education and ability. He had been a Methodist minister and was an effective public speaker. In spite of his education and talents, there were charges of poor management during his term of office, and subsequent events have tended to show that ill advised action was taken during the strike of 1901.

The Amalgamated president today is P. J. McArdle. McArdle is a young bar mill heater from Muncie, Indiana, and he has an exceedingly difficult position to fill. He is very much in earnest and gives the impression that he can be counted upon to live up to the best traditions of the national leaders from Bishop on.

CHAPTER X

THE GREAT STRIKES

IT has been pointed out that neither employers nor employes have worked with singleness of purpose toward a solution of the labor problem in the iron and steel trade. Each side has contributed something toward a solution, but the thing most desired by each and most sought after has been control. The organization of the Sons of Vulcan in 1858 was the real beginning of the struggle; before that the employer was supreme. The end is not yet in sight. There were evidences of unrest before 1858 when the first organized effort for control was begun by the workingmen. The strike of the Pittsburgh puddlers in 1849–1850 is said to have been the first great labor demonstration in the iron industry in America. The first contest of importance after the organization of the Sons of Vulcan occurred in 1865, and this resulted in a victory for the men. From that time the struggle was on in earnest. Various contests occurred before the "amalgamation" took place in 1876. Each of the separate unions had difficulties from time to time, and it was this fact, as has been pointed out, that led to the formation of the Amalgamated Association. The study of labor conflicts in this chapter is limited chiefly to those in Allegheny County, Pennsylvania, and to the period since 1880. This is the period of development of the great steel mills and the period of the most important contests.

The year 1882 was a strike year. On the twenty-first day of June, 1882, Senator Morgan of Alabama, speaking in the United States Senate, on a resolution for the appointment of a committee "to investigate strikes," made the statement that there were at that time 100,000 men on strike in the United States, including 700 steel workers at Homestead, Pennsylvania, who had gone on strike March 6. There were also large numbers of iron workers on strike in Cleveland, Ohio, and St. Louis, Missouri.*

* Congressional Record, 47th Cong., Vol. 13, Part 5, p. 161.

The Homestead plant was completed by the Pittsburgh Bessemer Steel Company in 1881 and began to make Bessemer steel. By October, two lodges of the Amalgamated Association had been organized there.* The company took prompt action and announced that every employe must sign an agreement not to join any labor organization, and if already a member, to withdraw before January 1, 1882, or leave the employ of the company. The union men refused to sign the agreement, and this led to the strike, though there were only 475 men on strike according to Secretary Martin of the Amalgamated Association, instead of 700, as stated by Senator Morgan. The question of unionism was soon dropped by the company and a reduction in wages became the point of controversy. The strike was marked with considerable feeling on both sides. Strikers occupying company houses were evicted to make room for strike breakers, whom the company proposed to bring in. On the other hand, some turbulence among strikers was reported from Homestead and there were manifestations of bitterness toward non-union men. The strike was finally terminated on March 20. The company agreed to take back enough men to fill out one shift or crew of men; in other words, to run half union. The wage difficulty was to be submitted to a conference of employers and men, a decision to be reached within thirty days.† This seems to have been the first instance of a labor controversy in a steel mill in Allegheny County.

In the summer of 1882 there was a general strike in the iron mills over the wage question, the center of the conflict being in Pittsburgh. The old scale ended June 1, and the strike was on from that time until September 20. In the latter part of May, 1882, the usual conference between the wage committee of the Amalgamated Association and the Pittsburgh manufacturers had been held, and the representatives of the Association had asked an advance over the scale of 1881–1882. The old scale gave the puddler a minimum base price of $4.50 when bar iron sold at $ .02½ per pound. Rolling muck iron was one-eighth the price of

---

* Journal of Proceedings, 1882, p. 795.

† This account of the Homestead difficulty is taken from reports found in the Pittsburgh *Commercial-Gazette*, in the issues of Feb. 28, March 2, 6, 7, 9, 13, 14, 15 and 20, 1882.

puddling, and the price of rolling on bar mills was $ .68¾ per ton. The puddlers claimed that they could not make over $700 per year on the old scale* and the men asked for a base price of $6.00 a ton on a $ .02½ card for puddling, and $ .75 for bar mill rolling. The muck rollers' scale was left unchanged. Later a demand was made for an advance in sheet rolling also.† On June 1 only three manufacturers in Pittsburgh,—Hussey, Howe and Company, Singer, Nimick and Company and Carnegie Brothers and Company,—had accepted the new scale, while at least 22 of the leading employers of the district, with pay rolls aggregating over 18,000 men, had refused the advance and their men were on strike.‡

In anticipation of the strike, the iron manufacturers held a meeting in Pittsburgh which was attended by "nearly every manufacturer of iron west of the Alleghenies," and an organization was formed to fight the Amalgamated Association. § President Jarrett of the Amalgamated Association was strongly opposed to the strike because he did not think that market conditions were such as to make success probable, but he was overruled by the rank and file. The Association made a strong effort to center the fight on the Pittsburgh manufacturers. They attempted to destroy the unity of the opposition by offering to run the mills outside Pittsburgh if they would agree to adopt the Pittsburgh wage scale when that was finally settled upon. This plan was not successful to such a degree as to break the strength of the Pittsburgh manufacturers, and on September 20 the strike ended, the men accepting the scale of 1881–1882 without change. On September 13, the finishers had held a meeting and voted in favor of ending the strike. On September 14, the puddlers held a separate meeting and voted to compromise on $5.75. This was rejected by the manufacturers and on September 19 conventions were held in the Pittsburgh, Wheeling and Youngstown districts, chief battle grounds of the strikers, and it was voted to accept the old scale. Thus ended the last general strike in the iron business. From that time the steel mills were to occupy the center of the stage, with respect both to commercial importance and to labor conflicts.

---

* Pittsburgh *Commercial-Gazette*, June 5, 1882.
† *National Labor Tribune*, May 27, 1882.
‡ Pittsburgh *Commercial-Gazette*, June 1, 1882.   § Ibid., May 24, 1882.

The Edgar Thomson Steel Works, built at Braddock near Pittsburgh by Carnegie Brothers and Company in 1875, was the first plant to manufacture Bessemer steel in Allegheny County, and it was also the first battle ground in the struggle for control in the steel industry. The plant was started as a non-union mill, but unionism gained a foothold in 1882. The union activity in Braddock, however, was never of a sort to alarm the employers. The company first took up the cudgels against unionism in 1885, and by the middle of 1888 had laid it low. Since then there has been no interruption to absolute control by the employers.

To trace the history of unionism more in detail in this first steel plant of the Pittsburgh District: On March 11, 1882, a lodge of the Amalgamated Association was formed at Braddock and before the end of the following year a local of the Knights of Labor also was organized. The main point of difference between the Knights of Labor* and those bodies affiliated with the American Federation of Labor is that the Knights organized by industries, rather than by trades, so that an iron and steel local would include all men working in a single mill, both skilled and unskilled. I was told by an old steel worker, who was a member of the Amalgamated lodge at Braddock in 1882, that this local also embraced all sorts of workingmen, including common laborers and gas producer men. If this is correct, it shows the influence of the Knights of Labor upon the Amalgamated Association, leading it to break down its policy of admitting only tonnage men, in order to meet the competition of a rival organization. The presence of two organizations does not seem to have produced satisfactory results. In discussing a reduction in wages that had been announced to take effect January 1, 1884, and which both organizations had accepted, a Pittsburgh labor paper† stated that the Braddock men had had their wages reduced steadily for the last five years, and declared that this was due to weakness, owing to the division of the union men into two separate organizations.

* The Knights of Labor succeeded in forming organizations in several of the smaller iron mills in Pittsburgh as well as at the Edgar Thomson, in the early eighties, but they never became strong enough to be much of a factor in the mills of the Pittsburgh District.

† *National Labor Tribune*, December 22, 1883.

In January, 1885, extensive changes were made in the Edgar Thomson plant. New machinery of the most improved type was installed, the most important being automatic roll tables for the blooming mill and improved devices for drawing and charging at the heating furnaces. Some years before this time—in 1879 the older steel workers say—the Edgar Thomson plant had been put on the eight-hour system. Superintendent Jones had established the eight-hour day at that time because orders were very heavy and, conditions being such that almost every position involved heavy physical labor, he had resorted to the eight-hour system in order to get out the orders.* The eight-hour system seems to have prevailed after that most of the time until 1885. In January, 1884, the mill ran double turn,† but at the end of the year the men were back on the eight-hour system.‡

The files of the daily and labor papers of Pittsburgh furnish rather fragmentary accounts of what occurred at Braddock during that winter of 1884–85, and the men who were employed there at the time give conflicting testimony about it. It appears, however, that in December, 1884, a notice signed by General Superintendent Jones was posted at the Edgar Thomson works, which stated that the works would close down for an indefinite period on December 16, and that all employes not notified to the contrary would be paid in full and discharged.§ This threw about 1600 men out of work.‖ Meanwhile, improvements were being installed and it was reported that a good many men would be permanently thrown out of employment. Either in December, 1884, or in January, 1885, the company proposed a new scale of wages to the men which involved a heavy reduction and a change back to the double-turn system. The dropping out of one full crew

---

* The following, said to be an extract from a letter by Captain Jones, appears in Bridge's Inside History of the Carnegie Steel Company (pp. 188, 189): "I soon discovered it was entirely out of the question to expect human flesh and blood to labor incessantly for twelve hours, and therefore it was decided to put on three turns, reducing the hours of labor to eight. . . . This proved to be of immense advantage to both the company and the workmen, the latter now earning more in eight hours than they formerly did in twelve hours, while the men can work harder constantly for eight hours, having sixteen hours for rest."

† *National Labor Tribune*, Jan. 19, 1884.

‡ Ibid., Feb. 7, 1885.   § Ibid., Dec. 20, 1884.

‖ Pittsburgh *Chronicle-Telegraph*, Dec. 18, 1884.

of men and the new machinery together would, it was thought, involve a heavy reduction in the labor force. It was said that the four heating furnaces had required 23 men on each turn, or 69 on three turns. With the new appliances there would be required six men on each turn or 12 on two turns, thus displacing 57 men. On the rail mill the 21 men on each turn were to give way to six men, so that the work of 63 men was to be done by 12. Sixty-two chargers were also to be done away with; and the whole number of men displaced would be not less than 300, as the converting department and the blast furnaces were also to go on double turn.* These estimates were probably not accurate, for the same authority announced two weeks later that 1500 men were then employed.† The men at first refused to accept the terms proposed, but they were not well organized. Many of them, fearing discharge on account of the new machinery, had withdrawn from the union before the mill shut down in December, in order to make themselves solid with the management, which was thought to be opposed to unionism. The company seemed to be in no hurry to start the mill. Andrew Carnegie, in an interview, said that the workmen were to blame for the suspension. "They allow other Bessemer mills to work at less wages than we pay." He referred to a mill at Harrisburg which was selling rails at $27. "We cannot do it, and must close rather than sell rails at less than cost. . . . I do not know when they (Braddock and Homestead) will be started, but not until the rail market improves and we can run and sell at a profit, or until the Amalgamated Association gains control of the other mills in the country and makes better wages in those establishments."‡ Early in February, the men accepted the terms of the company and went to work at a heavy reduction in wages and on a twelve-hour basis. It was reported that the cut in some departments would average 50 per cent. A workman was quoted as saying that men who had made $120 a month with an eight-hour day the year before, were now getting $60 a month for a twelve-hour day.§ President Weihe of the Amalgamated Association in January persuaded Captain Jones to agree to meet a committee representing the men. Later

* *National Labor Tribune*, Feb. 7, 1885.   † Ibid., Feb. 21, 1885.
‡ Pittsburgh *Chronicle-Telegraph*, Jan. 2, 1885.   § Ibid., Feb. 5, 1885.

Jones is alleged to have refused to meet them and to have required the men to sign individual contracts.* Soon after this the two Braddock lodges of the Amalgamated disbanded.†

The company pronounced itself once more able to compete with non-union mills, and the Edgar Thomson plant was again put in operation.

Thus ended the first important controversy over labor matters at Braddock. As a controversy it was insignificant, for very little resistance was made.

At the end of the year 1885, Superintendent Jones was quoted as saying that prospects were very favorable, and it was reported that there would be a return to the eight-hour day.‡ At the beginning of the new year, however, the company granted a 10 per cent advance in wages, with a continuation of the twelve-hour day, and these terms were accepted by the men in the steel works.§ But the intelligent and aggressive Irishmen in the blast furnaces wanted to return to the eight-hour system of 1884 and they refused the offer of the firm. As a result 700 blast furnacemen were discharged and the furnaces were banked.‖ The company succeeded in bringing in enough non-union men to operate some of the furnaces, but by the middle of the month the whole plant was tied up because the converter men refused to work the iron turned out by the strike-breakers.¶ The strike then became a general contest for an eight-hour day, and early in April, 1886, the company conceded the point and the whole plant went to work on three turns. Three hundred additional men were required.** The eight-hour day thus established continued in operation for two years. There was some disagreement over the wage settlement in January, 1887, and it was submitted to arbitration,†† but the hour question was not an issue.

During the year 1887, a rail mill of the newest type was built at Braddock, and other improvements such as would further displace men‡‡ were installed in the plant. On December 16, 1887, ten

* Journal of Proceedings, 1885, p. 1545.   † Ibid., 1885, p. 1538.
‡ National Labor Tribune, Dec. 12, 1885.   § Ibid., Jan. 9, 1886.
‖ Ibid., Jan. 9, 1886.   ¶ Ibid., Jan. 16, 1886.
** Ibid., April 3, 1886.   †† Ibid., Jan. 1, 1887.
‡‡ Ibid., Jan. 22, 1887; July 9, 1887.

days before Christmas, notices were posted in the mill announcing that the plant would close on the following day for "annual repairs." In the rail mill the notice read, "employes, not otherwise notified, will consider themselves discharged." On December 28, the conference committee of the Knights of Labor presented their scale to the company. No reply was received for six weeks, when a 10 per cent reduction was offered, hours to remain as before. This was rejected by the men. Jones offered to arbitrate the matter and the men signified their willingness to arbitrate for a six months' scale, so that the scale year might end July 1 each year instead of January 1, as heretofore. This offer was rejected by Jones, who later refused to arbitrate at all.* In March, the Knights of Labor sent a committee to New York to interview Andrew Carnegie. He received them and proposed a reduction of 10 per cent in the steel department and 8 per cent in other departments, together with a return to the twelve-hour day. These terms were necessary, he told them, to enable the Edgar Thomson plant to compete with the Chicago rail mills, which were nearer the market and where a twelve-hour day then prevailed.† In April, Carnegie went to Pittsburgh and made a proposition of a sliding scale of wages, based on the selling price of steel rails. A committee of workingmen were to be appointed who should inspect the books each month to determine the base of wages for the next month.‡ At the same time he announced that the plant would start non-union, and the men must sign an agreement not to join nor remain members of any labor union.§ In May, Carnegie refused to meet a committee or hold any further conference,|| and about the middle of the month, after being out all winter long, the men accepted the terms and went back to work. This ended unionism in the Edgar Thomson plant. In the twenty years that have elasped since that time there has been no organized effort of any importance on the part of the employes to regain the right to collective bargaining.

* Proceedings, Quarterly Meeting, District Assembly No. 3, Knights of Labor, April, 1888.

† Pittsburgh *Commercial-Gazette*, March 30, 1888.

‡ *National Labor Tribune*, April 7, 1888.

§ Proceedings, Quarterly Meeting, District Assembly No. 3, Knights of Labor, April, 1888.

|| *National Labor Tribune*, May 5, 1888.

During the several controversies at Braddock, Carnegie kept assuring his employes that the reductions proposed by him were necessary because other competing mills were paying lower wages or the men had a longer working day. The *National Labor Tribune*, the official organ of the Amalgamated Association,* took the same view and, pointing out that the question ought to be threshed out in Chicago rather than in Pittsburgh, it urged a temporary settlement at Braddock in 1888 and then a campaign for higher wages and shorter hours in the other steel mills of the country.† In the same vein Captain Jones said to the Braddock workmen in April, 1888: "I candidly charge the Knights of Labor with gross dereliction of duty when, after establishing as a general rule the eight-hour day, they lie down supinely and make no effort to have it established at rival establishments."‡ It would seem that Carnegie was correct in his contention that other mills had an advantage in labor cost (at least so far as men paid by the day were concerned) when they were operating with two shifts of men while the Edgar Thomson plant had three. It would appear, however, that in the end he went his rivals one better. The table opposite presents wage figures for blast furnace workers, taken from the files of the *National Labor Tribune*§ and arranged to show the labor cost for certain positions for twenty-four hours. This table does not by any means show the labor cost for each furnace, for a full furnace crew is not taken, nor does it show the number of men in each position. It is sufficient, however, for purposes of comparison. In 1887 the Carnegie Company was paying $46.35 for one man's labor in each of these enumerated positions, during each twenty-four hours. At Chicago, the labor cost for twenty-four hours for men in similar positions was $43.60. The aggregate was thus just a trifle over 6 per cent higher in Braddock than in Chicago. Carnegie's men worked eight hours, the Chicago men twelve. But that 6 per cent constituted an advantage, and so he held a readjustment was necessary if the works were to resume. That readjustment, accepted by men who had been out of employment all winter, called for reduced rates and a twelve-hour day at Braddock; and the labor cost for one

* *National Labor Tribune*, March 31, 1888.   † Ibid., April 7, 1888.
‡ Ibid., April 14, 1888.   § Ibid., April 28, 1888.

TABLE 3.—COMPARATIVE WAGES AND LABOR COST FOR CERTAIN POSITIONS IN BLAST FURNACES, AT BRADDOCK AND CHICAGO

Positions	Daily Wage at Braddock Three Turns 1887	Labor Cost at Braddock Three Turns 1887	Daily Wage at Chicago, Two Turns 1887	Labor Cost at Chicago, Two Turns 1887	Daily Wage at Braddock Two Turns 1888	Labor Cost at Braddock Two Turns 1888
Keeper	$2.40	$7.20	$3.25	$6.50	$2.86	$5.72
1st helper . . .	1.80	5.40	2.60	5.20	2.28	4.56
2d helper . . .	1.70	5.10	2.45	4.90	1.94	3.88
3d helper . . .	1.70	5.10	2.45	4.90	1.71	3.42
Stove tender . .	1.70	5.10	2.45	4.90	2.00	4.00
Cinder snapper .	1.50	4.50	2.30	4.60	1.60	3.20
Barrowmen . . .	1.60	4.80	2.10	4.20	1.83	3.66
Cagers . . .	1.65	4.95	2.10	4.20	1.89	3.78
Barrow fillers . .	1.40	4.20	2.10	4.20	1.54	3.08
Total labor cost for positions given . .	..	$46.35	..	$43.60	..	$35.30

117

man's labor for twenty-four hours in each of the enumerated positions was cut to $35.30, nearly 19 per cent (18.8) below the labor cost for the same positions in Chicago.

The first attempt at unionism in the plant of the National Tube Company at McKeesport was made the same year that Braddock was organized. A lodge of rolling mill men was formed May 27, 1882.* During that summer they inaugurated a strike which tied up the whole plant. On July 31, the company posted a notice to the effect that all men who did not report a desire to retain their positions by noon on August 1 would be discharged. It was also declared that the intention of the company was to employ only non-union men thereafter.† It is evident that the company was able to maintain its attitude, for the lodge disbanded December 9, 1882, because the "company could get all the non-union men it wanted."‡ Since that time the attitude of the company has been uncompromising in its opposition to unionism. It was reported the following year that an "iron clad" was required of every employe of the company.§ There have been occasional lapses into unionism from time to time since 1882. In 1886, and again in 1891, the Amalgamated Association reported the organization of lodges at McKeesport, but they seem to have been short lived and to have accomplished little. In 1901 a last stand for unionism was made. This was the only large steel plant in Allegheny County involved in the strike against the United States Steel Corporation of that year. Since that time there has been no attempt at organized activity on the part of the men.

Homestead, as has been stated, was organized in 1881. For the first few years unionism was not strong there, but after the

* Journal of Proceedings, 1882, p. 795.

† Pittsburgh *Commercial-Gazette*, Aug. 1, 1882.

‡ Journal of Proceedings, 1883.

§ "Iron clad" agreement required at McKeesport plant, National Tube Works Company: "I, —————— in consideration of agreement of even date, herewith and hereto annexed, hereby agree and pledge myself not to become a member of the Amalgamated Association of Iron and Steel Workers, nor of any other secret organization of a similar purpose or character, and to work irrespective of any rules or orders laid down or issued by them or any of them. In case I am at present a member of any such secret order, I hereby agree and pledge myself to withdraw. This agreement to hold good during continuance of agreement hereto annexed, unless sooner determined, when the same shall be void and without effect." (*National Labor Tribune*, June 9, 1883.)

middle of the decade there was a considerable growth of union spirit. In 1887 there were four lodges of the Amalgamated Association in the plant; in 1889, six; in 1890, seven; and in 1891 and 1892 there were eight lodges. Carnegie, Phipps and Company purchased the Homestead plant in 1883, and down to 1889 there was no strike nor any labor trouble of importance. There was a severe cut in wages in 1884,* but upon the whole the men were satisfied with their pay throughout the decade. The hour question does not seem to have been an issue. In 1886 an eight-hour day was inaugurated in the blooming mill.† The rail mill went on eight hours in 1887 and changed back to double turn in 1888. In 1889 the only departments having the eight-hour day were the blooming mill and the Bessemer departments; all the other departments were on double turn,‡ as they had been practically all of the time since the plant was built.

After the period of harmony a serious difficulty arose in 1889. The issue, deferred at that time by the signing of a three years' contract, came to the front again in 1892. The Homestead strikes of 1889 and 1892 were the most important and most far-reaching in their effects upon the steel industry of any difficulties that have arisen in the steel mills of the country, and they are worthy of careful consideration. The rate scales by which the men's earnings were calculated per ton were arranged locally. There was so little uniformity among the steel mills that a special scale was drawn up for each mill and a conference held with each manufacturer. Until 1887, the scale year had ended on December 31 of each year, but the Association succeeded in getting a change so that the steel scales should expire thereafter on June 30, as did the iron scales. This point was of importance to the Association, for they claimed that they were in a much better position to negotiate in the summer than in the winter. There are more men available in winter and so in case of a strike, the company would have an advantage which it would not possess in June, in securing men to take the strikers' places. The winter season is a bad time for a strike, moreover, because living expenses are much greater than in summer and in consequence the workmen cannot hold out so long.

* *National Labor Tribune*, Jan. 26, 1884.
† Ibid., July 24, 1886.   ‡ Ibid., April 27, 1889.

The steel manufacturers, on the other hand, preferred to have the year end with December because their fiscal year ended at that time. They claimed also that midsummer agreements handicapped them in booking orders, because they could not know whether there would be a readjustment of wages in the middle of the year. These contentions may serve to throw light upon one phase of both Homestead strikes.

In May, 1889, Carnegie, Phipps and Company proposed a new agreement for the Homestead plant which involved, besides other radical changes, three things which the employes were not willing to accept without opposition. It called for a sweeping reduction in rates, including all the employes of the plant excepting common laborers. Second, the scale proposed was to be in force from July 1, 1889, to January 1, 1892, so as to have new scales date from the beginning of the year. Finally, it required that each employe should sign the scale individually, and this meant practically a renunciation of the principle of unionism, for the whole strength of unionism rests upon collective bargaining. The company also proposed a sliding scale system for determining wages, similar to the system in operation at Braddock. The men's tonnage rates were to be based on the selling price of 4 x 4 steel billets, $25 per ton being the minimum base, below which the selling price should not affect the wage rates. The average price of billets for the preceding month was to be determined at the end of each month and upon this average price wages for the next month would be based.

The Homestead lodges met and rejected the scale and referred the matter to the convention of the Amalgamated Association which met in Pittsburgh in June, 1889. The convention appointed a committee to take the matter up with Carnegie, Phipps and Company, and this committee held several conferences with the company, but without result, for the latter would not modify its demands. On July 1 the scale year ended and, no new scale having been agreed upon, the men went out on strike.

Meanwhile the company had been advertising through the papers for workmen, and on July 10 the sheriff of Allegheny County attempted to bring to the works a carload of workmen who had been secured by employment agents in Pittsburgh. The strikers were patrolling all of the approaches to the plant and when these men alighted from the train they gathered in such numbers that the strikebreakers were afraid to attempt to enter. On July 12, the sheriff brought 125 deputies to Homestead and expected to take charge of the works. As before, the strikers assembled in front of the gates a thousand or two strong, and refused to move so that the deputies could pass in. After a few hours the deputies gave up the attempt and left Homestead.

At this juncture, with excitement running very high, and all communication broken off between the company and the Amalgamated Association, Sheriff McCandless succeeded after some negotiation in bringing representatives of the opposing parties together again in conference. The reopening of the conference had a quieting influence and in a few days more the strike was settled and the men went back to work. The settlement was in most respects a victory for the men. A reduction in rates was agreed to for the 23-inch, 33-inch and 119-inch mills. In other departments, rates were left unchanged or were advanced. There was no attempt to end the scale year in January and the principle of unionism was maintained. The sliding scale was adopted, based on 4 x 4 billets, with $25 the minimum. The scale was to be adjusted each three months, according to the selling price of 4 x 4 billets during the preceding three months, and, finally, it was agreed that the scale thus arranged should be in operation three years—from July 1, 1889, to June 30, 1892. So the truce was arranged and the controversy stilled for the time.*

The strike, for the most part, seems to have been well managed and the conduct of the strikers orderly. The accounts given in the daily press seem to indicate that there was little disorder, even when it might naturally have been anticipated.† There was a report of one man being roughly handled,‡ but this seems to have been the only instance of open lawlessness. What the strike might have become had it been prolonged, it is difficult to say. It was reported that on July 13 the employes at three other mills of the Carnegie Company—Edgar Thomson, Upper Union and Lower

* Full accounts of the strike of 1889 are to be found in President Weihe's report, Journal of Proceedings, 1890, pp. 2962–2977; *National Labor Tribune*, May 25, June 15, July 13, July 20, 1889; and Pittsburgh daily papers, May, June, July, 1889.
† Pittsburgh *Commercial-Gazette*, July 13, 1889.   ‡ Ibid., July 12, 1889.

Union—voted to go out on strike and remain out until the Homestead trouble was settled. It was also rumored that all railroad employes were ready to strike against handling Carnegie products, and that the employes of the H. C. Frick Coke Company were ready to walk out.*

There was such general satisfaction over the working of the new sliding scale that the Amalgamated Association in the convention of 1891 voted to adopt the system and try to establish it in all steel mills under its jurisdiction.† Nevertheless the scale became a bone of contention because of the fluctuations in the price of billets which took place during the term of the contract. When the scale was signed in July, 1889, steel billets were selling at $26.50. The price began to advance immediately and by December, 1889, it had reached $36. The price at the close of 1890 was $25.75 and in 1891 it fluctuated between $26.50 and $25.25. In January, 1892, the price was $25. It then fell to $23 in March, to $22.40 on June 3 and by the latter part of June it was $23.75.‡ It will be remembered that $25 was the minimum base. When billets were selling for $24 or $23, wages were being paid as if the price were $25. The scale did not slide downward after the price fell below $25, but there was no maximum above which wages ceased to advance with the selling price. This was one of the points of controversy in the Homestead strike of 1892.

It is not necessary to give here a detailed account of the various aspects and developments of the strike of 1892.§ That has been done until everyone who is interested in the labor movement in the United States is somewhat familiar with the story. Note, however, that a few events of an unusual nature served to fan the prejudices of the time, and these still obscure to many, who would like to be fair-minded, the real issues involved. The so-called battle between the Pinkerton men and the strikers and the subsequent treatment of the Pinkertons have done much to color

* Pittsburgh *Commercial-Gazette*, July 15, 1889. † Journal of Proceedings, 1891, p. 3649. ‡ *American Manufacturer and Iron World*, July 1, 1892. §References on the Homestead Strike.—Taussig, F. W.: *Economic Journal*, 3 : 307. Curtis, G. T.: *North American Review*, 155: 364. Oats, W. C.: *North American Review*, 155 : 355. Powderly, T. V.: *North American Review*, 155 : 370. Weeks, J. D.: *Christian Union*, 46: 113. Bemis, E. W.: *Journal of Political Economy*, 2 : 369. Bemis, E. W.: *Social Economist*, 3 : 108, 163. Testimony before Congressional Investigating Committee, Miss. Doc. No. 335, 52nd Congress, 1st Session. Report of Congressional Committee, Report No. 2447, 52nd Congress, 2nd Session.

popular opinion in the matter. The attempt upon the life of Chairman H. C. Frick of the Carnegie Steel Company by an anarchist from New York, a stranger in Pittsburgh and a stranger to the Amalgamated Association, also served to cloud the situation.

In most respects the strike of 1892 was a continuation of the conflict of 1889. The points over which, there was controversy were practically the same. The company proposed a reduction in the scale of the men employed on the 119-inch plate mill, the 32-inch slabbing mill and in the open-hearth departments. The second proposition was that the scale should be in force for one year and six months, thus terminating January 1, 1894, instead of in midsummer. The third proposition was the reduction of the minimum base of the scale from $25 to $23, per ton, for 4 x 4 billets. This third proposition, in its original form, was that the minimum should be reduced to $22, but before the strike had actually begun, Frick authorized a change to $23 in reply to a conference committee of the union, who offered to come down from their original demand for $25 to $24 as the minimum base.

There is no question about these being the controversial points—reduction of wages and of the minimum base, and change in the date of terminating the scale. These were the points that were considered in conference and apparently they were the issues over which the contest was waged. But there was another issue, and this must be kept in mind in any attempt to understand the bitterness of feeling in the Homestead strike. That issue was unionism. The union methods that were most distasteful to the employers have been mentioned. The arbitrary and arrogant spirit of some of the men in the local lodges was, it is generally admitted, more in evidence at Homestead than in any other important plant. It was undoubtedly due to this spirit that the officials of the Carnegie Company were not in an over-conciliatory mood at the beginning, and that when the men would not accept their terms they demanded a dissolution of the union.

On the other hand, there was every reason why the men could be expected to resist energetically any effort to break the power of their organization. Those who had misused the power that the union secured for them would resist because such power is too sweet to be lightly given up. The better class of workers, however greatly they might have deplored the unreasonable actions of some of their fellow workmen, would naturally stand with them against any attack from outside; for with all its defects, as business and government are now constituted, collective action is the workman's only sure defense against injustice. Especially is this true where large numbers of workmen are employed by a great corporation, with a correspondingly wide gulf between the source of authority and the individual employe.

There were circumstances that bred suspicion in the minds of the steel workers and led them to prepare to battle for something more important for the time than wage schedules. In January, 1889, H. C. Frick purchased the interests of D. O. Stewart in the Carnegie firm and became chairman of Carnegie Brothers and Company, later the Carnegie Steel Company. Frick had previously been chiefly interested in coke manufacture; the H. C. Frick Coke Company was one of the largest producers of coke in the Connellsville district. There had been labor difficulties in the coke fields, and rightly or wrongly, Frick was regarded as the implacable foe of organized labor; therefore the steel workers viewed with apprehension his entrance into the steel business. It may have been a coincidence that within six months after Frick had become a member of the Carnegie firm, the Homestead men were involved in the first serious difficulty that had ever come between them and the management, and that after all the previous years of amicable relations, the firm was demanding a dissolution of the union and the signature of individual contracts. It looked suspicious, however, and when in 1892, at the expiration of the contract signed in 1889, another conflict seemed imminent, the men looked upon it as a renewal of the campaign for the destruction of the union.

Negotiations for the new scale were begun in February, 1892, the men presenting a scale to the company. A few weeks later the company presented a scale to the men providing for a reduction. A number of conferences were held, and on May 30 the company submitted an ultimatum to the effect that if the scale were not signed by June 24 they would treat with the men as individuals.* That this meant that the men must accept the scale

* Journal of Proceedings, 1893.

by June 24 or the plant would become non-union is clearly indicated by Frick's testimony to the Congressional investigating committee on July 12, 1892:

> "After the 24th of June when these workmen refused to make terms with us, we concluded it would be necessary to protect our own property and secure new workmen, whom we had plenty of applications from."
>
> Q. "Non-union men you mean?"
>
> A. "We did not care whether they were union or non-union, but we wanted men with whom we could deal individually. We did not propose to deal with the Amalgamated Association after that date, as we had plainly told them."*

Again, in an interview with a reporter, Frick was credited with a statement defining his attitude of opposition to the Amalgamated Association in even stronger terms.† A conference was sought by the Amalgamated men in the latter part of June, and one was held on June 23, 1892, in the office of the Carnegie Steel Company in Pittsburgh. It was at this time that the concession was made by each side with respect to the minimum base, Frick offering $23 and the Amalgamated Association coming down to $24. These were the only concessions made and upon no point was there agreement; when the strike began on June 29, the members of the Amalgamated Association in Homestead believed that they were going into a fight to determine their right to united action.

The early engagement of Pinkerton men to take charge of the works indicated the preparedness of the Carnegie Company to attempt to crush out unionism. It was brought out in the testimony of H. C. Frick‡ and that of Robert A. Pinkerton§ before the Congressional investigating committee, that before the last conference was held between the representatives of the Amalgamated Association and the Carnegie Steel Company, negotiations were already under way with the Pinkertons. The last conference with

---

* Mis. Doc. No. 335, p. 33, House of Rep., 52d Cong., 1st Sess.

† "I can say with greatest emphasis that under no circumstances will we have any further dealings with the Amalgamated Association as an organization. This is final." (Pittsburgh *Post*, July 8, 1892.) The interview is printed in full in Frick's testimony before the Congressional investigating committee, pp. 30–33.

‡ Mis. Doc. No. 335, 52d Cong., 1st Sess., p. 42.

§ Ibid., p. 201

the men was held June 23, and nothing was accomplished. On June 25, Frick wrote to Robert A. Pinkerton of New York acknowledging Pinkerton's letter of June 22, the day before the conference, and stating that the Carnegie Steel Company would want 300 guards for service on July 6 to prevent interference with the operation of the Homestead plant. Frick and Pinkerton both testified that several days, possibly a week or more, before the letter of June 25 was written, a representative of the Pinkerton agency had been in Pittsburgh, having come from New York at Frick's request for the purpose of conferring with him. No definite arrangement was made at this time, but it is significant that several days before it was positively known that the Amalgamated Association would not accede to all of the propositions of the company, arrangements were being made for the engagement of guards to take charge of the Homestead plant.*

It is the belief of many of the men who engaged in the Homestead strike that Frick deliberately sought the conflict because he wanted to drive the union out of Homestead. It can scarcely be denied that the evidence tends to support this view, and there can be no doubt that before the strike began, the issue had become clear. Before it had been in progress ten days, wage questions and all other controversial points were forgotten and it became a struggle for the maintenance of the union.†

I have dwelt at some length on this point because it is vitally necessary to an understanding of the bitterness and determination manifested on both sides. If it is not yet clear why the destruc-

---

* Frick also testified before the Congressional committee (p. 34, Report of testimony) that the fence which was built around the plant in May, 1892, was erected as a defence against possible violence.

† The responsibility for the anti-union policy on the part of the company is placed on the shoulders of Carnegie himself by J. H. Bridge, at one time Carnegie's secretary and later a partisan of Frick when the latter and Carnegie were at loggerheads. On page 204 of his book "Inside History of the Carnegie Steel Company," (N. Y., Aldine Book Co., 1903) he reproduces a draft of a notice to the Homestead employes, which is presumably authentic, written by Andrew Carnegie on April 4, 1892, and sent by him to Frick at Pittsburgh. This notice was to the effect that the Homestead works would have to be non-union after the expiration of the contract then in force, which ran until June 30, 1892. The author states that Frick disapproved of the notice and so it was not given out. On page 205, what is represented as a letter from Carnegie, dated June 10, 1892, is reproduced, in which the advice is given that conferences should be refused, and that if the union should refuse the scale proposed by the company the non-union notice should go up on June 25.

tion of unionism was considered important enough to precipitate such a prolonged and bitter contest, perhaps the later chapters, bearing on the non-union régime and what it has come to mean, may help to explain it. On the other hand, Frick's evident determination to crush out the union may perhaps be understood in the light of the facts regarding union tactics described in Chapter IX.

After the strike began the men could not have done more to furnish apparent justification for Frick's course than they did when they practically took charge of the borough government at Homestead and defied the authorities of county and state. By their refusal to allow sheriff's deputies to enter upon the mill property and their treatment of the Pinkerton guards they struck organized labor a severe blow.

As to the issues that were the apparent cause of the difficulty there is opportunity for much difference of opinion. Frick claimed that a reduction in rates was necessary because of improved processes which had increased output without requiring any increased physical labor. These improvements had, however, done away with certain positions and so required the employment of fewer men* and decreased labor cost per ton of product. Frick refused to give the Congressional investigating committee any information as to labor cost,† but he stated that the company had lost money for more than a year on every ton of slabs, blooms and billets that it had sold.‡ Yet Bridge publishes a table showing the net profits of the Carnegie Company to have been $4,300,000 in 1891 and $4,000,000 in 1892.§ It appeared in the Congressional investigation that the Carnegie Company was capitalized in 1892 at $25,000,000. On this basis the net profit in 1891 was 17.2 per cent and 16 per cent in 1892, after all the losses incident to the strike. These figures do not cry for wage retrenchment.

However, it is difficult to say what is a fair wage for an industry. That is a matter upon which doctors disagree. It can probably be stated academically that justice may be reached by such a division of the returns to industry as will insure approximate

* Congressional Investigation, p. 29.
† Ibid., pp 26, 30, 165.   ‡ Ibid., p. 163.
§ Bridge, J. H.: Inside History of the Carnegie Steel Company, p. 295.

equality of opportunity among the various groups that make up society. As industry is conducted today, it is usually impossible to learn whether such a division has been made, so a discussion of the ethics of a wage reduction is, within certain limits, impracticable. As between different groups of workingmen, however, it may readily be determined whether their wages are such as to provide them with equality of opportunity with respect to each other. A study of the wage schedule submitted by Frick to the Congressional investigating committee does not reveal any set standard of fixing rates. If, for example, the readjustment had raised the wages of those at the foot of the scale and lowered the wages of those at the top, there would have been a clear principle involved. It has been generally supposed and widely stated that this was the intention of the Carnegie Steel Company in proposing the new scale. Frick said in his testimony that in the 119-inch mill the men receiving the highest wages were the ones who received the greatest reduction.* This is true only in the sense that the men at the extreme foot of the scale were not reduced. Among those whose wages were reduced, there seems to have been no attempt at an equitable leveling process. The three rollers in the 119-inch mill were cut about 44 per cent, so that their average monthly earnings† were reduced from $272.28 to $153.64. In the same mill there were thirty shearman's helpers whose average earnings were cut from $92.76 to $43.65, a cut of 53 per cent. In the 32-inch slabbing mill the two rollers were reduced from $198.42 a month to $166.67, a cut of 16 per cent. In the same mill the two second helpers on the heating furnaces were reduced 32 per cent—from $86.92 a month to $58.80. In the two open-hearth departments the twenty-four melters, who were receiving $6.00 per day, were to receive no reduction whatever, while the first helpers in No. 1 open-hearth department were cut from $3.28 per day to $2.92, and second helpers were cut from $3.14 a day to $2.37. In open-hearth department No. 2 the first helpers were to be reduced from $4.32 per day to $2.85, and second helpers from $3.37 to $2.37. These

---

* Mis. Doc., No. 335, 52d Cong., 1st Sess., p. 162.

† Based on figures for May, 1892, submitted by Frick. Page 5 of testimony before Congressional committee, op. cit.

are a few examples of the inequalities of which the wage schedule was full.*

With these issues before us, it is necessary to do no more than state briefly the most important events. On July 6, the three hundred men that Frick had engaged from the Pinkerton agency reached Homestead from Ashtabula, Ohio, where they had congregated. They arrived at a station on the Ohio river below Pittsburgh near midnight on July 5. Here they embarked on barges on the river and were towed upstream to Pittsburgh and thence up the Monongahela river to Homestead, which they approached at about four o'clock on the morning of the 6th. The Homestead workmen had been warned of their coming and when the boat reached the landing back of the steel works, nearly the whole town was there to meet them and prevent their landing. What followed will probably never be known with exactness, for it is doubtful whether there could be any impartial observers. It was not a time for calm and deliberate judgment. The Homestead men had been working in the mill at that place, many of them, since it was first built. They had seen it grow from a small beginning to one of the finest and best equipped plants in the world. They were proud of the plant and proud of the part that they had had in its progress. Over the hills rising from the river were their cottages, many of them owned by the workingmen who lived in them; and now these homes were in jeopardy. They could have gone back to work at any time, of course, by accepting the terms of the company. But that meant giving up their union, which to a union man is equivalent to self-disfranchisement. So when the Pinkerton men came, the Homestead steel workers saw in their approach an attempt at subjugation at the hands of

---

* At this point I wish to correct an error that has had very wide acceptation. It is often asserted that the Homestead workmen received such wages that their yearly incomes ran into the tens of thousands. A late work on metallurgy, by an engineer of distinction, gravely alleges that Homestead men who went into the strike were getting $30,000 a year. (Campbell, H. H.: The Manufacture and Properties of Iron and Steel, pp. 428, 429.) In all the testimony of Frick before the investigating committee, in which he submitted many wage figures, the highest quoted were the earnings of one roller, who received in May, 1892, $279.30 for twenty-three days' work. Frick admitted that May was above the average in tonnage. At that rate this man would have earned $3,280.50 in a year of 270 days, which Frick told the committee was the average number of working days (p. 51). But this man was the highest paid. The lowest received $1.40 a day.

an armed force of unauthorized individuals.* A mob of men with guns coming to take their jobs, coming to take away the chance to work, to take opportunity away from their children, perhaps to break up their homes—that is what passed through the minds of the Homestead men that morning. How far wrong they were, how perverted their judgment, I do not attempt to say. I only desire to explain their point of view, if possible, and show why men, ordinarily law-abiding, should slip revolvers into their pockets that morning.†

Yet the tragic events of July 6, 1892, were disgraceful in the extreme to organized labor, and no less so to organized capital. During the day a half dozen men were killed and more were wounded. The Pinkerton men finally surrendered, upon a promise from the leader of the strike, Hugh O'Donnell, that they would be conducted in safety from the town. They were then permitted to land from the barges and were formed in line to march to a building in the centre of the town to await a special train.

It may be, as O'Donnell testified, that the leaders were unable to protect the Pinkertons, but it is a deep and standing reproach, nevertheless, to the name of organized labor, that throughout the march of about four blocks the men were attacked on all sides. They practically ran the gauntlet through an angry mob of men, women and boys who assaulted them in the most cowardly manner; they were defenseless and many of them were severely injured. Strange to say, not a few of their assailants were women. The majority report of the Congressional investigating committee said of what followed:

> The character of the injuries inflicted on the Pinkertons in some cases was too indecent and brutal to describe in this report. Whatever may have been the character of these men, or the offense which they had committed against the people of Homestead, the indignities to which

* The Pinkertons had not been sworn in as deputy sheriffs and had no standing as peace officers.

† "While public sentiment has rightly and unmistakably condemned violence, even in the form for which there is most excuse, I would have the public give due consideration to the terrible temptation to which the workingman on a strike is sometimes subjected. To expect that one dependent upon his daily wage for the necessities of life will stand by peaceably and see a new man employed in his stead is to expect much." (Andrew Carnegie, *Forum*, Vol. I, 1886, p. 549.)

they were subjected, when prisoners and defenseless, are not only disgraceful to that town, but to civilization as well; and there is no evidence that any attempt was made upon the part of their captors for their protection, except as stated by Mr. O'Donnell, who did not see it. No brave man or good woman will maltreat a prisoner who is disarmed and has no chance to defend himself.*

After thus condemning the workmen for their conduct, the majority report turns to the responsibility of the company for what had occurred:

> But in the negotiations with the committee of Amalgamated workmen for the renewal of the contract, we do not think that the officers of the company exercised that degree of patience, indulgence, and solicitude which they should have done, by way of minute explanations of reasons why the company proposed a reduction of wages. Mr. Frick, who is a business man of great energy and intelligence, seems to have been too stern, brusque, and somewhat autocratic, of which some of the men justly complain, and which led to a rather abrupt termination of the negotiations. We conclude from all the surroundings that he, who is not the only manufacturer thus affected, is opposed to the Amalgamated Association and its methods, and hence had no anxiety to contract with his laborers through that organization, and that this is the true reason why he appeared to them as autocratic and uncompromising in his demands. If, as he claimed, the business of the company, on account of a fall in the market price in the product of the works, required a reduction of the wages of the employes, he should have appealed to their reason, and shown them the true state of the company's affairs. *We are persuaded that if he had done so an agreement would have been reached between him and the workmen, and all the trouble which followed would thus have been avoided*"† (p. xi). . . . . Had Mr. Frick and his learned attorneys urged the sheriff and aided him by their counsels, though his efforts may have been futile and even puerile—if they had joined him in an appeal to the governor, and if Mr. Frick had gone to Governor Pattison in person and laid the case before him, instead of employing the Pinkertons in the first instance—we believe the governor would, as he finally did, in the discharge of his

* Report No. 2447, 52d Congress, 2d Session, p. ix.
† The italics are mine.

131

plain duty, have sent a sufficient force to enable the sheriff to have taken possession and delivered to the Carnegie Company their property, to the end that they might have operated their mills in their own way *and have avoided the riot.** Men of wealth and capital, as well as the poor mechanics and laborers in this country, must learn to respect the law and the legally constituted authorities, and have recourse to these to redress their wrongs and enjoy their property, in preference to undertaking to do these things by private or personal instrumentalities (pp. xi, xii).

The trouble which began in Homestead soon spread to other mills. The Carnegie mills on 29th and 33d Streets, Pittsburgh, struck in sympathy. Duquesne, which had been non-union from the beginning, was organized in July and most of the men came out for a few weeks. Other mills in Pittsburgh having no connection with the Carnegie Steel Company ceased work, and altogether, it was a summer of strikes in the Pittsburgh steel mills. The strike at Homestead was finally declared off on November 20, and most of the men went back to their old positions as non-union men. It had been a long, costly struggle. The funds of the Association were depleted, winter was coming on and it was finally decided to consider the battle lost.

So the death knell of unionism was struck for the steel mills of the United States. The Carnegie Steel Company took the opportunity to break with the union in all of their plants at the same time. The other Pittsburgh steel mills that had been on strike became non-union also. Where the great Carnegie Steel Company led, the others had to follow; from this time on, we find the union being steadily but surely crowded out of the steel industry. Jones and Laughlin, today the largest independent steel company in Allegheny County, eliminated unionism from their plant in 1897. The panic of 1893, following the Homestead strike, dealt another blow to the Amalgamated Association. There were 24,068 members in 1891. In 1894 there were 10,000. All of the steel mills of Allegheny County, except a few small ones, were put upon a non-union basis before 1900, and there remained to the organization the iron mills west of Pittsburgh,—for

* The italics are mine.

132

in Pittsburgh, iron mills, as well as steel, became largely non-union between 1890 and 1900,—the large steel mills of Illinois, and a large proportion of the sheet, tin and hoop mills of the country.

As times grew better in the latter part of the decade the organization began to recoup its membership. There was no trouble over scales and everything was peaceful. But in 1900 there came rumors of a gigantic consolidation in the steel industry, including nearly all the large steel companies of the country. The Amalgamated officials were alarmed. In any such combination, the Carnegie Steel Company, now the arch-enemy of unionism, would easily be first, and would, they feared, insist on driving the union out of every mill in the combination. It occurred to President Shaffer and his associates that the propitious time to make their demands would be while the new corporation was forming. Anxious for public confidence, anxious to float its securities, it could not afford a labor controversy. Accordingly when the new scales were to be signed in July, 1901, the Amalgamated Association demanded of the American Tin Plate Company that it sign a scale for all of its mills, and not merely for those that had been regarded as union. This was agreed to, provided the American Sheet Steel Company agreed to the same proposition. The latter company refused and a strike was inaugurated against the Amercian Tin Plate Company, the American Sheet Steel Company and the American Steel Hoop Company, subsidiary companies of the United States Steel Corporation. In conferences held on July 11, 12, and 13, with these companies, the companies offered to sign for all tin mills but one, for all the sheet mills that had been signed for the year previous, together with four sheet mills in addition that had been formerly non-union. and for all the hoop mills that had been signed for the year previous. This advantageous offer was foolishly rejected by the Amalgamated Association men, who demanded all the mills or none. The strike then was on in earnest.

The strike did not have that popular support at the beginning that previous controversies of the Association had received, and on August 6, President Shaffer alienated most of the public sympathy remaining, by calling on all men who sympathized with the union movement in all the mills of the Corporation, to come out on strike, regardless of signed contracts.* In 1900 the convention, probably anticipating a struggle with the combinations then being formed, passed an amendment to its constitution which read, "Should one mill in a combine or trust have a difficulty, all mills in said combine or trust shall cease work until such grievance is settled."† Such a clause, if it were inserted in the scale book, which contains the contract between the firms and the men, could not be criticised, excepting, perhaps, upon grounds of policy. But it was not inserted in the scale book, and the constitution is not generally considered a part of the contract. Consequently, when in the strike of 1901 against the United States Steel Corporation President Shaffer called out the men in the mills not concerned in the original strike, he was complying with the constitution, but he was asking unions whose representatives had signed contracts to break them.

In some of the mills the men obeyed their leader and walked out, but the men in the mills of the Illinois Steel Company refused to break their contracts. Officers of the union finally persuaded the men employed in the mills at Milwaukee and Joliet to go on strike. The men at South Chicago, however, could not be persuaded and President Shaffer revoked their union charter, thus reading them out of the organization. This action hurt the prestige of the Amalgamated Association.‡

* August 6, 1901, Shaffer issued the following call:
"Brethren: The officials of the United States Steel Trust have refused to recognize as union men those who are now striving for the right to organize. The executive board has authorized me to issue a call upon all Amalgamated and other union men in name and heart to join in the movement to fight for labor's rights.
"We must fight or give up forever our personal liberty.
"You will be told that you have signed contracts, but you never agreed to surrender those contracts to the United States Steel Corporation. Its officers think you were sold to them just as the mills with contracts and all.
"Remember before you agreed to any contract you took an obligation to the Amalgamated Association. It now calls on you to help in this hour of need.
"Unless the strike is closed on or before Saturday, August 10, 1901, the mills will close when the last turn is made on that day.
"Brethren, this is the call to preserve our organization. We trust you and need you. Come and help us, and may right come to a just cause." (*Iron Age*, Aug. 8, 1901, p. 21.)
† Article 17, Section 23.
‡ The clause referred to is still to be found in the constitution, but the word "shall" has been changed to "may." Art. XVII, Sec. 22. See Appendix II, p. 253.

134

The strike call did not have the effect that had been hoped for and by the middle of August it was evident that the Association had made a mistake. Instead of finding their task easier because the United States Steel Corporation had just been formed, they found that corporation ready to bring all its tremendous power against this organization. They had gone into a fight with one of the greatest combinations of capital in the world, and they were not strong enough to win. President Shaffer offered to arbitrate the whole matter, but the proposition was rejected and at the end of August the strike was declared off. The outcome was a defeat for the union; instead of gaining ground it finally signed the scale for a smaller number of mills than before, ten formerly union mills becoming non-union.

So today the Amalgamated Association is again more than anything else an iron workers' organization. Its largest membership comes from the iron mills of Ohio, Indiana and Illinois. It still has a foothold in the sheet and tin mills, but it does not number in its jurisdiction one large steel mill where heavy material is handled.

Since the year of my investigation there have been noteworthy developments. When the annual contract between the Amalgamated Association and the American Sheet and Tin Plate Company expired at the end of June, 1909, the latter refused to sign another contract and refused to have any further dealings with the union. The men in the union mills promptly went out on strike and succeeded in tying up a number of sheet and tin plants, though the larger number were operated with non-union men. The men held together remarkably well, but in August, 1910, after nearly fourteen months, the strike was declared off by the Amalgamated Association. This action marked the absolute elimination of unionism from the mills of the United States Steel Corporation.

At the Convention of the American Federation of Labor, held at Toronto, in November, 1909, President McArdle of the Amalgamated Association introduced a resolution, which was passed, declaring the United States Steel Corporation to be the greatest enemy of organized labor, and calling for a conference of labor leaders to devise ways of organizing all of the mills of the Corporation. These labor leaders held several conferences and issued an appeal to all labor unions in the country to aid in the work of organizing. The executive council of the Federation also levied a tax on all its members of ten cents per member, to provide funds for the work.

Resolutions were drawn up denouncing the methods of the Steel Corporation in its relations with its employes, and these were presented to President Taft, and to the governors of the states where the Corporation has mills. In the resolutions addressed to the President, he was petitioned to urge Congress to provide for a government investigation of the relations existing between the Corporation and its employes. A resolution was passed by the United States Senate during the session of 1910 (S. R. 237) directing the Federal Bureau of Labor to investigate industrial conditions in the iron and steel industrv and report to the Senate.

PART III

THE EMPLOYERS IN THE SADDLE

CHAPTER XI

INDUSTRIAL ORGANIZATION UNDER THE NON-UNION RÉGIME

IN tracing the events in the struggle between employers and employes for control in the steel industry, I have devoted the greater space to the policy of the employes. Although the union never attained a position of absolute control, it was strong enough to put into practice many of its policies, and to that extent they could be examined and judged. The employers, on the other hand, have now throughout the greater part of the industry secured absolute control. It is accordingly possible to speak with more assurance regarding their labor program.

Left free to manage their affairs as they saw fit, as outcome of the strikes of the nineties, the steel manufacturers carried to new lengths their internal policy of reducing cost by increasing output and lessening dependence upon human labor. Time was utilized as it never had been before in this industry, and every known mechanical device was introduced that would increase speed, cut down waste, or overcome halts in production. In the last eighteen years, machinery has transformed the industry, eliminating much hand labor and discounting human skill.

This tendency to make processes automatic has resulted not only in a lessened cost with an increased tonnage, but it has also reinforced the control of the employers over their men. When the roll tables were introduced they threw many roughers and catchers out of employment; beyond that, they lessened the importance to the employers of the men remaining. Men can learn to pull levers more easily than they can reach the skilled mastery of a position where the greatest dependence is on the man and the least on the machine. Accordingly this development has lessened the value to the employer of all the men in a plant and at the same time has made the job of every man, skilled and unskilled, to a greater or less degree insecure. The enormous increase in immigration in the last two decades has added to this insecurity, for it has made unskilled men easy to get. Thus both the job and the wage of the steel worker are to a certain extent jeopardized.

It is not to be inferred, however, that the present-day policies of the steel companies are possible only because unionism has been overthrown. This is by no means true. Many of them were enunciated long before the Amalgamated Association had lost its power, and while they have been more widely extended, they are not altered in principle. The practice of using the best known mechanical methods was never, so far as I know, opposed by the union in this trade. The only incident of such a nature that has come to my attention was when the executive committee of the Association in 1885 recommended to the lodges that they accept a reduction in puddling in order to make iron cheaper than steel. This reduction, the committee stated, "if accepted by the Association will also stop very materially the introduction of steel in general to supersede iron." The proposal was rejected by the lodges.*

The question of improved machinery and its bearing upon the labor situation is of great importance everywhere, but nowhere more than in the steel industry. There has been a policy of daring, almost to the point of recklessness, that probably no other industry can duplicate. No change has been overlooked that would put a machine at work in place of a man;† thousands of men have been displaced in this way since 1892, and yet the industry has so grown that more men, in the aggregate, are employed than ever before. Ingot manipulation, which does away with a large number of men around the blooming mills, and makes possible the use of a larger ingot; the overhead electric crane; larger and more powerful engines; the substitution of electric power for steam—all these

---

* Journal of Proceedings, Amalgamated Association, 1885, p. 1577.

† "It is around Pittsburgh that the methods have been developed in blast furnaces and rolling mills which have become known as 'American Practice,' and I believe it is but the truth to state that these standards have in the main been established by the Carnegie Steel Company. . . . . The principle at Pittsburgh was to destroy anything from a steam hammer to a steel works whenever a better piece of apparatus was to be had, ... and the definition of this word 'better' was confined to the ability to get out a greater product. . . . . . Thousands of dollars are spent to dispense with the labor of one or two men." Campbell, H. H.: The Manufacture and Properties of Iron and Steel, pp. 470, 471.

are improvements that have been introduced within the last sixteen years; all have increased output; most of them have displaced men.

The aim today seems to be to make the whole process as mechanical as possible. Fifteen or twenty years ago a large proportion of the employes in any steel plant were skilled men. The percentage of the highly skilled has steadily grown less; and the percentage of the unskilled has as steadily increased.* The plants of the Carnegie Steel Company in Allegheny County employ in seasons of prosperity an aggregate of over 23,000 men. Of these about 17 per cent are skilled, 21 per cent semi-skilled, and 62 per cent unskilled, according to the classification employed by the company.† I do not know the exact standards used in determining these divisions as to skill, but from other data at hand it would appear that in the industry as a whole the percentage of what would be lumped roughly as common labor is even larger. In wage schedules furnished me from the office of a leading steel company, it was found that of 2,304 men employed, only 125, or 5.43 per cent, received over $5.00 a day.‡ A wage classification of this sort may not be a sufficient basis for an absolute judgment, but one is justified in assuming that where there are few highly paid men there are relatively few skilled positions.

The successful operation of a plant is not, however, in the hands of so small a group of men as might be inferred from these figures. Skill is not confined to the skilled positions. In every department of mill work there is a more or less rigid line of promotion. Every man is in training for the next position above. If all of the rollers in the Homestead plant were to strike tomorrow, the work would go on, and only temporary inconvenience, if any, would be suffered. There would simply be a step up along the line; the tableman would take the rolls, the hooker would manipulate the tables, perhaps one of the shearman's helpers would take the hooker's position, and somewhere, away down the

* The reference here is to the men engaged in the operating processes. With the development of the big machines, the staff of machinists, electricians, repair men, mill-wrights, etc., has of course increased.

† Table A, Appendix X, p. 349.

‡ See Chapter XII, Wages and Cost of Living.

line, an unskilled yard laborer would be taken to fill the vacancy in the lowest position involving skill. The course would vary in the different styles of mills, as the positions vary in number and character, but the operating principle is everywhere the same. In the open-hearth department the line of promotion runs through common labor, metal wheelers, stock handlers, cinder-pit man, second helper and first helper, to melter foreman. In this way the companies develop and train their own men. They seldom hire a stranger for a position as roller or heater. Thus the working force is pyramided and is held together by the ambition of the men lower down; even a serious break in the ranks adjusts itself all but automatically.

It is this coördination, this effort to combine harmony and permanence with control and efficiency, that presents one of the hardest tasks to the superintendent of a labor force. Whether the employes are of a single nationality or of many races, serious difficulties arise, and, as suggested above, the immigration factor enters into the problem for both employer and employe. It is sometimes held that better results from the standpoint of management are secured where there are many races grouped together. In the Pittsburgh District this condition has come about through the enormous Slavic immigration of the last fifteen years. There were Slavs and Magyars in the Pittsburgh District longer ago than fifteen years, but it has been within that time that these people have monopolized the unskilled positions in the steel mills. The displacing of the Irish in the blast furnaces, already touched upon, has occurred within twenty years. Fifteen years ago the laborers were largely English-speaking. Today one is surprised in passing through a Pittsburgh steel mill if he comes across an American, a German or an Irishman among the unskilled laborers.

Undoubtedly many of the unskilled English-speaking laborers of a decade ago have gone into the skilled trades. But this does not explain the presence of Slavs and Huns exclusively in the unskilled positions. The phenomenon is even more puzzling when it is noted that the newer immigrants are not working for less pay for a day's rough work than the races they replaced. The money wages paid for common labor in the Pittsburgh steel

Drawn by Joseph Stella

A New-comer

IMMIGRANT DAY LABORERS ON THE WAY HOME FROM WORK

mills have been going up during the period referred to. How far this increase has been offset by a rise in the cost of living will be discussed in the next chapter.

The most apparent causes back of the Slav and Magyar monopoly of the unskilled positions in the steel industry are five in number: first, the overwhelming Slavic immigration of the last fifteen years, due to causes in this country and abroad not connected with the steel industry; second, a system of petty graft, for which the steel companies are not responsible, but which as a body they have failed to eliminate; third, false standards which have made Americans feel that it is a disgrace to work on a level with a Slav; fourth, conditions in the industry itself which have caused the more ambitious workmen to abandon it when there was not room for promotion; fifth, the apparent fact that the steel companies have definitely sought this class of labor.

As to the first reason, it is noteworthy that English, Irish and German immigration began to fall off at just about the time that the steel industry began to expand so rapidly and at the same time to introduce automatic processes. This created a tremendous market for unskilled labor just as the field of immigration was shifting from northwestern to southeastern Europe. Slavs coming to America to perform unskilled manual labor, and finding it in the steel industry, sent for their relatives and neighbors. These automatic accretions, through letters and friends returning to the old country and spreading the tidings of where work is to be had, are at once the most natural and most widespread factors in mobilizing an immigrant labor force.

But this does not explain why the Slav came to monopolize the unskilled positions, when there were still American boys and sons of English and Irish immigrants already on the ground who might conceivably be looking for work. The four remaining factors, noted as apparent causes, throw light on this point.

The grafting system has its roots partly in the fact that the Slav is willing to work for less than an American and partly in his ignorance. The foreman in charge of a gang of laborers who is addicted to the grafting habit usually has a confederate in the gang itself, a Slav who has been in America long enough to know the ropes, and who conducts the negotiations. If there is an opening for another man, the confederate goes to some green foreigner who has just arrived and tells him that he can get him a job; the job is for sale, however, and he cannot have it unless he is willing to pay the price. The newcomer is given to understand that it is the custom to sell jobs in this country, and that the transaction is in no way unusual. Accordingly the price is paid, the confederate takes out his commission, the balance is handed over to the boss, and the man goes to work. With some foremen this is the end of the transaction, but with others it is only the beginning. There are many stories current of how the bosses are "treated" every pay day, or of cases of beer and boxes of cigars sent to their homes. It is said that there are foremen who let it be known when their larders need replenishing, and in some mysterious way the necessary provisions are delivered, with bills marked paid. I was told of a foreman whose men bought him a piano, paying for it in instalments out of their scant earnings. Many of these tales are undoubtedly fabrications. Probably the majority of the labor foremen are men who would no sooner be guilty of such despicable graft than they would rob a bank. But no one can deny that the practice does exist, and has existed for years. Back in the eighties there was excitement in the hard coal regions of Pennsylvania over mine bosses selling jobs to Hungarians at $1.00 apiece.* Gullible "Hunkies" have been known to pay $5.00, $10 or even $25 for a job in the steel mills. There can be no doubt that this practice has had an influence on the extent to which the Slav has entered the iron and steel industry. A grafting foreman will hire the men who will submit to the system, and there are none who submit as readily as the new immigrant.†

But this factor would not have been sufficient to bring about the present condition. A more fundamental influence has

---

* *National Labor Tribune*, April 19, 1884.

† It should be noted that every effort is made, probably by all of the steel companies, but certainly by the United States Steel Corporation, to eliminate this system. If a foreman guilty of this practice is discovered, he is instantly discharged. The superintendent of the Ambridge plant of the American Bridge Company recently said that he believed grafting was practically eliminated from his force and that it could not persist in any large way unless tolerated by the management. In recent years five foremen have been discharged at his works. It was this system, on the other hand, which constituted one of the chief grievances of the employes of the Pressed Steel Car Company, in their strike at McKees Rocks in 1909. In January, 1911, a Carnegie Steel Company foreman pleaded guilty to conspiracy, as result of charges brought by the chief detective of the company against him and against a merchant mill superintendent for mulcting the laborers under them.

been at work the last twenty years. There are many men occupying the highest positions in the mills who tell with pride that they made their start as common laborers. Today the young American who starts in the lowest position with the intention of working up is rare. The Slavic peasant, accustomed to subservience to authority, and taught it by all the force of tradition, is distrusted and disliked by his more independent American neighbor. Stolid and willing, living amid unsanitary surroundings, hoarding his earnings and spending only for immediate necessities, he is misunderstood and despised by the more liberal, wideawake Anglo-Saxon, until "Hunky" has come to be a convenient designation and a term of opprobrium as well. Many American boys fancy that they degrade themselves by entering into competition with a Slav for a job. Accordingly, lacking experience and hence skill, they shut themselves out of the avenues of approach to the better mill positions. As several skilled men have expressed it to me, the result to a considerable extent has been "to demoralize the American boys." Feeling superior to the Slav, some come to feel superior to work itself. Conscious disdain of toil, as such, is probably rare, but there can be no doubt of its existence. The young Americans are too many of them taking what the mill workers speak of as "pencil jobs," as opposed to manual work. They weigh metal, keep time, and perform services where they can wear good clothes and look like office men instead of laborers. There is little chance for promotion in these positions, the pay is poor, but many seem to be satisfied with their white collar distinction from the man in overalls who draws twice as much money on pay day. Some of the successful mill workers are sending their sons to college and technical schools, whence they emerge fit to fill the better positions in mill work; to these the Slav is no obstacle. For boys, however, who have their own way to make, and to whom more aggressive ideals have not been personified with equal alluringness, there is danger that they will allow false pride to make them dependent, poorly-paid clerks, instead of self-respecting and respected workmen.*

* "It was absolutely necessary to get Hungarians to do work which other men would not undertake in digging foundations and building the ———— plant," writes a former manager. "When it was ready to run, the men who had been

A fourth reason for the predominance of the Slav in the un-skilled labor positions lies in the nature of the industry itself. Long hours, much overtime, and the hardest work, are required of the unskilled laborers. No man with much imagination or desire for self-improvement is willing to work seven days in the week, ex-cept as a temporary expedient. The Irish were not driven out of the blast furnaces by a fresh immigration with lower standards of living; rather the conditions in the industry—the twelve-hour day, the days and weeks without a day of rest, the twenty-four-hour shift—made the life intolerable. They could make as good a living working fewer hours a day, and only six days in the week, in other positions and in other industries. So the Irish worker went out and the Slav came in.*

The fifth reason given for the increasingly large number of Slav and Magyar laborers in the mills was that the steel com-panies apparently sought them. Whether or not they have at different times actually encouraged foreign laborers to immigrate, it is known that immigrants have been encouraged to locate in the Pittsburgh District. H. C. Frick testified in 1892 that foreign labor had been definitely sought by the coke manufacturers.† It was reported in 1885 that Italian laborers were being brought to McKeesport to lay pipe at the National Tube Works.‡

The preference of the companies for this class of labor is indicated by the attitude of the foremen. Most of them say that they prefer Americans, yet, as far as I could learn, they make no effort to secure American labor. Even those foremen who hire their own men, directly, employ Slavs. Holding that alien labor is distasteful to them, it seems incredible that they should not attempt to secure a different class of men if they were absolutely free to hire whom they will. Of course, there are the counter-influences already

unwilling to do the work required were quite ready to take desirable positions in the mill, leaving the Hungarians out. We treated them [the immigrants] fairly, and so far as they were capable gave them places in operating the mill."

　*An Irish foreman who began as a laborer in a Pittsburgh blast furnace fifteen years ago tells me that then the laborers were nearly all Irish. Of fifty Irishmen who worked at the same furnace then, he is the only one left today. The others, he says, left because of the long days, the Sunday work, and the low wages.

　†Senate Investigation of Labor Troubles, 52d Cong., 2d Sess., Report 1280, p. 158.

　‡National Labor Tribune, Jan. 31, 1885.

mentioned,—that Americans will not work with the Slavs, and that the conditions are not to their liking. But the former did not obtain until within recent years, and the latter does not apply even now to all departments. There are many desirable labor positions through which intelligent and faithful men might expect to rise. A hint as to causes was contained in a letter which Captain Jones, manager of the Edgar Thomson works, is reported by Bridge to have written back in 1875: "My experience has shown that Germans and Irish, Swedes and what I denominate 'Buckwheats'(young American country boys), judiciously mixed, make the most effective and tractable force you can find."* Nearly thirty years later, soon after the unions in the sheet and tin mills went on strike in July, 1909, the same note was struck in advertisements which appeared in Pittsburgh papers for men to work in non-union tin mills. One such advertisement contained the statement, "Syrians, Poles and Roumanians preferred." The advertisements were inserted by a Pittsburgh employment bureau, but it was evident that the men were wanted for the Steel Corporation mills.

These straws may help explain why the mixed races of east Europe are not unwelcome to the steel companies. It is certain, at any rate, that the workingmen in the mills are divided racially into many groups.

By the eastern European immigration the labor force has been cleft horizontally into two great divisions. The upper stratum includes what is known in mill parlance as the "English-speaking" men; the lower contains the "Hunkies" or "Ginnies." Or, if you prefer, the former are the "white men," the latter the "foreigners."

An "English-speaking" man may be neither native American nor English nor Irish. He may be one of these or he may be German, Scandinavian or Dutch. It is sufficient if the land of his birth be somewhere west of the Russian Empire or north of Austria-Hungary. A "Hunky" is not necessarily a Hungarian. He may belong to any of the Slavic races. "Ginny" seems to include all the "Hunkies" with the Italians thrown in. The clearest division, then, runs between these two groups—the one largely

* Bridge, J. H.: Inside History of the Carnegie Steel Company, p. 81

Teutonic and Celtic, the other largely Slavic. Between them there is little sympathy.

But there is not complete unanimity among members of these large groups. There are vertical as well as horizontal divisions. In the "English-speaking" group one would expect to find some friction between the Teuton and the Celt. This seems to be manifested chiefly by the dislike of the native American and the English for the Welsh workingman. Among the "foreigners" there is more to create dissension. The Magyar is traditionally at outs with his Slavic neighbors. The Finn, the Pole, the Slovak, and the Lithuanian all have their sectional jealousies. The church, too, creates a division according to creeds, the Greek Catholic being opposed to the Roman, and both viewing the Protestant with suspicion. With such a heterogeneous collection of races and religions it can readily be seen that united democratic action, embracing the majority of the labor force, must be difficult and beset with conflicting elements.

Whatever it was that grouped the labor force as it is today, the grouping is favorable to continued control on the part of the employer.

It will be interesting to watch the future of the Slav in the steel industry. At present there seems to be little tendency on the part of the foremen and superintendents to promote a Slav workman to the higher position even if he is fitted for it. On the contrary, during the depression of 1907–1908, skilled Americans who were out of work because of the suspension of certain departments in the mills were given laborers' positions, where opportunity offered, in preference to the Slavs who had formerly held the jobs. I was unable to learn of any Slavs who had worked up to positions as rollers or heaters in the Pittsburgh mills. This is due without doubt to the poorer industrial equipment of the immigrants as well as to the unwillingness of the foremen to give the better positions to them; but it is the general impression among the mill workers that a Slav will not be promoted so long as an English-speaking man is to be secured.* The time may come, however,

* An official of one of the steel companies, familiar with all departments of mill work, after reading this statement, wrote me as follows: "This is perfectly natural, quite apart from racial feeling. The skilled men are those from whom

148

when there will be no one but Slavs for the positions, and in the open-hearth departments this situation seems to be rapidly approaching. A new man is put to work in the cinder pit; from here he is promoted to be second helper and then first helper. Practically all of the cinder-pit men now are Slavs, the majority of the second helpers are Slavs, and it would seem to be only a question of time when the first helpers and even the melter foremen will be men of these races promoted from the lower positions. This is the thing that the English-speaking men dread, believing, as they do, that the result will be a constantly lower scale of wages.

the foremen are chosen. Foremen must know English, among other reasons being that they have more or less clerical work in connection with orders, employment records, and general mill regulations. The foremen also are many of them in training for positions as superintendents, most of whom were at one time in foremen's positions. In short, the organization is much like that of the army, with the necessary distinction between the commissioned officers and the ranks; and the unskilled foreign labor appreciate that, just as in Europe, they have small hope of securing commissions in the army. As is perfectly well known, many (a very large proportion) of these unskilled men, especially the Slavs, have no 'stake' in the country and do not expect to remain in the United States. Those who do and send their children to the public schools will, in the second and third generation, be absorbed into the general mass of 'Americans,' whose progress in the steel industry or any other will depend solely on individual fitness and adaptability."

'WANT ADS' APPEARING IN PITTSBURGH GAZETTE-TIMES, JULY 15,
1909, DURING STRIKE IN U. S. STEEL CORPORATION TIN MILLS
Note in small advertisement near foot of column, "Syrians, Poles and
Romanians preferred"

Detached Brick Dwellings.   Four rooms and bath. $2700 to $2800

Detached Frame Houses. $5000 to $7000

HIGH GRADE TYPES OF COMMERCIALLY BUILT HOUSES IN MILL TOWNS

CHAPTER XII

WAGES AND COST OF LIVING

THERE are a few steel workers—perhaps a score—in the Pittsburgh mills whose earnings amount to $15 a day. That fact generally makes a stronger impression when heard for the first time than does the fact that there are thousands in the steel mills of Allegheny County who receive less than $2.00 a day. The old reputation of the steel industry as one of exceptionally high wages is false so far as the rank and file are concerned; neither, on the other hand, should it be singled out as an unusual type, as an industry in which the majority of the men are paid at the lowest rates. To get at any understanding of the situation, we must know the groups into which the wage-earners fall, what the tendency in wages has been for each group, and the proportion of the working force at present falling in each. And first of all, as a basis for judgment as to the trend of effective earnings, it is necessary to regard them in relation to the trend of prices of the necessities of life.

Bulletin No. 75 of the United States Bureau of Labor shows that at no time during the previous seventeen years were prices as high as in 1907. The average wholesale prices of certain commodities, usually classified as necessities, was 22.1 per cent higher in 1907 than in 1892.* The increase has been distributed rather uniformly, the rate of advance of most of the necessities of life being about the same as that of the average for all commodities. Food products were 13.7 per cent higher in 1907 than in 1892, clothing 16.2 per cent higher, lumber and building materials 42.9 per cent higher, and house furnishing goods 11.3 per cent higher.†

* From 1897, which was a low-ebb year for prices in the decade 1890–1900, this increase was 44 per cent.

† Bulletin No. 75, Bureau of Labor, March, 1908, p. 295. Figures were based on wholesale prices of 258 commodities divided into nine groups as follows: Farm products, Food, Cloth and Clothing, Fuel and Lighting, Metals and Implements, Lumber and Building Materials, Drugs and Chemicals, House Furnishing Goods, Miscellaneous.

These figures apply to the country as a whole, without regard to local conditions that may affect the situation. So far as Pittsburgh, and with it, Allegheny County, is concerned the figures are probably inadequate, as in 1907 the average price of necessities was higher here than in other cities of the same rank.

House rent is an item in the cost of living for a majority of the working population, and the rise of 42 per cent in the cost of building materials in the seventeen years doubtless explains in part at least the advance in that direction. Pittsburgh real estate dealers say that many rents have doubled in the last five years, and in the same time taxes in some of the mill towns have so advanced that people have been deterred from buying or building who might otherwise have done so, believing that taxes, repairs and water rates would be nearly as high as house rent. In many of the surrounding mill towns rents are as high as in Pittsburgh. A good frame house of six rooms, with a bathroom, and running water in the kitchen, rents for $25 to $40 a month, according to the location. Such houses and better ones are occupied by some of the highly paid steel workers, some of the comparatively few men whose earnings are over $5.00 a day. I know employes of the Steel Corporation who live in houses that they built for themselves which would command $40 and even $50 rent if the owners wished to vacate them.

But the majority of mill men do not live in such houses. I should say that the average English-speaking mill worker's home contains about four rooms and not infrequently is without plumbing. Such a house may be rented for $16 a month. I found an iron worker's family occupying three rooms on the second floor over a store on the corner of a congested street, with the din of the mill just two squares away. The only approach to the place was through a dirty court and up a rear flight of stairs. This flat, absolutely without plumbing, rented for $15 a month. With prices and rents steadily rising, it is hard for the family of a man earning not over $3.00 a day to keep their standards in the face of a fight with the dirt and ugliness and smoke-laden atmosphere of a congested mill neighborhood.

The effect of the rent situation has been to drive many of the wage-earners' families from the streets to the alleys and from the single house with its bit of lawn and yard to the flat. It has herded the foreigners together in houses and single rooms; and has brought forth in comparatively small mill towns evils of congestion hardly to be looked for outside of a large city. The workmen receiving the lowest wage, the unskilled laborers, huddle near the mills, where they can economize by living in cramped quarters and in lodging houses, and where they are saved the necessity of paying carfare. Here they are never spared from the confusion except for a twenty-hour period from Saturday evening to Sunday evening. But this is respite from the noise, not from the soot, for the stacks pour forth their black clouds almost without ceasing. The better paid men live farther away from the mills, the more fortunate of them on streets shaded, and attractive with bits of lawn, some living miles away over the hills where there is little to remind them of the din of industry. Those who live at a distance have to pay for it, of course, by long street-car rides, and they have less time at home than those who live near their work.

In the price of food stuffs as well as in taxes or rents, the Pittsburgh steel worker feels the pressure of the high cost of living. The country is very rough in every direction from the city, and there is little farming land, so the industrial towns cannot depend upon local truck gardeners to supply their tables with vegetables, nor upon a near source of production for their eggs, butter and fruit. One Pittsburgh family of my acquaintance have, for some years, been buying their potatoes and supplies in Michigan, and much of their clothing and house furnishings in Chicago, and have been able to get them delivered at their home at a cost below what they would have had to pay if they had purchased them at retail in Pittsburgh.

To balance the advanced costs of living,* wages should have advanced in proportion. The average wage paid in all industries throughout the country should have advanced 22 per cent over the prevailing wage of 1892 to give the wage-earners in 1907 as great a purchasing power as they had at the earlier date. The year 1892 is an important one in the steel industry as marking the overthrow of the union in several of the largest plants in the Pitts-

* For a presentation of the family end of the wages problem, and of the cost of living in the Pittsburgh District, see Homestead: The Households of a Mill Town, by Margaret F. Byington, a companion volume of The Pittsburgh Survey.

burgh District, and the consequent assumption by the employers of all responsibility for labor conditions. It is also important as marking the beginning by the employers of a series of reductions in rate scales which have apparently continued down to the present. In certain mills there were reductions in 1894, and in others in 1896. There seems to have been no general reduction throughout the nineties, but the whole body of skilled workers received occasional cuts in rates throughout the period. In 1904 there was a general reduction, said to average 10 per cent, in the wages of employes of the United States Steel Corporation, and although this was restored to a majority of the working force in 1905, it was not restored to many of the skilled workers. Day laborers were raised in 1907, but at the beginning of 1908 there were a considerable number of individual reductions among tonnage men in mills of the United States Steel Corporation, and in 1908 and 1909 wage cuts were general in the independent mills.

Since 1892, as shown by Table 4, there has been a decline of 60 and 70 per cent in the tonnage rates governing important positions in the plate mills at Homestead.

TABLE 4.—TONNAGE RATES IN PLATE MILLS, HOMESTEAD, 1889–1908*

Position	Cents per Ton, 119-inch Plate Mill			Cents per Ton, 84-inch Plate Mill		Per cent of Decline since 1889–92
	1889–92	1892 [Feb.]	1894 [Feb.]	1905–07	1908 [Feb.]	
Roller	14.00	12.15	6.00	5.50	4.75	66.07
Screw-down. . .	11.50	9.55	3.70	4.11	3.82	66.78
Heater	11.00	9.55	5.25	4.29	3.99	63.73
Heater's helpers . .	7.50	4.85	2.22	2.50	2.09	72.13
Tableman . . .	10.00	6.94	3.20	3.29	2.74	72.60
First shearman . .	13.00	9.85	4.09	..	..	..
Second shearman .	8.50	6.80	3.41	..	..	..
Shearman's helpers .	5.50	3.47	2.27	2.16	1.70	69.09
Hookers . . .	8.50	6.08	2.72	2.75	2.40	71.76
First leader . . .	7.75	5.21	2.95	..	..	..
Second leader . .	7.25	4.47	2.56	..	..	..

* E. W. Bemis, writing in 1894, gave a list of reductions in the 119-inch plate mill at Homestead, that appear in the first three columns of the table. (*Journal of Political Economy*, Vol. II, p. 338.) In 1905 this mill was made over into an 84-inch mill, and the rates in the fourth column were paid. The fifth

Revolutionary changes in machinery and method, no less than the elimination of the Amalgamated, have been the occasion of these repeated reductions in the scale and have materially modified the effect upon the earnings of employes. The outcome can be better understood by dividing the employes of the steel companies roughly into three classes. The first is the unskilled labor paid at day rates. As in most industries, this is numerically the largest class, comprising about 60 per cent of all employes. At the opposite extreme are the men of highest skill, headed by the rollers and heaters, who have gangs working under them and are practically foremen. These men represent not over 5 per cent of all employes. The remaining 35 per cent are what I call the real steel workers. They are not foremen, but they are men skilled in steel manufacture. In contrast to the 5 per cent above them, their earnings are very moderate, and in contrast to the 60 per cent below them, these men are individually essential to the industry and it is essential to them. They could not enter any other industry without a reduction in earning power, because they are skilled only as steel workers, while the 60 per cent in the unskilled class can dig ditches or heave coal any day just as well as they can throw chains around piles of steel billets or shovel scrap into furnaces.

The wages of the first of these three classes, the day laborers, have increased in the last few years. In 1892 they received 14 cents an hour at Homestead. In 1907–08 their pay was 16½ cents an hour in the mills of the United States Steel Corporation—an advance of 18 per cent over the hourly pay of 1892. This increase fell short by 4 per cent in keeping pace with the increased cost of necessities as indicated by the Bureau of Labor Bulletin. In the Jones and Laughlin plant in Pittsburgh in 1907 the rate was 15 cents.

With the exception of these unskilled laborers and such day men as machinists and molders working at their trades in the plants, the steel mill employes are paid by the ton. It is necessary

column shows the rate that was instituted in February, 1908. I have not been able to secure the rates for the years intervening between 1894 and 1905. The rates in the fourth and fifth columns were given in a letter written by a Homestead steel worker to a labor paper (*National Labor Tribune*, Feb. 6, 1908). I have been able to check them up through other sources, and they may be relied upon as substantially accurate.

to distinguish very clearly between these rates paid per ton and the earnings of the men per day who turn out the tonnage. As an example of the effect of the change in tonnage rates upon the employer's labor cost on the one hand and the men's earnings per day on the other, we can compare the rates paid on the 119-inch plate mill at Homestead in 1892 with rates paid in 1908 in Homestead plate mills which may be said fairly to correspond to it in character. The tonnage rates were cut an average of over 65 per cent in these 15 years, as shown in Table 4. The effect of these cuts in the scale upon the labor cost and earnings per day in certain positions is shown in Table 5, on the following page.

Although earnings of workmen in these mills have not declined in any such degree as has the rate per ton, there has been a substantial reduction in daily earnings, and a considerably greater reduction in daily labor cost. The one plate mill at Homestead in 1892 was operated with three crews of men each working eight hours, while the four plate mills now in operation in the plant have two crews working twelve hours each. If the rate had not been reduced, there would have been no reduction in the labor cost per day even though the change in shifts was made that eliminated one-third of the men employed on the mill. As it was, the reduction in the rate made it possible for the management to effect a saving of from 30 to 60 per cent in the labor cost per day for the positions named in 1907, as against that of 1892. On the other hand, if the rate had not been reduced there would have been a corresponding increase in daily earnings* with every increase in output due to increased speed, improved machinery, or other cause. But with the changes in rates, the daily earnings of the men in the crews fell off from 5 to 40 per cent. Had they continued on an eight-hour basis, their loss must have been much greater than that. As it was, they were not able, despite the increased tonnage they handled, to maintain their old income even by working twelve hours in 1907 as against eight hours in 1892,— an increase in the working day of 50 per cent.

The data given as to these plate mill crews illustrate how rate cuts have lessened the earnings of the highly skilled men. Another illustration: Frick furnished to the Congressional in-

* See page 189.

TABLE 5.—SHOWING REDUCTION IN DAILY EARNINGS AND IN LABOR COST FOR CERTAIN POSITIONS ON PLATE MILLS AT HOMESTEAD, 1892–1907*

POSITION	AVERAGE DAILY EARNINGS PER POSITION					LABOR COST PER POSITION IN 24 HOURS				
	May, 1892, 119-inch Mill (8 Hours)	1907, 84-inch Mill (12 Hours)	Per cent of Decline, 1892-1907	Oct. 1, 1907, 128-inch Mill (12 Hours)	Per cent of Decline, 1892-1907	May, 1892, 119-inch Mill, 3 Crews	1907, 84-inch Mill, 2 Crews	Per cent of Decline, 1892-1907	Oct. 1, 1907, 128-inch Mill, 2 Crews	Per cent of Decline, 1892-1907
Roller	$11.84	$9.90	16.39	$8.44	28.72	$35.52	$19.80	44.26	$16.88	52.48
Screwdown . . .	8.74	7.39	15.45	......	......	25.22	14.78	41.40	......	......
Heater	8.16	7.72	5.39	7.21	11.64	24.48	15.44	36.93	14.42	41.09
Heater's helpers . .	5.80	4.50	22.41	4.09	29.48	17.40	9.00	48.28	8.18	52.99
Tableman . . .	7.75	5.91	23.74	......	......	23.25	11.82	49.16	11.16	60.80
First shearman . .	9.49	......	......	5.58	41.20	28.47	......	......	......	......

* The averages for the 119-inch mill for May, 1892, were taken from the testimony of H. C. Frick before the Congressional committee that investigated the Homestead strike. The amounts actually earned by different persons in the same position were added together and the sum was divided by the total number of days worked. For example, the first roller in the list worked 24 days in May, 1892, and earned $259.05; the second worked 22 days and earned $278.50; the third worked 23 days and earned $279.30. Thus we have a total of 69 eight-hour days for one roller and $816.85 paid in wages. Dividing we have $11.84 as the average daily earnings of rollers on the 119-inch mill during May, 1892. The average for the 84-inch mill in 1907 was found without difficulty, for we had the rate per ton paid in 1907 as given in the previous tables, and it was ascertained that the average output each twelve hours in 1907 was 180 tons. The daily earnings of employes in the 128-inch mill, October 1, 1907, were secured from an authoritative source.

vestigating committee in 1892 wage figures for the 23-inch structural mill of the Carnegie Steel Company at Homestead, so that
comparison is possible for certain positions in this department
with figures for 1907 secured from an authoritative source. Such
a comparison shows a substantial reduction for heaters and rollers.

TABLE 6.—AVERAGE EARNINGS PER DAY AT DIFFERENT PERIODS
AND PER CENT OF DECLINE IN 23-INCH STRUCTURAL MILL,
HOMESTEAD

	May, 1892 *	Oct. 1, 1907	Per cent of Re-duction, 1892–1907
Roller . .	$11.09	$7.38	33.45
Heater. .	5.65	4.98	11.86

With respect to the scales for the skilled workers since 1892,
let me quote an operating man of one Pittsburgh company:

It is perfectly true that the tonnage rates, and in some
instances the actual daily earnings of skilled laborers, have
been largely decreased. The reason for this is, mainly, the
tremendous increase in production, due to improved equipment, representing very large capital investment, enabling
the men at lower rates to make equal, or even higher, daily
earnings. At the same time the daily earnings of some of
the most highly paid men have been systematically brought
down to a level consistent with the pay of other workers,
having in mind skill and training required and a good many
other factors. That the systematic reductions have been
made with perfect justice could probably be denied, but there
is no such thing as absolute perfection, and it is believed that
on the whole the changes have been fair and right.

In other words, there has been a consistent policy on the
part of the management, not only to cut rates so that with the
increased production the earnings of the tonnage workers should
not go up to exorbitant figures, but to cut the rates for the
highly skilled men still further, so that the earnings for these
positions should be brought down to a figure nearer the common
average.

With regard to the middle class men, the 35 per cent who
are the "real steel workers," I have not sufficient data to justify
general conclusions. Efforts to secure from a representative company comparative data covering a period of years in Allegheny

* Mis. Documents, No. 335, 52d Congress, 1st Session.

County and applicable to this middle group, were unsuccessful.*
Such data as I have, however, as will appear below, do not indicate
that their earnings have kept pace with the advanced cost of living.

Figures for the open-hearth department at Homestead indicate that the men receiving lower wages have not sustained as
heavy reductions as the better paid men. It is a little difficult
to make a comparison because the organization of the department
has been changed since 1892. At that time there was a melter
for each furnace, who was paid at the rate of $6.00 a day. There
is now at Homestead one foreman melter for three furnaces, whose
earnings averaged in 1907 a little over $9.00 per day. But the first
helpers, who are doing practically the same work as was formerly
done by the melter, averaged in 1907 about $5.00 per day.

The average for all employes in the open-hearth department
was, in contrast to these better paid men, about the same in
1907 as in 1892 — $2.70 as against $2.78.†

But that the lower tonnage men sometimes suffer as deep,
or even deeper, wage cuts in a period of readjustment as the men
at the top, is illustrated by the irregularities in Table 7, which
shows the reductions put in force in the 84-inch mill in Homestead
in 1908.

The heater, whose rate was $4.29 per 100 tons, was reduced
about 7 per cent, while his helper, whose rate was a little over one-
half that of the heater, was reduced over twice as much—16 per

* A similar request was presented more recently at the office of the chairman
of the United States Steel Corporation, by whom valuable data, in response to
other requests made at the same time, were placed at our disposal. It was stated
that no statistics or data giving wage rates for typical positions, including monthly
earnings of employes in such positions, from 1892 to date, are compiled or readily
available. In further explanation, the statement was made that: "Such information does not constitute a part of the regular statistics compiled by us, and the
only way we could get at the data would be to go back to original time books and
payrolls and compile the figures. This would be a very large task, as you can well
understand, and would require many weeks' work at least, even if the original time
books were available, which is doubtful. Such records are stored away in various
places and very frequently are, after three to five years, destroyed for lack of
storage room."

† The total amount of wages in both mills of the open-hearth department in
1892, after deducting monthly salaries, was $27,904.10. The total number of days'
work actually performed in the month of May, 1892, was 10,034.25, which gives an
average daily wage of $2.78 for each man. (From Frick's statement, Mis. Doc.,
52d Congress, 1st Session, No. 335, pp. 11–18.) The average daily earnings per
man in the open-hearth department at Homestead, October 1, 1907, were $2.70.

cent. The roller, the highest paid man on the mill, received a reduction amounting to nearly 14 per cent, while the shearman's helpers,—who were, with the exception of the salter and the cold roller, the lowest paid employes in the list,—had their earnings cut over 21 per cent, the heaviest reduction in the mill.

TABLE 7.—REDUCTION IN RATE PER 100 TONS ON 84-INCH MILL AT HOMESTEAD, 1908

Position	Rate per 100 Tons, 1907	Rate per 100 Tons, 1908	Per cent of Reduction
Salter. . . .	$2.00	$1.90	5.00
Heater . . .	4.29	3.99	6.99
Screwdown . .	4.11	3.82	7.06
Cold roller. . .	2.07	1.90	8.21
Craneman. . .	2.50	2.23	10.80
Marker . . .	2.76	2.45	11.23
Gaugeman. . .	2.76	2.45	11.23
Hookers . . .	2.75	2.40	12.73
Roller . . .	5.50	4.74	13.82
Helper . . .	2.50	2.09	16.40
Tableman . . .	3.29	2.74	16.72
Shearman's helpers	2.16	1.70	21.30

On the other hand, an operating man in one of the constituent companies of the United States Steel Corporation showed me figures indicating that the average earnings of the employes in his company had advanced 13 per cent between 1901 and 1908. This covered the actual earnings per man per day for the men in the works, including superintendents, clerks and foremen. This increase, he said, was brought about partly by actually raising the rates of the men paid by the day, partly by increasing the proportion of the men paid tonnage rates (by which they were enabled to make greater earnings than when paid by the day), and partly by increases in the productive capacity of the equipment due both to investment in improvements and to improved management. His figures covered plants situated in six of the northern states, the total number of men employed varying from 20,000 to 26,000.

In judging of the significance of this increased average wage, it may be well to trace the movement of wages since the organization of the Steel Corporation. The United States Steel Corporation was organized April 1, 1901, and business was good until the summer of 1903, when there was a check, and on the ground that "earnings had fallen off to a point barely sufficient to pay fixed charges" a general reduction in wages was announced, applicable to all employes and averaging 10 per cent, to go into effect January 1, 1904. The old rate was restored April 1, 1905, to men paid by the day, but not to all tonnage men. The statement has been made, that with the exception of a few very highly paid men, the rate was completely restored, but out of about one hundred men with whom I talked, who had been affected by this general cut, none had got their old rate back. January 1, 1907, the day men received an advance, the rate for unskilled workers, who constitute the bulk of the working force, being raised to 16½ cents an hour.* During the two years following there was no general adjustment of wages, though the rates for individuals and departments were at different times reduced. For instance, while plants were shut down or run on part time during the depression of 1907–08, and men were laid off in large numbers, there was no general horizontal decrease in pay by the Steel Corporation, then or during the depressed period of 1909, although nearly all of the principal competing steel companies are reported to have made such decreases.† On this point the Corporation took a firm stand as a collective organization.

It is to be noted, however, that the Braddock men, paid on a sliding scale, which fluctuates with market prices, suffered losses in their tonnage rates corresponding to the fall in prices. Further, while the Carnegie Steel Company did not announce any change in wages at the beginning of January, 1908, the Homestead men learned with great surprise in the latter part of the month that a reduction was to go into effect February 1. This reduction affected most of the skilled departments. The open-hearth furnace men escaped, but plate-mill men received reductions varying from 3 per cent to 22 per cent. The wage figures for the 84-inch mill shown in Table 7 give an idea of the reduction as it affected the plate mills. This mill I take as fairly typical. Some employes in the structural mills received even heavier reductions.

As the net result of this movement in rates during the years from 1892 on, I was told by practically every man in this middle

* During this period, the principal commodities sold by this company were said to have decreased in average price 15 per cent (comparing 1905 with 1901, the decrease was 20 per cent). These percentages were given me as based on the net returns drawn from the company's books.

† In 1907 the Jones and Laughlin Company reduced the wages of a large number of men. It was reported that nearly all their rollers were cut 40 per cent.

group with whom I talked in 1907 and 1908 that his earnings had been going steadily down for a number of years. A banker in one of the mill towns told me that since 1892 the earnings of this group had declined to a very considerable degree. These statements are not dislodged by the 13 per cent advance for all the men employed by a given company, mentioned on page 159, for such a general average for all employes must be affected by what may have happened to the wages of common labor on the one hand and the highly paid men on the other, and does not afford sufficient means for judging the actual movement of earnings in the important intermediate group.

It will be remembered that if the steel workers of 1907 in any and all grades were to have the same purchasing power that they had in 1892, it was necessary that their earnings be advanced 22 per cent. How does the case stand? The unskilled laborers received an advance amounting to 7 per cent in the Jones and Laughlin plant and 15 per cent in the mills of the United States Steel Corporation. The men at the top, the "aristocrats" of labor, have had their earnings reduced since 1892. This is an admitted fact. There are many of them who have had more taken from their daily earnings in the last fifteen years than the total daily wage of an unskilled man. The earnings of the intermediate men may have advanced in certain individual cases, but such evidence as I was able to gather indicated at best a stationary condition, and if compared with the increased cost of living, a downward tendency. Steel workers, in common with all consumers in America, experienced during the fifteen years an unprecedented rise in the cost of the necessaries of life. Wages in the steel industry have lagged behind this rise in prices. Whether or not the large body of English-speaking steel workers were getting less money wages than they did at the beginning of the period,—on this point we have found divergent testimony,—it seems fairly clear that at the end of it they were less well off as to the purchasing power of a day's earnings—as to real wages—than they were at the beginning.*

* Since this chapter was written, in May, 1910, announcement was made of a general increase in wages for all employes of the United States Steel Corporation. It was described as approximating 6 per cent over existing rates. Common laborers' pay was increased in the mills of the Corporation in the Pittsburgh District from 16½ cents an hour to 17½ cents. This is an increase of 25 per cent over the 14-cent rate paid in 1892.

This discussion has given us something of a perspective by which to regard the wages prevailing* at the close of this period not only of rising prices but of unexampled prosperity.

The annual report of the United States Steel Corporation for 1907 gives the total number of employes of all companies as 210,180, and the total amount paid in wages and salaries during the year 1907, as $160,825,822. This would indicate about $765 as the average yearly earnings of employes of the Corporation, but this sum is too high, for the total included salaries as well as wages. If all salaries, from President Corey's down to that of assistant superintendents, were deducted, the average yearly earnings of wage-earners would be considerably less.

As before, averages are deceptive, and we must look to the wage groups and know the number of men in each if we are to gain an understanding of the situation. Figures furnished by an official of one of the leading companies for five departments of one large plant, for October, 1907, throw light on the matter. The number of men employed in these departments was 2,304. I feel the more justified in basing conclusions on these figures because investigation convinces me that they are in general somewhat in advance of wages paid in the other mills of the Pittsburgh District. Table 8 is based upon the figures thus secured, which appear in the appendix in the form submitted by the company. †

A glance will show that the majority of the employes were at the lower rather than at the higher extreme of wage payments. In the five departments included, a trifle over 5 per cent of the working force received over $5.00 a day. The tabulations indicate that 71 per cent received $2.50 or less and nearly 23 per cent earned from $2.51 to $5.00 a day. These figures are interesting, but not altogether typical, as they cover five departments in which the proportion of highly skilled men is probably larger than in the plant

---

* The compilation of wages for the iron and steel industry covering the period since 1890 made by the Federal Bureau of Labor has been compared with the results reached in the text and tables appended. The latter have been gone over with officials of the Pittsburgh companies, and such discrepancies between the two sets of figures as occur are probably to be explained by the Bureau's method of taking isolated occupations over the entire country with respect to which the processes have changed but little; whereas my statistics are for typical positions in one locality.

† See Appendix IV (II), p. 301.

TABLE 8.—DISTRIBUTION OF DAILY EARNINGS IN CERTAIN DEPARTMENTS OF A TYPICAL STEEL MILL IN ALLEGHENY COUNTY

Name of Department	Number of Employes Receiving:											Total
	Under $2.00	$2.00-$2.50	$2.51-$3.00	$3.01-$4.00	$4.01-$5.00	$5.01-$6.00	$6.01-$7.00	$7.01-$8.00	$8.01-$9.00	$9.01-$10.00	$10.01-$12.00	
Open-hearth	1280*		22	158	48	82	..	2	10	6	2	1,610
Bessemer	27	79	60	10	2	..	..	3	..	..	..	181
Structural mill	73	18	41	12	7	..	..	2	..	..	..	153
Blooming mill	71	21	22	23	4	..	4	..	..	..	..	145
Plate mill	49	37	42	55	18	6	2	4	2	..	..	215
Total	1655		187	258	79	88	6	11	12	6	2	2,304
Percentages	71.83%		8.11	11.20	3.43	3.82	.26	.48	.52	.26	.09	100
	71.83%		22.74%			5.43%						

* This figure, 1280 men, is an undistributed remainder. For 1,077 twelve-hour men in the open-hearth department, I did not have classified daily earnings. Their average, $2.32 per day, was readily obtained, however, as the company gave me the total number of twelve-hour employes in the open-hearth department (1,517) and the average daily earnings of the same ($2.76). They also furnished me with the actual daily earnings of 440 twelve-hour men filing what they denominated the "important positions" in the department. These 440 men are entered in the proper columns in the table. Of the 440, the 110 lowest paid were earning $2.50 per day, or less. Therefore, it is probable that few, if any, of the 1,077 men remaining were earning above that amount or they would have been so designated. Most of the 1,077 would fall in the under $2.00 group, as the large majority of open-hearth men are unskilled laborers. In that group also fell the earnings of 93 ten-hour men averaging $1.80 per day.

as a whole, and of course they do not embrace the yard laborers and many other unskilled men at the lower end of the full payroll.

With respect to the former, I have figures from other sources: Rollers and heaters are the best paid of all the regular mill workers, often receiving more per day than the superintendent of the department, who hires and discharges them. I have reliable wage figures for rollers on nine mills at the Homestead plant, including two structural mills, four plate mills, two slabbing mills and one blooming mill. The average daily earnings of rollers on these seven mills was, in 1907, $8.22. In wage figures that I have for five mills at the same plant, including three plate mills, a blooming mill and a structural mill, the heaters' average daily earnings in 1907 were $6.90. There are 16 rolling mills in the Homestead plant, and as all are operated on the two-turn system, the regular rollers in the entire plant number 32. There are probably about 60 heaters employed in these mills, and I make the statement without fear of its being challenged that the total number of rollers and heaters together required to man the Homestead plant is not over 100, or about 1½ per cent of the whole number of employes at this plant in 1907. This 1½ per cent of the Homestead steel workers who (exclusive of foremen) received the highest wages paid in the plant averaged between $6.00 and $8.00 for each working day in 1907.

In three rolling mills at Homestead which are typical of the Carnegie Steel Company mills, six shearmen were the only men besides superintendents and foremen, rollers and heaters, who received over $5.00 per day in 1907. The 120 first helpers in charge of the 60 open-hearth furnaces at Homestead, averaged $5.10 per day during the month of October, 1907. In the Bessemer converting mill, the highest wage paid in 1907, below that of the general foreman, was $4.27 to the blower. In the mills to which these figures apply there were no other positions, exclusive of supervisory positions, paying as much as $5.00 per day. They may be considered fairly typical for Allegheny County, although data in my possession respecting the other large works in the county show somewhat lower averages. They go to show that the proportion of employes receiving a daily wage of $5.00 or over in 1907 was under 4 per cent.

With respect to the unskilled group, earning less than $2.00 a day, we have the census of the largest company in Allegheny County. This places the proportion at about 60 per cent.

There remain, then, 36 per cent whose daily earnings were between $2.00 and $5.00.

I have sketched roughly what has befallen the pay of the men employed in one great American industry during a period of marvelous industrial concentration and mechanical advance, of rising costs of living and lowering prices of output. The figures for 1907 show us the share of the unexampled prosperity which at the close of that period came as each day's earnings to the groups of workers making up the labor force, and the numerical significance to attach to each of those groups.

CHAPTER XIII

THE WORKING DAY AND THE WORKING WEEK

IT was pointed out in an earlier chapter that a fruitful way to reduce costs, from the production standpoint, is to eliminate wastes. To accomplish this, as well as to increase output per unit of capital, the steel mills operate day and night, and steel making is held to be essentially a "continuous industry."

In old fashioned iron mills, although continuous operation is possible, a period of idleness between shifts is not a serious matter. But the steel mills deal with larger tonnage and larger machines. The heating furnaces cannot be allowed to grow cold, lest they crack, and the gas is kept burning even through an extended stoppage of the works. In recent years it has become even more important that there shall be as little waiting time as possible, on account of the development of open-hearth steel making. In these furnaces, which hold from 50 to 100 tons of molten steel, a shut-down involves considerable loss. Since the furnaces are operated continuously, the rolling mills must also be operated continuously in order to take care of the ingots. Accordingly there has been no easy ten-hour compromise in the steel industry. The mills are operated twenty-four hours in the day, and to man them the crews must work either in two shifts of twelve hours each or in three shifts of eight hours.

The history of the working day in the rolling mills has been traced in a general way up to 1892, in the chapter devoted to the policies of the Amalgamated Association. By the "heat system" of the puddlers, a ten-hour day came to be universal in iron mills. The heat method was adopted to some extent in the steel mills, but continuous furnaces made it unnecessary to pay any attention to the number of heats; early in the eighties the twelve-hour day was already customary in the non-union mills. The union steel mills kept the heat method in operation, with a working day about ten hours in length in some mills though not in all, for some time after continuous operation became possible. It is difficult to appreciate today the various elements that entered into the question of the length of the working day in the eighties, or the causes that led to action in some quarters or lack of action in others. Old steel workers who were employed at the Edgar Thomson plant at Braddock thirty years ago, say that an eight-hour day was established there in 1879 without any activity on the part of the employes, because orders were so heavy that the company wished to increase output by putting on a third crew of men.* As a result of the various causes which have been described in the earlier chapter, the situation had so shaped itself that by 1890 almost all of the sheet mills had recognized the eight-hour day, while the twelve-hour day was becoming universal in the other steel mills. In most plants the Bessemer men, the blooming mill crew, and many of the smaller mills worked on an eight-hour schedule.

In some of the Pittsburgh blast furnaces also the eight-hour day was introduced in the eighties. It was reported in the census of 1880 that in the Lucy furnaces, owned by Carnegie Brothers and Company, there had been a change from a twelve-hour to an eight-hour day because the increase in production had made the work too severe for twelve hours.† In 1886, writing in *The Forum*, Andrew Carnegie said: "At present every ton of pig iron made in the world, except at two establishments, is made by men working in double shifts of twelve hours each, having neither Sunday nor holiday the year round. Every two weeks the men change to the night shift by working twenty-four hours consecutively."‡ These two establishments were, apparently, the Lucy and Isabella furnaces in Pittsburgh, owned by the Carnegie Company. During the summer of 1886 the employes at the Edgar Thomson furnaces struck for an eight-hour day and succeeded in getting it temporarily, going back to twelve hours in 1888. In commenting on the strike the *National Labor Tribune* reported that the twelve-hour

* See note on page 112, Chapter X, for Superintendent Jones's statement.
† Tenth Census, Vol. XX, Statistics of Wages, p. 123, note.
‡ *The Forum*, Vol. I, 1886, p. 544.

day had been tried in the Lucy furnaces in 1885 and had been found impracticable. If it had been successful, it was to have been adopted in the Isabella furnaces also.* These seem to be the only experiments in a shorter working day in blast furnaces, but they were abandoned before 1890, and since that time a twelve-hour day has been universal in pig iron production.

Sunday work has been general in blast furnaces in this country from the beginning. It has been rather the exception in rolling mills, however, until within the last fifteen years. There was Sunday work in some of the steel mills at an earlier date, but it was abandoned at Homestead in 1882 as a result of local agitation.† The Edgar Thomson plant seems to be the only one that has always been operated during a portion of Sunday. Since 1880, at least, this plant has been starting its furnaces Sunday afternoon and beginning to roll steel by six o'clock or earlier.

The Amalgamated Association of Iron and Steel Workers was opposed to Sunday work and waged effective warfare against it. In the convention of 1882 they adopted a resolution opposing Sunday work and calling for a cessation of work in steel mills from Saturday evening until Monday morning.‡ A similar resolution was passed in 1883.§ As a result of their determination they were able to report in 1887 that in no mill under the jurisdiction of the Amalgamated Association did the men begin to roll iron or steel on Sunday afternoon.||

In the years immediately preceding the strike of 1892, then, a majority of the iron and steel workers, exclusive of blast furnace men, had their Sundays free in Allegheny County. No work was done in the union mills from Saturday night until Monday morning, except repairs and other work that was unavoidable. The week-day schedule of hours was, on the other hand, far from uniform. While the twelve-hour day was most nearly general, ten-hour positions were numerous and a very considerable number of positions were operated on an eight-hour schedule.

Beginning with 1892 a new order prevailed. The strike years were the pivotal years in the policies of the steel com-

* *National Labor Tribune*, Jan. 9, 1886, p. 4.   † Ibid., May 13, 1882, p. 4.
‡ Journal of Proceedings, 1882, p. 995.   § Ibid., 1883, p. 1253.
|| *National Labor Tribune*, Jan. 29, 1887, p. 4.

panies. The Carnegie Company thereafter began to introduce the twelve-hour day wherever possible. In 1892 the blooming mill, the converting department, and the 119-inch mill at Homestead were operated on the eight-hour basis. After the strike all the rolling mills were put on twelve-hour shifts.* The substitutions in other mills were made more slowly, but the eight-hour day is now practically gone in the Pittsburgh steel mills. In 1897, Jones and Laughlin broke with the union, and this company has been slowly and steadily lengthening hours ever since that time. A number of the departments had an eight-hour day, but one at a time they have practically all gone over to the twelve-hour system. In 1908, during the depression when work was slack, this company put all of its men on a twelve-hour day. This was the only plant in Allegheny County during that time with no eight-hour men in the Bessemer department.†

With the lengthening of the working day has come an increase in Sunday work in rolling mills. Mills that had customarily begun to roll steel at 6 a.m. Monday morning, began to roll at midnight, which brought the furnace men out several hours earlier to get the steel hot. Then the mills began to roll at 6 p.m. on Sunday and in 1907–08 most of the steel mills of the Pittsburgh District were as actively at work at 5 p. m. on Sunday as at any hour in the week, some departments beginning at 4 o'clock. At the plant of the National Tube Company at McKeesport there had been no Sunday work up to the strike of 1901. When operations were resumed, the company required the men to come out Sunday evenings. This is today the only tube mill under the United States Steel Corporation where Sunday night work is done.

Some years ago work on Saturday night and Sunday was paid for at an extra rate. Such a policy tends to penalize a mill administration for any overtime work and to that extent auto-

* Statement of A. C. Dinkey, now president of the Carnegie Steel Company, before Senate Committee on Education and Labor, 57th Congress, 2d Session, Document No. 141, p. 393.

† In 1909, when the steel business was again on a prosperity basis, the blooming mill rollers and the Bessemer men went back to the eight-hour schedule. The heat in the latter department is so great that it is usually conceded that a twelve-hour day is too long. It was tried in the Bessemer department at Braddock in 1885 or 1886, and the Duquesne plant tried it in 1890, but in both cases they soon went back to eight hours for the more difficult positions.

matically serves to diminish it. Millwrights, pipe fitters and others of this class of workmen, when under the jurisdiction of the Amalgamated Association, were paid at the rate of time and one-half for all overtime work. Extra pay was given for overtime at Homestead even up to seven or eight years ago. The practice has now been stopped in all the Pittsburgh steel mills.

The situation at present, or rather as it existed in 1907–08, as the direct outgrowth of these policies, can best be understood by considering the various departments of the industry. Steel mills are so complex and such a variety of work is done, that no sweeping statement can be made in regard to the hours of labor. It is certain, however, that the eight-hour day does not flourish here. After ten months' residence in the Pittsburgh District, and careful search throughout that time for the facts of the industrial situation, I can state with assurance that, outside of sheet mills, the eight-hour day was, with few exceptions, to be found only in the Bessemer departments. At the Edgar Thomson plant at Braddock 45 rail straighteners worked in three shifts, with 15 men in each shift, and in the Schoenberger plant of the American Steel and Wire Company, the blooming-mill rollers, as well as the converter men, had an eight-hour day. The same was true at the Edgar Thomson works and in the Jones and Laughlin plant, but in the other large plants all rollers had a twelve-hour day. Generally speaking, the eight-hour day was confined to the one department where the Bessemer converters are operated, and where those men who are exposed to the greatest heat usually worked in three shifts. Their number was not large. After extended inquiry, in which I talked with all grades of workmen and with men in authority, I could find only 120 eight-hour men in 1907 * among the 17,000 employes in the three largest plants of the Carnegie Steel Company in Allegheny County, a trifle less than three-fourths of one per cent.*

The prevailing working day is twelve hours for the men who are actually engaged in the processes of manufacturing and working steel, skilled and unskilled workmen alike.† The yard laborers and machinists are the apparent exceptions. The former are supposed to do day work and to do it on a ten-hour basis, but their

---

* This was when the mills were running full, before the financial depression.

† It should be noted, however, that there are large numbers of ten-hour

hours vary with the demands of the season. The working day is extended and a night shift is put on when orders are heavy. It is probable that with these gangs overtime is the rule rather than the exception in prosperous times when all departments are crowded; and such conditions governed generally in the mills for the four years previous to November, 1907. To illustrate, in October of that year, as I learned from an authoritative source, the yard men in a blast furnace plant earned about $2.00 a day. They were paid at the rate of 16½ cents an hour, and to earn that amount they could not have worked less than twelve hours a day. Molders and machinists have a regular ten-hour day in theory, but the machinists, being also repair men, are sometimes obliged to work much longer. A repairing job has to be finished before the men can leave it, and this quite frequently necessitates a continuous twenty-four-hour period, while sometimes the men work thirty-six hours or longer, without rest. Payroll figures of one of the big steel mills near Pittsburgh showed the schedules of hours in six departments to have been as follows in October, 1907:

TABLE 9.—WORKING DAY OF EMPLOYES IN A STEEL MILL, OCTOBER, 1907.—BY LENGTH OF WORKING DAY

Duration of Work- ing Day	Number of Employes	Per cent in Each Group
Eight hours . . .	9	0.24
Ten hours . . .	721	19.31
Eleven hours . .	68	1.82
Twelve hours . .	2,935	78.63
Total . . .	3,733	100.00

(See Appendix IV, p. 300, for wage schedules from which these figures are derived.)

With nearly four-fifths of the workmen on a twelve-hour schedule, working longer hours from time to time, it is fair to say that the twelve-hour day prevails.

It is not enough, however, to state the prevailing length of the working day. Before we can understand what a day exacts of a steel worker we must know whether he is employed six, seven or eight days in a week. In this connection I use the word "day"

men in the pipe mills of the National Tube Company at McKeesport, and in the cold-rolled shafting department at the Jones and Laughlin plant; also in works fabricating structural material which are not, of course, properly steel-making plants.

in two senses. The operating day, from the standpoint of the mill, is twenty-four hours long and there are seven in a week. The prevailing working day of the steel workers is twelve hours in length and there are fourteen of them, from Sunday morning to Sunday morning.

The work of the rolling mills, shaping and working the steel bars and billets, I found going forward six full operating days in the week, shutting down Saturday evenings at six o'clock and beginning at the same time Sunday evening. Accordingly, each of the two shifts of men who work in the rolling mills had a week of six working days, and a weekly period of rest which was modified by the change of shifts from day to night. The shift that went on at 6 p.m. Sunday was composed of the day men of the previous week, who had been off duty twenty-four hours. The former night shift, that finished its work Saturday morning, was the day shift of Monday. In this way each shift had twenty-four hours of continuous rest one week, and forty-eight hours the next. But there were exceptions to this schedule which will be brought out later.

The manner of operating the open-hearth furnaces is such that it is hard to generalize for that department. The furnaces were usually operating from Sunday morning to Saturday night, thirteen working days. Saturday night there was usually no work done, but a low heat was kept on the furnaces. On Sunday morning the full heat was turned on. One or two men could do the necessary work in the morning and the full crew did not report until noon or later. The time schedule was correspondingly irregular. In some of the plants the Sunday crew remained on duty until Monday morning. This involved twenty-four hours for the charger and second helper, and shaded down to about fifteen hours for a part of the crew. I refer here to the plants where the ordinary stationary open-hearth furnaces, with capacity varying from 30 to 60 tons, are found. The Talbot open-hearth furnaces were a different proposition, very much larger than the ordinary furnace, and were operated continuously.*

* The only Talbot furnaces in Allegheny County in 1907 were in the Jones and Laughlin plant. Here there were five, each with a capacity of 200 tons, and four more, to have 250 tons capacity each, were in process of construction. A feature of the Talbot furnace is that the molten steel is poured into the ladle by tilting the furnace. These furnaces were going seven operating days in the week.

Investigation and information from authoritative sources, covering about half of the open-hearth furnaces in Allegheny County, showed that in an open-hearth plant about 25 men are employed to a furnace. There were 132 open-hearth furnaces in the county in 1907, and there must have been twenty-five times that number of employes, or about 3,300. These are hard to classify on account of the varying periods of Sunday work as described above. In the Talbot furnaces the crews alternated between six days and eight days a week, but in the other style of furnaces in a given week one crew worked six days, and the other six days and from three hours to a full day over. That is, on alternate weeks a man had Sunday work. One-half of the total force then, or approximately 1,600, were at work each Sunday.

The only department in the industry similar to the Talbot furnaces in respect to weekly schedule is the blast furnace, at the beginning of the whole process. There are 44 blast furnaces in Allegheny County, and unless a suspension is caused by some extraordinary or unforeseen occurrence, every one is in blast 365 operating days in the year, not excluding the Christmas and Fourth of July holidays that the other workmen still enjoy. Furnaces may be banked occasionally and still operated with a fair degree of success, but the likelihood is much greater that if the blast is taken off and the furnace banked, it will act badly when it is again "blown in." American engineers are agreed that to avoid great loss blast furnaces must be operated continuously. In a typical plant where the number of men employed was given me from the payroll, I found that about 40 per cent of the men worked on the day turn only, and that the other 60 per cent were divided into two shifts working alternate weeks day and night. Accordingly 30 per cent of the total force were on duty at night and 70 per cent during the day. With the 40 per cent force there were seven full working days in every week. On account of changing the shift, the 60 per cent force experienced periodical variation, but they averaged seven days of work a week. These percentages are of course approximations, based on the practice in this typical plant.

In this plant there were 200 men, on all shifts, to each furnace, but other figures that I have indicate that the average number of men to a furnace, in the Pittsburgh District, is nearer

180. Using the smaller figure, it appears that there were about 8,000 men employed in 1907 at the 44 blast furnaces in Allegheny County.

In the 132 open-hearth furnaces, there were, as we have seen, 3,300 men working on seven days in each alternate week, or 1,600 every week. Of the 8,000 men in the blast furnaces, all were seven-day men, and about 5,000 worked the long turn every alternate week. Accordingly there were in 1907 a total in these two departments of the iron and steel industry of well towards 10,000 men working on seven days in each week.

For other departments it was harder to make estimates, but the situation as regards Sunday work is by no means set forth when we have discussed blast furnaces and open-hearth plants. The heating furnaces are never allowed to grow cold. Whether the suspension be the ordinary one, from Saturday night to Sunday night, or whether it be a shut-down for many weeks, the fires are not allowed to go out, and men are on duty tending gas, changing the flame from one side of the furnace to the other. In the open-hearth department the second helpers take turns tending gas on Saturday nights. In the soaking-pits and the re-heating furnaces, either the heater or some of his assistants remain with the furnaces all through the period of suspension. Sometimes this involves a twenty-four-hour shift, and sometimes that is avoided, but Sunday work is inevitable. In 1907–08 Sunday was the repair day. Repairs were made through the week, but everything that could possibly wait was left until Sunday, so that no time might be lost in the mills, and so that the repair men might work without being endangered or impeded by moving machinery. This practice was not defended by some of the men in authority, but the efforts made to stop it were without practical result. In a normal year the steel mills are crowded with work. Sunday was, the year of my inquiry, a day for clearing up, for tardy departments to get even with swifter ones. Often the mills rolled out the finished product faster than the shears or the transportation department could take care of it. Then there was great activity of traveling cranes and narrow-gauge or dinkey engines, and when the rolling mills began again on Sunday evening everything was cleared away, and all departments were ready for another week. Whenever there was construction work of any sort it was customary for it to go on without interruption until it was finished. Loading cars and unloading them frequently continued on Sunday, and for all this work many laborers, crane men, engineers, firemen, millwrights and machinists, besides the regular mill watchmen, were on duty seven days in the week.

I have shown that there were about 8,000 seven-day men in blast furnaces and 1,600 in the open-hearth furnaces of Allegheny County, a total of 9,600 men. Sunday workmen are seven-day workmen, when the mills are running full, and it is evident that the number would be very much larger if we were to add those named in my last paragraph. Three hundred such men to each of the five largest steel plants in the county would be a very conservative estimate,—over 7 per cent of the employes in those plants. If we apply that percentage to the 70,000 mill workers in the county, it would give us about 5,000. Add this to the number already secured, and we have in round numbers 14,500, or one man out of five as the total number of Sunday and seven-day workmen in the mills and furnaces of the county in the year studied. This is a minimum estimate.*

Added to and intensifying the evils of Sunday work is the "long turn" of twenty-four hours that comes every second week to 60 per cent of the blast furnace workers and to many others. This is involved in the variations referred to on a previous page. The men average seven working days a week by working six days one week and the next week eight. Every Sunday the shifts change about. The men on the night shift give place on Sunday morning to the men on the day shift, and these work through

* Since the initial publication of this report, there has been a stiffening up in practice in the United States Steel Corporation mills. In March, 1910, the executive officials made it known that they would thereafter rigidly insist that a minute of the Finance Committee passed in 1907, but hitherto a dead letter, should be lived up to in all operating departments. The text of the resolution, etc., in this connection is shown in Appendix VI. The full significance and effect of these rulings cannot be known at once. They cover a large number of the 3,500 miscellaneous workmen mentioned above, but apparently leave the 9,650 blast furnace and open-hearth furnace workmen on the same schedule as before. At the first annual meeting of the American Iron and Steel Institute, in May, 1910, W. B. Dickson, First Vice-President of the United States Steel Corporation, declared the seven-day week a reproach upon the steel industry, and a committee was appointed to inquire into the feasibility of a compulsory six-day week for the men in blast furnace and other continuous departments. (See Appendix VI, p. 325.)

until Monday morning, a full twenty-four hours, so as to change to the night shift for the week succeeding, while the old night shift changes to the day. The men who get through Sunday morning have a twenty-four-hour interval. Theoretically they have a day of rest, but they must choose between trying to take advantage of it without resting from a twelve-hour night of work, or going to bed and waking, later, to find most of the precious day of freedom gone. This is a schedule that applies to about 5,000 blast furnace men in Allegheny County, to mill-wrights, furnace tenders and watchmen in all mills, whose numbers it is impossible to estimate, and to machinists and repair men as necessity may require.

To sum up, the weekly schedule in 1907–08 in the Allegheny County plants was as follows:

   I. Blast Furnace Department: For 60 per cent of the force 72 hours one week, 96 the next; average week, 84 hours. For 40 per cent, 70 to 84 hours.
  II. Bessemer Department: 48 hours for a few, 72 hours for the majority.
 III. Open-Hearth Department: 78 to 84 hours.
 IV. Rolling Mills: 72 hours for 95 per cent of the force, 84 to 91 hours for 5 per cent.
    The seventy-hour, eighty-four-hour and ninety-one-hour schedules indicate seven-day work.

The necessity of maintaining intact the industrial organization has accounted in part for the insistence of the companies that Sunday work shall not stop under any circumstances. Workmen told me that it was easier to get excused on any other night than Sunday. In some of the mills men are discharged if they refuse to work on Sunday. During the depression of 1907 and 1908, when the mills were idle a large part of the time, it was still the general custom in the Pittsburgh District to begin to roll steel on Sunday evenings, and this was true even when it was known that there were not orders enough to keep the mill running through the week. The Jones and Laughlin plant was notorious in this respect. Mills would be started on Sunday evening, when they did not have over twenty-four hours' work ahead, and would shut down on Monday evening. In November, 1907, the workmen claimed that one of this company's mills was operated to its fullest capacity, working through Saturday night and shutting down for only twelve hours on Sunday, while another mill in the plant that could have done the same kind of work stood idle.

In such a discussion of working hours, the question of holidays comes to mind. Twenty-five years ago these were more numerous in the steel industry than they are today. Legal holidays were observed, and the custom of shutting down the mills on account of the annual picnic of the Amalgamated Association has already been mentioned. That is all a thing of the past. There are only two holidays in the steel industry today, Christmas and the Fourth of July, and even these are denied to the men of the blast furnace crews. My first glimpse of the works of the Carnegie Steel Company was on September 1, 1907. I passed through Homestead on my way to Kennywood Park, where the trade unionists were holding their celebration of Labor Day. Business houses in Pittsburgh were closed, and the whole city was on its way to the various parks. But in Homestead there was no cessation in the clamor of the mills. The Edgar Thomson plant in Braddock across the river was enveloped in smoke as we passed. There was a holiday for all except the steel worker.

The effect of these long hours is discussed in a later chapter. That it is unnecessary for such conditions to exist is evidenced by the experience of other countries. A comparison with European practice is illuminating. A recent writer* on the subject of American industrial conditions reports more overtime and Sunday work in America than in either Germany or England, and fewer holidays. The working day is longer in America than in England, and less time is allowed for meals. The eight-hour day has been developed much farther in England than in America, and it has, he states, been very successful. America has not a single blast furnace with an eight-hour work day, but furnaces in the north of England have the eight-hour day in successful operation.

The open-hearth furnaces are operated on the twelve-hour basis in Allegheny County, and as far as I have been able to learn, on that basis everywhere else in the United States. With a few exceptions they have always been operated on that basis. In Wales, on the contrary, there are a number of open-hearth plants

* Shadwell, Arthur: Industrial Efficiency, Vol. II, Chapter 7, p. 80–113.

where an eight-hour day is established. John Hodge, M. P., secretary of the British Steel Smelters, Mill and Tin Plate Workers, is authority for the statement that there are seven establishments in Wales and two in England where the three-shift system is in operation. In one plant it has been in operation twelve years, in another ten, but in a majority the practice has been adopted within the last three or four years. Where the system has been adopted in recent years, the men accepted the same tonnage rate that they had before, and so voluntarily reduced their earnings one-third. In England the system is reported by Mr. Hodge as satisfactory, and the eight-hour work day is growing in popularity.

In 1904, when there was a bill before Congress providing for an eight-hour day in government contract work, a representative of the Carnegie Steel Company stated to the Senate Committee on Education and Labor that an eight-hour day in open-hearth furnaces would be impossible on the ground that the workman in charge has to remain with his furnace through an entire heat. "If the crews were changed just at the time a heat was about being completed, the steel would undoubtedly be spoiled, because the men coming would not understand the conditions that had prevailed all the way through the process."* The English and Welsh experience renders this position untenable. But a little knowledge of present-day practice in the twelve-hour mills is sufficient to convince one that the statement quoted is groundless. The shifts change without regard to the condition of the heat, and at all stages in its progress, on regular, previously understood hours. If this were not the case, the crews would have to make the change whenever a heat is poured, and that would almost necessitate an eight-hour day, for in the open-hearth plants around Pittsburgh

* Hearings before Senate Committee on Education and Labor, second session, 58th Congress, 1904, p. 363; statement of A. C. Dinkey, now president of the Carnegie Steel Company. In connection with Mr. Dinkey's statement, the testimony of W. E. Corey, now president of the United States Steel Corporation, given four years earlier, is interesting. The following is to be found on page 176 of the report of hearings on the eight-hour bill by the Committee on Labor of the House of Representatives in 1900.

Mr. Furuseth: "In the matter of smelting furnaces, and open-hearth furnaces and blast furnaces there is no serious obstacle to working an eight-hour shift, is there?"

Mr. Corey: "No. I would say there is no serious objection that cannot be overcome. There are objections that have been mentioned here before the committee; but I believe that those troubles and objections could be overcome."

178

there are usually about three heats in twenty-four hours. I have no hesitancy in saying that there is no difficulty attendant upon changing the shift at the end of eight hours that is not also present in a change after twelve hours, and in this statement I have the support of every open-hearth workman to whom I have put the question, and that of competent men who are not workmen, including foremen, superintendents and executive officials.

Some of the rolling mills in England are also operated on the eight-hour system. According to Mr. Hodge, one mill where the system has lately been introduced is now rolling as much steel in eight hours as it formerly did in twelve. There is little opportunity for such a comparison in this country, but in one case that came to my notice the same experience was reported, and I had opportunity to verify the report by the statements of both the company officials and the employes. The Sharon Steel Hoop Company, located at Sharon, Pennsylvania, is an independent company engaged in the manufacture of hoop steel and cotton ties. They employ about 1200 men in their plant, about 150 of whom are engaged on the three finishing mills. These, from the time the plant was built up to 1904, had worked on the two-turn system. As in other hoop mills, a day's work was ten hours, the mill stopping three times during that period for about half an hour each time, to give the men opportunity to rest. The work requires such speed and agility that it was held to be impossible for men to work continuously ten hours, consequently the finishing mills were idle five to seven hours out of the twenty-four.

But in 1904 a change was made. The finishers were, for the most part, members of the Amalgamated Association of Iron, Steel and Tin Workers. As usual the company signed their scale, but did so with something of a protest, for they said it was higher than that paid in non-union mills, with which they must compete. An officer of the union suggested that the company secure an advantage by putting on a third crew and eliminating the periods of idleness. This was a revolutionary suggestion, for there was no other hoop mill in the country operating with three crews. It was doubtful whether the plan were feasible or possible. When the men heard of it they objected. Their wages are based on tonnage, and they thought an eight-hour day would mean less output and lower wages. The company, however, decided to give the plan a trial.

When the men drew their first pay, they found that their earnings were not reduced. They had turned out as much tonnage in eight hours as they had previously in ten. It may have taken longer to convince the company that the plan was a good one, but it does not now care to go back to the old system. Instead of there being a period of idleness every day, the mills are operated continuously. There are no stops except to change rolls or to make repairs. The rest periods have been eliminated, and the half hour for lunch as well. Instead, the company has provided "spell hands," so that the men are relieved in turn and each one has an occasional rest with plenty of time for lunch, without stopping the mill. This makes it necessary to employ larger crews than formerly so that the labor cost per ton of product is larger than under the old system, but the general superintendent informed me that the saving in fuel is so great and the profits are so increased by the larger output per day that the extra labor cost is insignificant.

I visited Sharon and made careful inquiry as to the effect of the eight-hour day. I was much surprised at the unanimity with which the system was endorsed, not only by the mill people, but also by the citizens not directly interested in steel manufacture. The general opinion seemed to be, and it was verified by my own observation, that the eight-hour day had made for better morals and higher intelligence on the part of the working-men. Of course, this instance does not concern a large mill, and even if it did, it would hardly be safe to draw conclusions from a single example, especially with reference to an increased tonnage. However, it is an interesting case, and worthy of consideration.

The seven-day week seems, at first, a more difficult problem than the long day, for blast furnaces, at least, must be operated on Sundays. Not only so, but foremen report that large numbers of men prefer to work seven days in a week, and even ask to do so as a privilege.

Without doubt this is true, but those who make such requests are usually either foreigners who are trying to save money and go back to Europe, or workingmen definitely settled in this country who feel they need to earn more each week in order to secure proper comforts for their families. The former ought not to be allowed to set standards for America, and the latter condition ought not to exist. In a tariff-protected industry men should not have to work seven days in a week in order to support their families.

But even if men prefer to work on Sundays simply because they are greedy for the extra pay, it cannot properly be cited as an excuse for the practice. It is a degrading system of work that affords no opportunity for rest, and, in spite of the technical necessities of continuous operation, it is not necessary that men should work continuously. Because a blast furnace has to be in commission seven days a week is no final reason why any blast furnace man need work over six. An addition of one-seventh of the working force would make it possible to give each man one day of rest a week. This is a practice required by law in continuous industries in half a dozen foreign countries.

CHAPTER XIV

SPEEDING UP AND THE BONUS SYSTEM

ONE of the most impressive things about steel mills is their seemingly limitless possibilities. The history of steel manufacture is a history of breaking records, and no sooner has some mill performed the "greatest feat ever known" than another mill performs a greater one. The record outputs of thirty years ago are insignificant in comparison with the average production of today. The growth in output of blast furnaces during the last fifty years has already been pointed out; in the last fifteen years alone the average tonnage per furnace has doubled. The Bessemer converter output has increased as rapidly; the open-hearth furnaces have made substantial advances in recent years; and rolling mills have doubled and even trebled their tonnage since 1890. In 1892 hoop mills were limited by the Amalgamated Association to 450 bundles of cotton ties to a turn. In Painter's Mill, Pittsburgh, the union was defeated in that year, and the plant was changed from two turns to three, the men continuing to roll 450 bundles to a turn. In 1908 this mill was operated by two shifts working eleven hours each, and 1,300 bundles were being turned out by each shift. A blooming mill at Duquesne that was rolling 300 to 400 tons in twelve hours in 1892, rolled in 1908, 900 to 1,200 tons in the same time. One of the merchant mills at the same plant has more than doubled its output in five years. It was turning out 100 tons in twelve hours in 1902, and in 1907 it was averaging between 250 and 300 tons. The structural mills at Homestead have doubled their output since the early nineties. A shearsman at Homestead told me that while his shears handled 200 tons in twenty-four hours in 1893, they now take care of 600 tons in the same time. In 1886 the Edgar Thomson steel works were rolling out 600 tons of rails in twenty-four hours,* and it was considered one of the leading mills of the world. At present mill No. 1 at this plant has a capacity of 100 tons an hour, and it averages 2,000 tons or over in twenty-four hours.

Thus it is seen that great advances have been made in the production of steel. New machinery and improved processes have gone far toward achieving the standards that have been reached. The great changes of the past twenty years have already been discussed. Along with the improved machinery there has been increased power. An ingot is handled more rapidly in the blooming mill than it used to be; fewer passes through the rolls are necessary, for it is "broken down" more at each pass. There is greater economy of time now than in former years; additional furnace capacity has been provided, and rolling mills do not have to wait for hot steel as was once the case. But not all of the credit of the increased output can be given to the machinery; a very great deal, though just how much no one could well say, is due to increased intensity of physical effort. In the hoop mills, where output has more than doubled, there is practically no change in operation from that of twenty years ago. Roll changing can be accomplished more quickly on account of the overhead crane, but this is practically the only improvement. In the sheet mills, where output has doubled in the last twenty years, there has not been in that time a single important change in machinery or method.

The standard of efficiency required and maintained in the mills has grown along with the growth in the tonnage. The steel mills today offer an excellent demonstration of the theory of the survival of the fittest. The steel workers are men of strong, sturdy constitutions; they must be, for when they begin to fail they cease to be steel workers. Often I was told by workmen of forty and forty-five that they had been at their best at thirty years of age, and that at thirty-five they had begun to feel a perceptible decline in strength. The superintendents and foremen are alert in detecting weakness of any sort, and if a man fails appreciably, he expects discharge. A few years ago a general order was reported to have been sent from headquarters to all mills of the Carnegie Steel Company directing the superintendents to accept

* National Labor Tribune, April 24, 1886.

no more men over forty years of age in any department, and in some departments to hire only men of thirty-five and under.* In the rules for its pension department adopted January 1, 1902, the American Steel and Wire Company has this provision: "No inexperienced person over thirty-five years of age and no experienced person over forty-five years of age shall hereafter be taken into the employ of the company." There is a provision for suspending this rule in case of "special" or professional services,† thus indicating an expectation of physical deterioration on the part of mill workers at an age when professional men are esteemed capable of discharging their duties. Employes sixty-five years of age who have been in the service of the company ten years or more, may be retired and placed on the pension list.‡

By this process of eliminating the unfit a high standard of physical efficiency is maintained, but that in itself is not sufficient to secure the results desired. A strong man is no better than a weak one, unless he uses his strength; so by methods both direct and indirect the workmen are stimulated or "speeded up" to as rapid a pace as is possible.

It is necessary in any employment that the men do their work with reasonable alacrity. It is one of the duties of any foreman to eliminate the drones and to keep up the efficiency of his force. But in the steel industry the demand is for more than reasonable and ordinary efficiency.

In the first place, the men engaged in the processes are all paid piece rates—an incentive in itself to output; but this in the steel industry has never been strong enough to produce the results secured by other methods. It is augmented by the fact that each man's rate is paid on the tonnage gotten out by the crew, so that his fellow workers are interested in the effort he puts into his part of the job. A man at the re-heating furnaces cannot escape attention if he "soldiers" on his job. If the furnaces are not run to their capacity, the rolling mill gangs will soon notice the falling off in their supply of hot steel for rolling. If the rolls

* Pittsburgh *Dispatch*, September 26, 1904.

† Regulations of Pension Department, American Steel and Wire Company, No. 6.

‡ Op. cit., No. 3.

are slow, they block the furnaces, and so on down the line. In all the different departments of mill work there are gangs, each man dependent upon the others in his gang, and each gang dependent upon other gangs. From the wages standpoint the strain is great, for if one man is slow he reduces the tonnage and hence the earnings of a hundred other men. From the production standpoint the strain is perhaps greater, for on each man rests the necessity for handling the steel as fast as it comes. The procession must not be halted. Put a strong, swift man at the head of the first gang and the steel does its own driving.

Common laborers are usually divided into gangs of convenient size, and over each gang is a foreman who is commonly referred to as the "pusher," because his main duty is to "push" the men, and urge them to keep up to a rapid pace.

Every foreman is on the alert to keep his department up to a high standard; in the skilled departments as well as the unskilled the men are urged on by those in authority. The tonnage rates paid the skilled men incite them, as we have seen, to work for large outputs, but the foremen do not hesitate to add their influence. "Look at those stopper setters and the steel pourer," said a Bessemer blower and foreman to me as I was watching them fill the molds with the molten steel. "They're on tonnage, and you'd think that would be an incentive to them to work pretty hard, but they have to be driven just the same." A British observer, after a visit of the British Iron and Steel Institute to the United States in 1890, wrote of the American steel mills: "The 'bosses' drive the men to an extent that the employers would never dream of attempting in this country. There are trade unions,* but they do not seem to be able to protect the men in this respect. The bosses have the faculty of driving the men and getting the maximum of work out of them, and the men do not seem to have the inclination or the power to resist the pressure."†

This constant pressure of bosses, aided by the gang itself, is the direct stimulus which has been superimposed upon piece rates in the steel industry. In contrast to this direct, active pressure, are indirect stimuli which have even greater influence

* This was before the destruction of unionism in the steel mills.
† James Kitson, *Contemporary Review*, Vol. 59, p. 629.

in boosting output. One of these is a skilful use of the spirit of emulation. It was used years ago in the infancy of the business. When a mill broke a record, the men who accomplished the feat were praised, their names sometimes published in the trade journals, while superintendents of other mills taunted their men with the disgrace of being beaten. This would rouse all the skilled men to greater activity, and another mill would establish a new record. For years a piece of steel plate, cut to the shape of a huge broom, was kept suspended above the Edgar Thomson blast furnaces at Braddock, as a symbol that all competitors had been swept aside and that these furnaces were producing more pig iron a day than any others in the world. This made a strong appeal to the men and they were constantly on edge to retain that record.

In the same way the Bessemer converter men in one of the steel mills near Pittsburgh were constantly induced to break their former records. They kept raising the pace until finally, when it had reached a very high point, the superintendent told them that having demonstrated their ability to produce that much steel it would thereafter be expected of them. Consequently the system is well established today. Superintendent is pitted against superintendent, foreman against foreman, mill against mill. When a record is broken it means simply that the goal to be struggled for has been set ahead. In the mills of the Carnegie Steel Company two months in each year, usually March and October, are known as "record months," and are sacred to the breaking of records. The mills are pushed to the limit; every possible advantage is given in the way of perfect equipment, and all known obstacles are removed beforehand. Some departments are run straight through the month without an hour's stop, and all are run overtime. If records are broken, the superintendent passes cigars!* The new record has an effect, for what is done in March and October is of course possible in April and November.†

* The largest single order of one of the leading Pittsburgh cigar companies comes each month from a steel plant.

† "The largest pay in the history of Homestead steel works, and the largest ever made by the Carnegie Steel Company, will be distributed next Friday and Saturday among the 7,000 men employed at the Homestead steel works and its auxiliaries—the Howard axle works and the Carrie blast furnaces. This pay will aggregate $308,000, and is larger than usual because of the records broken last month at the plant." (Pittsburgh *Post*, Nov. 13, 1907.)

In all the speeding up, it is readily to be seen that superintendents and foremen are the major factors. The forces that move them to action influence in turn the increased physical effort that has been noted. Of course emulation is a factor with foremen and superintendents as well as with workmen. Competition for positions is sufficient to keep them alert, for if one superintendent does not make good, some other one can. These are negative forces, however; the positive ones range from gifts and extra favors to the bonus system of the United States Steel Corporation.

The effect, upon some foremen, produced by the gift of a fat turkey on Thanksgiving or Christmas is really surprising. Extra favors shown have a far-reaching effect, too, and this is understood and acted upon. "Why anybody should complain about the Steel Corporation is more than I can see," said a foreman with whom I had been discussing certain phases of the prevailing discontent. "They certainly treat me fine. Only the other day the superintendent came around and asked me my address, and I know what that means. There'll be a turkey left up at my home the day before Thanksgiving." I had been sitting in his parlor talking with the foreman and his wife, and when I rose to leave my host offered to walk down the street with me. His wife suggested that, since he was going out, he might see about a woman to help her clean house next day. "Why, what's the use?" he said protestingly. "I'll send a laborer up from the mill and he can help you as well as not." So it was arranged, and I suppose some stalwart Slav earned his $1.98 the next day scrubbing floors instead of wheeling pig iron.

These have their influence, but the important thing behind the activity of the bosses in the mills of the Steel Corporation is the bonus system. This, it should be understood, is distinct from the so-called profit-sharing scheme involving the issue of stock to employes, which will be described in a later chapter. Both plans were inaugurated in 1903 and embodied in the same circular letter of that year.* There is an essential difference between the two. From the standpoint of the administrative interests of the Corporation, the stock issue plan is for the purpose of creating greater stability among the employes, by making it an object for them to

* Appendix V, p. 306.

remain continuously in the employ of the Corporation, and for the purpose of increasing the spirit of loyalty. The bonus system is a plan which incidentally seeks these ends, but which is essentially a system of cash and stock rewards to foremen, superintendents, and others for services of various kinds. As expressed in the initial circular of 1902, the finance committee had been "endeavoring to devise some comprehensive plan under which those of you (officers and employes) who are charged with responsibility of managing and directing the affairs of the corporation, or of its several subsidiary companies, shall receive compensation partly on the profit-sharing basis." During the year preceding the announcement, changes and adjustments were made in the salaries of the men occupying official and semi-official positions, and it was announced that thereafter they were to "share with the stockholders in any profits made after a certain amount of annual net earnings shall have been reached." Directly in line with this general relationship between surplus profits and the size of the total bonus to be distributed, it is generally understood that the greater part of it is paid for getting out a big tonnage. Fifty-two out of 72 recipients in a representative plant were classified as superintendents, assistant superintendents and foremen. There is nothing in the statement of the plan, or in its practical workings as I found traces of them in the Pittsburgh District, which would keep the speeding up occasioned by this incentive from going beyond the bounds of reasonable efficiency, or which, in the absence of trade union organization, would safeguard the rank and file against the demands of an unscrupulous superior; it becomes an inducement to men in authority to drive those below them.

In 1906, $3,300,000 was distributed; in 1907, $3,000,000; and in 1908, $1,500,000.* When such sums are divided among those "charged with responsibility in managing the affairs of the corporation," it is possible to give a substantial slice to each. It is reported in Pittsburgh that a foreman or the superintendent of a department receiving a salary of $2,500 a year is likely to get about $500 in bonuses, an amount large enough to be worth working for; and there can be no doubt of the efficiency of the system in leading those in authority to speed up the men below.

* See Appendix V, p. 323.

All these forces have been factors in the marvelous growth in the daily production of steel. We have seen how the piece-rate wages and the gang system have been supplemented by direct and indirect incentives; how the spirit of emulation has played its part in leading the men to do their utmost in producing a constantly larger tonnage. We have seen the effect of the record months, and how back of all stand the men in authority, egging their subordinates to ever renewed efforts, doing all in their power to increase the tonnage, receiving extra money rewards if they do it. It remains to point out the greatest factor of all in the "speeding-up" system. My belief is that the tonnage system of payment in itself would never have been sufficient to call out the speed which now prevails. But when the rate is judiciously cut from time to time, the tonnage system of payment becomes the most effective scheme for inducing speed that has yet been devised.

That the rate of pay per ton of product should be reduced during the last fifteen years was inevitable. Had it remained the same during that time, the earnings of skilled men would be swollen today. For example, the rate paid to rollers on the 119-inch plate mill at Homestead in 1892 was said to be 14 cents per ton.* The 119-inch mill has been remodeled in late years into an 84-inch mill, and in 1907 the rate paid the rollers in this mill was 5½ cents,—a cut of over 60 per cent in the rate. But the tonnage had increased, and in spite of the cut, the roller was able to make $9.90 a day in 1907. If he had been paid at the old rate, he would have received over $25 a day. This example illustrates one reason for the cutting of the tonnage rates. The statement is sometimes made that in certain skilled positions, workmen would receive over $100 a day if they were now paid the tonnage rate that obtained fifteen years ago. Such statements are probably the result of mere guessing. At any rate, I do not know of any facts that would tend to substantiate them. But while the tonnage rate has been cut to correspond with the rapid increase in the output, a careful inquiry soon reveals the fact that the reductions have often preceded the advance in output, and have more than kept even with it. It was stated above that the rollers on the 84-inch mill at Homestead

* *Journal of Political Economy*, Vol. II, p. 338.

received $9.90 a day in 1907, but in 1892 the rollers on the 119-inch mill were paid $11.84 a day.* This is a decline of 16 per cent in actual earnings; in certain positions the reduction has amounted to over 20 per cent. As pointed out in the chapter on wages, while there is divergent testimony as to whether the earnings of the great body of skilled men have gone up or down, it is an admitted fact that the earnings of the most highly skilled men have been intentionally cut down in the last fifteen years. It should be noted here, once more, that this statement of reduction does not apply to all departments; in some positions wages have advanced in the last decade. The day men, that is, men who are paid by the hour or by the day instead of by the ton, have had their wages advanced in recent years, while the rates if not the earnings of all tonnage men were declining. This fact is significant. All workmen whose efforts have a direct, appreciable bearing on the day's output are paid by the ton. The day men are the unskilled laborers, engineers, and others who are not able to affect the product so much by lagging or "soldiering." The skilled men occupy the strategic positions and rate-cutting is a most effective leverage, in connection with the other devices, for increasing the output.

Whatever a man's earnings may be, whether high or low, he adjusts himself to that basis and it becomes his minimum of comfort. The man who has had six dollars a day and is reduced to four, experiences a hardship never realized by a man on three dollars a day, who has never had a chance to develop four-dollar tastes. A reduction in wages means sacrifice, and the desire to get back to the old basis after a reduction is stronger than is the desire to enjoy a higher wage than the accustomed average. The steel companies have been good judges of human nature in this respect. The mere possibility of greater earnings than any yet enjoyed would never have been sufficient to rouse the men to the degree of effort desired. Only a reduction could furnish the required stimulus, for that made it necessary to struggle to reach once more the old wage which had become the minimum of comfort.

* Investigation of Homestead Strike, Miscellaneous Documents No. 335, 52d Congress, 1st Session, p. 5.

I should not wish to underestimate the factors other than speeding that have increased output. Early in this chapter mention was made of some of the mechanical elements in the advances, and I refer to them again to correct any possible misapprehension. In two departments especially it would appear that speeding of the men has been a minor factor. These are the blast furnaces and the open-hearth steel furnaces. In both departments there is considerable waiting time, during which the men watch and hold themselves in readiness to do whatever may be necessary, according to the stage of development of the process. Here, at least, the more important elements in greater outputs appear to be mechanical devices and scientific developments in processes, and the visitor may be impressed with the leisureliness of the work going forward in the great half-open sheds.

In a measure the same may be said of rolling mills. In some cases physical toil has been lightened by new devices, but in almost every case where this is true responsibility has become heavier. The hot strain on back and muscles has been eased only to make way, often, for increased nervous strain. More and more the demand is upon nerve control and swift judgment. Dependence is still upon human strength. It is not entirely due to the marvelous ingenuity of American engineers that steel production has increased at such a remarkable pace. The speed of the men who man the plants has played its part. Devices to develop it, possibly not bad in themselves, become in their combination, when there is no restriction of the length of the work day other than the full round of the clock dial, a schedule of overstrain; and they become, when there is no common organization of the men to balance them and resist encroachment, a system of exploitation. There is a human element in large outputs that does not appear in statistics of tonnage. The steel companies know just the relation between this human element and the tables of statistics, hence the "pushers," the fostering of foolish rivalries, the orgy of overtime in the "record months," the stifling of natural considerateness in the bonus system, and the playing upon human necessity in the cutting of the tonnage rates. The result of it all is a system of speeding, unceasing and relentless, seldom equaled in any industry, in any time.

Boss of the Crew

Swimming Tank

Assembly Hall

"Gym"

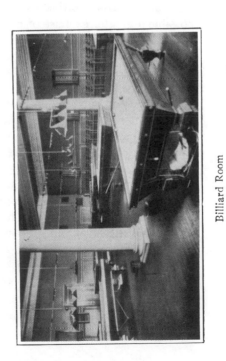

Billiard Room

RECREATIONAL EQUIPMENT OF CARNEGIE LIBRARY AT HOMESTEAD

CHAPTER XV

THE LABOR POLICY OF UNRESTRICTED CAPITAL

THAT there has come about a reversal in relations between employer and employe in the steel industry is apparent. Before 1901 there was a national union which dealt with individual employers. Now there is one great corporation whose negative action, at least, practically fixes standards for the whole industry. This national corporation deals not even with local associations; it deals with individual workmen. In former years the Amalgamated Association had some advantage over employers because the latter were not organized. This advantage was greatly modified, however, by the existence of large companies, such as the Carnegie Steel Company and the National Tube Company, before the United States Steel Corporation was inaugurated. Yet lack of co-operation between the different employers made possible a greater exercise of power on the part of the union than would otherwise have been the case. Now, on the other hand, there is practically no bar to the domination of the employers. The independent mills of the Pittsburgh District followed the lead of the Carnegie Steel Company and the other companies that are now in the combination, in breaking with the union and in their subsequent action, so that today conditions are practically uniform in all steel mills, under the absolute and unregulated control of the employers. The purpose of this chapter is to set forth in a more rounded way how the employers have used this power, viewed from the standpoint of labor conditions.

Entirely apart from unionism or non-unionism are certain arrangements which may be termed employes' benefit policies. A paternalistic spirit appeared early in the history of the Carnegie Steel Company. In 1883 the employes in the Edgar Thomson works at Braddock received a cut in wages which was accepted without any complaint. A notice was then posted by Mr. Carnegie—to show his appreciation, it was said—to the effect that he would furnish coal to his employes at one to two cents per bushel below the market price. To those who owed money on houses or lots he offered a 25 per cent reduction on the January, 1884, instalment.* Since then the arrangement has become general in the Carnegie mills of delivering coal to employes at cost. A more considerable plan has been that of loaning money to employes for the purpose of building homes. In the nature of the case it is an advantage to a mill-town employer to have property-owning employes. The labor force is more stable and there is less likelihood of a strike, the employes not wishing to jeopardize their positions after a house has been acquired, lest they have to move. This building-loan plan was inaugurated by the Carnegie Company long before the union was eliminated, and is continued to-day. Loans up to two-thirds of the value of the property are made to employes to aid them in buying houses. Interest is charged at the rate of 5 per cent per annum plus the state tax. A considerable length of time is given in which to repay the loan, and the payments are taken out of the pay in such amounts as the employe may direct.†

Together with this loan feature is a savings department maintained by the company. At the outset, it was believed that deposits would be virtually offset by the amounts loaned house builders; but it did not work out that way, the loans not equaling the deposits. Accordingly, while any employe who wishes to do so may open an account, the extension of deposits has not been encouraged for a number of years. Deposits of any amount not lower than a dollar will be accepted, and interest is paid upon them usually in excess of the prevailing rate among banks. In 1908 it was 5 per cent. The number of depositors is 1,100.

In Homestead and Munhall, where the Carnegie Company owns a number of houses, it has proved itself a good landlord‡ in

---

* *National Labor Tribune*, Dec. 29, 1883, p. 4.

† In 1910, 165 employes had loans with the company.

‡ See Byington's Homestead: The Households of a Mill Town, Chapter II. For a description of Painter's Row, where the company had not such a happy record as a landlord, see The Pittsburgh District, a companion volume of The Pittsburgh Survey.

comparison with some of the small owners of rented properties in these boroughs. The houses are kept in good repair, water is furnished, and connections are made with the company mains through which gas is furnished to the tenants at a cost of about five cents per thousand feet less than is charged by the gas company. The company rents these houses at a figure 30 to 40 per cent below that charged by other landlords. There is always a waiting list of those who are desirous of moving into a company house.

The American Bridge Company controls a number of houses in Ambridge, the National Tube Company in Lorain, the American Sheet and Tin Plate Company developed the better property at Vandergrift along town planning lines, and the Indiana Steel Company has a land system at Gary, etc.; but the Steel Corporation, especially in Allegheny County, has not in any sense worked out a common housing policy* in its relations to the towns which its plants call into being or hold together. In many of them unsanitary and uneconomical dwellings prevail, while the congested immigrant lodgings are disease-ridden.

In the field of insurance and pensions, the American Steel and Wire Company has stood out as the one subsidiary company of the United States Steel Corporation which has maintained a pension system. This went into effect in 1902, and provides for the retirement and pensioning of all employes sixty-five years old, who have been in the service of the company ten years, and all employes between fifty-five and sixty-five years of age who have been ten or more years in the service of the company and have become physically disabled. The amount of a pension is determined by adding, for each year of service, one per cent of the average regular monthly pay for the ten years preceding retirement. Thus, by way of illustration: if an employe has been in the service of the company for 40 years and has received an average for the preceding ten years of $50 per month regular wages. his pension allowance would be 40 per cent of $50, or $20 per month, There is a minimum of $5.00 a month, and the highest pension now paid is $58.63 a month. At the close of April, 1908, there were 342 pensioners who were receiving a total sum of $3,886.62 each month, an average of $11.36 each.

* In developing its new steel plant at Woodlawn, below Pittsburgh, the Jones and Laughlin Company has (1910) gone into an extensive house building scheme.

In a larger field, covering not only superannuation but fatalities and serious injuries, the Carnegie Relief Fund of $4,000,-000 has benefited the employes of another constituent company. From this fund injury benefits* have been paid out beginning one year after the date of incapacity; death benefits have been paid of $500 to families dependent upon single men, $500 to widows, and $100 additional for every child under sixteen; and modest pensions to employes retired because of old age or incapacity. Of the 21 pensioners resident in Homestead in 1908, the average monthly allowance was $11.06, the highest was $18, the lowest, $5.65. Altogether, of the million dollars in interest paid out since 1901, 40 per cent has gone for pensions. The fund was a personal gift in 1901 by Mr. Carnegie to the men in the works which he at one time controlled. "I make this first use of surplus wealth upon retiring from business," he wrote, "as an acknowledgment of the deep debt which I owe to the workmen who have contributed so greatly to my success." The fund has applied to all the employes of the Carnegie Steel Company, but has been as distinct from that company as the Carnegie Library at Braddock or the Carnegie Institute in Pittsburgh, and cannot properly be considered as a company policy or enterprise.

So far as compensation for accidents is concerned, the payments made by the constituent companies of the Steel Corporation in Allegheny County in the year studied, July 1, 1906,–June 30, 1907, did not differ materially from those customary among other large companies of the district. In 33 out of 60 cases of married men killed in plants controlled by the Steel Corporation, it contributed nothing over funeral expenses, to take the place of the wages of the dead breadwinners; in 17 out of 28 cases, the same was true of their chief competitor, the Jones and Laughlin Steel Company; proportions corresponding in a rough way with the generalization true of the Allegheny County employers as a whole. In over 50 per cent of the· cases studied, both married and single, no share whatever of the lost income was borne by the employer. The main economic loss in half of all the year's in-

---

* At first injury benefits were paid beginning two weeks after the accident, but these payments had to be discontinued, as the income from the fund did not hold out.

dustrial accidents staid where it first fell—on the families of the men killed at work.*

TABLE 10.—COMPENSATION PAID BY EMPLOYERS TO DEPENDENTS OF 168 MARRIED MEN KILLED IN WORK-ACCIDENTS IN ALLEGHENY COUNTY, JULY 1, 1906, TO JUNE 30, 1907

Name of Employer	Nothing	$100 or less or funeral expenses	$101–$500	$501–$1000	$1001–$2000	$2001–$3000	Unknown	Total
American Steel and Wire Co.. . . .	..	..	4	1	..	..	..	5
National Tube Co. . .	..	6	3	1	1	..	2	13
Carnegie Steel Co.† . .	10	17	8	3	2	2	..	42
Jones & Laughlin Steel Co.	7	10	4	3	2	2	..	28
Pressed Steel Car Co. .	3	3	3	..	..	..	1	10
Other Companies . .	30	23	14	1	..	..	2	70
Total	50	59	36	9	5	4	5	168

During the publication year of this volume, the United States Steel Corporation has announced two important developments in the way of a relief plan and a pension system which, so long as a man remains an employe, will help protect his family against the hazards of industry and will make some provision toward his old age. On May 1, 1910, the Corporation introduced for one year's trial a plan of relief for injured employes which provides for regular uniform payments in case of injury or death by accidents of employment.‡ This may be considered a striking development of the generous policy of certain employers in making accident settlements where the present Pennsylvania law recognizes no liability. In this plan, too, there is the advantage to the workman of knowing definitely what he may expect. The "relief"

* For a full discussion of the causes of work-accidents and their compensation in the Pittsburgh District, see Work-Accidents and the Law, by Crystal Eastman, a companion volume of The Pittsburgh Survey. Similar proportions were found true in Erie County (Buffalo) in 1909, by the New York State Employers' Liability Commission, which in 1910 secured the first compensation laws enacted in the United States.

† Exclusive of Carnegie Relief benefits.

‡ For detailed provisions see Appendix VII, p. 330.

of which the company bears the whole expense is roughly from 18 months to three years' wages in case of the death of a married man living with his family,* and from 35 per cent of wages up to $2.00 per day in case of disability, limited to one year. These rates are much higher than those regularly paid by any large employer in the Pittsburgh District whose policy in dealing with accident cases was revealed in the cases studied by the Pittsburgh Survey.

Distinct from its accident relief, announcement has been made of another important plan on the part of the Steel Corporation. The Carnegie Relief Fund with its endowment of $4,000,000, and a fund created by the Steel Corporation of $8,000,000, have been consolidated under the name "United States Steel and Carnegie Pension Fund."† An administrative board composed of four members representing the Carnegie Fund and eight members representing the Steel Corporation will manage this joint fund, the income from which will be devoted to pensions for retired employes. The Carnegie Relief Fund discontinues benefits in cases of injury and accidental death among employes of the Carnegie companies arising after May 1, 1910. In other words, the Carnegie Relief Fund will, from now on, operate as part of a larger fund for purposes of superannuation, while the accident relief is to be maintained by the Corporation as a regular business charge.

In connection with the special subject-matter of the next chapter, and apart from the benefits to be derived by the employes from these two marked developments of Corporation policy, it should be noted that certain administrative advantages attach to them. After an employe has been five years with the company, the amount of relief his family is entitled to in case of death is increased 3 per cent with every year of service. All pension systems, when carried out by a single employer, are, of course, wholly dependent upon length of continuous service. They give

---

* The English Workman's Compensation Act provides for a compensation equivalent to three years' wages, provided the amount does not exceed £500; a law passed by the New York state legislature in 1910, covering certain hazardous occupations, calls for a compensation equivalent to four years' wages. In the case of unmarried men and of the many thousand immigrants whose families are living abroad, the amount of payment is left to the discretion of its company managers by the Steel Corporation.

† In effect January 1, 1911. For detailed provisions see Appendix VIII, p. 336.

stability to a labor force, but they do it at the sacrifice of the mobility of that labor. A man will think twice before giving up a job with a pension attachment for something immediately better; he will be loath, especially as he gets along in service, to risk discharge; he will not join a union, offhand at least, if joining means discharge. These administrative advantages have, no doubt, had their weight in the inauguration of the pension scheme; but it should be said that the relief plan for the most part is singularly clear-cut and free from secondary entanglements.

A plan that appears to be closely allied with these in spirit is the so-called profit-sharing system of the United States Steel Corporation. This is a profit-sharing scheme and something more. In fact, the purposes of the plan have been so perverted as to secure for the Corporation greater potential control over its employes. The system will receive attention in a later chapter.

In the policy of the United States Steel Corporation regarding the prevention of accidents a great change is going forward. I mentioned accidents, in a brief way, in an earlier chapter, and pointed out some instances of neglect of safety in the mills. Such conditions are now being met by a positive, constructive policy of safeguarding machinery and reducing the possibility of accidents as far as possible, and to this end the co-operation of foremen and workmen in committees of safety has been consciously enlisted.* The Jones and Laughlin Company has, in contrast, mani-

---

* See article by David S. Beyer, Chief Safety Inspector, American Steel and Wire Company, describing the work developed under a central committee of safety appointed by the United States Steel Corporation, May, 1908, published as Appendix III in Eastman's Work-Accidents and the Law, a companion volume of The Pittsburgh Survey. A later development has been the overhauling of hospital equipment and staff for the treatment of accident cases. In November, 1909, the Carnegie Steel Company appointed a chief surgeon under whom the work of fifty or more company physicians is being systematized; a standardized emergency hospital unit is to be installed in each plant, and the major surgical work for the mills in the Pittsburgh District has been centered in a new city hospital where the operating facilities are complete and specialists are within call. By means of record cards and reports the professional treatment of each case is audited, and foremen are not permitted to let the patient return to work before the physician's certificate shows that he is ready for it. Thus, relapses are prevented. It is too early to review the features of this co-ordinated hospital service. The first improvements reported as a result of it have been in the direction of cutting down infections to a minimum and putting an end to crude treatment of wounds either by local company doctors or by fellow workmen; also in applying advanced methods in surgery to the multiple fractures sustained in heavy mill work.

fested considerable indifference to methods of reducing the danger of accidents. In 1908, at the time that this study was made, their South Side plant was badly overcrowded, and there were many dangerous machines which lacked proper guards. Similar conditions were to be found in some of the older plants of the United States Steel Corporation, but the work of overhauling them and equipping the machines with protective devices was being pushed after years marked, from the standpoint of saving life, by similar disorganization and neglect.*

These plans illustrate the administrative and, to a degree, the human advantages which have come with combination in the steel industry. In the first place, as illustrated by the safety work, inventions and adaptations instituted in one plant may at once be made the common property of many; an expert staff can be set at the exact study of difficult problems with the whole run of the Corporation's mills as their laboratory; and standards once adopted, whether of safety inspection, accident compensation, or surgical service, may be enforced by executive act so as to affect 200,000 men instead of waiting for enlightenment to soak through to the understanding of a hundred independent managers. Again, the private owners of the 90's faced a wracking competition, but profits went wholly into their own pockets. The directorate and executive officials of the Steel Corporation bear a different relation to the year's proceeds. Their personal incomes are not affected in inaugurating a relief fund, for example; and whether or not their sense of economic justice may be enlisted as between stockholder and wage-earner, they can bring a more detached and far-seeing judgment to the disposition of the surplus, at least in so far as a given share may serve to stimulate or keep intact the working organization of which they are parts. These advantages have been illustrated in a number of ways in the past five years and they are a hopeful element in the years ahead. But it should be noted that they are in a field apart from

---

* The work which the National Tube Company, the American Steel and Wire Company, the Carnegie Steel Company and the American Bridge Company are doing in the Pittsburgh District in the direction of safety work, is not only an example for other employers, but a practical argument for an adequate system of factory inspection and workmen's compensation which will bring the practice in all industries to a high level—and keep it there.

the main currents of labor management, and that they have their reverse side in the impersonal dead wall confronting a superintendent or manager, who may, for example, believe that the twelve-hour day is as senseless from a business standpoint as it is from a human standpoint, and who would abolish it, if he could manage the shop as his own. For the inertia of corporation control, which has given compelling effect to such changes as those noted, gives rigid uniformity to bad standards as well as good, and gives widespread coercive force to operating policies which in themselves, or in the form in which they are inaugurated, are socially destructive. And to affect them the individual workman, to a far greater degree than the individual manager, is helpless.

As already indicated, the break with unionism had no direct bearing on the policies which have thus far been cited. Some of them were initiated by the employers during the time of greatest union strength. But there are other conditions which have come into being that would certainly have been opposed if the men had retained their collective power.

One of these is that internal organization of the industry which, in eliminating waste of all kinds and introducing mechanical changes, has also put the entire control of the mills back into the hands of foremen and superintendents, so co-ordinating the labor force as to make it most easy to control and most difficult to unionize. Another is the wages policy, which, while advancing the wages of common labor, has brought down the earnings of men of highest skill; which has anticipated increased output with cuts in the rates, and which has suffered the whole wage movement, unprodded by union demands, to lag behind the advances in prices of family necessities.

With the employers no longer penalized by having to pay extra for overtime, the day's, the week's, and the year's work has been lengthened. Now the twelve-hour day is the working schedule for the majority;* the seven-day week in 1907–08 claimed at least 20 per cent of all employes; and the twenty-four-hour

* The Jones and Laughlin Company changed from a twelve-hour to an eight-hour schedule in a few positions in 1909, but this was merely a restoration of the conditions existing before the panic, and did not alter the fact that the great majority of their employes work a twelve-hour day.

shift comes once every two weeks for large numbers. One of the leading steel presidents in Pittsburgh told me that he, personally, was opposed to a twelve-hour day, and that wherever possible his men worked ten hours. The impracticability of a universal ten-hour day in the plants is, however, apparent, when one recalls that the steel industry is continuous, operating through the twenty-four hours of the day and night. And in its absence, the twelve-hour shifts are the rule.

Added to these adverse conditions under the employers' régime, we have noted the speeding up system in all its ramifications; the "pushers," who drive the common laborers; the gang system at the furnaces and at the rolls, which, combined with the tonnage system of payment, makes the steel blooms and billets do their own driving; the cash rewards given to the foremen and superintendents in the Corporation mills for helping to keep up the tension; and, finally, the judicious cuts from time to time in the rate of pay per ton, which make the men put forth the last ounce of energy to prevent a wage loss. All these, together with the heat and the danger of accident, result in overstrain and exhaustion, both mental and physical.

The final outcome of this régime of exploitation may not be known in this generation. It will do injury to the physical health not alone of individuals, but eventually of society. Even more serious, however, is its influence on the mental and moral natures of the men concerned.

Let us look at the situation as it is reflected in the everyday life of the men, remembering that the depleting consequences of long hours are in direct proportion to the stress of the work that engrosses them. The immediate effect of such a working schedule is on the home. Many a steel worker has said to me with grim bitterness, "Home is just the place where I eat and sleep. I live in the mills." Theoretically, the steel workers are in the mills twelve hours on each turn, from six to six; in practice, though, there is considerable latitude about the time of changing. It has come to be quite a general custom in certain departments for the men to work longer at night than on the day turn. The men prefer to work the longer shift at night because such leisure as they have when on the night shift comes at a time when it is hard to use it to advantage. They come home in the morning and go to bed, getting up at about four o'clock in the afternoon. There is little opportunity for pleasure or social intercourse before it is time to go to the mill again. By the time supper is eaten, most of the free interval is gone. The steel workers are united in saying that "on the night shift you can't do anything but work, eat and sleep anyhow." So home pleasures and social pleasures alike are entirely lacking during a full half of the time. Whatever opportunity for enjoyment of the home there may be, must come in the alternate weeks on day shift.

The manner of dividing the twenty-four hours of the day into two turns varies. Judging merely from observation, I should say that the most general adjustment is an eleven-hour day and a thirteen-hour night. At Homestead, however, most departments have a ten-hour day with a fourteen-hour night, and there are many positions throughout the district where the shifts change at six o'clock morning and evening, making a straight twelve-hour turn for both shifts. With an eleven-hour day, a man's work begins at seven in the morning. Most of the skilled workers live at least a half-hour's ride on the cars away from the mill, so if the man is to get to his work by seven, his breakfast must be ready at six o'clock, and he must be up and dressed before that. At six in the evening he is relieved by his "buddy," the man who holds the same position on the opposite shift. If he cares about his appearance, he will take fifteen minutes making himself presentable for the street, and if his car is not delayed he may reach home by a quarter before seven, having been absent twelve hours and fifteen minutes. But between six and seven the rush is at its height, and the man who can take the first car that comes along is fortunate. Sometimes one has to wait for half a dozen cars to go by before he can find one with any standing room left. With the best of luck it will be after seven before he can sit down to his evening meal. This is the program of a day that has been outlined to me again and again by the steel workers until I am sure it is neither overdrawn nor unusual in any way. When I asked about the evening, the usual reply was: "Well, I am mostly too tired to go out anywhere. I read the paper a little while, but I soon get sleepy and I go to bed so that I can get up early enough the next morning." And this is the alternate week of comparative leisure!

The wife of the steel worker, too, has a hard day, and even a longer one than her husband's. To prepare a breakfast by six in the morning she must rise not later than half past five. The family cannot sit down at the supper table until seven or later, and after that the dishes must be washed. There is little time for husband and wife to have each other's company. It is only by an extra exertion that they can spend an evening out together, and the evening at home is robbed of much of its charm by the projection of the domestic duties beyond the time that would be required if the meal were served earlier. The father, too, has little time with his children. If they are quite small, he may go for weeks without seeing them except in their cribs. What the ultimate social effect will be of this stunting of family life may only be conjectured.

Not only is home life threatened, but other healthy influences in the mill towns feel the blighting effect of the twelve-hour day. Opportunity for mental culture would seem to be ample in the mill towns. Each has its Carnegie Library. Big, splendidly equipped affairs are the libraries in Homestead, Braddock and Duquesne. Each has its auditorium and music hall with a fine pipe organ, where lectures and concerts of high grade are held. There is a club in connection with the library in each of these towns, and membership in the club is open to all. The dues are small, and the privileges of the baths, bowling alleys and billiard tables are open to members. The attendance at the baths, especially in summer, is large.

In the libraries themselves there is a good stock of books and periodicals, the supply on metallurgy and mechanical arts being especially ample. Books may be drawn, of course, and read in the home. But the steel workers seldom make use of these privileges. There is a great deal of prejudice against the gift of Mr. Carnegie on account of the several labor conflicts that have occurred in the mills formerly controlled by him; this has its effect, but it is not alone sufficient to bar out the workingman. The trouble is the same as that which has already spoiled half of the home life, and bids fair to blight the rest. There is not enough energy left at the end of a twelve-hour day to enable the average man to read anything of a very serious nature, and the reading done by even the most intelligent does not extend much beyond the limits of the daily paper. As for lectures and concerts, —to attend them would necessitate a change of clothing and a preparation for which a weary twelve-hour man has little heart. The difficulties that must be met before these cultural opportunities can be enjoyed are usually too great to be overcome. The following, taken verbatim from my notes as written out just after each interview, are typical examples of the experience and feeling of skilled steel workers. In each case the thought expressed is that of the man himself, and usually the words are his also. The interviews were written out in the third person for convenience.

(A) November 26, 1907.—The hours of labor in the mills are altogether too long. On account of the time consumed in going to and from the mill, this man is away from his home fourteen hours every day. He seldom gets out to any social affairs. Practically all of his time is spent in the mills or in bed.

(B) December 6, 1907.—The men all work on the two-turn system. By arrangement with his "buddy," however, when on day turn this man goes to work at 7 a. m. and works until 5.30 p. m. This gives a little extra time every other week. It does not give so much time, though, that he feels like going out often to social affairs or to places of amusement, in the evening. He cannot go out and feel much like work the next day. He usually goes to the lectures at the Carnegie Library, but to little else. No man who works twelve hours, he says, has time or energy to do much outside of his work. His life is lived in the mill.

(C) December 14, 1907.—Working on the two-turn system, this man is obliged to get up at 5.45 in the morning in order to be at the mill at 6.50. He must stay there until 5.30 p. m., and then in order to make himself presentable he must bathe, as well as he can without proper facilities, and change his clothing, so it is after six when he gets home. He gets through supper some time after seven, and soon after that gets sleepy. If he sits down to read, he will fall asleep over a paper or a book. He has not read a book through in three or four years. Some years ago he read several of Shakespeare's plays, and while he was doing this he sat down to his reading each evening after supper and did nothing else. This is the only systematic reading he has done for years. He never uses the library, and the other mill men do not use it either. As a rule, they do not care for it, but they could not use it even if they wished to do so, for their hours are too long to permit the use of a library. They have a lecture course in the library, and every year have some of the best talent in the country, but this man seldom goes. The library and the lecture course are fine things for business men, women and children, but they are absolutely useless, so far as the mill men are concerned.

(D) January 10, 1908.—The hours are long in this man's department and the work is hard and hot. There is no rest, no pleasure, no time to one's self. He works from 7 a. m. to 5.30 p. m. when on day turn. On Sundays they go to work at 6 p. m. and work until 7 Monday morning. Sometimes he has to work on Sundays during the day in order to catch up with the mill. This does not happen more than three or four times a year, as a rule, but he has to come out whenever called. He has purchased a 60-acre farm, and expects to move on it in the spring. He doesn't expect to make as much money as he is getting now, but he will be free. He will have some time at home, and have his Sundays free, and won't have to work when he is sick.

In these leaves out of plain men's lives we get the meaning of the labor policies of unrestricted capital. The employers chafed under trade union rules and said they were not free to manage their own business. They are now free to manage their own business and they have managed it in the manner described. There can no longer be any sharing of responsibility for conditions with the men. The employers took that responsibility from the shoulders of their employes when they drove out unionism, and now they "decide what is good and put it into effect before the employes have a chance to express themselves."*

Having described the working-out of the labor policies of the steel companies, we may search for the causes that developed them. These causes were primarily economic. Such labor policies were mapped out and developed as would best meet the "exigencies of business."

The motive back of the destruction of unionism was desire for administrative control. That control did not rest entirely in the hands of the employers so long as there was a strong organization among their employes. One purpose of unionism is, or should be, to bargain with employers and to protect employes from unjust demands. To that extent a union has a clear moral right to a voice in determining labor conditions. It appears from the evidence that I have been able to gather that the Amalgamated Association of Iron and Steel Workers, in the days of its power, went further than this, and demanded a share in administrative control inconsistent with necessary business methods.

* Quoted from a conversation with a prominent employer.

But it was not alone because the steel companies wished to rid themselves of these improper restrictions that they crushed out unionism; they wished also to be free from the proper and legitimate activities of the union.

This latter becomes evident when we consider what has been done by the employers when free from union control. They have not stopped with introducing a necessary and proper discipline in their plants, but have taken advantage of their unlimited control to introduce the negative and destructive policies summarized above. Like the union, which in the days of its strength sometimes demanded all of the benefit of an increase in tonnage due to a new invention, and would not accept a reduction in the rate of pay, the steel companies are now demanding all of the benefit of increased tonnage, whether due to inventions or to physical effort, and will not permit any proportionate advance in workmen's earnings. More than this, they are taking advantage of the situation to exact far more of the worker than was expected of him years ago, and it is my belief far more than is expected now in other industries.

The causes that developed the present labor policy were, as stated above, economic in their nature. But a proper economic policy from the standpoint of the individual may be absolutely uneconomic from the standpoint of society. Such men as have plundered our forests and wasted our coal deposits have followed out an economic policy individually sound, but that policy is today denounced as at enmity with the public good. If the man who wastes and destroys *natural* resources is a public enemy, what of the corporations that exploit *human* resources?

If the employes could be charged formerly with a share of the responsibility for conditions in the steel industry, that time has gone by. The employers accepted the full burden of that responsibility by driving out unionism; they have increased their accountability by their stern measures designed to retain for themselves the control now exercised.

A repressive régime that makes it impossible for men to protest against conditions that are inimical to their welfare serves now, and has served since the destruction of unionism, to keep the employers in the saddle.

CHAPTER XVI

REPRESSION

IT now becomes necessary to discuss the reasons for the apparent acquiescence of the steel workers in existing conditions. The obvious deterrent to collective action on their part is the fact that they are non-union. But that merely suggests the question: Why don't they organize? To understand the absence of united action and resistance to the policies of the companies one must understand the obstacles that stand in the way.

In the first place, there is the so-called profit-sharing system of the United States Steel Corporation. This plan was announced by the Corporation to take effect in 1903. There were at that time about 168,000 employes of the Corporation, and these were divided, according to annual earnings, into six classes. It was provided that 25,000 shares of preferred stock should be set aside, and during January, 1903, the employes should have opportunity to subscribe, each one for as many shares as he wished, within the limits of a sum represented by a certain percentage of his annual salary.

Every year since 1903 there has been an additional stock issue, and the employes have usually over-subscribed the amount of stock allotted. Since the beginning, the number of shares allotted employes in each year has been as follows:

Year	Shares	Year	Shares
1903	47,551*	1908	30,450
1904	31,644	1909	{ 17,960 preferred
1905	18,180		{ 15,387 common
1906	24,001	1910	24,580
1907	27,150		

The total number of employes subscribing each year was as follows:

* All the stock issued has been preferred stock except in 1909, as shown.

Year	Employes	Year	Employes
1903	26,399	1907	14,163
1904	9,912	1908	24,562
1905	8,494	1909	19,123
1906	12,192	1910	17,363

These figures cannot be added up to show the total number who hold stock, for the same employes have subscribed in different years. The total number of employes holding stock of the Corporation in April, 1910, was 27,641, of whom 17,835 had fully paid for their stock.

The terms of purchase are very advantageous. Stock is to be paid for in monthly instalments, to be deducted from wages in such amounts as the subscriber may designate, not to exceed 25 per cent of the monthly wages or salary. Three years are allowed for full payment and 5 per cent interest is charged on deferred payments. In the allotments of stock, preference has been given the employes whose incomes fall in the lower classes, although at least one full share of stock has been allotted each subscriber. No employe has ever been refused. Of the six classes designated, 25.69 per cent of the stock has been subscribed by the sixth class (workmen with an income under $800 per year, or, roughly, under $15 per week, in which, as we have seen, fall 71 per cent of the labor force). Skilled men, foremen and minor superintendents would fall in the fifth class, which has subscribed most heavily—56.38 per cent. Officials earning over $2,500 have subscribed the remaining 17.93 per cent. Of these, those earning over $5,000 have subscribed 6.91 per cent.

A plan by which the great working force of 200,000 employes can share in the year's profits of the United States Steel Corporation commends itself for its fair intent. It is possible that a plan by which, as here, employes can share through a system of stock ownership, open to all, has advantages over a percentage based on wages or output. Such a plan, as is often urged, may tend in entirely natural ways to a community of interest between men and management.

But other factors have been injected into the stock ownership plan of the United States Steel Corporation which remove it from the class of straight profit-sharing. On these factors it must be judged. The full text of the original offer appears in the appendix.* In order to show the superimposed features which differentiate this plan from straight profit-sharing, I will quote from it briefly:

> As soon as the stock shall have been fully paid for, it will be issued in the name of the original subscriber and the certificate will be given to him, and he can then sell it any time he chooses. But as an inducement for him to keep it and to remain continuously in the employ of the Corporation or of one or another of the subsidiary companies, and to have the same interest in the business that a stockholder or working partner would have, the following offer is made, viz.:
>
> If he will not sell or part with the stock, but will keep it and in January of each year, for five years, commencing with January, 1904, will exhibit the certificate to the treasurer of his company, together with a letter from a proper official, to the effect that he has been continuously in the employ of the Corporation or of one or another of its subsidiary companies during the preceding year, and has shown *a proper interest in its welfare and progress,*† he will during each of such five years receive checks at the rate of five dollars a share per year. . . . .
>
> If he shall remain continuously in the service of the Corporation or of one or another of its subsidiary companies for five years, at the end of the fifth year the Corporation intends that he shall receive a still further dividend, which cannot now be ascertained or stated, but which will be derived from the following source, viz.:
>
> All who subscribe for stock in January, 1903, and commence to pay for it, but who discontinue at any time during the five years, of course will not receive the $5.00 per share for such of the five years as remain after they discontinue. The Corporation will, however, pay into a special fund each year the $5.00 payments that would have been made to such subscribers had they continued. This fund shall be credited with 5 per cent annual interest, and at the end of the five years' period the total amount thus accumulated will be divided into as many parts as shall be equal to the number of shares then remaining in the hands of men who shall have continued in such employ for the whole five years, and the Corporation will then by its own final determination award to each man *whom it shall find deserving thereof*† as many parts of such accumulated fund as shall be equal to the number of shares then held by him under this plan.

* Appendix V, p. 306.   † Italics are mine.

By 1908, when the first "extra dividend" was declared, the 26,399 employes who had subscribed in 1903 for 47,551 shares of stock, had dwindled to 5,409 employes holding 12,339 shares of stock, entitling them to participation in the fund. The extra dividend amounted to $65.04 a share.

In 1909 the extra dividend was distributed to 4,085 employes holding 16,019 shares, for which they had subscribed in 1904, the amount per share being $19.10. In 1910, 3,731 employes holding 9,624 shares of stock subscribed for in 1905, received $16.80 on each share.

Each stockholder sharing in these extra dividends had previously received the $5.00 bonus on each share for five years preceding—$25 on each share. He had also received regular 7 per cent dividends, $35 during the five years, a total net return of $60 on each share for the five-year period. With the extra dividend added, the net returns per share during the five-year periods ending with the calendar years 1907, 1908, and 1909 respectively, were $125.04, $79.10 and $76.10. Stock was sold to employes in 1903 at $82.50 a share, in 1904 at $55, and in 1905 at $87.50. Accordingly the total returns in the first five years on the investments made in 1903 amounted to 142.9 per cent. On the 1904 investments 143.8 per cent was realized in the five years, and on the investments of 1905 the returns were 86.97 per cent.* In other words, stock purchased in 1903, 1904 and 1905 yielded a yearly return for five years of 28.6 per cent, 28.7 per cent and 17.4 per cent, respectively. After five years, regular 7 per cent dividends were paid.

There can be no doubt of the value to the employes of the stock issue plan as a business proposition. An average net return on an investment of 17 to 25 per cent per year, for the first five years, and after that 7 per cent, is not bad. In spite of this there is not unanimity of feeling regarding the plan among the employes of the Steel Corporation. Some who hold stock criticise the policy very severely, while they admit that it is a good investment. This criticism is not all of it logical, perhaps. Some of it is aroused by the mere fact that the plan was worked out by capitalists, whose every move is regarded by certain classes of men in a

* See Appendix V, p. 306.

sinister light. Others are logical in their reasoning provided they are correct in their premises, and when they see the United States Steel Corporation giving with one hand and taking away with the other they connect the two in their minds, and they do not view the dividends with pleasure. Many of the men with whom I talked spoke bitterly of the stock issues. One of the Homestead men said to me: "Many of the workingmen have been fooled by the preferred stock plan, and they really believe that the company has meant to do great things for them, in giving them the bonus besides the regular dividend. But I want to tell you that the first stock issue in 1903 was followed by a cut in wages in 1904* that made up to the company several times over all the extra bonuses they will pay in five years. The plan is to keep the men quiet, and it does it too. No stockholder wants to try to organize a union when the terms of the agreement state that only those who show a proper interest in the affairs of the company will receive a bonus."

There are employes who jump to the conclusion that the stock issues and the savings department of the Carnegie Steel Company, and all such plans, are for the purpose of finding out how much a workingman can save, and thus just how much of a wage reduction he can stand. A steel worker in one of the mill towns held that the reduction of 1904 in his mill took from each class of workmen almost exactly what the representatives of each class had been paying each month on their stock. A letter published in a labor paper from a Homestead steel worker just after the reduction in wages went into effect in February, 1908, is a good example of the sentiment entertained by many of the skilled workmen in the employ of the Corporation. A part of it reads as follows:

> With a blare of trumpets the United States Steel Corporation has announced a large distribution of profits to its preferred stockholders, especially to its employes, but nothing has been said about the big reduction in wages at its Homestead plant which took effect February 1, 1908. This is the second heavy cut in wages at this plant since the preferred stock scheme was devised by the big corporation, and will amply reimburse the United States Steel Corpora-

* See p. 160.

tion for its generosity to its workmen. The present reduction averages about 20 per cent.* How does this strike you after their last year profit, amounting to $160,000,000 net earning to 1907? †

Another steel worker, in discussing this same reduction in a letter to the same paper remarked, "The United States Steel Corporation is making a grand-stand play in giving away cash bonuses on preferred stock. Any man with two spoonfuls of horse sense knows that when they give away one dollar they know where they are going to get another in its place." ‡

Whether or not there has been a connection between extra dividends and wage reductions, I have no light to help the reader to judge, but the workman who pointed out the effectiveness of the deferred dividend policy in promoting a passive acceptance of conditions was not far wrong.

Profit-sharing in principle is good. A scheme that recognizes that the employe is a vital and necessary part of the successful prosecution of the business, and therefore admits him to a share in the profits of an industry, is to be commended. Such a profit-sharing is only a fair recognition of the part played by the employe in making profits possible. But the stock-issue plan of the Steel Corporation is not that kind of profit-sharing.

In the first place, there is no suggestion that the special dividends and bonuses that the employe receives are, at best, other than kindly meant gifts distributed by a benevolent overlord. The whole tenor of the apparently inspired newspaper and magazine articles dealing with the subject is suggestive less of the spirit of wages than of almsgiving; and as such is a form of injustice. If the amounts distributed are a deserved and just remuneration for value received, then the Corporation is humiliating and misusing these men in pretending to *give* money instead of paying it.

A larger reason for condemning this stock-issue system is that it brings those employes who invest in stock more surely

* The writer was incorrect in supposing that this reduction was general throughout the plant. It affected the plate mills chiefly.
† *National Labor Tribune*, February 6, 1908.
‡ Ibid., February 20, 1908.

under the domination of the Corporation. The bonus paid each year for five years is to go to those who have shown "*a proper interest in the welfare and progress*" of the Corporation, and the extra dividends at the end of the five-year period are awarded to those whom the Corporation finds "*deserving thereof*." There is nothing to prevent an employe of the Corporation purchasing stock on the same basis as the outsider, but in that case he will receive only ordinary dividends. The extraordinary return received by the holder of employes' stock is based on his acquiescence as an employe. So long as his large profits are potentially dependent upon submission to every policy and project of the Corporation, so long will the principle underlying these special bonuses be vicious. It is said that they have been distributed automatically, and that the phrasings I have italicized in the announcement have never been employed as a basis for excluding a man from the benefits. But those provisions have been repeated in every announcement year after year, and as far as the psychology of control goes, their actual employment is immaterial. If a man refrains from doing a thing because he fears they may be called into action in his case, the provisions are effective. Would a stock-holding employe be showing a "proper interest in the welfare and progress" of the Corporation if he should protest and encourage his fellow workmen to protest against Sunday work? I do not know, for I have never met a stock-holding employe who had tried it. Nor have I met one who had tried to bring his fellow employes together into an association for purposes of collective bargaining; but I have no illusions in regard to such an employe being considered "deserving" of extra stock bonuses.

Efforts to encourage loyalty in a working force have much to commend them, from the standpoint of administrative efficiency. They may make for the smooth running of a plant, for increased productivity, and better returns for stockholders and men. But a plan which penalizes independent thinking and democratic action does not make for healthy progress. That the profit-sharing plan has been subordinated to this ulterior purpose is further affirmed by the practical repetition of its worst features in the bonus system. There only officials are concerned, many of them the minor operating heads upon whose independence and fraternalism, in the absence of trade union activity, the men must depend for the working out of common justice in the plants. A share of the year's bonus is held back in the form of stock. In remains with the company for five years and if a man leaves his position, or is discharged in this time, he forfeits it. Similarly he forfeits the special bonus distributed at the end of each five-year period.

But the positive influence of these systems of rewards, binding the working force to the company, is supplemented by the negative influence, far more sinister, of a system of espionage.

I doubt whether you could find a more suspicious body of men than the employes of the United States Steel Corporation. They are suspicious of one another, of their neighbors, and of their friends. I was repeatedly suspected of being an agent of the Corporation, sent out to sound the men with regard to their attitude toward the Corporation and toward unionism. The fact is, the steel workers do not dare openly express their convictions. They do not dare assemble and talk over affairs pertaining to their welfare as mill men. They feel that they are living always in the presence of a hostile critic. They are a generous, open-hearted set of men, upon the whole; the skilled men are intelligent and are able and glad to talk upon a variety of subjects. But let the conversation be shifted to the steel works, and they immediately become reticent. It is safe to talk with a stranger about local option, the price of groceries, or the prospect of war with Japan, but it is not regarded as safe to talk about conditions in the steel industry. Concerning the most patent and generally known facts, intelligent men display the most marvelous ignorance.

Everywhere, even among the comparatively unintelligent, there is the same suspicion. One evening as I was walking on one of the streets of Munhall, the borough in which the Homestead steel works are located, I overtook a workman, dinner-pail in hand, on his way to the mill. I inquired of him the location of the street I was seeking, and as it lay further down the hill, I walked with him. We exchanged a few commonplace remarks, and as there had just been announced a reduction in wages affecting a large number of men, I spoke of that to see whether he would talk about it. His attitude immediately changed from cordiality to suspicion. "I don't know anything about it," he answered, shortly. "I haven't heard of any cut." Yet the reduction was being discussed in every steel worker's home in Homestead and Munhall. On another occasion I was walking through the Homestead steel works. Passing through the yard, I encountered a water-carrier, a man of little mental alertness apparently, so I thought I would see whether he would exercise the same discretion that I observed among the skilled workmen. I walked with him a short distance and asked him about the dangers of mill work. He never had heard of any dangers. When I asked him if accidents did not occasionally take place, he looked at me suspiciously and said, "I have never seen anybody hurt."

When I met the men in their homes, too, there was suspicion to be broken down. Sometimes I could not get an opportunity to see the man whom I was seeking. Business engagements would suddenly be remembered which prevented an interview. Several men refused to talk about mill work. A highly paid employe of the Corporation refused even to see me. I had been at his house, and finding that he was out, I left word that I would return at a specified hour. Returning at the time named, my ring brought the housewife to the door, who told me that her husband was at home, but that he would not see me or talk to me because the company had forbidden its employes to talk with strangers about mill work. Repeatedly I interviewed men who answered my questions guardedly, evidently in great perturbation of spirit, as if they feared that my visit boded them no good. Sometimes when meeting a workingman, and explaining to him my desire to talk over industrial conditions, he would say protestingly, "But I haven't anything to say against the company," although I had not once mentioned the company. On several occasions, at the close of an interview in which only the most careful statements had been made, my canny informant chuckled in evident relief, "There—I haven't told you anything against the company, have I?" One man, of long experience as a steel worker, who gave me a better insight into mill conditions than any other one person, remarked: "I used to write for labor papers a great deal, and sometimes I fairly burn to do it now—to declare before the world, over my own signature, the facts about working conditions in the steel industry. But I can't. It wouldn't be safe."

In spite of all this fear, when I got an opportunity for a

quiet talk with the men so that I could show them my letters
of introduction and explain my mission, I usually found them
sympathetic and helpful, for they said: "We cannot tell about
these things ourselves; we cannot write for the papers about our
long hours and the unjust restrictions; but we want the public to
know and we are glad to tell you—but *never mention our names.*
We must not lose our jobs, for that is all we have." I remember
one man who had evidently been waging a battle, during all of our
conversation, between his habitual caution and his desire to tell
his true feelings. He went with me to the door as I left and followed me out onto the porch into the night, closing the door behind him. Then, certain that no one, not even his family, could
hear him, he said, anxiously, "Now you won't ever mention my
name in connection with this, will you?"

This self-repression, this evident fear of a free expression of
personality, manifests itself in other ways than in a hesitancy to
talk with strangers. The men do not talk much with each other
about mill conditions. There is little discussion of politics—that,
too, could easily bring a man into dangerous waters. There is
considerable socialistic sentiment in all of the mill towns. One
encounters it not infrequently in going about among the steel
workers. I met more socialists in Homestead and Munhall than
elsewhere—enough to lead one to expect to find a local organization there. There may be as many in the other mill towns,
yet in the four more important steel centers, McKeesport, Duquesne, Braddock and Homestead, there was not in 1907 a trace
of a socialist local. I wondered at this until a Homestead steel
worker told me that they simply had not dared to have a local
within the borough. To be known as a socialist the men thought
would be to court discharge, and most of the Homestead socialists
held membership in a Pittsburgh local. I have since learned
that in the campaign of 1908 a local was organized in Homestead.

These skilled steel workers are very much like other Americans. They are neither less nor more intelligent, courageous, and
self-reliant than the average citizen. Their extreme caution, the
constant state of apprehension in which they live, can have but
one cause. It is the burnt child that dreads the fire. It would
hardly be expected that the loss of one strike, disastrous though

it was, should have so disheartened the workers that they would never attempt to revive collective bargaining. It has been through a series of such attempts that the men have learned to respect the vigilance and power of their employers, and they have learned the cost of defiance.

In 1895 it was reported in the Amalgamated Association Convention that the Homestead steel workers had received "another reduction, ranging from 48 per cent to 60 per cent." A meeting with a thousand men in attendance had been held January 16 to protest, and officers of the Amalgamated Association had addressed the meeting. The next day the Carnegie Steel Company "discharged men by fives and tens for daring to attend a public meeting." Secret meetings were then held, and 25 men employed in the 119-inch mill were organized into a lodge of the Amalgamated Association. It was not long before the officers of this lodge were discharged, and the president of the lodge was told that it was for organizing. In concluding his report, Vice-President Carney of the Amalgamated Association stated that the company was spending large sums of money in order to maintain a system of espionage. One man in each ten was thought to be a spy.* Other similar occurrences have taken place at Homestead. On April 29, 1899, "T. J. Shaffer Lodge, No. 13," was organized there.† When the convention of the Amalgamated Association met in May, it was reported that some of the members of this lodge had been discharged and the men were on strike for the right to organize.‡ It would appear from the fragmentary account given by the president of the Amalgamated Association that the agitation had been started to protest against Sunday work. On September 30, 1899, the lodge disbanded.§ Again in 1901, according to an officer of the Amalgamated Association, a secret organization was formed with a thousand members. The movement was discovered and several hundred men were discharged. In the other Carnegie mills near Pittsburgh there has been more acquiescence in the past than at Homestead. Less determined efforts have been made to re-establish unionism at Braddock

* Journal of Proceedings, 1895, p. 4882.
† Ibid., 1899, p. 5596.   ‡ Ibid., p. 5567.
§ Ibid., 1900, p. 5795. See Appendix III, p. 298.

and Duquesne, but all such movements have been sternly repressed.*

The McKeesport mills of the National Tube Company, and the Dewees Wood plant of the American Sheet and Tin Plate Company, have fought the Amalgamated Association for twenty-five years with the weapons now used by the United States Steel Corporation—lockout and discharge. Repeated efforts have been made to organize both mills, with every attempt finally ending in failure. In 1901 the last effort was made in both plants. When the strike was over the president of the lodge in Wood's mill was refused re-employment, and today it is a matter of common report that he is blacklisted in every mill of the Steel Corporation.

These instances serve to illustrate the attitude of the Corporation toward organization on the part of its employes. The independents are not far behind. It will be remembered that Jones and Laughlin broke with the union in 1897. An employe of this company told me of an attempt in 1906 to hold a meeting to protest against Sunday work, but with no intention of organizing as a trade union. The men who were interested in the matter had engaged a hall. Word was carried to the company. The superintendent called the men together from the departments where the agitators were supposed to be and ordered them, with threats of discharge, to abandon the plan. When the time for the meeting came, a foreman, with several mill policemen, stationed themselves where they could see every man who went into the hall. As a result, no one attempted to go to the meeting.

The steel companies seem to be opposed to any independent activity on the part of the men if it has any connection with their work. A few years ago, a workman told me, a petition was circulated among steel mill workers at the National Tube Works in McKeesport, asking for a change to an eight-hour day, at the same tonnage rate as before, being in effect a request for a shorter working day with a corresponding cut in wages. A large proportion of the employes signed the petition, but it was never presented, for the company let it be known that it did not look upon

* At Duquesne in 1901, 60 men were reported to have been discharged for joining a union. (*Independent*, Sept. 5, 1901, p. 2071. Cf. *Iron Age*, Sept. 5, 1901, p. 37.)

the matter with favor; so the movement was dropped. A Braddock employe told me that either in 1906 or 1907, a similar petition was drawn up by the men employed about the heating furnaces in the Edgar Thomson plant. The men sent it, through their foreman, to the general superintendent of the plant. It was refused, apparently without consideration. No formal reply ever reached the men.

The officials of the steel companies make no secret of their hostility to unionism, and I have been told by two leading employers that they would not tolerate it. Any movement toward organization, they assured me, would mean discharge. That this was no idle boast is evident from the record of all attempts at organization since 1892.

All of the steel companies have effective methods of learning what is going on among the workmen. The Jones and Laughlin Company has some organization that keeps it sufficiently informed as to the likelihood of sedition breaking out, and the United States Steel Corporation has regular secret service departments. Its agents are thought by the men to be scattered through all of the mills of the Corporation, working shoulder to shoulder at the rolls or furnaces with honest workmen, ready to record any "disloyal" utterances or to enter into any movement among their fellows. The workmen feel this espionage. They believe it exists, but they do not know who the traitors are. It may be that the friend of long standing who works at the next furnace is one of them, or, possibly, the next-door neighbor at home; they do not know. Is it any wonder, therefore, that they suspect each other and guard their tongues?

This book is not intended to be condemnatory except as the facts speak for themselves. There may be considerable defense, from the standpoint of shop management, for much that has been pointed out to be socially bad. But no justification of any sort presents itself for this "spy system."

Let us look at it clearly and understandingly. It is detective work of a different stripe from that which would weed out grafting among foremen, or would protect tools and metals from theft. The steel companies have large properties which they must protect. But I assume that neither the officials of the Jones and Laughlin Company nor the directors of the United States Steel

Corporation would bribe a bookkeeper in a competing company to give them its trade secrets. If a representative of organized labor during a recess in a conference with an employer were left alone, on his honor, in the employer's private office, and he took advantage of the opportunity to examine the correspondence lying on the desk, I have no doubt that these same steel company officials would agree with me that such action was despicable. They would be right. That is the other side. What do they think of buying information about their workmen, not intended for them; of sending paid spies into the workmen's committees? Such things are justified in war. Does war exist in western Pennsylvania?

PART IV

THE STEEL WORKERS AND DEMOCRACY

CHAPTER XVII

CITIZENSHIP IN THE MILL TOWNS

THE question next arises—and the answer must determine our judgment of the employers' policies—what does it all mean to the men and the families of the men who work in the mills? What is the effect upon standards and ideals, down deep in the heart of the community life?

Steel making is carried on in a score of mill towns in the Allegheny and Monongahela valleys. In these towns, more clearly than in the greater city of Pittsburgh, the influence both of the labor conditions and of the policies of suppression are to be seen. With the men deprived of collective action through work-organizations, do the older social institutions of church and town afford channels through which democratic action and ideals may find expression and conditions be improved, or are they too benumbed by the influence of the administrative policies we have outlined?

In the industrial district surrounding Pittsburgh a wonderful opportunity exists for organized Christian service. But the churches do not see this opportunity because their point of view is individual, not social. There are in the churches of Allegheny County ministers who are doing heroic service, but there are too many, preaching every Sunday to steel workers' families, who never have stepped inside a steel mill and who do not know a Bessemer converter from a puddling furnace. It is because of this lack of knowledge of some of the real problems of life that the ministers sometimes deliver their heaviest blows against secondary evils while the prime wrongs, the ones that dry up the roots of the community life, may escape their wrath. To make my point clearer, I will refer to one of the biggest problems in the steel mills today—that of Sunday work. There is no doubt of the evil of the practice that makes men toil seven days in the week. Its results are bad physically, intellectually and morally. The ministers have combatted Sunday work, but they have directed their energies more frequently against drug stores, confectionery and fruit stores and amusements, than they have against the United States Steel Corporation with its thousands of employes working the "long turn." They have, it is true, requested the superintendents of the steel mills to eliminate Sunday work as much as possible, but there has been no determined effort to enforce the Sunday closing law against the steel works, as there has been in the other quarters named. This is partly due to the fact that the ministers have not informed themselves properly as to the extent of Sunday work. Some of them are in possession of the essential facts, but many others seem to be in almost complete ignorance.* Another reason is the fact that the steel companies are considered too powerful for successful attack. If this be true, we are in a bad way. If the forces of righteousness in a community dare not attack corporate wrongdoing, but must devote their energies only to the small offender, the time will not be long deferred when the hands of those who would see justice done will be effectually tied.

I speak of this attitude of mind of the leaders of the churches because of the effect of it upon the workers. I would not criticise the churches because they do not prevent Sunday work in the mills. It is quite true that they cannot do that—not in a day. The fact, however, that the ministers do not generally understand the workingman's problem, and do not seek to understand, well enough to sympathize fully with the hardships of their lives, has tended to make the workers lose interest in the church. Even deeper has been the estrangement which has arisen because of the hesitancy of the clergy to speak as boldly against the large offender as against the small.

There is an instinctive feeling among the steel workers that the church is "on the other side." The thought that the church people "do not understand" has led to bitterness. A steel worker during the slack times in the winter of 1908, spoke to me of the

---

* This can scarcely be urged in extenuation since the publication of the findings of the Pittsburgh Survey in *Charities and The Commons* in January–March, 1909, and in the Pittsburgh newspapers.

practice of starting the mills on Sunday evening when it was known that they would be idle again before the end of the week. "And still the good church people," he remarked, "wonder why we don't go to church." Another man told me that the minister of the church of which his wife was a member had urged him to attend more frequently. He replied that he was too tired from his week's work to go to church Sunday morning, and Sunday evening he was back at work again in the mill before church services began. He asked the minister why he didn't "do something to get him a chance to go to church." I must quote the statement of a skilled steel worker who gave utterance to what was expressed to me numbers of times, though not always with the same amount of feeling:

> There are a good many churches in this borough, supported generally by women. The preachers don't have any influence in securing better conditions for the men and they don't try to have. They never visit the mills, and they don't know anything about the conditions the men have to face. They think the men ought to go to church after working twelve hours Saturday night. They could accomplish a lot if they would try to use their influence in the right direction. Let them quit temperance reform until they get better conditions for the men. It is no time to preach to a man when he is hungry. Feed him first, then preach to him: so with the workingman. Get a decent working day with decent conditions for a man, then ask him to stop drinking. Let the preacher find out how the men work; go and see them in the heat and smoke and heavy toil; let them notice the crushed hands, broken arms and amputated limbs and find out what the workingman is up against, and then try to better his condition.

Of course, the hostile attitude toward the church of some of the workingmen is not entirely reasonable, although it is a feeling characteristic of the majority. They are defiant, and they make demands beyond the churches' strength. There are, on the other hand, a good many steel workers who are loyal members of churches, and the church would, I think, have the confidence of all if it would boldly withstand industrial oppression and corporate wrongdoing in the spirit of the Man who violently drove the money changers out of the temple and who denounced to their

225

faces those who laid heavy burdens upon the poor. Then the church could also serve to keep the best spirit alive in the homes in spite of the long working days, and it might help to provide for the social life of the mill men who are now almost entirely barred from the better forms of social observance.

Thus it was that my residence in the mill towns brought it home to me that three institutions organized to promote enjoyment and progress are not, in these communities, exerting their proper influence. As was shown in an earlier chapter, the schedule of hours does not permit the home and the library to fulfill their natural functions. We have now seen how lethargy within and pressure without are tending to nullify or misdirect the influence of the church.

But this does not mean that the workingmen in the mill towns have no opportunity whatever for pleasure or society. It is only the moral and intellectual forces that are insulated. Young men who work in the mills cannot have their spirits utterly dampened by a long working day, and they often take trouble to dress for an evening's entertainment or to meet their friends socially. This does not last long, for youth itself is not long-lived in the steel mills; but whether young or old, men cannot thus easily be deprived of the social instinct. It is essential that they should meet together somehow and somewhere in fellowship and in relaxation from their work. The saloon and the lodge remain as the social centers for the steel workers.*

There are other reasons, to be sure, than the desire to mingle with one's fellows, for the popularity of the saloon; drinking is traditional among iron and steel workers. But there is no doubt that the craving for companionship is one of the strongest reasons for its hold upon a community of workingmen. The nature of mill work is such as to make the saloon habit one of the most natural ones in the world. Practically every man is affected by the heat even if he does not have a "hot job." The whole atmosphere is such as to induce perspiration and enhance thirst. All the workers drink water in great quantities as long as they are in the mill. Sometimes a man drinks too much, so that he leaves

* For description of the fraternal orders see Homestead: The Households of a Mill Town, by Margaret F. Byington.

Photo by Hine

A MILL TOWN SALOON—THE SOCIAL CENTER

Unpaved Street in Foreign Quarter of Mill Town

at the end of a day's work feeling half nauseated. Such a man steps into a saloon for a glass of something to set his stomach right. Or if a man does not overdrink during the day, he is still chronically thirsty, and it is to satisfy a real longing for drink that he stops for his beer. The dust of the mills, too, that the men have been breathing for twelve hours, sends another quota to their beer or whiskey to clear out their throats. Then comes the largest contingent of all, the men wearied with the heat and the work, some almost overcome and dragging their feet. These feel the necessity of a stimulant, and they get it day after day, regardless of the waste of physical and nervous energy involved in keeping themselves keyed up to their work by an artificial aid. I do not think I am far wrong when I say that a large majority of steel workers sincerely believe that the regular use of alcoholic drinks is essential to keep them from breaking down. It is seldom a pleasure-seeking crowd that fills the saloons after the whistle has blown at the end of a turn. The men line up at the bar, each one taking one drink and paying for it himself. The first line of men put down their glasses and leave, and the bar is filled again with a second group. There are very few who take more than one drink on coming from the mill.

There is more conviviality on Saturday nights and after pay days than on an ordinary midweek night. Then is the time the men relax; then the treating is done. The saloon becomes a social center and the men find the fellowship that they crave. It is a following of the line of least resistance that makes the saloon supplant all better forms of social life. A man does not need to change his clothing and get a shave before he is made welcome here. He may come covered with the grime of the mill and not feel out of place. In slack times, when the mills are not running, the saloon becomes a regular meeting place, and men go there primarily for companionship, the drinking becoming secondary. Ordinarily one does not see very much drunkenness. The men want to be fit for work the next day. On the eve of a holiday some will go too far, but these are most likely to be the unskilled workmen. The only men whom I found in a state of intoxication when I looked for them at their homes were blast furnace men—men who had been working for months without a holiday or a Sunday.

227

The men I refer to had had a brief holiday and they spent it in the only way they knew. The better class of steel workers, who view their fellows with a sympathetic eye, explain the holiday intoxication of a certain element in the industry as a logical result of steady work and the long day. After weeks and months of work, twelve hours a day, and no holidays, a man gets far behind in his accumulation of the pleasure that he feels to be his due. When a holiday comes it is all too short to collect the overdue bill; pleasure of a concentrated sort must be sought in order to make up for lost time.

As a result of all these cumulative promptings, the saloons take more of the steel worker's money than do many of the legitimate business interests of the mill towns. During 1907 there were 30 saloons in Duquesne, a mill town of 10,000 or 12,000 population. I was told in 1908, by one who was in a position to know, that the leading saloonkeeper in this borough drew from the bank, regularly, every two weeks, just before pay day, between $200 and $300 to be used as change in anticipation of the bills of large denomination that would be handed over the bar. Braddock, where the Edgar Thomson steel works are located, had in 1907, 65 saloons. Braddock and North Braddock together had a population of about 25,000. I was told that a considerably larger sum was required for change on pay days here than in Duquesne, the average to each saloon being $500, making over $30,000 in all. I cannot vouch for the truth of this statement—it was a report which reached me indirectly and may be only an expression of some one's opinion and not based on facts. But information in regard to the situation in McKeesport in 1906 came to me through such channels that there can be little doubt as to its accuracy. McKeesport had about 40,000 people in 1906, and 69 saloons. On the Thursdays preceding the semi-monthly pay days, which fall on Fridays and Saturdays, the three leading saloon-keepers of the city were accustomed to draw from their bank accounts from $1200 to $1500 each in dollar bills and small denominations, to be used as change. Other saloonkeepers drew varying amounts, and the totals thus drawn each fortnight footed up to $60,000. On the Mondays after pay days the saloonkeepers usually deposited double the amount drawn. These periodic leaps in deposits never failed to coincide with pay days, and the inevitable conclusion is that about $60,000 of the steel workers' wages were regularly expended in the saloons within the two days. If this seems overdrawn, let me cite the case of George Holloway, who was blacklisted in 1901 after leading a strike in the Wood plant of the American Sheet and Tin Plate Company in McKeesport. With what was generally understood to be borrowed funds—for Holloway was left almost penniless by the strike—he started a saloon in McKeesport. I saw and talked with him in the fall of 1907, and he told me that in 1905, four years from the time of entering business, he had sold out. He has established a son in a saloon in the west, and with the rest of his family he is now living in McKeesport on the income of his investments, a retired capitalist.

The liquor situation in an American town bears a very direct relation to the political life. This is true in these boroughs. In earlier chapters we have seen how the steel companies deny the employes the right to organize in unions. In spite of this, the situation is not hopeless so long as the workingman is secure in his possession of the ballot. It is commonly understood that the United States Steel Corporation is the dominant force in politics in the mill towns, except in McKeesport, where authority seems to be divided with the brewing interests.*

Repeatedly I was told that workmen have been discharged at Duquesne for refusing to vote the way the company wished. I was told by one employe that he had been called into the office of his superintendent and remonstrated with for working against the company ticket, and an indirect threat was made of discharge. I was told by men of unimpeachable standing in Braddock, who were not steel works employes, that in the spring of 1908, preceding the May primaries, men were induced to vote for the candidates favored by the Corporation by promises of a resumption in industry if the right men were nominated. But the

---

* In McKeesport, during the strike of 1901, when the threat was made that the Dewees Wood plant would be dismantled on account of the alleged hostility of the people of the town, the mayor issued a statement in which he charged that the property of the Steel Corporation in this city was assessed at 40 per cent of its market value, while the houses of the citizens were assessed at 70 per cent. (*Outlook*, August 17, 1901, p. 889.)

most damaging testimony that I received regarding the interference of the Steel Corporation in politics came from a source
clearly authoritative.

For obvious reasons I cannot give my informant's name.
"A short time before the primaries of May, 1908," he said, "orders
came from the New York office of the United States Steel Corporation, to the general superintendent of the Edgar Thomson plant
at Braddock, directing him to order the department superintendents to line up their employes for the Penrose candidates for the
legislature. The general superintendent called a meeting of the
department superintendents and delivered the orders. This
created considerable dismay, for local option was an issue in the
primaries and the Penrose candidates were opposed to local option.
Some of the superintendents were already prominently identified
with the local option party and had been assisting in organizing
the campaign. How they could with honor or self-respect abandon
the issue at this point was not clear to the officials. But the answer
to the objections was clear and to the point. They were told that
their first duties were to the Corporation. They must, accordingly,
break any or all promises and work for Penrose, because the
United States Steel Corporation needed him in the Senate."

After this information had come to me, I received other
corroborative testimony. I had a talk with a man who had been
prominent in the local option campaign previous to the primaries
of 1908 at Braddock. I wrote down what he said, and after he
had read my manuscript he indorsed every word. His statement
was as follows:

> The most damnable feature of the whole campaign
> was the attitude of the United States Steel Corporation.
> There is not such a perfect political organization in the
> country as the steel trust. They aim to control the politics
> of every borough and town where their works are located,
> and usually they do control. They plan their campaigns
> far in advance; they are laying their wires now to control
> the borough council three years ahead. You ought to see
> the way they line up their men at the polls and vote them by
> thousands. What does a secret ballot amount to? In every
> ward in this borough the steel works employes are in the
> majority. There are two or three foremen in nearly every

ward, and it is up to them to round up the vote. If there are not enough foremen in a ward, they send them over from the next ward to help out. Naturalized foreigners can be handled easily, but so can men of three and four generations of American blood. These men have been so long dominated by the Corporation that they dare not disobey. They have a sort of superstitious feeling that somehow the boss will know if they vote wrong. And the workingmen are not the only ones that can be managed. Before the May primaries we perfected an organization in this borough to fight for local option. Several of the foremen and assistant superintendents in the mills were among our most active workers. Some of them helped in the speaking campaign. One day an order came that the thing must stop. The United States Steel Corporation needs to have Boies Penrose in the Senate, and the political life of Penrose is bound up with the liquor interests of the state. So a blow to liquor is a blow to Penrose, and the steel trust cannot have that. So the superintendents and foremen were ordered to line up their men for Penrose and the saloon. One young man who had been speaking in the campaign refused to stop, and he was called into the office and plainly told that he must either quit local option or quit the mills. That was not unusual though. The bread and butter argument is always used. As a result, the local optionists were badly broken up. The speaking campaign practically stopped and men whom we had counted on and who had been with us, actually turned around and made a show at least of opposing local option. Then the company gave it out that if the Penrose candidates to the legislature were nominated, the mill would be likely to resume operations, and the men who had been idle half or two-thirds of the time since October, clutched at that half promise like drowning men.

It is probably unnecessary to add that Penrose carried Allegheny County.

In the chapter on repression I showed how through policies of seducing and spying, the Steel Corporation kept a strong hand on the men to prevent any collective or outspoken action with respect to the terms of their employment. A negative policy—that of enforcing silence. It is a policy of sitting on the safety-valve. A policy which runs parallel to it is here described. If the first was repression, this other is coercion.

231

CHAPTER XVIII

THE SPIRIT OF THE WORKERS

UNDER common conditions workingmen are apt to develop common feelings with respect to some of the deeper and more fundamental questions of their lives. This is especially true in a crisis or a peculiarly aggravated state of affairs, when minor differences are forgotten and feeling is keen. This was so at Homestead in 1892 when H. C. Frick sent the armed Pinkerton guards to drive the striking workmen off the company premises; it was so in Homestead again in February, 1908, when with the panic at its height and the mills operating on barely one-fourth time, the Carnegie Steel Company cut wages 10 to 30 per cent of men who were not, during those months, earning enough to live on. It has been so at different times in the Monongahela valley in the last decade when men have been discharged and then blacklisted for meeting in a public hall to form an organization.

Since 1892 a common feeling has been slowly making headway. The lengthening of the working day, the choking of democratic institutions, and the coercive sway of the employers have worked out more than a well organized industrial machine. The years from 1892 down are illuminated here and there with flashes of indignation. These have died away and the public has forgotten, but each time the embers have glowed a little redder, a little more surely. Among the many fine workingmen that I grew to know in Pittsburgh was one whose gentleness of breeding and native courtesy would have marked him in any company. I asked him once how far socialism had progressed in the mill towns. His eye suddenly flashed as he answered, "Ninety-nine per cent of the men are socialists, if by that you mean one who hates a capitalist."

The steel worker sees on every side evidences of an irresistible power, baffling and intangible. It fixes the conditions of his employment; it tells him what wages he may expect to receive and where and when he must work. If he protests, he is either ignored or rebuked. If he talks it over with his fellow workmen, he is likely to be discharged. As a steel worker said to me, the same one quoted above, "The galling thing about it all is the necessity of accepting in silence any treatment that the Corporation may see fit to give. We have no right to independent action, and when we are wronged there is no redress."

But I would not leave the impression that the steel workers, taken all together, think alike and act alike. That the overwhelming majority of them, in both Corporation and independent mills, are resentful and bitter toward their employers, no one who has mingled with them enough to catch their spirit can deny. As to everything else, however, there are differences. The presence of many races is enough, in itself, to make one expect to find ideas and hopes of many different kinds. But if we take the English-speaking workers alone, we shall still find little unanimity of thought.

Viewed from the standpoint of their attitude toward their working conditions, there are four classes or groups among the English-speaking workers. This classification will perhaps seem arbitrary and artificial, but it is made only as a help in interpreting their outlook upon the future in its bearing upon this one great problem of their lives. Their views as to religion or art or education may create more or fewer divisions. But with these we are not now concerned.

No great problem, whether social or other, can be worked out with success without enthusiasm and hope. The difficulty of reaching a solution of the labor problem in the steel industry is augmented by a certain element among the workers with whom hope is dead and enthusiasm forgotten. There are a large number of whom this is true. They are the older men, generally, who have hoped, years back, and waited, for a revival of something like democracy in western Pennsylvania. But " Hope deferred maketh the heart sick." The years have done their work, and these men, with spirit dead, face a future in which they expect nothing and ask for nothing. They look dull-eyed on a world from which the brightness is gone. Writers have always loved to make use of striking epithets in describing the power wielded by forceful men who are counted the successful ones of their times. Latterly we have heard much of "merchant princes" and "captains of industry." Kindred to these is the term "iron-master." It is a name to roll over one's tongue, and suggests might and power. But it has a grim significance to those who know the men upon whose toil these strutting "iron-masters" have raised themselves. To them the name does not suggest heroics.

This group of workers who have lost hope, while numerically considerable, is small compared with the whole number of employes. Among the most of the steel workers there exist varying kinds and degrees of hope, but only the second and third groups in my classification can be termed specifically hopeful.

The first of these is the smallest; necessarily so, for it is composed of those who have been financially successful to such an extent as to be measurably independent and correspondingly indifferent to conditions in the industry. Among the highly skilled men, the 2 or 3 per cent who earn $5.00 and over a day, there is a considerable proportion who have invested their savings wisely and who are able in consequence to look forward to retiring to a life of less activity, and to an old age spent in comfort on the income of their investments. I found three or four such men. They were owners of real estate, and derived such a comfortable sum from the rentals of houses and other buildings as to be rather unconcerned about wage reductions. There are other workmen almost equally indifferent to labor conditions; men who have saved a considerable amount from their earnings, but not enough to live on without some additional income. I talked with some who had purchased farms and intended moving onto them, and others who were preparing to do likewise. To these men a wage reduction is an inconvenience in so far as it may defer the day of entrance upon the new field of livelihood. It will be observed that in the attitude of this group there is nothing that gives promise of improvement of the labor conditions. If these men are hopeful they are so as individuals, and their activities are directed toward the solution of an individual, not a social, problem.

The third group in my classification is made up of the socially hopeful. To the comparatively few only is the hope of individual independence open. A majority of the workmen feel

Drawn by Joseph Stella

IN THE GLARE OF THE CONVERTER

GROWN GRAY IN THE SERVICE

that it is only through their efforts and that of the community at large, together launched against the opposing powers, that their industrial freedom is to be won. In spite of the period that has elapsed since there was any form of union activity in the steel mills, there is still a firm belief on the part of a great many that some day the mills will be all unionized. The argument favoring this opinion is logical enough. The situation is growing intolerable, the workmen say; there is a limit to human endurance, and when that point is reached it will have become so patent even to the dullest minds that strength lies only in united effort, that the men will rise as one, organize, and make their demands. These demands, with the strength of the united workers behind them, cannot, they hold, be safely refused.

Not all of the socially hopeful workmen look to trade unionism to secure to them what they consider their rights. As the years have gone by since unionism was overthrown, and each year has seen the control of the employers grow more certain, and nearly absolute, many have turned to politics as the way out. Under such conditions, radicalism finds fertile soil and socialism is making slow but steady headway. Just how far it has gone would be difficult to say. There is a deep unrest among the voters in the mill towns with regard to things political, and in this uneasiness or dissatisfaction there is a marked tendency in the direction of theories commonly called socialistic. This situation has grown not so much from a study of socialist literature, and an intellectual acceptance of the principles involved, as it is a turning away from an adherence to a political organization that has invited the support of the workingmen, yet failed to interest itself in any important legislation for their benefit. Of course, many believe that sometime laws will be enacted by a republican legislature affording more protection to workingmen, though when or why this is to occur they do not explain. Most of the Pittsburgh steel workers vote the republican ticket, because they see no immediate hope of success through a workingmen's party; but they are ready to accept any political theory that promises something worth while to labor. If the workmen in the mills were once convinced that in an approaching election there existed a possibility of the election of the socialist candidates, there would follow what could not adequately be termed a landslide; it would be an avalanche.

I have mentioned three of the groups in my classification. The fourth I approach with some hesitancy, partly because of a lack of data, partly because of a certain tendency on the part of many people to regard as sensational, and hence untruthful, statements of fact that run counter to their own experiences or desires. It must be remembered that I do not set absolute limits to my classification, and when I state that there is a group of workmen in the steel district whose social philosophy involves physical resistance, I make no claims beyond the fact that I found such opinions among the steel workers. How widely they may prevail, I do not know. They do exist, however, and it seemed to me significant that some of the most intelligent and thoughtful workmen should hold the view, as they admitted to me, that the only way out of a situation that is fast growing intolerable is through an appeal to force. This opinion was clearly expressed to me by only a few, a bare half dozen, but many others intimated, without expressing themselves openly, that they held similar views. The few, however, were among the better class of workmen, and the thing that excited my wonder was that even one should mention it to an outsider.

An incident in a conversation that I had with a father and son together impressed me in some ways more than anything else that I encountered during my stay in the Pittsburgh District. It was a family of intelligence and breeding. That it was a profoundly religious family was evident. The father had been telling me about his experience in a long life as a workman, and he discussed the present industrial situation with a face flushed with indignation. The son had sat silently acquiescent in his father's analysis of existing conditions, but following the conversation with close attention. Finally, addressing both, I asked what in their judgment would be the outcome of the unrest and discontent, the reasons for which had just been so strongly set forth. There was silence for a moment, and then the father shook his head sadly and said, "There is no way out. There will be no change." But the son cried out through set teeth, "Yes! there is a way out, and it is through an armed revolution."

In one or another of these four groups it may safely be assumed that most of the English-speaking steel workers belong. The groups may, and probably do, overlap more or less, but I think I am right, in a broad sense, in the classification. I am certain that these are the leading or ruling opinions current today within the limits indicated.

It is not necessary for me to attempt to interpret the minds of the immigrant workmen. That has been done by others in the Pittsburgh Survey far better qualified to speak. It is necessary to refer to them, however, that we may keep freshly in mind the leading aspects of the labor problem in the steel mills. The so-called English-speaking workmen number less than half of the total employed. Fully 60 per cent of the workmen are immigrants, the Slavic races largely preponderating. Most of these are unskilled laborers; few of them are citizens; a majority are unable to speak the English language. The way in which this mass of illiterate, unassimilated foreigners complicates the labor problem in the steel mills has been pointed out in an earlier chapter.

In a sense the immigrants are an unknown factor in the problem. It would seem, as has been pointed out before, that their presence in such large numbers would have a tendency to make more stable the existing conditions in the industry. But a good case also might be made for an opposite thesis. A skilled American-born workman pointed out to me that the foreigners occupy a strategic position, and that a new union movement might naturally start from among them that would be irresistible. The foreigners already have organizations through which they could work, in the fraternal orders that are everywhere to be found among them as auxiliaries to their churches; and so compact are their organizations and so loyal are they to their churches, that a priest might easily give the word that in a short time would tie up the whole industry. While this view fails to take into account the lines of cleavage between Protestant and Catholic, and between the Roman church and the Greek, it is worthy of consideration. The strength of the organizations under the banner of any one of these creeds is enough to be formidable.

In the summer of 1909 there was a demonstration of the spirit of immigrant workmen that opened the eyes of the public

237

to qualities heretofore unknown. For many weeks at McKees Rocks they persisted in their strike against the Pressed Steel Car Company. It had been thought that the Slavs were too sluggish to resist their employers, and unable to organize along industrial lines. It was proved in this conflict that neither theory was correct; and, stranger still, it was demonstrated that American-born and immigrant workmen can and will work side by side for common ends. It is encouraging to note the awakening of social consciousness among the Slav workmen; it is quickening to catch the spirit of their leaders; but it must be remembered, too, that they are as a body ignorant and illiterate. When they become fully awake to their power, they may be an element of strength added to the cause of social justice, or they may be a menace to life and property in their indiscriminate fury.

I have told in these chapters the facts as I found them in the Pittsburgh District. And yet in the face of them all, I know that there are some who will deny the existence of any labor problem, or of any injustice in the institutions of society, that may not be remedied by individual effort. I have heard a minister, a man of rare talents and usefulness, say from his pulpit that there need be no suffering nor discontent among the working people, because in a single Western state, he alleged, there is enough unused land to provide sustenance for them all if they would leave the cities and occupy it. I have been assured by employers that it is impossible for any great injustice to exist in an industry because the workmen can always quit their jobs and find others. If these statements were true, they would represent a poor makeshift for a social program. The best they offer is a way of escape from unwholesome conditions, while the real evil is not attacked. But the statements are misleading at best, and they suggest a theory with reference to the labor problem that is utterly unsound. They fail to note that the labor problem is social, not individual. They assume a mobility on the part of labor that does not and cannot exist; they are ill considered and unfair.

It is not to be assumed that the minister would desire the wheels of industry to be stopped. When, therefore, he advises dissatisfied city workmen to go to the farms, he is instead of offering a suggestion designed to relieve society of a burden, recommending a transfer of the burden from the shoulders of one group to those of another. The movement would be impossible without greatly increased immigration, in order to fill the places of those who have gone to the farms; and if the overhanging industrial evils were not attacked, the new contingent would have to escape to the land after a time. The logical following out of this theory would eventually involve the appropriation of the last vacant farm; what would be the remedy when this enforced stationary condition arrived, it remains for the supporters of the theory to explain.

The suggestion that the right to quit offers anything in the way of refuge from unjust conditions reveals ignorance of the true facts. Young, unmarried men may shift about quite freely without incurring great danger, and many of them do. But married men cannot jeopardize the interests of their families by leaving the known for the unknown. Even skilled men cannot be sure of finding readily other positions in their own trades, and to begin again, as apprentices, to master other trades is of course out of the question. Beginners' wages are not sufficient to support families. Many employers prefer married men because they are more stable, and this is merely another way of saying that married men dare not quit, and so do not make trouble.

To be effective, the right-to-quit theory would have to be accompanied by absolute mobility on the part of labor. For many reasons this cannot exist, and any theory that requires such mobility for its justification is blind. The minister, the banker, the man of affairs, when they take the attitude mentioned, are unconsciously measuring all workmen, from the poorest, most illiterate laborer up, by their own standards, and out of their own experiences. It is nothing to the business man to travel from Boston to St. Louis, and to know the demands of trade over thousands of miles of country; it is easy for the student or the professional man to acquaint himself with localities where opportunity is relatively good. Such men, with their wide outlook on life, their unusual opportunity to know industrial conditions, and their exceptional equipment, find that America is rich in opportunity. They blame the factory or mill hand, bound to twelve daily hours of toil, and without any of the means for discovering the most advantageous industry, because he does not know all that they know. It would be as reasonable for an engineer to scorn a professor of Greek for not knowing how to build a bridge.

This attitude is unfair because it subjects workingmen to tests that their more favored critics are not willing to meet. Home means much to the educated man and to the man of affairs. He will not lightly tear himself loose from the city or the locality where all his closest friends reside and go so far away that they perhaps may never follow, and he may never return. Is it a small thing that the working people also love their homes and the associations of years? The home community often means more to a workman of slender means than it does to those more fortunate, for he knows just who are the trusted friends there who can be counted on in disaster. It cannot be made to sound very impressive to a New York or Pennsylvania workman, that there are good chances on the farms of Iowa or the Dakotas.

Those who defend existing conditions in the steel mills and in other similar industries have another favorite argument. It is the "high wage" theory. A certain foreman in one of the Pittsburgh mills had this theory, and he undertook to become my guide on a tour of the mill, in order that he might demonstrate its truth to me. He showed me a Hungarian laborer sitting on a box with nothing for the moment demanding his attention. This man was idle half the time, I was told, and drew $2.00 a day. We passed an engineer, dozing in the cab of his dinkey engine, and it appeared that he received $3.50 a day for doing that. We came to where a heat of steel was being poured, and men were pointed out to me by my guide, working in the glare of the metal, who were getting $5.00, $6.00 and even $7.00 a day, and some of them were known to be dissatisfied. To my guide it was an evidence of depravity. But I had noticed some things as we wandered about to which he had not directed my attention. Perhaps he was too familiar with the mill to notice them. A stopper had not been set correctly in a ladle, and when they turned a converter down and poured steel into this ladle a roaring flood of it escaped through the tap hole and made a pool on the ground. I looked about for the two-dollar-a-day laborer and was relieved to find that he had escaped to a place

A YOUNG MILL-WORKER: SLAV

Skilled Steel Worker—American Born

of safety. But when I passed that way a half hour later, he was down below the converter working with the mass of steel, now hard, getting a chain about it so that it could be dragged away. I wondered what would happen then if there should be another escape of steel, and how much satisfaction it would be to him in such a case, that he had received $2.00 a day and had sat on a box half the time. About the same time one of the highly paid vesselmen was struck by a tiny drop of molten steel—it was a very small drop, and his wages were good, he ought to have been satisfied—but he caught the drop in his eye and he came with his face distorted with pain to get aid from some one. The little piece of steel was embedded in the membrane of the eyeball, and my foreman friend removed it for him with the point of his pencil, and turned again to go on with his discussion of the high wage theory. The dozing engineer did not come to grief while I was near, but I wondered why he dozed. Was it in the second half of a twenty-four-hour shift, or had he made the mistake of going to the theatre or reading a book the evening before?

There are many intelligent people, with wider experience in life than this zealous foreman, who earnestly contend, and honestly, too, that wages vary not only according to skill required, but according to the comparative degree of danger of different occupations, and that if a workman is sent to a disagreeable or dangerous task his higher wages are a recompense. From both parts of this theory I must dissent. Men are not recompensed according to the degree of risk involved in their trades. The insurance companies themselves are able to measure occupational risks in a steel plant only in the most general way; some do it not at all. At best, they can determine a class risk, not an individual one, and the workman's problem is individual; he cannot measure his personal risk. He would be no better off if he could, because his bargaining power is not equal to that of his employer. Over half of the men killed in work-accidents in Allegheny County in the year studied by the Pittsburgh Survey, were earning less than $15 a week. Moreover, an unskilled man who starts to work in a steel mill begins at the wages of common labor, although he may be put in a dangerous place. But it is the latter part of the theory that is most false and most pernicious,—the idea that high wages can properly be balanced against injustice, and that if wages only be high enough, any sort of labor conditions may be justified.

It was shown in the chapter on Wages and the Cost of Living that steel workers are not highly paid. But even if their earnings were very high, it would be folly to claim that they are compensated for their lack of opportunity to live the lives of normal men who work a normal day and rest at night, or for their lost privileges of free speech, or for their stolen political rights. These are things for which you cannot pay a man.

But here, as in every other phase of the labor problem, the social aspect overshadows the individual. Were a man to consider himself recompensed by high wages for long hours and lack of touch with the world or for extreme danger, society is not thereby recompensed. Men stunted, whether physically or mentally, are a burden to the communities in which they live; and the man or the industry that has placed a barrier before a man's growth is to that extent a social enemy. For the rearing of children, strong in body and mind, with aspirations toward mental and moral growth and with ideals that shall make for honest citizenship, there is need of strong fathers and mothers, healthy in body and mind. There must be time in the home for the development of a sentiment not wholly concerned with bread-winning. That person, or corporation, or set of ideas that stands in the way is a public enemy, and there is none greater.

Enough has been said to make the workmen's point of view clear. No reasonable person will deny that, to speak mildly, unfortunate conditions prevail in the steel mills. These are the result of a growth or evolution through a period of years; and the important thing to be considered now is the direction that this growth is to take in the future. It would seem that if conditions remain as they are at present, or grow worse, some kind of determined and effective opposition must eventually be encountered by the employers.

There are three ways in which the workers may interpose this opposition, the three that have already been mentioned: trade unionism, politics, revolution.

The action of The American Federation of Labor on

November 15, 1909, in its convention at Toronto, referred to in Chapter X, indicates that efforts are making along the line of trade unionism. A beginning has already been made in political activity. There was an attempt in the presidential campaign of 1908 at common action on the part of union labor. The attempt was not very successful; but it may be expected that in the United States, as in England, organized labor will play an increasingly important part in politics. The Pittsburgh steel workers are very nearly ready for a political movement. They are inwardly seething with discontent, and the time is not far distant, if indeed it has not already arrived, when with a leader who understands how to gain their confidence they will flock from the standards of the old parties in a way that will be a severe shock to the machine politician.

The workingmen of Pittsburgh or any other American community could not be roused over night to the point of serious, premeditated, revolutionary violence. Agitation alone, however persistent, could never accomplish it; but if the treatment that the steel companies are now employing toward their workmen be indefinitely prolonged, it will be hard to predict the ultimate action of the workers. Under such circumstances, if there should ever be a violent outbreak of any sort, the Corporation officials will not need to look far for the cause. Revolutions, however, do not necessarily involve violence. And through either the trade union or the political movement or through some other means, there is bound to be a revolution erelong that shall have as its goal the restoration of democracy to the steel workers.

APPENDICES

APPENDIX I

DOCUMENTS RELATING TO THE AMALGAMATION OF THE UNIONS IN THE IRON AND STEEL INDUSTRY

I. THE FIRST MOVE TOWARD AMALGAMATION [1874]

(From the National Labor Tribune, Dec. 26, 1874, p. 1, c. 1.)

LOUISVILLE, KY.—The Rolling Mill Men of Louisville, Kentucky, and New Albany, Indiana, have met together to devise remedies for the present depression. They propose a National Organization to be composed of representatives from all branches and departments of skilled labor in the mills. The object of this organization is to "establish a scale of prices more uniform, that cannot be altered by any man, or set of men, save the men who make them."

The first meeting was held over three weeks ago, which was well attended. The expression was unanimous for united action by all branches of skilled mill labor. The difficulties and drawbacks incident to the successful development of the iron trade, and the many acts of injustice resorted to by the leading men in it were set forth. The second meeting was held two weeks ago, when a committee was appointed to draft preamble and resolutions.

On Monday of last week the third meeting was held in New Albany, when the following address and resolutions were presented and passed:

LOUISVILLE, Dec. 10, 1874.

From the employees of the Louisville and New Albany rolling mills to their brother workmen in the various rolling mills in the United States:

We have been for some time reflecting seriously over the demoralized condition of the iron market and the serious effects of this demoralization on the price of labor. We have made inquiries among ourselves as to the real cause of this state of things, and, after much deliberation on the subject, have come to the conclusion that there are many causes, some of which we will endeavor to explain according to our understanding of the case:

First—The credit system which has been originated by a set of wild and indiscreet speculators, who, by their recklessness, brought on a panic that fell upon us like an earthquake, and those who were not swallowed up and lost were left shattered wrecks upon the surface, and it will require the labor of years to place them again on a sound foundation.

Now some scrutinizing person might ask, in what way does this affect us so long as we get our pay for labor? We answer, in many ways; two of which we will endeavor to explain to the best of our judgment:

First—It has paralyzed every branch of industry, and, second, has depreciated the price of labor, which always was and always will be the result of a suspension of manufactories, and, in fact, all other industrial pursuits.

Second—The want of co-operation, confidence, sympathy, and unanimity among ourselves. In the absence of these essential elements there are and have always been in our midst crime, destitution and want; the committal of crime often occurring for want of a kind, judicious friend to advise with in the hour of adversity. How many thousands of poor, depraved creatures to-day would have been good and useful members of society if they had been connected with some organization of workmen who would assist them in time of need and console them in the hour of despair.

Third—The competition between iron manufacturers has become so great that many unscrupulous iron masters force their iron upon the market at rates which compel them to reduce the price of labor to sustain them, and, in the absence of unity among ourselves, and for want of a consolidated organization of all the skilled labor, the men in many instances submit to the nefarious schemes of their employer, and suffer their pay to be reduced. This results in either a strike or a general reduction, and in either case, proves detrimental to our interest and ruinous to the iron trade.

Again, there are a number of mills which have their own stores, and in many instances of the kind, we are obliged to take our pay in store goods at whatever rates they may think proper to make. Some, also, give depreciated paper, and are thereby enabled to undersell the market, leaving those mills which pay the cash to do one of two things—either to shut up their mills or force their men to a reduction of wages.

Now, as we have given a part of the evils as we understand them, we will endeavor to give the remedy to the best of our ability and judgment.

We would most respectfully suggest the propriety of a consolidation of all the skilled labor of the rolling mills in the United States, and, in order to do this, effect the immediate organization of all the skilled labor not already organized, and appoint delegates to meet in National Convention to establish a scale of prices more uniform, that cannot be altered by any man or set of men, save and except the men who make them. Therefore, be it

Resolved, That it is the sense of this meeting that every mill in the United States respond to the above call. Another meeting was held last Tuesday, at which preparation was made to prepare a pamphlet for distribution over the United States, among all the mills, asking for the co-operation of all interested.

The Boilers have already a powerful organization. The Iron and Steel Workers Association is also a strong organization. Perhaps if we began by getting harmony of action between these two organizations the rest of the work would be comparatively easy.

We are glad to see this revival of interest in organization. It betokens better times. It awakens inquiry and starts men to thinking and acting. Whether the proposed plan is the wisest, in the light of all the experience at our command, is a question for consideration. This is not the time to try experiments. The Boilers have had twenty years experience and have perfected an organization which others can imitate with safety. The Heaters and Rollers might form an alliance with them for offensive and defensive purposes. This point gained, all is gained that mere organization can accomplish.

The other results aimed at can then be reached. Grievances can then be redressed, and abuses can be removed. We desire all movements to be dictated by wisdom in the light of experience, and we will watch the proposed movement with great interest.

II. CIRCULAR OF 1875 TO THE HEATERS AND ROLL HANDS OF THE UNITED STATES

Columbus, Ohio, April 20, 1875.

AMALGAMATION

To the Heaters and Roll Hands of the respective National Unions of the United States:

We, the Executives of the above organizations, have, from past experience, been forced to believe that it is of vital importance to ourselves and trade that the above organizations amalgamate, for the better protection of their interests, they being identical. The events of the past year are conclusive evidence of the necessity for a more thoroughly united effort on the part of all Iron Workers, to put in practice the principles they profess. Every day's experience teaches more fully the advantages of combined organization, and the hopeless condition of labor, unless prompt and decided action be had looking to its future liberty and rights. The feeling and desire of such a step is fast gaining prevalence among the members of both bodies; in fact is almost unanimous, as their correspondence will show.

In order to consummate the above, and at the request of many members of both organizations, we have concluded to submit the following suggestions to every Subordinate Lodge under their jurisdiction, soliciting their deliberate consideration thereon; the result to be sent to the respective Executives.

First. That in view of the depressed condition of the iron trade, also the very limited financial resources of our members, and believing as we do that economy is one of the prime features of good government, we suggest that it is inexpedient for the Heaters and Roll Hands to hold their National Convention this year, thereby saving the enormous amount of money necessary to carry on said conventions.

Second. Seeing that the sentiment of the Heaters and Roll Hands, together with their executives, is almost unanimous in favor of amalgamation, we suggest that there be a committee of three appointed from each organization, in addition to the three already appointed, to draft a code of laws which shall govern us as an amalgamated body.

Third. The time has come. The great mass of iron-workers fully understand and favor amalgamation as the only safe ground in which they can stand, and to hold conventions for no other purpose than to discuss a question which all are prepared to accept, would involve us in an unnecessary expense which, at the lowest estimation, would amount to two thousand five hundred dollars. Under existing circumstances we suggest the advisability of waiving both conventions.

Fourth. We suggest the propriety of the committees being called together as soon as possible, leaving it to the chairman of said committees to decide as to the place of meeting.

Fifth. And that the expenses of each committee be defrayed by their respective Grand Lodges.

249

Do not lay this circular aside or *place it on file*, until you have taken *some action* to secure the representation of your organization.

Yours fraternally,

ADAM W. SCHADA, W. G. S.
RICHARD SULLIVAN, W. V. G. S.
BEN. F. SPANGLER, G. R. S.
DAVID A. PLANT, G. Pres't.
JNO. FITZSIMMONS, V. G. Pres't.
WILLIAM MARTIN, G. Rec. Sec'y.

III. CIRCULAR LETTER OF 1876 TO THE IRON AND STEEL WORKERS OF THE UNITED STATES

Pittsburgh, Pennsylvania, August 21st, 1876.

Fellow Workmen:—

It affords me pleasure to announce the Amalgamation of the three National Organizations representing the Iron and Steel Workers of the United States, viz: The Grand Lodge Associated Brotherhood Iron and Steel Heaters, Rollers and Roughers of the United States, The National Union Iron and Steel Roll Hands of the United States, and the National Forge United Sons of Vulcan of the United States. The new Organization will be known as the Amalgamated Association of Iron and Steel Workers of the United States, a Society which we have reason to know will enable us to protect our interests and meet our wants with greater ease certainty and satisfaction than is possible under separate Organizations.

Our old Societies served as schools of instruction and discipline wherein the frequent contests about wages for years past have taught our membership the great value of compact organization. Our growth has been retarded by the recurrence of strikes and lockouts precipitated upon us by employers who saw a favorable opportunity to divide us, or array one branch of mill labor against the other. Employers have sought to make unionism odious by getting working men divided and causing a loss of mutual confidence. They have done this for two reasons, First, to prevent unity of action, which would enable us to secure the full value of our labor, and, Second, they hoped thereby to establish in our divided condition a standard of wages based upon what the cheapest labor could be hired for.

American working men are excusable for taking a higher and broader view of this question. They believe the duties that devolve upon them call for liberal wages, more moderate hours of labor, and that they should not be required to toil for a mere animal existence. They believe that the pressure for low wages and long hours of toil in our trades arise, in a great measure, from the unjust overreachings of capital which has contrived to make men subservient to machinery, instead of making machinery subservient to the elevation of man.

Our experience has demonstrated that the want of compact organization has invited many of the struggles through which our trades have passed. We have battled with this tendency and weakness in many of our fellow men, and have endeavored to show them the error of their course, and the justness and advantages of unionism. We have struggled for the spread of trades organizations, because it elevated the standard of wages from what grasping capitalists and employers would demand and enforce to a standard made necessary by the duties and requirements demanded of citizens of a republic. Many of our men in not providing for a rainy day, and who are indifferent on the subject of steady employment, have opened the way, in many cases, for a breach in our ranks, which has often caused those demoralizing defeats, which have retarded and discouraged the growth of Trades Unions. These and many other reasons impressed themselves on the minds of the members of our late Unions, until a very general desire arose for an Amalgamation of all branches of skilled mill labor, in order that we could have unity and harmony of action and lessen the possibilities of strikes and lockouts.

Correspondence was opened up between the different Organizations, and the feasibility of Amalgamation was thus established.

I will not recite all the steps which preceded the final Amalgamation. The work done is great, but it still remains with you to say how productive of good it will be to you individually and collectively.

Eternal devotion and watchfulness will be the price of our success. The several Organizations representing the skilled labor of our mills have formed a junction, and are now moving forward, hand in hand, and working for the good of each and all; but will still need the same devotion, courage and sacrifices as before.

To my brother Officers I can freely say: while you require no urging to do your duty, yet a great responsibility rests upon you. Be punctual and prompt in your attendance, just in the discharge of your duties, calm and friendly in all your official relations. Make your Lodge room an interesting place for all, and encourage a full attendance of all the membership.

To our Union men, where no Organization already exists, I say: quietly canvass among yourselves, Heaters, Rollers, Boilers and all qualified persons, and have a Lodge instituted so that you can be in communication and co-operate with the Association. Let me urge this action on you, it is for your own good and you should not delay it.

To the Heaters, Roll Hands and others, who work in places where there has been no separate Organization, I have to say: go into the Lodge room and become one of us in the manner prescribed by our Constitution. The Boilers, in those localities, should take the initiative in this matter and fraternally welcome all eligible persons, and when with us make them feel at home and know that, although only recently associated, we are all old in Unionism.

To those who have always held aloof from our Organizations I have a few kind words. What is good for your fellow workmen in the Union is also good for you. You get the benefit of their Organization and struggles and should help support it by your dues, your counsel, and your intelligence. Your absence is only a constant temptation to your employer to attack us. Let me earnestly urge on you to consider this matter and put yourself right before your fellow workmen and right before yourself. Membership in our Association has been, is now, and always will be an honor. Non-membership will soon become a badge of unfitness for membership.

The honest brave men who have toiled a long life through for Trades Unionism and justice will not be discouraged by any apathy, or any opposition. They mean to make labor a power. We seek to establish no unjust or arbitrary rule, to impose no arbitrary determinations, to exact no concessions not demanded by justice. We seek no conflicts, but will avoid them when possible. We seek to gather and hold power enough to make ourselves respected by our employers and the community at large.

We believe that labor is noble and holy, and we shall defend it and ourselves from degradation, and divest it of evils to body, mind, and estate, which ignorance and greed have imposed. In using this power of organized effort we but emulate the example of capital. We mean no antagonism with capital. We hope to lessen the long tedious hours of mill labor, and ultimately secure to each laborer the full reward of his toil. To this end *Compact Organization is imperative.* Fellow workmen, energy is needed. I appeal to each of you to give this subject your constant attention. Be true to your principles of right and justice, manifest a self-sacrificing spirit for our cause, and stand firmly by your fellow men in all coming struggles.

Let intelligence light our pathway, and zeal carry us over the difficulties that may await us. Our Organization *must* be made a success. The responsibility rests upon all. Let us each resolve to act well our part. Personal and continued zeal and effort is needed and nothing else will do.

The opportunity is now presented to the Iron and Steel Workers of the United States to place themselves above the danger of defeat, disorganization and oppression. The watchword has been spoken. Every man is a link in the chain that binds us together. Let us feel the responsibility that rests upon us and emulate each other in fraternal unity. By such fraternity the true harmony—the harmony of labor and capital that grows out of equality and mutual respect and dependence will spring into life and power. Let our standard never fall, our courage never falter, until we reach that fast approaching time.

Brothers, give us your undivided support. Let us join hands and move forward.

Fraternally submitted,

Jos. Bishop, *President*

103 Fifteenth Street, South Side, Pittsburgh, Pa.

APPENDIX II

THE AMALGAMATED ASSOCIATION

I. Development of Rules and Machinery

The first Constitution of the Association was adopted in 1876, at the first convention. There was some discussion over a clause in the first section which included helpers among those eligible to membership. The Sons of Vulcan had not admitted helpers to their organization, and they were somewhat opposed to doing so in the new union. The other unions that came into the amalgamated body included helpers among their numbers, so after some debate, the section was adopted. The list of those eligible to membership has been expanded from time to time, but it has always been exclusive. Since 1889 no one has been specifically barred excepting common laborers, and these may be admitted by the subordinate lodges. In practice, however, common laborers are very seldom admitted.

The second section of the first article of the constitution, which stated the purpose of the association, elicited much discussion in the convention of 1876. The section, as reported by the committee, declared it to be the purpose of the association to obtain certain rights by means of "arbitration or conciliation, or by other means. . . . that are fair and legal." Controversy arose over the word "arbitration," and it was voted to drop it, leaving "conciliation" as the means of settling disputes. By conciliation was meant the meeting with employers in conference and the open and fair discussion of differences. This was the method that the Sons of Vulcan had been employing from the beginning with excellent results and it is still employed without material change. Within the last few years, however, an arbitration feature has been adopted which adds greatly to the merit of the system.

The most important matter which comes up for discussion each year is the wage question. The scale runs for a year, the scale-year ending July 1. If changes are desired, notice must be sent to the secretary of the national lodge before the third Tuesday in March. The secretary has all proposed changes compiled and printed, and a copy is sent to every subordinate lodge, so that the delegates whom the lodge sends to the convention may be duly instructed. From the delegates chosen by the various lodges, the president of the association appoints a wage committee of about twenty-five, endeavoring to make it fairly representative of the various trades. This committee meets a few days before the opening of the convention, in the city where the convention itself is to be held, and it formulates a scale to be presented to the manufacturers for signature. Formulating a scale means much more than deciding on the wages that are to be asked for the ensuing year. The scale book includes, besides the wage scales themselves, a long list of footnotes which deal with the conditions of employment, the length of working day, the number of pounds of iron to be put into the furnace at one time, the settlement of disputes, the amount of work to be done in a day and a countless number of other regulations of great importance to the workmen. There are usually a good many suggestions regarding alterations of footnotes, and as the committee has to pass on all of these its task is no easy one. When the convention meets—and to the end that there may be ample time for discussion and negotiation it meets early in May—the committee is ready with its report; the whole scale with the footnotes is considered point by point; each proposal is of course subject to amendment or rejection, and new proposals may be substituted. Having passed the convention, the scale is ready for the consideration of the manufacturers. Previous to 1909 for a considerable number of years conferences had been held with the Western Bar Iron Association, with the Republic Iron and Steel Company, with the American Sheet and Tin Plate Company and with independent sheet and tin manufacturers. Since 1909 there have been no conferences with the American Sheet and Tin Plate Company.

The Bar Iron Association is composed of certain independent manufacturers of the West. The Republic Iron and Steel Company is a corporation embracing a large number of formerly independent iron and steel plants. The scale accepted by these two organizations is the scale under which wages are paid in all union mills for the next year. The conference committee has full power to modify the scale approved by the convention. The manufacturers of course come into the conference with a scale that they are willing to sign; and the outcome is usually a compromise between the two scales.

In recent years the Amalgamated Association and the employers have adopted a so-called "continuous operation" arrangement. In former years it used to be understood that if on the first day of July no scale had been signed the men would cease work until an agreement should be reached. Under the continuous operation agreement the men go on working under the old scale. Provision is also made for arbitration. If the manufacturers' and workingmen's committees fail to reach an agreement within ten days after the scale year ends, a "board of conciliation" is formed. The manufacturers and the Amalgamated Association severally select single representatives, and from a list mutually agreed upon these two representatives choose a third. This board of three decides all points in controversy. Neither side is obliged to accept the findings of the board, but objection to the findings cannot be made with very good grace, and none has ever been made. This agreement has been in force since 1902; but the Republic Iron and Steel Company withdrew from it in 1908, and there are indications that the plan may be abandoned.

It should be noted further, that a sliding scale of wage payments is maintained, so that wages fluctuate with the price of bar iron. The system was worked out by Miles Humphreys and the Sons of Vulcan over forty years ago, and the changes since introduced are not material.

THE AMALGAMATED ASSOCIATION

For a number of years, in the later seventies and early eighties, the Amalgamated Association threshed out the wage question with the Pittsburgh manufacturers, and the settlement reached in these negotiations was accepted by the manufacturers of the Ohio Valley and the West. A higher rate, however, was paid in the West. In Cincinnati, Cleveland and Chicago the wages paid for puddling were a dollar a ton higher than in Pittsburgh. Apparently the main reason for the difference was that skilled men were scarce in the West and a higher wage had to be paid in order to attract them.

In the earlier history of the Amalgamated Association, when there was no manufacturers' association, the scale was taken to the leading iron manufacturers in turn. If Jones and Laughlin, Moorehead, McCleane and Company, and a few others signed the scale, the rest began to fall into line.* Later, an association of Pittsburgh manufacturers was formed for the purpose of conferring on the scale, and this association came in time to include manufacturers outside of Pittsburgh. None of the manufacturers' associations, however, have been long-lived; each, as a rule, has come into existence for the purpose of holding conferences, and has ceased to exist after the conferences have been held. This is a rule, however, to which the Western Bar Iron Association appears to be an exception.

In the Amalgamated Association, the revenue of the national lodge comes from fees for organizing new lodges and from membership dues. Every member, regardless of wages, pays $1.00 per quarter to the national lodge, and there are monthly dues which vary in proportion to wages received. Members earning not more than $2.50 per day pay 60 cents per month; those earning more than $2.50 and less than $5.00 pay 80 cents per month; and those earning more than $5.00 pay $1.00 per month. With a membership of 10,000 these dues provide a considerable revenue. In 1907 the receipts amounted to over $135,000. This has been the method of raising funds since 1905. In the earlier years of the association no attempt was made at grading dues; there were uniform membership fees for all regardless of the amount of daily wages.

In 1903 a death-benefit fund was established by appropriating to that purpose ten per cent of the money then in the treasury. In order to maintain the fund, each lodge was required to pay an assessment of twenty cents per quarter for each member. On the death of a member in good standing $100 was paid to his heirs. A member in good standing was interpreted to mean one whose obligations to his lodge and to the national lodge had been discharged and who had been a member at least three months preceding his death. At the convention of 1908 the insurance system was put on a new basis and its scope was widened. It now provides for sickness, accident and disability benefits, besides the death benefit, and it grades the death benefits from $100 to $500 according to length of period of membership.

* It is interesting to note that Carnegie Brothers and Company were always among the first to sign the scale. From the birth of the Amalgamated Association in 1876 until 1889 there was no serious difficulty between the Carnegie Company and its employes. Then, inside of three years, the Carnegie Company was twice involved in labor troubles which for bitterness exceeded anything the iron and steel industry had ever known; and when the second contest was over, the Amalgamated Association was shorn of its strength.

The executive organization of the association has been changed from time to time as the organization has grown or as policies have changed. In 1876 the association elected a president who was also to act as secretary, a vice-president for each of the eight districts, a treasurer and three trustees. To the president was voted a salary of $1500 per year; for the other officers no salaries were provided. After a few years the president found that he could not attend to the business of the association without help, and he appointed a secretary. The convention ratified his choice and voted a salary to the secretary, and after 1880 the position was made elective. As the organization grew in strength and importance, the other officers, excepting the trustees, were also put on salary. This was done for two reasons: that the officers might devote all of their time to the service of the association and that they might be independent of their jobs in the mills. The duties of the various officers have been practically unchanged from the beginning. The president, in addition to his ordinary executive duties, is interpreter of the constitution, and on questions of interpretation his decisions are final. He is also an organizer and is expected to spend much of his time in the field.

The duties of the vice-presidents are similar: they are expected to promote the interests of the association within their special fields, and they frequently act as mediators. The whole territory covered by the iron and steel industries was divided at first into eight districts, later into ten; and until 1905 there was a vice-president for each district. In 1905 the system was changed: vice-presidents were elected not for districts but for divisions corresponding to the different branches of mill work, and there were created the boiling, finishing, sheet and tin divisions, with a vice-president at the head of each division, while one division only remained territorial—the Eastern. In 1908 the number of divisions was reduced to two, the boiling and finishing division and the sheet and tin division.

The only national officers not provided for in the original constitution are the editor of the official *Amalgamated Journal*, an assistant secretary and an insur" ance secretary. At the present time the officers and their annual salaries are as follows: president, $2160; secretary-treasurer, $1800; assistant secretary, $1440; two vice-presidents, $1440 each; insurance secretary, $1200.

The subordinate lodges have the usual executive officers, but the most important organ of the lodge is the mill committee, which is composed of three members on each "turn" or shift. The mill committee represents the men, and it is through the mill committee that the employer communicates with the lodge. All controversies are adjusted, if possible, by conference between the mill committee and the employer. It is the duty of the mill committee to guard the interests of the association and to enforce its rules.

If a member has a grievance he reports it to the mill committee; the matter is investigated, and an attempt is made to effect a settlement. If no settlement is attained, a meeting of the lodge is called; and if the matter is considered of sufficient importance it is reported to the vice-president of the division, and no action is taken until the vice-president has had time to investigate. If the vice-president is unable to settle the difficulty and the matter is serious enough, he calls together the executive committee to decide whether or not a strike shall be authorized. The executive committee consists of the president of the national lodge, the vice-president of the division who acts as chairman, the deputies to the vice-president and the president and two members of the lodge primarily concerned. If the executive committee decides to authorize a strike the men may cease work. Authority to terminate a strike is lodged in the same committee. After an authorized strike has been in operation for two weeks, the members on strike are entitled to $4.00 per week from the protective fund of the national lodge, provided there is $10,000 or over in the treasury. The payments continue for thirteen weeks; after that they cease unless ordered continued by the president. In order to provide funds for a strike the national secretary-treasurer has the right to levy a tax upon the members under a graduated percentage system, dependent upon the number of men on strike and upon the daily wage of the taxable members.

II. Make-up of Amalgamated Association, as Shown by Changes in Article I of its Constitution

Section 1: [Adopted 1876.] This Association shall be known as the National Amalgamated Association of Iron and Steel Workers of the United States, consisting of Puddlers, Boilers, Heaters, Roll Hands, Nailers, Helpers and Shinglers.

The convention of 1879 added to the list "Nail Feeders, Hammermen, Knobblers, Roll Turners, Tin Men, Picklers, Annealers, Washmen, Assorters, Hot and Cold Straighteners, Wire Drawers, Tackers, Shearmen working by the ton, Furnace Builders, Blacksmiths, Machinists and Engineers directly connected with Iron, Steel or Tin Works."

Section 1: [Adopted 1882.] This Association shall be known as the National Amalgamated Association of Iron and Steel Workers of the United States, consisting of Puddlers, Boilers, Heaters and their Helpers; Roll Hands except Drag Outs on Muck Mills; Nailers, Spike Makers; Nail and Spike Feeders, Hammermen, Shinglers and Knobblers, Refiners, Roll Turners; also Picklers, Annealers, Washmen, Assorters and Tin Men in Tin Mills; Hot and Cold Straighteners and their Helpers; Gaggers and Drillers working by the ton; Chargers, Pull-Outs; Hot Bed Men and Clippers in Rail Mills; Wire Drawers, Tackers, Spring Makers, Spring Fitters, Axle Turners, Water Tenders, Rivet Men, Axle Makers, their Heaters and Helpers; Heaters and Welders in Pipe Mills; Gas Makers in Crucible Steel and Iron Works, after they have been working at the business one year; Shearmen in Bar, Plate, Sheet and Nail Mills; Engineers and Blacksmiths directly connected with Iron, Steel or Tin Works, also Stockers, Chargers, Cupola Tenders, Speigel Melters, Runnermen, Vesselmen, Bottom Makers, Ladlemen, Pitmen, Cindermen, Stagemen and Blowers working by the ton and Pipe Fitters connected with Bessemer Steel Works. Also Keepers and their Helpers, Bottom Fillers, Top Fillers, Engineers, Iron Men, Cindermen and Water Tenders at Blast Furnaces directly connected with Bessemer Steel Mills.

It will be observed that the list is still exclusive. The men of highest skill directly concerned in working iron or steel were first admitted, then a wider circle were made eligible, but skill was the test of eligibility. Lines were intentionally drawn barring out the men of lesser skill and the laborers. For example, drag outs on muck mills are particularly named as not being eligible to membership, heaters and welders in pipe mills were to be admitted but the dozen or more men besides in each furnace crew were not considered. Engineers, blacksmiths and a few of the blast furnace men occupying the better positions were to be admitted if they were connected with iron, steel or tin works. Keepers and engineers employed at isolated furnaces would be ineligible. In 1889 the list of those who might become members of the Amalgamated Association was made to include "all men working in and around Rolling Mills, Steel works, Nail, Tack, Spike, Bolt, and Nut Factories, Pipe Mills and all works run in connection with the same, except laborers, the latter to be admitted at the discretion of the Subordinate Lodge to which application is made for membership."

III. Constitution and General Laws of the Amalgamated Association of Iron, Steel and Tin Workers of North America

(Instituted August 4, 1876. Affiliated with the American Federation of Labor, December 13, 1887. Adopted as amended by National Convention at Detroit, Mich., May, 1909, and will remain in force until August 1, 1910.)

PREAMBLE

"Labor has no protection—the weak are devoured by the strong. All wealth and all power center in the hands of a few, and the many are their victims and their bondmen."

So says an able writer in a treatise on association, and in studying the history of the past the impartial thinker must be impressed with the truth of the above quotation. In all countries, and at all times, capital has been used by some possessing it to monopolize particular branches of business until the vast and various industrial pursuits of the world are centralizing under the immediate control of a comparatively small portion of mankind. Although an unequal distribution of the world's wealth, it is, perhaps, necessary that it should be so.

To attain the highest degree of success in any undertaking, it is necessary to have the most perfect and systematic arrangement possible; to acquire such a system it requires the management of a business to be placed as near as possible under the control of one mind; thus the concentration of wealth and business tact conduces to the most perfect working of the vast business machinery of the world. And there is perhaps no other organization or society so well calculated to benefit the laborer and advance the moral and social conditions of the mechanic of the country, if those possessed of wealth were all actuated by those pure and philanthropic principles so necessary to the happiness of all. But, alas, for the poor of humanty, such is not the case. "Wealth is power," and practical experience teaches us that it is a power too often used to depress and degrade the daily laborer.

Year after year the capital of the country becomes more and more concentrated in the hands of the few; and, in proportion, as the wealth of the country becomes centralized, its power increases and the laboring classes are more *impoverished*. It, therefore, behooves us as men who have to battle with the stern realities of life, to look this matter fair in the face. There is no *dodging* the question. Let every man give it a fair, full and candid consideration, and then act according to his honest convictions. What position are we, the iron, steel and tin workers of America, to hold in society? Are we to receive an equivalent for our labor sufficient to maintain us in comparative independence and respectability, to procure the means with which to educate our children and qualify them to play their part in the world's drama?

"In union there is strength," and in the formation of a National Amalgamated Association, embracing every iron, steel and tin worker in the country, a union founded upon a basis broad as the land in which we live, lies our only hope. Single handed we can accomplish nothing, but united there is no power of wrong that we may not openly defy.

Let the iron, steel and tin workers of such places as have not already moved in this matter organize as quickly as possible, and connect themselves with the National Association. Do not be humbugged with the idea that this thing cannot succeed. We are not theorists, this is no visionary plan, but one eminently practicable. Nor can injustice be done to anyone. No undue advantage should be taken of our employers. There is not, there cannot be, any good reason why they should not pay us a fair price for our labor, and there is no good reason why we should not receive a fair equivalent therefor.

To rescue our trades from the condition into which they have fallen, and raise ourselves to that condition in society to which we, as mechanics, are justly entitled; to place ourselves on a foundation sufficiently strong to secure us from encroachments; to elevate the moral, social and intellectual condition of every iron, steel and tin worker in the country, is the aim of our National Association. And to the consummation of so desirable an object, we, the delegates in the Convention assembled, do pledge ourselves to unceasing efforts.

CONSTITUTION AND GENERAL LAWS

ARTICLE I

NAME AND OBJECT

Section 1. This association shall be known as the AMALGAMATED ASSOCIATION OF IRON, STEEL AND TIN WORKERS OF NORTH AMERICA, and shall be composed of all men working in and around rolling mills, tin mills, steel works, chain works, nail, tack, spike, bolt and nut factories, pipe mills, and all works run in connection with the same, except laborers, the latter to be admitted at the discretion of the subordinate lodge to which application is made for membership. Any person employed at any job controlled by this association shall be eligible to membership whether he be a stockholder or director.

Sec. 2. The object of this association shall be the elevation of the position of its members; the maintenance of the best interests of the association; and to obtain by conciliation, or by other means just and legal, a fair remuneration to members for their labor; and to afford mutual protection to members against broken contracts, obnoxious rules, unlawful discharge, or other system of injustice or oppression.

ARTICLE II

JURISDICTION AND GENERAL OFFICE

Section 1. This association shall have supreme jurisdiction where there are at present, or may be hereafter subordinate lodges located, and shall be the highest authority of the order within its jurisdiction, and without the sanction no lodge can exist, or any scale of prices be recognized in any mill except the regular adopted scale of wages of this association.

Sec. 2. The general office of the association shall be located in the city of Pittsburgh, Pa., and it shall be required that the President and Secretary-Treasurer of the National Lodge shall reside in the city where the general office is located.

ARTICLE III

NATIONAL LODGE ELECTIVE OFFICERS AND THEIR DUTIES

Section 1. The elective officers of the National Association shall be a President, who shall also be Organizer; a Secretary-Treasurer, an Assistant Secretary, Managing Editor of *Amalgamated Journal,* two Vice Presidents, one for the Boiling and Finishing Divisions and one for Sheet and Tin Divisions, and three Trustees, who shall hold office until their successors are elected or appointed.

Sec. 2. The President shall be elected from among the delegates at convention, or those who have been delegates at any previous convention, or who ever held office in the National Association previous to the adoption of this article, and shall be an active member in good standing. The President shall instruct all new members in the workings of the association, and superintend the workings of the order throughout its jurisdiction. He shall sign all official documents whenever satisfied of their correctness and authenticity, and appoint Vice Presidents temporarily from among the deputies, or Trustees of the National Lodge, where vacancies occur. He shall have power to visit any sub-lodge and inspect their proceedings, either personally or by deputy, and require a compliance with the laws, rules and usages of this association, and if any sub-lodge shall refuse or neglect to place any of their books, documents or any information in their possession in the hands of the President or his deputy, whenever required by either of them, for any information or investigation he may deem necessary, the President may fine or suspend the sub-lodge immediately and report his action to the Secretary-Treasurer of the National Lodge, who in turn shall report the same to the Vice President of the division or the district in which the lodge is located, and to all sub-lodges in the association as soon as possible. He shall submit to the Secretary-Treasurer at the end of each month an itemized account of all moneys, traveling and incidental, expended by him in the interest of the association, and at the end of his term of office he shall report his acts and doings to the National Convention. He shall preside over all national and special conventions, over all national and special conferences, and enforce the laws thereof. He shall have the casting vote when equally divided on any question, but shall not vote at other times except at the election of officers. He shall appoint officers *pro tem.*; he shall, when called away to attend to any duties pertaining to the affairs of the association, notify the Secretary-Treasurer of its object, his destination, and where he could be reached by telegram or other communication from the National office, a record of which shall be kept, and in case the National President is absent from his office and his whereabouts not known for one week to the National office force, they shall at once notify the First Vice President to take possession of the office and provide for an election according to our laws. He shall make out and announce the following committees:

On Western Scale of Wages, consisting of twenty-eight (to be selected with a view of having the various classes of trades represented thereon according to their approximate number in the association), together with the President and Secretary-Treasurer of the National Lodge; on Steel Workers' Wage Scale whose report shall have precedence over all others; on Appropriations; on Report of the President and other Officers; on Ways and Means; on Auditing; on Secret Work; on Grievances; on Claims; on Appeals; on Constitution and General Laws; on General Good of Order; on Mileage; on Death Benefit Fund.

He shall be required to devote all his time to the interests of this association; he shall give a bond of five thousand dollars ($5,000) for the faithful performance of his duties, and for his services shall receive such sum as the National Convention shall determine.

Sec. 3. In the event of any body of manufacturers desiring to meet representatives of our association any time after December of any scale year to discuss and arrange scale or scales for the following scale year, the President shall select a committee to hold such conference; but in no event shall said scale or scales be signed until a minute report shall be sent to all sub-lodges strictly interested in said scale or scales, and that they be approved by the succeeding National Convention, and such scale or scales shall always commence on July succeeding and end on the 30th day of June following date of commencement.

Sec. 4.   After the scale has been signed by the manufacturers and the Amalgamated Association, under no consideration shall any board of officials or any official of the Amalgamated Association be allowed to grant manufacturers any deviations from scale as signed for the scale year, and no special expanded conference shall have power to change the base of scales of any craft without the consent of the majority of all members of lodges belonging to said craft.

Sec. 5.   The Secretary-Treasurer shall be elected from among the delegates at convention or those who have been delegates at any previous convention, or who ever held office in the National Association previous to the adoption of this article, and he shall take charge of all books, papers and effects of the general office. He shall furnish all elective officers with the necessary letter heads and stationery. He shall convene and act as Secretary of the National Convention, keep all documents, papers, accounts, letters received, and copies of all important letters sent by him on business of this association, in such a manner and place, and for such purpose as the National Convention shall direct. He shall collect and receive all moneys due the National Association, and shall send to each sub-lodge a statement of their financial standing with the National Lodge, together with the credentials at least two weeks before Convention convenes. He shall draw warrants for money paid out by him, which shall be signed by the President. He shall deposit all moneys belonging to this association in bank in his name as Secretary-Treasurer of the Amalgamated Association of Iron, Steel and Tin Workers, and before any money thus deposited can be drawn, each check must be signed by him as Secretary-Treasurer, and countersigned by the President and resident Trustee of the National Lodge. He shall submit to the National Association a complete statement of all receipts and disbursements during the term of office. He shall prepare a quarterly report of the financial transactions connected with the National Association, and furnish each sub-lodge with a copy of the same. He shall register the names of members who have received strike or victimized benefits, and the amount each member has received. He shall close all accounts of the National Association on the 31st day of March in each year, and all moneys received or disbursed after said date shall not be reported in the general balance account at the next National Convention. He shall, after the adjournment of each National Convention, prepare a report of the proceedings of the Convention with a general account of all moneys received and disbursed, a copy of which shall be furnished gratis to each subordinate lodge in good standing. He shall give a bond of twenty-five thousand dollars ($25,000) for the faithful performance of his duties, and for his services shall receive such sum as the National Convention shall determine.

Sec. 6.   Upon the death, resignation or removal of the President of the National Lodge, the First Division Vice President shall immediately assume the duties of the President and notify the other Vice President, who shall meet, and in conjunction with the National Lodge officers, shall elect a successor for the unexpired term.

Sec. 7.   Upon the death, resignation or removal of the Secretary-Treasurer of the National Lodge, the President thereof shall immediately take charge of the books, papers and effects of the general office, and notify the Divisional Vice Presidents, who shall meet, and, in conjunction with the National Lodge officers, shall elect a successor for the unexpired term.

Sec. 8.   Two Vice Presidents shall be elected by regularly elected delegates to Annual Convention, one to represent the Boiling and Finishing Divisions and one to represent the Sheet and Tin Divisions, said candidates shall be fully qualified to fill the position to the satisfaction of the delegates, and shall at time of election be a member in good standing and holding some job in the craft he aspires to represent, unless he be present incumbent.

They shall devote all their time to the interests of the association in organizing new, and building up depleted lodges of their division, and shall settle all disputes and render decisions, as is the present custom. They shall keep a daily record of their proceedings and expenses, and send a correct report weekly to the National Lodge. Their expenses shall appear in quarterly statement, and copies of any and all decisions be sent to District Deputy and lodges of his division, and each Vice President shall read an annual report of his official acts to the Annual Convention.

At any time the National Executive Board shall have positive evidence of any Vice President's incompetency to fill the position to the best advantage of the association, the National Executive Board shall have the power to dispose of him, according to Article XIV of the Constitution, and the National President shall appoint some deputy from that division until a successor shall have been elected by the General Executive Committee.

Vice Presidents shall receive $1,440 yearly, plus railroad and hotel bills.

DEPUTIES

Sec. 9. Each Vice President shall appoint one deputy to each of the present districts from his division, said deputy shall be a member in good standing, and holding a job in some mill in district as designated in his division, he shall act in conjunction with Vice President in settling all disputes, and rendering of decisions, in absence of Vice President. Sections 2, 3 and 4 of Article XXXIV of Constitution shall have first been followed.

In case of sub-lodge having trouble, said deputies shall, at any time the Vice President, in conjunction with the National Executive Board, deems advisable to advance the interests of the association, devote such time as the Vice President, in conjunction with the Executive Board, thinks best, in the capacity of Organizer. Said deputy shall at time of appointment be a member in good standing and holding some job (designated in his division) in some mill in the district for which they shall be appointed, they shall be competent to fill the position, and should the Vice President, in conjunction with the National Executive Board, see that any of the deputies are incompetent or through dereliction and conduct bring reproach upon the association, they shall be discharged and said vacancy shall be filled by appointment as in first instance.

At any time deputies are filling the position of Organizer they shall keep a correct record of their proceedings and forward same weekly to Vice President of their respective divisions, who shall include same in his report and shall while on duty receive time lost plus railroad and hotel expenses.

Sec. 10. It shall be the duty of the Board of Trustees to receive and to hold the required bonds of the President, Secretary-Treasurer and Assistant Secretary, which shall be five thousand dollars ($5,000) for the President; twenty-five thousand dollars ($25,000) for the Secretary-Treasurer, and two thousand five hundred dollars ($2,500) for the Assistant Secretary. They shall also, in conjunction with the President and Secretary-Treasurer, audit all accounts of the National Lodge every three months, which settlement shall be final for each quarter. A copy of each settlement shall be sent to each sub-lodge by the Secretary-Treasurer of the National Lodge, in which shall appear the individual expenses of the National Lodge Officers, including the deputies and members of the Executive and Conference Committees of the several districts, and these settlements shall be referred to the Committee on Auditing at each National Convention. For the faithful performance of their duties the Trustees shall give a bond of five thousand dollars ($5,000) each, which shall be deposited with the President.

Sec. 11. The National President, Secretary-Treasurer, Assistant Secretary, Managing Editor, Divisional Vice Presidents and Resident Trustee shall constitute an Executive Board, who shall have jurisdiction over all matters and subjects not clearly defined by law.

Sec. 12. The National Lodge Officers, Deputies, Executive and Conference Committees shall, at the end of each quarter, present to the Secretary-Treasurer of the National Lodge an itemized report of their average lost time in the mill and all traveling and other necessary expenses incurred by them in the discharge of their duties, and two dollars and fifty cents ($2.50) per day, when the mill is not working, will be allowed for service, which shall be paid by the National Association. (See Section 9 of this Article.)

Sec. 13. The term of office for the President, Secretary-Treasurer, Assistant Secretary, Managing Editor and Trustees of the National Lodge, also the Vice Presidents of the several divisions shall not expire until the first day of October, after a successor to either of them has been elected or appointed, and the salaries of the President, Secretary-Treasurer and other officers shall remain as decided upon by each Annual Convention, and continue in force for one year, commencing October 1, following each annual session.

Sec. 14. The association shall adopt an official button, the design to be the same as the National Lodge seal, of enamel of different colors and gold finish. They shall have it patented or copyrighted, or both, and same shall be the property of the Amalgamated Association, and no others shall be allowed to sell said buttons.

Sec. 15. At each convention a full quota of delegates of the A. F. of L. Convention shall be elected from the floor of the Convention.

ARTICLE IV

FORMATION OF SUB-LODGES AND REPRESENTATIVES

Section 1. Any sub-lodge composed of at least ten practical workmen, as provided in Section 1, Article I, who are of good character and who are eligible to membership in this association, shall, after obtaining the approval of the Vice President of the district or division and also of the National President, be entitled to a charter of the same upon payment of $25.00, and two dollars per member, which is to go to Benefit Fund. Each member shall sign the Constitution and comply with all the rules therein contained.

Sec. 2. After receiving said charter (which must not be named after any living person) they shall also be entitled to a representation in the National Convention as follows: A sub-lodge with less than one hundred members shall be entitled to one representative; a sub-lodge with one hundred and twenty-five members shall be entitled to two representatives, and one representative for each additional hundred, and each lodge must send one delegate, and may send its full quota of representatives if it so desires.

Sec. 3. Each representative to the National Convention shall be entitled to one vote, but cannot vote unless present at the meeting when the vote is taken.

Sec. 4. One of the representatives shall make out and forward the quarterly report of the lodge which he represents to the Secretary-Treasurer of the National Lodge, together with all assessments levied by the President of the National Lodge, on or before the thirtieth day of September, the thirty-first of December, thirty-first of March, and the thirtieth of June next succeeding the session of the National Convention in which they have last served, and in case neither of the representatives nor the lodge forward their quarterly report for June thirtieth, September thirtieth, or December thirty-first within six days after the same becomes due, said lodge shall be deprived of all strike benefits and the password during said quarter; and any lodge failing to forward its report for March thirty-first on or before April tenth shall be deprived of the strike benefits and the password for said quarter, and shall not be entitled to a seat in the succeeding National Convention. Delegates, elected to represent their lodges at the Annual Convention, shall not be prevented from coming by managers on account of scarcity of men to keep the mills going, or from any other cause.

Sec. 5.   In order to insure a duplicate quarterly report the Corresponding Representative of each sub-lodge shall send to the General office both the original and duplicate reports, and the latter shall be returned when corrected (if corrected) to the sub-lodges.

Sec. 6.   All lodges failing to forward reports as above shall be charged with all assessments according to the number of members on the preceding report.   And any lodge failing to send in their quarterly report for two successive quarters shall be deprived of strike benefits for six months.

Sec. 7.   The Corresponding Representative of each lodge shall send a report to the general office of the association once a week, stating how the mill is running, the number of men, standing turns, etc., the same to be published in the "Amalgamated Journal."   And in order to educate our members, one of the delegates shall, at each regular meeting, expound one Article of the Constitution.

ARTICLE V

NATIONAL CONVENTION

Section 1.   The National Convention shall meet annually on the first Tuesday in May, at 10 o'clock A. M., at such place as shall from time to time be designated by the preceding Annual Convention.   A quorum for the transaction of business shall consist of one-fourth of the whole number of representatives-elect.

Sec. 2.   Prior to the assembling of the Convention a program of business shall be sent to each subordinate lodge by the Secretary-Treasurer of the National Lodge, six weeks prior to the date appointed for the calling of the Convention. The program shall contain any suggested alterations or amendments to the laws, and any that shall have been sent by sub-lodges under their seal to the Secretary-Treasurer of the National Lodge, and any resolutions bearing upon questions of law or prices not contained in the program, shall not be entertained at the Convention unless by consent of two-thirds of the delegates, except on base of scale.

Sec. 3.   In order to facilitate the business at Convention, the names of delegates-elect shall be sent to the Secretary-Treasurer of the National Lodge, who shall enter the same on the roll of delegates for Convention, and at the opening thereof shall call the roll, when each shall answer to his name.   As the delegates arrive at Convention they shall present their credentials to the Secretary-Treasurer, who shall examine the same, and at the termination of the calling of the roll he shall state whether all present are entitled to seats.   All disputed or contested seats shall be referred to a special committee, who shall proceed to investigate forthwith, but no contest shall be recognized unless those contesting have properly notified the sub-lodge to which they belong of their intentions, and have properly applied to the Secretary-Treasurer of the National Lodge, which application shall bear the signature of the Recording Secretary of the said lodge and seal thereof. Any delegate to the National Convention absenting himself (except in case of sickness of self or family), the President shall call upon the alternate-elect to fill the unexpired term.

Sec. 4.   Should the National Convention assemble without quorum, it can transact no business; but may issue an address to subordinate lodges, with a view to secure a full representation at an adjourned meeting or at the next stated meeting of the National Convention.

Sec. 5.   At each of the annual sessions an executive session with closed doors shall be held.   The first business at the executive session shall be devoted to the consideration and adoption of a scale of prices, and during such session no person shall be present except the representatives of the National Convention.

Sec. 6.   The National Executive Board may, at their discretion, call an extra session of the National Convention, provided a request to that effect be made by a majority of the subordinate lodges.

Sec. 7. All necessary expenses, except mileage, incurred by the representatives to the National Convention, including wages, shall be defrayed by their respective lodges.

Sec. 8. The Secretary-Treasurer of the National Lodge shall negotiate with the various railroad companies for reduced rates for delegates attending the National Convention, and such reduced rates shall be the actual amount the delegates shall receive for their mileage, which shall be paid by the National Lodge.

Sec. 9. Any lodge not sending a delegate to the National Convention shall be fined the sum of fifty dollars ($50) unless a reasonable excuse is offered. A lodge with its members on strike is a reasonable excuse for not sending a representative to the National Convention, and should not come under the $50 fine.

Sec. 10. The Convention shall place the construction on laws adopted by the Convention.

ARTICLE VI

ELIGIBILITY TO NATIONAL CONVENTION

Section 1. Representatives to the Annual Convention shall be elected by sub-lodges annually at the first regular meeting in the month of April, and shall hold their office one year, commencing the first annual seesion following said election. The written ballot shall be used in balloting, and where but one is to be elected, and there should be no election on the first ballot, all but the two highest shall be dropped. Where there are two or more delegates to be elected, each ballot shall contain the names of candidates sufficient to comprise a full delegation, but when one or more of the candidates in nomination has received a majority of all votes cast, said candidate shall be declared elected, after which balloting shall continue; each subsequent ballot shall contain a sufficient number of names to complete the delegation, but when a candidate has received a majority of all the votes cast he shall be elected and on each ballot the candidate receiving the lowest number of votes shall be dropped. They shall also elect an alternate to insure a representative of the lodge in case the representative elect fails, from any cause whatever, to attend.

Sec. 2. To be eligible as representative to the National Convention candidates must be clear on the Secretary's books up to and including the night of election; must be working at some trade specified in Section 1, Article I, must have served six months in office in the Sub-Lodge they aspire to represent either as President, Vice President, Recording Secretary, Financial Secretary, Treasurer, Corresponding Representative, Journal Agent, Chairman of Mill Committee, or delegate to a Central Labor Union, Trades Council or Labor League, and must have attended two-thirds of the meetings of the Lodge during the year, or such part thereof as he has been a member of such Lodge. Ex-delegates who have not forfeited their good standing in the organization, and who have not refused to serve their Lodge as an officer, and who are clear on the Secretary's books up to and including the night of election, and who have attended two-thirds of the meetings of the Lodge during the year or such part thereof as he has been a member of such Lodge, are eligible.

This not to conflict with Article VI, Section 4, of the Constitution.

This law, however, does not apply to Lodges not organized long enough for the officers named to have served six months in office.

Sec. 3. Any member allowing himself to become suspended must, after reinstatement, comply with Article VI, Section 2, to be eligible as a representative to Convention.

Sec. 4. Representatives to the National Convention shall, after their term of service in that capacity expires, be permanent members of the same so long as they retain their good standing in any sub-lodge (proof of which they shall present), and said lodge retains its connections with this body. They may discuss any question and be eligible to any office.

Sec. 5.   Any subordinate lodge being in arrears to the National Lodge, the same shall be deducted from the mileage of the representatives of each lodge to the National Convention.

Sec. 6.   No delegate shall be allowed a seat in Convention coming from a mill that has been in operation three months with the scale unsigned, unless permission has been given by the Advisory Board.

ARTICLE VII

REVENUE

Section 1.   The revenue of this association shall be derived as follows:

For organizing a subordinate lodge the sum of twenty-five dollars ($25.00) shall be charged, and two dollars ($2.00) per member, which is to go to the Benefit Fund, said sums to be paid at the time of organization.   The supplies to be furnished a newly organized sub-lodge, which the organization fee of twenty-five dollars ($25.00) is intended to cover, shall be: One charter, 1 seal, 3 rituals, 25 constitutions, 10 annual working cards, 10 withdrawal cards and 8 quarterly report blanks.   Additional supplies shall be charged for as follows:

For issuing a duplicate charter (for one destroyed) to a subordinate lodge, $5.00; remodeling an old seal, $4.50; rituals, $1.00 each; constitution and general laws, 5 cents each; quarterly report blanks, 5 cents each; scale of prices, 5 cents each; withdrawal cards, 5 cents each; annual working cards, 5 cents each; honorary cards, $1.00 each.

Sec. 2.   In order to create a fund to meet the expenses of the National Association, the quarterly tax to the National Lodge shall be $1.00 per quarter for each member, and the following system of collecting dues shall be adopted: Members earning $2.50 per day or less shall pay 60 cents per month; over $2.50 and less than $5.00, 80 cents per month; $5.00 and upwards, $1.00 per month, and 25 cents extra per month, which is to go to Benefit Fund.

Sec. 3.   In order to create a fund for the support of victimized members or such members as may be engaged in legalized strikes, it shall be required that each member of the association shall pay to his lodge, for the Protective Fund, the sum of twenty-five (25) cents per month.   All moneys so received to be used only for the purpose specified.

Sec. 4.   At the last stated meeting in each quarter the Financial Secretary of each lodge shall report to the lodge the correct number of members on his books taxable to the Protective Fund for the quarter, when an order shall be drawn on the Treasurer for a sum equal to seventy-five cents for every member on the books thus reported by the Financial Secretary, and the sum thus drawn on the Treasurer, together with the per capita tax and benefit fees, shall be given to the Corresponding Representative, who shall, as soon as possible, forward the same to the Secretary-Treasurer of the National Lodge, who shall receipt therefor.

Sec. 5.   Any member who is sick or out of employment during the period of one full month shall be exempt from paying the twenty-five (25) cents per month to the Protective Fund until he recovers from his sickness or finds employment. But members out of employment must report the fact to their lodge at every regular meeting, or be charged with the twenty-five (25) cents per month to the Protective Fund.

Sec. 6.   All moneys due the National Association shall be forwarded to the Secretary-Treasurer thereof by draft (on New York, Philadelphia or Pittsburg), express, postoffice order or registered letter.

ARTICLE VIII
AMALGAMATED JOURNAL

Section 1.   The Journal Agent shall send to the Managing Editor, after each stated meeting, the names and street addresses of all members initiated, admitted by card, withdrawn or suspended.   He shall receive such remuneration as the Sub-Lodge may determine.   Every member in good standing shall be entitled to receive his Journal, or have it sent to any address he may desire.   The Journal Agent shall endeavor to secure subscriptions from non-members and solicit advertisements from the local merchants for the Amalgamated Journal and further its interests in every way possible.   He shall send a weekly report of the operation of the mill, etc., and such other information as will benefit the organization.

Sec. 2.   The official Journal of the Amalgamated Association of Iron, Steel and Tin Workers of North America, known as the Amalgamated Journal, shall be issued weekly by and under the supervision of the Managing Editor of the Amalgamated Association of Iron, Steel and Tin Workers, and the said official journal shall be furnished weekly to each member of the Amalgamated Association of Iron, Steel and Tin Workers at the rate of 37½ cents per quarter, and each local shall make an appropriation as the subscription price for each member per quarter, and collect the same, and that said quarterly subscription shall be forwarded to the Secretary-Treasurer as part of the quarterly per capita tax.

Sec. 3.   The Managing Editor shall make all rules and regulations as to the rates for advertising and all other matters pertaining to the publication of said official journal, subject to the supervision of the National Trustees.

Sec. 4.   The Secretary-Treasurer shall make a report to the National Convention as to all matters pertaining to the publication and issuing of the official journal, and that the Managing Editor shall likewise make a separate report thereof.

Sec. 5.   Members of our own association shall be permitted to sign a *nom-de-plume* to economic and civic articles, and members of any other *bona-fide* labor union or ministerial calling shall be permitted to publish such articles in the Journal when they tend to strengthen the cause of the workingman and they are published with the signature of the writers, and no letter shall be published eulogizing any political party.

Sec. 6.   At the last stated meeting in December the President of each sub-lodge will appoint a Journal Committee of from three to five members, to serve during the following year, for the purpose of co-operating with the Journal Agent in setting forth to the merchants of the community the prestige of our official organ and its claims for a share of their advertising patronage.

Sec. 7.   The Journal Agent shall be elected at the last stated meeting in December to serve one year.

ARTICLE IX
EXECUTIVE COMMITTEE, ITS DUTY AND POWER

Section 1.   There shall be an Executive Committee in each district or division, consisting of the Vice President, his deputies, the President of the National Lodge, and the President and two members of the lodge where any grievance may arise, except for the signing of the yearly scales.   But no person shall be allowed to serve as a member of the Executive Committee who is personally or directly interested in any grievance that may come before said committee.

Sec. 2.   The Vice President of the district or division shall be chairman of the Executive Committee.

Sec. 3.   It shall be the duty of the Vice President after first having been notified by and under seal of the sub-lodge, to examine, in conjunction with the

Mill Committee, into both sides of any grievance that may arise before calling the Executive Committee together to legalize a strike. When a strike has been legalized the Vice President shall notify the general office of the same in writing.

Sec. 4. The Executive Committee, if upon investigation, finds it to the best interests of the association so to do, shall have full power to declare a strike which they have legalized at an end, and the Vice President shall report the same to the general office of the association.

Sec. 5. The Executive Committee shall have full power to open a mill that goes on a strike in violation of Sections 3 and 4 of this Article.

Sec. 6. Where a dispute arises as to the class of mill, the President of the National Lodge, with the Executive Committee, shall class the mill.

Sec. 7. Where there are two or more mills belonging to the same company in the same district or division or when, in the opinion of the Executive Committee, the interest of the association will be benefited thereby, the Executive Committee shall have power to call upon each lodge under said company, or in the district or division to send one delegate to a meeting to be held for the purpose of considering such matters as the Executive Committee may lay before it.

Sec. 8. All expenses incurred by the Vice Presidents, Deputies and Presidents of sub-lodges serving on Executive Committee shall be paid by the Secretary-Treasurer on the order of the President, attested by the Secretary-Treasurer of the National Lodge. All bills of deputies and Executive Committee shall be certified to by the Vice President.

Sec. 9. In settlement of local scales, or any scale legally referred to the District Executive Committee three members of the sub-lodge interested shall be appointed by the sub-lodge to assist the Executive Committees. Said members to act in an advisory capacity only, without vote, and to be paid by the local lodge.

ARTICLE X

STRIKE BENEFITS

Section 1. No sub-lodge under the jurisdiction of this association shall be permitted to enter into a strike unless authorized by the Executive Committee of the district.

Sec. 2. When the Executive Committee of a district or division finds it necessary, in accordance with the laws of this association, to legalize a strike in any one department of a mill or works, it shall be required that the men of all other departments shall also cease work until the difficulty is settled.

Sec. 3. When a strike has been legalized and the general office of the association has been properly notified of this fact in writing, the Secretary-Treasurer of the National Lodge shall at once prepare a printed statement of the facts in the case, as near as possible, and forward the same, under the seal of the National Lodge, to all sub-lodges, warning all true men not to accept work in such mills, shops or factories.

Sec. 4. Any subordinate lodge entering into a strike or lockout in the manner provided by the laws of this association, provided that the amount in the National Treasury is not less than ten thousand dollars ($10,000), shall receive from the Protective Fund the sum of four dollars ($4.00) per week for each member actually engaged in the strike in the mill over which the lodge has jurisdiction, provided they remain in the locality of the strike or notify the Corresponding Representative of that lodge of their location and their being unemployed each week while on strike, and have held membership in the association for six months, are not in arrears, and the lodge to which they belong is in good standing in the National Association. Except a strike has been legalized three months prior to July first, no benefits shall be paid to any member for any strike during the months of July and August. This section also applies to members who are standing turns in the mills on strike, and who hold no other situation except that on standing turns in that mill.

Sec. 5.   The National Secretary-Treasurer is empowered to levy an assessment as follows on all lodges when their respective mills are working one-fourth or more time during the month:

When 500 or any fraction thereof over 100 are on strike or locked out, members earning $2.50 per day, or less, 30 cents per month; members earning from $2.50 to $5.00 per day, shall pay 40 cents per month; over $5.00 per day, 50 cents per month; 1,000 or any fraction thereof over 500 members, earning $2.50 or less, 35 cents per month; $2.50 to $5.00, 45 cents per month; over $5.00 per day, 55 cents per month; 2,000 or any fraction thereof over 1,000 members, earning $2.50 or less, shall pay 40 cents per month; $2.50 to $5.00, shall pay 50 cents per month; over $5.00, 60 cents per month; 3,000 or any fraction thereof over 2,000 members, earning $2.50 or less, shall pay 45 cents per month; $2.50 to $5.00, 55 cents per month; over $5.00, 65 cents per month; 4,000 or any fraction thereof over 3,000 members, earning $2.50 per day or less, shall pay 50 cents per month; $2.50 to $5.00, 60 cents per month; over $5.00, 70 cents per month; 5,000 or any fraction thereof over 4,000 members, earning $2.50 or less per day, shall pay 55 cents per month; $2.50 to $5.00, 65 cents per month; over $5.00, 75 cents per month. Same to be charged to members by Financial Secretary at the end of each month and be governed by the same laws as dues.

All appeals for aid to members on strike must hereafter be sent through the National Lodge, and that the strike benefits and donations from sub-lodges shall also be paid through the National Office, all such donations received and paid out to be reported separately in the quarterly financial statement.

Sec. 6.   The Vice President of the division wherein said strike is legalized shall appoint, in conjunction with the Corresponding Representative, two responsible men, one to act as Treasurer, the other as Clerk.   All moneys paid to be accounted for on official sheets, one to be kept for inspection of sub-lodge, one to be filled out and promptly returned to National office each time benefits are paid.   If, upon investigation, it is found that benefits have been paid to a member not entitled to them, the lodge in which such member or members receiving such benefits held membership shall be held responsible for the amount paid, and said amount shall be charged up to the lodge.

Sec. 7.   No member shall be entitled to strike benefits for the first two weeks while on a legalized strike.   Payments of benefits shall date from the commencement of the fourth week after the strike has been legalized, and no benefits shall be allowed for the fraction part of the first week.

Sec. 8.   A member who has been suspended or expelled shall not receive any strike benefits (whether engaged in a legalized strike or is victimized) until six months after he has been restored to membership.

Sec. 9.   If any member or members, while receiving benefits from this association, shall work three or more days in one week at any job, either inside or outside of a mill or factory, he or they snall not be entitled to benefits for that week.   And any member on the benefit list, either on strike or victimized, refusing to work a third turn in a week, within a view of securing his benefits, his name shall, if proven against him, be stricken from the benefit list.   Members out of employment, or idle on account of repairs when strike takes place in one department of the mill (those that were idle previous to the commencement of said strike and were idle at the end of it) cannot be considered "on strike," nor entitled to strike benefits.

Sec. 10.   No member or members of this association shall be entitled to strike benefits for a strike in any mill or factory in which he or they have the mere promise of a situation.   This is to say, if a member has been promised a situation in a mill and said mill should go on strike before he began to work, he shall not be entitled to strike benefits during said strike.

Sec. 11. Any member engaged in a legalized strike, procuring a permanent situation elsewhere, forfeits his claim to strike benefits during the continuation of such strike.

Sec. 12. Strike benefits shall stop after the payment of the thirteenth week. Should, however, the exigency of the situation be such, as in the opinion of the President to demand it, he, with the Executive Board, may, at the expiration of the thirteenth week, extend payment for four additional weeks. At the conclusion of the time to which payment of benefits had been extended, if conditions are such as to clearly warrant it, further extensions of payment may be made, the length of time to which payment is extended to be determined at the time the order is given.

Sec. 13. Should a lodge be forced out on a strike or locked out through no fault of their own, immediately after a lodge is organized they shall be entitled to benefits the same as if organized six months; this not to conflict with Article IV.

ARTICLE XI

VICTIMIZED MEMBERS

Section 1. Should any member or members of this association be discharged (victimized) from his or their employment *for taking an active part in the affairs of this association*, either as a member of the mill or conference committees, or for otherwise being active in promoting and guarding the interests of this association, such member or members shall use his or their best endeavors with the manager to be reinstated, and failing in this, he or they shall then and there report such case to the chairman of the Mill Committee, who shall at once proceed to investigate the case as set forth in Sections 2 and 3 of Article IX. Should the committee fail to get the brother or brothers reinstated, they shall then carry the case to the lodge in precisely the same manner as in cases where the whole mill is involved in difficulty, and in no case of individual discharge (except the Mill Committee have good grounds to believe that the brother is discharged *for just cause*) shall such job be declared vacant until the Executive Committee of the district has decided the case.

Sec. 2. Should the Executive Committee of the district or division, after deciding the brother victimized, deem the organization unable to sustain a strike for his reinstatement, he shall receive from the Protective Fund of the association six (6) dollars per week for a period of eight (8) weeks and no longer, except in extreme cases, when it shall be left discretionary with the President of the National Lodge as to the length of time benefits shall be paid. If within the limit of the time (eight weeks) prescribed for the payment of victimized benefits a situation has been procured for him, either by himself or other members of the association, payment thereof shall immediately cease. The law applying to the payment of victimized benefits shall be the same as that governing the payment of strike benefits.

Sec. 3. If, upon investigation, it is found that victimized benefits have been paid a member not entitled to them, the lodge in which such member receiving benefits held membership shall be held responsible for the amount thus paid, and said amount shall be charged up to said lodge.

BENEFIT FUND

Benefits—Sick, Accident, Disability and Death

Sec. 4. Each sub-lodge shall at the end of each quarter draw from its treasury the sum of seventy-five cents for each member in good standing upon its books, to be collected from members as dues, the same to be sent to the Secretary-Treasurer of the National Lodge, along with the Protective Fund and Quarterly Tax. Said money to go to the credit of Benefit Fund, to be used to pay benefits hereinafter named. A member who has been in continuous good standing for six months, immediately preceding any sickness or accident following initiation, admission by honorary card, or reinstatement, and who is not indebted to the sub-lodge to an amount equal to three months' dues, except where such member has by action of sub-lodge (said action to be spread upon the minutes and entered upon Financial Secretary's Ledger) previous to any sickness or disability, been carried in good standing. Said action to be placed upon application for benefits. And who is not under any of the restrictions specified in these laws, shall be entitled, when taken sick or is disabled so as to incapacitate him from following his usual vocation, to the sum of five dollars ($5.00) per week, for a period of thirteen weeks, provided however, that such sickness or disability shall not have been caused by intemperance, debauchery, or other immoral conduct, but no benefit shall be paid for the first seven days' sickness following six months' good standing, or a fractional part of a week.

No member shall be entitled to receive benefits for a longer period than thirteen weeks in any one year, either continuous or periodical.

Sec. 5.   A member to be entitled to benefits from this fund must notify the Financial Secretary within one week from the time he became sick or disabled, when he shall be given the following form:

He shall fill out the first part of it down to the physician's report (leaving date line blank) and at the expiration of two weeks' sickness or disability, the physician, Benefit Committee, President and Financial Secretary shall complete the report (said report now to be dated two weeks after sickness or disability), and immediately thereafter forwarded to the National Office.

..........................19....

To the Officers and Members of........*Lodge, No*.........*A. A. of I. S. and T. W.*

   of North America:

(Give full name)

This is to certify, that I.., now

(Full address)

living at...and a member of

(Name of Lodge)

..............................No........, having paid all dues to....day

of..............................19...., and at present unable to work,

(State cause)

caused by ....

I was taken sick or disabled the...............day of...............

(Name place here)

19...., at....................................and secured the services of

Dr................................., whose address is..................

on the....................day of....................19....

(Signed)........................

(Full name of sick member)

271

PHYSICIAN'S REPORT

This is to certify, that I am a graduate of a school of medicine recognized by the state board of health and have waited upon.............................. in a professional capacity since the.................................day of ....19.... and report his condition such that it incapacitates him from following his usual vocation. Disease or cause of accident...

(Signed).....................M.D.

We, your committee report...

....

....
(Chairman)   (Member Sick Com.)   (Member Sick Com.)

....
(President)   (Fin. Secretary)   (Vice President)

————

Was sickness or disability caused by intemperance, debauchery or other immoral conduct?..................................
(Yes or No)

AFFIDAVIT

STATE OF .... }
COUNTY .... } ss.
CITY .... }

Personally appeared before me......................................

who is President of...

Lodge, No.......State..............and upon being duly sworn saith that the statements contained in the above certificate in the claim of............

....................Card No.......is true to his knowledge and belief.

Signed...........................

Street Address...............

[SEAL] Sworn to before me this...........................day of ....19....

....................Notary Public.

272

THE AMALGAMATED ASSOCIATION

(The Financial Secretary will give below exact copy of member's Ledger account for the past year, prior to sickness, accident or disability, but if he has been a member for a less period, give account for the full time he has been a member.

ABSTRACT OF LEDGER ACCOUNT OF

Name...................................... Card No...............

Year	Dues	Ass't	Fines	Tot'ls	Year Date of Am't Paym't Paid		Tot'ls	Remarks
			Balance due, $			Bal. to Credit, $		
Jan.								
Feb.								
Mar.								
Total Charges for quarter, $					Total Paym'ts for quarter, $			
April								
May								
June								
Total Charges for quarter, $					Total Paym'ts for quarter, $			
July								
Aug.								
Sept.								
Total Charges for quarter, $					Total Paym'ts for quarter, $			
Oct.								
Nov.								
Dec.								
Total Charges for quarter, $					Total Paym'ts for quarter, $			
Sum Total,					Sum Total			

Dr. On the first of each month charge on this side the monthly dues in advance, and all assessments or fines when levied.

Cr. On this side enter all dues and assessments, when paid, with exact date and full amount of payment, all on one line.

273

AFFIDAVIT

STATE OF .... ⎫
COUNTY .... ⎬ ss.
CITY .... ⎭

Personally appeared before me....................................

who is Financial Secretary of..

Lodge, No.........................State...............and upon being

duly sworn saith that the above abstract of Ledger [account in reference to the

standing of......................................Card No.......is true to

his knowledge.

Signed.............................

Street Address................

[SEAL] Sworn to before me this............................day of

....................................19....

....................Notary Public.

BY-LAWS AND RULES GOVERNING SICK AND ACCIDENT FUND

Must be a member in good standing continuously for six months.

Must be sick seven days before benefits start.

Lodge pays five dollars for thirteen weeks only in any one continuous twelve months.

Each week's sickness must be certified to by a physician. A member must notify the Financial Secretary within one week from the time he becomes sick or disabled, when he shall be given an original form blank. He shall fill out the first part of it down to the Physician's report (leaving date line blank) and at the expiration of two weeks' sickness or disability, the report shall be completed by the physician, Benefit Committee, President and Financial Secretary filling in their part of it (said claim to be dated two weeks after sickness began), and immediately thereafter forwarded to the National Office.

Each week thereafter a supplementary report, similar to front side of original claim, shall be filled out and forwarded to National Office at once on this form, as no notice will be taken if notified by any other form.

If a member fails to report himself sick or disabled within the time specified, benefits will not start until seven days after the date he reports.

If a member is in arrears to the amount of three months' dues he will not be entitled to benefits should he be taken sick or is disabled during said sickness, even though he pays up said arrearages, except as hereinbefore provided.

Blanks will be furnished free to members on request to the Financial Secretary of the lodge, either in person or by mail, and if a member fails to give such notification, benefits shall begin only from date the sub-lodge or its officers receive such notifications.

Upon the receipt of such notice the Financial Secretary, through the Corresponding Representative, shall send official report duly signed and sealed each week of sickness, to the Secretary-Treasurer of the National Lodge, and if the record in the National Office shows the member to be entitled to benefits, the Secretary-Treasurer shall instruct the sub-lodge to pay sick benefits to said member, and upon the termination of such sickness, the Secretary-Treasurer shall forward check to cover same.

Sec. 6. Sub-lodges shall arrange for a Benefit Committee to visit sick members, but in no case shall the committee consist of less than three members. The Benefit Committee shall in all cases see that a physician of good repute signs the certificate on benefit reports, giving date, nature and cause of sickness or disability. If a visiting committee is refused admittance to the house or not permitted to see the sick member, unless by order of the board of health, it shall not be obligatory to pay the member the weekly benefits until such restrictions have been removed. The visiting committee shall not be required to visit members having malignant or contagious diseases, but shall make statement on benefit claims covering such cases.

Sec. 7. Any officer or officers using his or their offices to get sick benefits for a member fraudulently, or any member obtaining such benefits fraudulently, shall be fined the sum of twenty-five dollars ($25.00), said fine to stand against said member on the books, and must be liquidated to entitle him to any of the benefits or privileges of this association.

A member who is indebted to the sub-lodge to an amount equal to three months' dues shall not be entitled to sick benefits until three months after said indebtedness shall have been paid, except as hereinbefore provided; or a member who has been suspended, until six months after such suspension shall have been raised. Arrearages shall mean any debt either to the sub-lodge or to the National Lodge, or both, for dues, fines, assessments, etc., either separately or collectively.

DEATH BENEFITS

Sec. 8. At the death of a member in good standing, the sub-lodge shall report the same to the National Lodge on the proper blanks. The Secretary-Treasurer will, if the claim be valid, draw from the Benefit Fund the sum of one hundred dollars ($100.00) for a member who has been in continuous good standing for three months immediately preceding his death; one hundred and fifty dollars ($150.00) for two years continuous good standing; two hundred dollars ($200.00) for three years continuous good standing; three hundred dollars ($300.00) for five years continuous good standing, and if a member shall have been in continuous good standing for a period of ten years immediately preceding his death, then the sum of five hundred dollars ($500.00) shall be paid, provided, however, that no member shall be entitled to the death benefit who is at the time of his death indebted to the sub-lodge to an amount equal to three months dues, except as hereinbefore provided, nor until three months after such indebtedness shall have been paid, and if suspended, until three months after such suspension shall have been raised. Arrearages shall mean any debt either to the Sub-Lodge or the National Lodge, or both, for dues, fines, assessments, etc., either separately or collectively.

Sec. 9. The death benefit is to be paid by the sub-lodge officers, to-wit: The President, Vice President and Recording Secretary, in conjunction with the Corresponding Representative, to the beneficiary. In the event the deceased member has not designated a beneficiary, then to the wife, or children, or father, or mother, or brothers, or sisters, or executor, or administrator of the estate of the deceased, and the receipt of one or more of the above named persons or representatives of the deceased, or other proofs of such payment to any or either of the aforesaid persons, shall be a full acquittance and discharge of all claims and demands against the sub-lodge or the National Lodge on account of the death of said member.

Sec. 10. A member in good standing means one who has been continuously a member of the organization three months immediately preceding his death, and whose name has been reported as being in good standing in the last quarterly report of his sub-lodge to the National Lodge next preceding his death, and on whom the insurance fee has been paid.

Failure of the sub-lodge to forward to the National Lodge a correct record at the proper time of all those in good standing, shall exempt the National Lodge from paying benefits on account of the sickness, injury, disability, or death of a member of such Sub-Lodge.

Sec. 11.   All questions and disputes arising on account of the payment or distribution of the Death Benefit Fund between the claimant or claimants, and the sub-lodge or the National Lodge, on account of the death of a member, shall be referred to the National Executive Board of the Association, whose decision shall be conclusive and final without appeal, except by permission of said Board, when an appeal may be taken to the next Annual Convention.

No claims shall be paid from the Benefit Fund unless the claims and proof of death shall have been presented within six months after the death of said member.

It is compulsory that all sub-lodges pay benefit dues on all members reported in good standing.

Sec. 12.   Members in good standing, retiring from mill work, and desiring to continue their insurance, for death benefit only, shall be permitted to do so, by withdrawing by honorary card and making application for silent membership on blanks to be furnished by the National Lodge, and upon acceptance of said application, shall pay to the National Lodge Benefit Fund, through their sub-lodge, the sum of $2.60 per year, which may be paid quarterly or yearly, and must be paid in advance, and any silent member failing to pay his fee on or before the date mentioned on the last receipt made out in his favor, shall immediately become a lapsed member and shall not again be permitted to become a silent member. Such members to be silent members only, but shall be subject to the same rules, regulations and penalties as a member holding full and active membership, provided, however, that no silent member shall be entitled to more benefits than the time his credit on account of his continuous good standing at the time of his withdrawal by honorary card would entitle him to; and be it further provided, that a member who is at present a silent member, shall not pay more than the present rate of $2.60 per year. Applications for honorary card and silent membership must be made on the same date.

Sec. 13.   That upon the death of the wife of a member, when such member shall have been in continuous good standing for a period of six months immediately preceding his wife's death, the sum of fifty dollars shall be paid to the husband, this amount to be deducted from the amount said member would be entitled to at the time of his death, provided, however, that this money shall only be paid if at the time of her death they are living together as man and wife. The time herein specified to be computed from October 1, 1908, and be it further provided, that if the member dies first the insurance on the wife ceases forthwith.

Sec. 14.   Any member who voluntarily or otherwise severs his connection with this organization, shall immediately forfeit all rights, claims and privileges to participation in this fund, except as provided for in Section 12 of this Article.

Sec. 15.   This law shall go into effect October 1, 1908, and the first quarter's insurance fee shall be due and payable for the quarter ending September 30, 1908. All members who are in good standing the required three months on October 1, 1908, shall be beneficiary to the amount of $100.00, but for all amounts above that the time shall be computed from October 1, 1908.

Sec. 16.   That where any sub-lodge fails to make out and forward their report at the proper time, and the claim of a member in good standing in such sub-lodge who is taken sick, disabled or dies, is disallowed on account of the failure of such sub-lodge to make out and forward their report at the proper time, the sub-lodge shall be held liable for the payment of said claim, and shall be charged against said sub-lodge's account at the National Lodge, and that where any sub-lodge is indebted to the National Lodge to an amount equal to the last quarterly report (as per report submitted) said sub-lodge shall be considered in arrears to the National Lodge, and no claim shall be paid on account of the death, sickness or disability of any member of such sub-lodge, until said arrearages shall have been paid.

Sec. 17.   Each member shall be required to sign a blank form giving the names of the person or persons to whom the benefit is to be paid, and in the event the member has not designated a beneficiary, and no legal heir can be found, then

276

the sub-lodge shall be entitled to not more than $100.00 to be used to defray funeral expenses, the balance, if there be any, shall be held by the National Lodge, and placed to the credit of the Benefit Fund.

Sec. 18.   Upon the total disability of a member in good standing, when such disability has not been caused by intemperance, debauchery or other immoral conduct, the Secretary-Treasurer shall pay, upon proof of such disability, one-half the amount said member would be entitled to in case of death as set forth in Section 8 of this Article.   A member who receives the disability benefit, said amount shall be deducted from the death benefit due said member at death.

A member shall be entitled to disability benefits only when he shall have complied with all the requirements as specified in Section 5 of this Article.

Sec. 19.   Upon the total disability of a member in good standing, the President, Financial Secretary and Corresponding Representative shall secure, from a reputable physician in his locality, a certificate setting forth the cause of said total disability, and said certificate must be sworn or affirmed to before a Notary Public, and attested to by the President, Financial Secretary and Corresponding Representative, said certificate to contain the correct lodge record of said member.

Blank certificates to be furnished by National Lodge.

All laws now in effect which may in any way conflict with any of the provisions of these laws shall be, and the same are hereby repealed.

In order to create a reserve or sinking fund to further make the beneficial features tenable, and to assure their permanency, the initiation fee shall be advanced to a minimum of five dollars, two-fifths of which shall go to the benefit fund, and a reinstatement fee of five dollars be charged, two-fifths of which shall also go to the benefit fund.

In the instituting of new lodges a charter initiation and reinstatement fee of not less than a sufficient amount to cover cost of organization supplies, and two dollars per member (which is to go to the credit of Benefit Fund), shall be charged. The charter to remain open for a period of thirty days.

ARTICLE XII

CONSTITUTIONAL DECISIONS AND APPEALS

Section 1.   All questions of constitutional character shall be referred to the Vice President of the district or division having jurisdiction over the sub-lodge sending it.   Sub-lodges, however, shall have the right to appeal from the decision of the Vice President of the district or division to the President of the National Lodge, whose decision shall be final, unless non-concurred in by two-thirds of the delegates present at the succeeding National Convention.   That all appeals and decisions and rulings be published monthly in the Journal, so as to avoid further appeals from lodges that do not know what the rulings are on many matters in our Constitution.

Sec. 2.   Individual members in good standing having a grievance of any kind before their lodge, and not being satisfied with the decision thereof, shall have the same right to appeal from the decision of the lodge, through the Vice President of their district or division, as set forth in Section 1 of this Article.   Notice of an appeal by individual members, however, shall be served on the sub-lodge from whose decision the appeal is made.

Sec. 3.   All questions referred to the Vice President of the National Lodge, as set forth in Section 1 of this Article shall be in writing, giving full details of the case.   These documents shall also bear the impression of the seal of the sub-lodge, and in such cases the seal shall be at the disposal of the individual member the same as with sub-lodge.

Sec. 4.   In the case of a sub-lodge being brought to trial before the District Board, with a member of the said Board as prosecutor, such a member shall not

277

sit on the case; the remaining members of the Board shall appoint one to serve in his place on that occasion.

ARTICLE XIII

SEALS

Section 1.   The seal of the National Association shall be peculiar to itself; subordinate lodge seals shall be uniform and furnished by the National Association, and all documents emanating from the National or subordinate lodge officers shall bear the impression thereof.

Sec. 2.   The sub-lodge seals shall not be used on any matter or documents when the sending of such matter or documents through the mails would be violating any of the postal laws.

ARTICLE XIV

CHARGES AND TRIALS

Section 1.   No subordinate lodge shall be expelled or suspended, or deprived of any of its rights or privileges, except as provided in this constitution.

Sec. 2.   If any subordinate lodge is found to be violating any of the laws, rules and regulations of this association, they shall be reported in writing to the Vice President of the district or division in which such subordinate lodge is located, by any member in good standing in this association.

Sec. 3.   When the Vice President has received notice of any subordinate lodge violating the laws, etc., as provided in Section 2, he shall, as soon as possible, proceed to investigate the case, and if he finds that the charges reported to him are correct, he shall at once notify the President of the National Lodge, and shall, without unnecessary delay, bring such lodge to trial before a Board of Investigation appointed by him, including the President of the National Lodge, the Vice President of the district or division, whose decision shall be final, unless non-concurred in by two-thirds of the delegates at the National Convention.

Sec. 4.   Before any sub-lodge can be put on trial by the President of the National Lodge, the latter shall serve the lodge to be put on trial with a full copy of the charges preferred against it in writing, not less than two weeks before the time appointed by him for trial of the case.

Sec. 5.   Any sub-lodge put on trial as set forth in this article shall place in the hands of the President of the National Lodge such documents as he may desire to further the investigation, and such lodge shall be entitled to produce such testimony bearing on the case as they may desire, and also to employ counsel, but such counsel must be selected from members in good standing in this order.

Sec. 6.   The Board of Investigation shall have full power to inflict such penalty for violation of laws, etc., as they may deem expedient in the case, and any lodge refusing to pay the penalty inflicted upon it by the Board of Investigation, their charter shall at once be forfeited until the meeting of the National Convention, when, if said convention reverse the decision of the Investigating Board, their charter shall be returned.

Sec. 7.   When any member or members of a sub-lodge have violated any of the laws of the association, charges shall be preferred against them in writing, signed by a member of this order, stating, besides the general offense, the specified particulars with reasonable clearness, a true copy of which shall be placed in possession of the accused at least seven days before the time appointed for trial by the committee.

Sec. 8.   The charges and certified copy of appointment for trial shall be placed in the hands of a special committee of not less than three members of the lodge, who shall notify both the accused and the accuser to appear before the committee for investigation, when they shall present such testimony as will bear upon the case.

278

Sec. 9. The committee shall keep a correct record of all the proceedings in the case, which they shall submit to the lodge, together with a report embodying their conclusion in form of a resolution, for the action of the lodge.

Sec. 10. If the accused or accuser fail to appear before the committee when duly summoned, they shall be reported guilty of contempt (if they have not sufficient excuse) and shall be subject to suspension or expulsion, on a vote of the majority present. But their failure to appear shall not preclude the committee from proceeding with the investigation, if the witnesses or other means of investigation are at hand.

Sec. 11. When a committee has reported charges sustained, the accused or accuser may present defense in the lodge, either personally or by counsel (the counsel employed must be members in good standing in this organization), and shall then, with the prosecutor, retire, when a vote by ballot shall be taken; first, whether the lodge will sustain the committee; second, if the lodge will adopt the recommendation of the committee. On which proposition every member present, except the President, shall vote, and a two-thirds vote shall determine the result.

Sec. 12. When charges are preferred against the President of the National Lodge, the Vice President of each district shall select one lodge in their respective district or division, from which lodge one delegate each shall be elected by written ballot. Said delegates shall constitute an investigation board, whose duty it shall be to investigate said charges, and if found guilty, said board shall have power to reprimand, suspend or expel from office; and a majority vote of said board shall sustain charges and convict.

Sec. 13. The Secretary-Treasurer and Trustees of the National Lodge, and also the Vice Presidents of the several districts or divisions shall be tried as provided in Section 12, at which trial or trials the President of the National Lodge shall preside. He shall previously give the date, place and hour of meeting.

ARTICLE XV

PENALTIES AND PRIVILEGES

Section 1. The President of the National Association shall issue a quarterly password through the Secretary-Treasurer of the National Lodge to each subordinate lodge in good standing. No lodge shall be entitled to or receive the password unless complying with Article IV, Section 4. And no member shall communicate the password to another, or use it for any purpose whatever, except to enter a lodge room, under penalty of expulsion.

Sec. 2. Where there are two or more lodges in one locality and the interests of the organization require their consolidation, they may join in forming a new lodge by a vote of the majority of the members present; *provided,* that there shall not be ten members of either lodge who are desirous of retaining its separate organization; the name of the lodge so formed to be decided by a majority vote of the lodges in joint session.

Sec. 3. Subordinate lodges shall have the power to reinstate their suspended members by the applicant paying the sum specified in Article XXIX, Section 2.

Sec. 4. All subordinate lodges having become suspended for non-payment of dues or otherwise violating the constitution, meriting suspension, may be reinstated by making proper application to the President of the National Association, and paying such sums as he may deem proper.

ARTICLE XVI

DEFUNCT LODGES

Section 1. Any subordinate lodge disbanding shall immediately transmit to the Secretary-Treasurer of the National Association all books, seal, charter and funds in their possession, and in the event of reorganization of said subordinate lodge, they shall be entitled to receive back the same, upon the payment of the usual charter fee, except the funds, which shall stand to their credit in the National Lodge books.

Sec. 2.   Any member of a former lodge now defunct, and of which the books, etc., have been returned to the general office (see Section 1 of this Article), who can procure a certificate of recommendation bearing the signature of the President and Corresponding Representative, together with the impression of the seal of any subordinate lodge to which he may make application, the Secretary-Treasurer of the National Association, shall issue a recommendation for such member to be reinstated into such subordinate lodge upon the payment of such sum provided for in Article XI, Section 19.

Sec. 3.   Any member of a defunct lodge shall, before being reinstated, pay to the Secretary-Treasurer of the National Lodge, the sum of $3.00, which amount shall be the maximum, same to be placed in the treasury of the National Lodge.

ARTICLE XVII

GENERAL SPECIAL RULES

Section 1.   Every member shall interest himself, individually and collectively, in protecting his trade, and the business of all employers who recognize, negotiate and are under contract with this association.   This, however, shall not be construed to mean that a member can work for anything less than the regular adopted scale prices, or in any other manner do what is detrimental to the established rules, customs, etc., of the association.

Sec. 2.   Every member of this association is strictly prohibited from employing helpers at a boiling, puddling or heating furnace, under the age of fifteen years.

Sec. 3.   When a roller or catcher leaves a job from any cause, the rest of the crew shall retain their positions.

Sec. 4.   All iron rolled on Sheet and Tin mills required to be sheared, shall be pulled up to the shearman's standing by the company, ready for shearing.

Sec. 5.   No person shall work at a scale job or constitutional job in any mill signing the Amalgamated Association scale who refuses to become a member of the Amalgamated Association and pay all dues, fines and assessments levied by same, and any member using his influence to disorganize his fellow workmen, or knowingly makes it difficult to carry out the objects of the Amalgamated Association, shall be tried as per Article XIV, Section 2.

Sec. 6.   Any mill under the jurisdiction of this association running double or treble turn three or more months in the year, shall be considered a double turn mill, and in the event of such mills going on a single turn, the work shall be divided; night turn roller to receive an equal share of work at night turn roller's wages.

Sec. 7.   Should any department of a mill working on single, double or treble turn be stopped through overproduction or other causes, the work shall be equally divided, except when a furnace is out for repairs.   It is, however, understood that any sub-lodge may, by a majority vote of those present, enact a law of their own to control the above subject.   But such law should not be made when there is a grievance pending, and any person taking a job on conditions shall be branded as a "black sheep."

Sec. 8.   This association will not tolerate any man holding more than one job.   One single furnace one turn, one turn of rolls double turn, one steel melting gas furnace one turn, to constitute one job, and all are expected to enforce this rule. Any man holding two or more separate jobs in violation of this section shall be stigmatized as a "black sheep."   By "two or more jobs" is meant where one man draws pay for two or more separate jobs at the same time.   No person shall be allowed to work two or more consecutive turns at his job in a mill or factory when there are members out of employment in the immediate vicinity who are fully qualified to do the work.

Sec. 9. Any member known to go to his work drunk, or who shall lose any work through drunkenness, and the foreman of the mill discharges him, no steps shall be taken by his lodge to reinstate him in his work. Any member acting in a manner detrimental to the interest of, or that will bring reproach upon, this association or its members, shall be reprimanded, fined, suspended or expelled from the lodge in which he holds membership.

Sec. 10. The members of this association shall not injure each other in their employment, such as undermining and conniving at a member's job, when such member is known to be standing out for his rights and trying to obtain those privileges which properly belong to the members of this association. Any member taking a job in such a way shall become unworthy of membership and be expelled from the association. No member of this association shall purchase tools or pay for any breakage that might occur in any mill. Any member being convicted of such shall become unworthy of membership and shall be expelled from the association.

Sec. 11. The several members of all lodges shall, as much as in their power, endeavor to establish and make permanent the same, and use all honorable exertions to secure employment for any member of this association in preference to all others. They shall also give a helping hand to each other in the works as much as it may be in their power to do so, and when it is the recognized time to start, at five (5) or nine (9) o'clock, or any other regular stated starting time, and the crew starts after the regular time, they shall stop work at the regular quitting time. After the crew has started and from breakage or other cause they are stopped for one (1) or more hours, they shall stop work at the end of the eight (8) hours from when they started.

Sec. 12. Except on questions of wages regulated by scale of prices, two weeks' notice shall be required from employers before a reduction can take place, and two weeks' notice shall be given when an advance is requested, and any rules agreed upon by the Mill or Factory Committee and company, *and ratified by a two-thirds vote of the lodge,* cannot be changed unless two weeks' notice has been given by either party.

Sec. 13. In voting on all questions involving the shutting down of a mill or factory for the purpose of sustaining a member who has been discharged, or for other causes, the written ballot shall be used.

Sec. 14. No member of this association shall be allowed to alter or change rules existing in any mill before submitting the desired changes to the lodge having control of the department for which the change is intended; and if a majority of all members of the lodge vote in favor of said change, the Mill Committee shall notify the superintendent of said change before the same goes into effect.

Sec. 15. Any members having worked at any of the trades in iron or steel mills or factories shall not be termed green hands, providing they are members in good standing in this association.

Sec. 16. Any person employed as foreman, puddle boss, superintendent or general manager of any mill or factory, or holding any of the above positions, together with a situation in the mill or factory, shall not be eligible to membership in this association.

Sec. 17. The members of this association shall, at the direction of the President of the National Lodge, refuse to work in any mill or factory where the manager, superintendent, foreman or puddle boss is deriving a direct benefit from the furnace, rolls, etc., in addition to his position as above, for which he receives a regular salary.

Sec. 18. Should any member of this association undertake to instruct an unskilled workman in any of the trades represented in this association, it shall be the duty of the Mill Committee to notify him that this association cannot tolerate such proceedings, and should he still persist in doing so, charges shall be preferred against him, and he shall be expelled or suspended, as the lodge may determine.

Sec. 19.   In each mill under the jurisdiction of this association, the company shall return to each tonnage-man, as soon as the turn is weighed up, a classified report of work done, or have same put in a convenient place in the mill, and any member shall have the privilege of seeing their turns weighed if they so desire.

Sec. 20.   Any member leaving a job to better his condition cannot claim his former job if he gets discharged or loses his new job on account of a shut-down.

Sec. 21.   All men are to have the privilege of hiring their own helpers without dictation from the management, and no member shall be permitted to discharge a helper, except for just cause, nor shall a member reduce the wages of a helper during the scale year.

Sec. 22.   Should one mill in a combine or trust have a difficulty, all mills in said combine or trust may cease work until such grievance is settled.

Sec. 23.   All steel, rod, or sheet bar mills shall cease rolling not later than 5 P. M. on Saturdays, and start at the usual hour.

Sec. 24.   Any sub-lodge located in any city or town where there is now established or to be established a Central Labor Union, Trades Council or Labor League, or other central labor body, organized for the purpose of benefiting organized labor, such sub-lodge should elect one or more delegates to such central labor body on such terms as they may decide.   The duties of said delegates shall be to look after the interest of their sub-lodge and its members, and the trade or craft governed by such lodge, make a report once each month, and perform such other duties as the lodge may require.   They shall hold office for six months, and their dues shall be paid by the sub-lodge to the central body, and shall be eligible to the office of Corresponding Representative.

Sec. 25.   All new mills starting after the scale has been signed be given three months to do the same.

Sec. 26.   On plate mill heating furnaces they shall change first and last each week.

Sec. 27.   Operations shall be suspended on the following holidays: Fourth of July, Labor Day and Christmas Day.

Sec. 28.   Members of the Amalgamated Association shall not be requested to use checks for going in and out of mill; but in such mills where they are required to use checks, the checks be retained and only presented on pay days at paymaster's window, for identification of holder, if necessary.

Sec. 29.   All finishers and assistant rollers must be members of the Amalgamated Association.

Sec. 30.   When a finisher or assistant roller takes turns rolling, he shall pay full dues to the local or sub-lodge where he is working.

Sec. 31.   Members of the Amalgamated Association are strictly forbidden to pay interest on money advanced by the firm, manager, foreman, agent, or to any one directly or remotely connected with the firm, under penalty prescribed in Section 1, Article XXXV of Constitution.

Sec. 32.   That all union men be given permission to work in any mill providing there is no strike at that mill; also, that he notifies the President or Secretary of the sub-lodge of which he is a member and that they notify the Vice President of that respective division and keep in good standing in the sub-lodge of which he is a member.

ARTICLE XVIII

SPECIAL RULES—BOILING, BAR AND FINISHING MILLS

Section 1.   When a vacancy occurs in the boiling department, the oldest boiler, if he so desires, shall have the preference of the furnace so vacated.   Five heats double turn, and six heats single turn, and in mill working three turns, five heats per turn shall constitute a day's work for boilers working common iron. The uniform charges for pig iron in a single boiling furnace shall not be more than five hundred and fifty pounds per heat, but in neither case shall this apply to furnaces working castings, for a double boiling furnace the charge for pig iron shall not be more than eleven hundred pounds per heat; for a "twin" furnace (where there are two doors on one side only, close together), the charge for pig iron shall not be more than twelve hundred and ten pounds per heat; for a Swindell furnace, the charge shall not be more than fourteen hundred and thirty pounds per heat; for a Siemens-Martin furnace not more than fifteen hundred and fifty pounds per heat; for a double furnace not more than twenty-two hundred pounds per heat. Castings in a single boiling furnace shall not exceed twenty-seven hundred and fifty pounds per turn on double turn, and thirty-three hundred pounds on single turn, and sixty-six hundred pounds for double furnaces on single turn. For fixing furnaces the men shall be given all the necessary pulverized ore the furnace requires. Mills using clay for blast doors, clay shall be in mill and in condition to use.

Sec. 2. Any iron worked in a boiling furnace taking more than one and three-quarter hours to make a heat shall be considered a grievance, which on demand of a majority of the members working hard iron, the Mill Committee shall report to the boss, in accordance with Article X of the Constitution; and if at any time within thirty days from the expiration of the above notice the iron shall again be as bad as when the notice was given, the Mill Committee shall report to the boss, and the night turn, if working double, shall finish their turn, and they shall then cease work until they get better iron.

Sec. 3. If upon investigation, any of the sub-lodges governing boiling departments are found to be allowing the violation of clause two (2) of the footnotes of the boilers' scale, or clause three (3) of memorandum of agreement, a fine of twenty dollars ($20) shall be imposed, and suspension from all benefits or protection of the organization, if necessary, and the names of such lodges shall be published in the financial statement.

Sec. 4. A fine of five dollars ($5) shall be imposed on any boiler or puddler who is known to put in any "jams" or "cheeks," "back walls" or "bridges," with brick or fire clay, and upon proof thereof, a fine of five dollars ($5), followed by suspension, shall be imposed upon any boiler who is known to violate this rule, and the names of such party or parties shall also be published in the financial statement. Such fines, when imposed, shall be collected from the member at the first regular meeting of his lodge succeeding the violation of this section. This section is not intended to prevent a puddler or boiler from putting a ball of fire clay in the jams, back walls or bridges during the week in order to keep his furnace working.

Sec. 5. Every member of the association is strictly prohibited from employing helpers at a boiling, puddling or heating furnace under the age of fifteen years.

Sec. 6. Furnaces working piles on boards shall not be allowed to charge while drawing.

Sec. 7. A fine of five dollars ($5) shall be placed on finishing mills who shall change pinions, crab, spindle or crab-box.

Sec. 8. Any member of a sub-lodge who has been appointed on Mill Committee shall receive proper recognition from the company while serving on said committee.

Sec. 9. Rollers and heaters having charge of trains of rolls or furnaces shall be compelled to give next job in line of promotion to the oldest hand, provided he is a member in good standing of the association. This is not to interfere with any local rule employed to govern the hiring of standard turn men.

ARTICLE XIX

SPECIAL RULES—SHEET AND JOBBING MILLS

Section 1.   All day hands on sheet and jobbing mills, who are members of this association, having any grievance, shall present the same to the roller or manager as the case may be, and if the trouble is not adjusted it shall be referred to the lodge, and if the lodge fails to settle the case it shall be referred to the Vice President of the district or division, and in case he cannot settle the difficulty, he shall call the Executive Board together, and in conjunction with the President of the National Lodge, they shall render a decision in the case, which decision shall be final.

Sec. 2.   Rollers on sheet mills shall hire their own help.

Sec. 3.   Where helpers are employed by heaters on sheet mills, they shall be paid not less than thirty-five per cent. of heater's wages.

ARTICLE XX

SPECIAL RULES—TIN PLATE MILLS

Section 1.   Any tin roller, or other member of his crew, who shall clean grease, or shall change rolls or other castings, or assist in any form, shall be fined not less than five dollars ($5.00) nor more than twenty-five dollars ($25.00) for the first offense, and for the second offense shall be expelled from the association, unless such work be paid for.

Sec. 2.   In case the Mill Committee has any doubt about a turn of work, the said committee shall have power to count how many pairs are in said turn of work and report such turn to the lodge.

Sec. 3.   Roughers on tin plate mills shall receive not less than 30 per cent. of roller's wages, doubler's helper to receive not less than 29 per cent. of doubler's wages, this work to be limited to running the furnace and dragging down pairs. The heater's helper to receive not less than 33½ per cent. of the heater's wages.

Sec. 4.   No helper on tin mills shall be allowed to help more than one man.

Sec. 5.   No catcher shall go down the pit to get grease to put on the roll necks; if he does he shall be fined not less than 25 cents for every offense.   Company shall furnish a man for that purpose.

Sec. 6.   All rollers, doublers and heaters on tin mills employing helpers through the summer months shall be compelled to keep them on through the winter, thus allowing the men holding the jobs the option of hiring helpers or not, as they choose.

ARTICLE XXI

SPECIAL RULES—STEEL AND ROD MILLS

In case any steel mills agree with their company to work pending a settlement of their scale, the employees of said mill shall receive their last year's scale of wages until their new scale is agreed to and signed by both parties.   A written agreement to this effect shall be drawn up and signed by both parties where work is done pending such settlement.   In case the company refuses to agree to the above, the mill shall cease work at the expiration of the old scale.   In case of an advance in their new scale, the same shall date from the expiration of the old scale.   In case of a reduction, the same shall date from time the scale is signed.

ARTICLE XXII

SCALE OF PRICES

Section 1.   Wherever practicable, steps shall be taken to provide a scale of prices for every trade or calling in each district, represented in this association, but no scale or price shall be considered by the Executive Committee or the Convention, unless the same has first been presented to and demanded of the firm.

Sec. 2. When it is found necessary that the scale of prices governing any department of a mill or factory needs revision, such department shall submit in writing to their lodge the alteration desired in their scale on or before the first meeting in the month of March. Each lodge shall then consider such desired changes, and shall vote by written ballot thereon and report the result in writing, under the seal of the lodge, to the general office of the association. No sub-lodge under the jurisdiction of this association, or members thereof, shall countenance the holding of meetings outside the lodge room for the purpose of agitating class legislation for advanced wages, and no lodge in this association shall receive or act on matters discussed, originated, or in any manner acted upon outside of the association relative to class interests.

Sec. 3. When all desired alterations to the several scales are received at the general office from sub-lodges, which shall be on or before the third Tuesday in March, the Secretary-Treasurer of the National Lodge shall get the same printed in pamphlet form, together with the suggested amendments to the laws, and forward a copy thereof to every sub-lodge six weeks prior to the meeting of the next annual convention.

Sec. 4. The proposed alterations to the several scales and amendments to the general laws as compiled and sent to the sub-lodges by the Secretary-Treasurer of the National Lodge, shall then be discussed in each lodge, and the action of the lodge be given to the delegates of the lodge, who shall carry the same to the National Convention.

Sec. 5. The suggestion pertaining to the scale of wages and contained in the programme of business shall be referred to the Wage Committee at the Annual Convention, and the President of the National Lodge is empowered to call the Wage Committee together in the place designated for the meeting of the Annual Convention, three or more days prior to the convening of the Annual Convention at his discretion, for the purpose of considering the scale suggestions and preparing a report thereon for the Annual Convention.

Sec. 6. In order to aid the Wage Committee in their work, the Corresponding Representative of each lodge must send to the general office, two weeks prior to the meeting of the committee a statement giving the condition of their mill, the amount of work done the last year, the feeling of the members of the lodge regarding wages for the next year, stocks on hand, if any, and what kind, and other information that will aid the committee and convention in arriving at proper understanding on the wage question, and any Corresponding Representative failing to comply with the provisions of this section shall be fined in the sum of $2.00 and his sub-lodge shall be notified of the same.

Sec. 7. To change the basis of any scale it will require a two-thirds vote of all the delegates present at the Annual Convention.

Sec. 8. In iron rail, steel-rail and converting mills, all departments in said mills shall have their several scales expire on June 30th, and when it is found necessary that the scale of prices governing any departments of such mills need revising such departments shall submit, in writing, to their lodge the alterations desired in their scale on or before the first stated meeting in March. Each sub-lodge directly interested in such scales shall then consider such proposed change at the first stated meeting in April, at which a vote shall be taken by written ballot, requiring a two-thirds majority to adopt, and if the committee appointed by the lodge fail to agree with the company, the case shall be referred to the Executive Committee of the district for final action. All tonnage-men working in large steel mills, working rails or soft steel billets, with an average output of three hundred tons and more, twelve hours, shall operate three turns of eight hours each.

Sec. 9. Unless the scale is signed in conference, three copies shall be sent out by the Secretary-Treasurer of the National Lodge, and when signed, one shall be kept by the firm, one by the lodge, and the third be sent to the General office of the association.

Sec. 10.   The scale, unless signed in conference, shall be presented to the manufacturers for signature by members of the Mill Committee representing each department one week prior to July 1st, the commencement of the scale year, and notice shall be given by them that unless the scale of prices be signed on or before June 30th, all departments of the mill and factory will cease work after the night turn has finished its turn, provided they start to work before 12 P. M., except roll turners and engineers.

Sec. 11.   Where there are two or more lodges working for the same firm and in the same plant, agreement on scales must be made by joint committee, and that one lodge or one department shall not be permitted to sign a contract or scale until the other departments have agreed, when the scale or contract shall be signed jointly, excepting when agreement is provided for by conference with manufacturers collectively.

Sec. 12.   When a stock of muck bar is on hand and the company does not wish to boil iron, the finishing mill shall run on after the scale is signed.   But when ready to boil every man shall receive his own job; if he does not, the mill shall cease work until he does.

ARTICLE XXIII

SUBORDINATE LODGE OFFICERS

The elective officers of a sub-lodge shall consist of a President, Vice President, Recording Secretary, Financial Secretary, Journal Agent, Treasurer, Guide, Inside Guard, Outside Guard and three Trustees, and in case of resignation or death of any of them, a successor shall be elected to fill the vacancy.

ARTICLE XXIV

NOMINATION AND ELECTION OF SUB-LODGE OFFICERS

Section 1.   The nomination of sub-lodge officers shall be made at the stated meeting preceding the night of election, also on the night of election. A member can be elected into office while absent, provided he has accepted the nomination.

Sec. 2.   To be eligible to the office of President, Vice President, Recording Secretary, Financial Secretary, Journal Agent, Treasurer or Corresponding Representative of a sub-lodge, all candidates therefor must have been members six months.   This shall not apply to lodges that have not been organized six months.

Sec. 3.   The election of officers, except Representative to the National Convention (see Section 7, Article V), shall be separately, by ballot, and shall take place at the last stated meeting in December and June, except the Recording Secretary, Financial Secretary, Treasurer, Journal Agent and three Trustees, who shall be elected annually at the last stated meeting in December.

Sec. 4.   The President shall appoint three members not in nomination for office, one as clerk and two as tellers of election, who shall receive the votes and count them in the presence of the lodge, and the clerk shall announce the result to the President, who shall in turn declare the names of the successful candidates to the lodge.

Sec. 5.   The officers-elect shall assume their respective duties at the first stated meeting after their election.

Sec. 6.   No member shall be entitled to vote who is three months in arrears for dues, assessments and fines, and no candidate shall be eligible for office unless he is clear on the Secretary's books up to and including the night of election.

Sec. 7.   The written ballot shall be used in balloting for all officers, and a candidate must receive a majority of all the votes cast before he can be declared elected. If there should be no election on the first ballot, all but the two highest shall be dropped. No member present shall be excused from voting.

ARTICLE XXV

INSTALLATION OF SUB-LODGE OFFICERS

Section 1. The installation of sub-lodge officers shall take place at the first regular meeting after election. Vacancies *pro tem.*, may be filled at any regular meeting by appointment by the President.

Sec. 2. Any member accepting an election in any subordinate lodge and failing to appear for installation, without a constitutional excuse, shall be fined the sum of fifty cents.

Sec. 3. No officer shall be allowed to vacate his chair until his successor has been installed.

ARTICLE XXVI

SUB-LODGE OFFICERS' DUTIES

Section 1. It shall be the duty of the President to preside at all meetings of the lodge, preserve order and enforce the constitution; he shall decide all questions of order, subject to an appeal to the lodge; he shall have the right to vote at all elections of officers, and when the members are equally divided on other questions he shall have the casting vote; he shall sign all orders on the Treasurer for such moneys as shall, by vote of the lodge, be ordered to be paid; he shall call special meetings at the request of the Mill Committee, or by request of ten members of the lodge in good standing, and perform such other duties as the lodge may require of him.

Sec. 2. It shall be the duty of the Vice President to perform all the duties of the President in case of the absence of that officer, and to assist in preserving order in the lodge.

Sec. 3. It shall be the duty of the Recording Secretary to record the proceedings of the lodge in a book kept for that purpose; to read all papers before the lodge, and draw and sign all warrants ordered by the lodge, and perform such other duties as the lodge may require.

Sec. 4. The Corresponding Representative shall answer all letters and carry on all correspondence which may be deemed necessary, abstracts of which he shall record in a book kept for that purpose, which at all times shall be subject to the inspection of the lodge. He shall also prepare and send to the Secretary-Treasurer of the National Association a quarterly report, as provided for in Section 4 and Section 6, Article XXII, and perform such other duties as the lodge may require of him. All necessary expenses incurred by him in the discharge of his duties shall be paid by the lodge.

Sec. 5. It shall be the duty of the Financial Secretary to receive all moneys due the lodge and pay the same to the Treasurer, from whom he shall take a receipt; he shall keep correctly the accounts of the lodge with its members, and shall at all times have his books open for examination by the Auditing Committee, and perform such other duties as the lodge may require of him.

Sec. 6. It shall be the duty of the Treasurer to receive from the Financial Secretary all moneys collected by him. He shall deposit all moneys belonging to the lodge in bank, in his name as Treasurer of ———— Lodge, No. ————, State ————, Amalgamated Association of Iron, Steel and Tin Workers, and before any money thus deposited can be drawn each check shall be signed by him as Treasurer and countersigned by the President, Recording Secretary and Chairman of the Board of Trustees of the lodge. He shall pay all warrants drawn on him by the President and signed by the Recording Secretary; keep regular and correct accounts of all money received and paid by him, and report the same at each

287

quarterly meeting; having his accounts open for examination by the Auditing Committee at any time when called upon; and at the expiration of his term of office (or sooner if called upon by the lodge so to do), deliver up all moneys, books, papers and vouchers in his possession to the Auditing Committee or his legally elected successor. Before entering upon the duties of his office he shall give bonds with such security as may be thought proper by the lodge for the correct and faithful performance of his duties.

Sec. 7. It shall be the duty of the Guide to see that all present are entitled to remain; take up the password, introduce candidates and attend to visiting members.

Sec. 8. It shall be the duty of the Guards to attend properly to the doors, inside and out, and see that none but members are admitted, unless permitted by the lodge.

Sec. 9. It shall be the duty of the Trustees to have charge of the hall and all property of the lodge, subject to the direction of the lodge, and perform such other duties as the lodge may require. They shall also hold the bond of the Treasurer, and see that said bond is legal.

ARTICLE XXVII
SUBORDINATE LODGE MEETINGS

Section 1. Stated meetings of sub-lodges shall be held not less than twice a month.

Sec. 2. Special meetings must be called by the President on application of the Mill Committee, or any ten members in good standing, or at any time the President himself may deem it necessary for the interest of the lodge.

Sec. 3. When special meetings are called, there shall be no business transacted except such as is specified in the call.

Sec. 4. Seven members shall constitute a quorum for the transaction of business at stated meetings, and ten members shall constitute a quorum at special meetings, and no intoxicating drinks shall be permitted to be served in any room when holding a business meeting.

ARTICLE XXVIII
APPLICATION FOR MEMBERSHIP

Section 1. Candidates for membership to sub-lodges shall be proposed by a member of the lodge in good standing, which proposition shall be made in writing, entered on the records and referred to a committee, whose duty it shall be to inquire and report in writing, at the next stated meeting of the lodge, as to the fitness of the candidate for membership. Candidates for membership working by the day or hour in steel mills shall apply to the lodge composed of men working by the day or hour in such mills, if one is in existence, and lodges composed of tonnage men shall receive application from such men in such mills. The Recording Secretary shall read the proof of the committee, and if it is favorable, the candidate shall be balloted for, and if all the balls are white, he shall be declared elected, but if two or more black balls appear against him, his case shall be referred to a special committee for investigation; and should the persons casting the black balls refuse or neglect to give their reasons for so doing to the special committee for the space of two weeks, and should the special committee themselves find no just cause for the rejection, they shall report favorable to his election, whereupon he shall again be balloted for, and if two-thirds of the votes cast be favorable he shall be declared elected, but if more than one-third be unfavorable he shall be declared rejected. Should either committee report unfavorable, they shall state their reason for so doing, and the lodge shall then receive or reject said reasons by a majority vote.

Membership shall date from time of initiation, admission by card, or reinstatement, and dues, fines and other moneys shall be charged accordingly.

Sec. 2.   It shall be the duty of the Corresponding Representative to notify the general office of the rejection of a candidate, and a person who has been rejected in any lodge shall not be proposed for membership in any other lodge for the space of six months thereafter.   And should the candidate apply to any other lodge for membership after the expiration of six months, it shall be the duty of such lodge to instruct their Corresponding Representative to inquire of the sub-lodge that rejected the candidate the cause of such rejection.

Sec. 3.   The member who shall propose a candidate for membership shall, at the time of making the proposition, pay to the Secretary one-half the amount of the initiation fee, which shall be returned in case the candidate is rejected.   Should the candidate be elected, he shall be admitted on payment of the balance of his initiation fee and signing the Constitution.

Sec. 4.   Should the candidate neglect or refuse to appear and be initiated for the term of one month after receiving notice of his election, unless prevented by sickness or other unavoidable occurrence, he shall forfeit his claim to membership, together with the amount paid at the time of his application.

ARTICLE XXIX

DUES AND OTHER MONEYS

Section 1.   Each new member of a sub-lodge shall pay an initiation fee of not less than $5 and for dues members earning $2.50 per day or less, shall pay 60 cents per month; over $2.50 and less than $5, 80 cents per month; $5 and upwards, $1 per month, and 25 cents per month which is to go to Benefit Fund, together with fines and other moneys.   The due card shall be sufficient notice of his arrears, and any member omitting to pay the same within three months shall be reported to the lodge by the Financial Secretary, whereupon the President shall, unless otherwise directed by the lodge, declare such member suspended.

Sec. 2.   A member suspended for non-payment of dues, shall be reinstated upon the payment of not less than $5, as provided in Section 19, Article XI, and such sum (not to exceed one year's dues, said one year's dues not to include special assessments), as the lodge may determine.

Sec. 3.   A member feeling incapable, by some unavoidable cause, to pay dues, fines and other moneys, shall report his cause to the lodge, who may exempt him from paying the same by a two-thirds majority.

Sec. 4.   Any lodge having charged any member full dues and accounts, shall forward the pro rata amounts due to National office.

ARTICLE XXX

MEMBERS IN ARREARS

Any member of a subordinate lodge three months in arrears, shall not be recognized by the Mill Committee in any grievance in which he may become involved during such arrears, even though he pay up his arrearages immediately before or after the trouble arises.

ARTICLE XXXI

FUNDS

Section 1.   The funds of each sub-lodge shall be used only for its legitimate purposes, and under no circumstances shall the funds of any sub-lodge be appropriated to, or divided among its members, except by permission of the National Secretary-Treasurer.

Sec. 2.   In order that the funds of the lodge may be had at as short notice as possible when required, it shall be the duty of the Treasurer to deposit in the bank all moneys over twenty-five dollars; the Treasurer shall draw the moneys thus deposited whenever it may be required to be used to pay orders regularly drawn on him by the proper officers of the lodge.

Sec. 3. All bills and other claims against the lodge must be presented at regular meetings and receive the approval of the same before payment.

ARTICLE XXXII
SUB-LODGE AUDITING COMMITTEE

Section 1. At the last stated meeting in June and December, each sub-lodge shall appoint three members for the purpose of auditing the accounts of the Financial Secretary and Treasurer.

Sec. 2. The Auditing Committee shall thoroughly investigate the accounts and report the same to the lodge at the first stated meetings in July and January, and the balance that the books call for shall be shown to the lodge by the Treasurer, or its equivalent in a certificate of deposit, or the account in a bank book.

Sec. 3. Should the Auditing Committee, through complication of account or otherwise, be unable to report, as provided in Section 2 of this Article, they shall nevertheless report to the lodge the condition of affairs, when the lodge shall grant such time as the exigencies of the case may require.

Sec. 4. It shall be the duty of all members to render the officers and committees of the lodge proper aid and influence in the prosecution of their duties.

Sec. 5. All committees not otherwise provided for shall be appointed by the President.

ARTICLE XXXIII
FINES FOR VARIOUS CAUSES

Section 1. Officers and members of subordinate lodges are required to be punctual in their attendance.

Sec. 2. Officers of subordinate lodges failing to attend the regular meeting of the lodge shall, for such omission, be fined twenty-five cents, unless satisfactory reasons can be shown, in which case the fine shall be remitted.

Sec. 3. Members of sub-lodges failing to attend meetings of their lodges for two successive meetings shall be fined the sum of ten cents, and any member failing to attend lodge for three months shall be fined one dollar, unless excused through sickness or some other unavoidable cause.

Sec. 4. Any member of a subordinate lodge failing to appear at the last stated meetings in June and December shall be fined fifty cents, unless he can give satisfactory evidence that it was impossible to attend.

Sec. 5. Any member of a subordinate lodge persisting in using unseemly language, or in any indecent manner give offense to a brother member, or by offensive conduct, shall be fined one dollar for the first offense, and if he still persists in the unmanly use of such language, he shall be excluded from the lodge room and will not be permitted to re-enter during the meeting.

Sec. 6. The chairman of any committee failing to report at the time required, unless further time be granted, shall be fined one dollar. Such fine, however, shall be remitted when satisfactory explanation is given.

Sec. 7. Any member entering a subordinate lodge under the influence of liquor shall, for the first offense, be fined one dollar, and double the sum for every subsequent offense.

Sec. 8. Any member of a subordinate lodge violating his obligation to this order, shall be liable to a fine of not less than three dollars, reprimand, suspension or expulsion, according to the decision of his lodge on a two-thirds majority vote.

Sec. 9. Any Corresponding Representative failing or neglecting to prepare and forward quarterly report of his lodge, or to attend to such other duties as pertain to his office, shall be fined two dollars; and any Corresponding Representative refusing to serve as such, after being elected delegate and attending Convention, shall be fined not less than five dollars.

Sec. 10. All fines thus imposed, if not paid at the time, shall be charged by the Financial Secretary to the person from whom due, and must be liquidated at the end of each quarter to entitle him to the privileges or benefits of this association.

Sec. 11. Any member or members of lodge or lodges working on Labor Day shall be fined not less than five dollars ($5.00), nor more than twenty-five dollars ($25.00) for the first offense; for the second offense the President shall take the charter from any and all offending lodges.

Sec. 12. All rollers and furnacemen are required to report to their lodge once a month the names of their crews or helpers, giving their standing in the lodge. Failure so to do, a fine of one dollar shall be imposed.

Sec. 13. Any tin roller found working without a screw boy shall be fined five dollars ($5.00) for the first offense, and for the second offense he shall be suspended or expelled from the lodge.

ARTICLE XXXIV

MILL COMMITTEE AND THEIR DUTIES

Section 1. Each sub-lodge shall have a Mill Committee consisting of three members, on each turn, from each department represented in the lodge, and any member in good standing in the lodge and holding a job in the mill where the lodge exists, can be appointed on the Mill Committee, whether at the meeting or not, provided he is twenty-one (21) years of age, and has been a member of this association one year, and all excuses from serving on said committee must be granted by a two-thirds vote of the lodge. This law shall not apply to newly organized lodges where the members have not held membership for one year.

Sec. 2. It shall be the duty of said committee to superintend and guard the interests of the association in their several departments, and any member found guilty of interfering, abusing, or insulting a member of the committee while in the discharge of his duties shall be fined $5.00 for the first offense, and for the second offense he shall be expelled from the lodge. When it becomes apparent that any advantage is being taken of our laws or any member of this association, and the committee of the department where this occurs has failed to adjust the difficulty with the manager of the works, after using all honorable means to bring about a settlement, they shall immediately call a joint meeting of the respective lodges, and all members of each lodge working in that mill shall be notified by the Mill Committee to attend same.

Sec. 3. At said special meeting the grievance pending shall be explicitly stated by the members of the committee, and if the joint meeting consider the grievance sufficient, the Corresponding Representative of the lodge having the grievance, shall, by instruction of his lodge, *under their seal, and in no other manner,* notify the Vice President of the district or division, and work shall continue until the Vice President has investigated the case.

Sec. 4. The communication sent to the Vice President, as set forth in Section 3, shall in turn be sent to the general office of this association by the Vice President as a guarantee that the sub-lodge has complied with the law prior to the Vice President going to investigate the case.

Sec. 5. In mills or factories where the manager, superintendent, foreman or boss absolutely refuses to recognize the Mill Committee in the settlement of any difficulty in which this association is interested, the committee shall immediately call a special meeting, as set forth in Section 2 of this Article, and carry out the instructions as laid down in Section 2.

Sec. 6. In each works the committee shall wait on each new workman when employed and ask him for his card. They shall deliver the same to the Secretary. But if he has not got a withdrawal card then 50 cents per turn shall be collected from him until he gets his card, and the lodge shall adopt any means within its power to collect the same, and if the man fails or refuses to get his card the lodge shall retain the money so collected; but if a man is not a member, then steps shall be taken to induce him to join.

They shall carefully watch and attend to any complaint that may suddenly arise in the works, or any other matters affecting the interests of the members, and when it is found that a manager, superintendent or foreman is using his or their influence in persuading men in the mills or factories not to join their association, they shall severally be notified by the Mill or Factory Committee that such action must be stopped.

ARTICLE XXXV
DISHONORABLE MEMBERS

Section 1. Any member robbing or embezzling from a brother involving wages, or monies of sub-lodge, or misapplying the funds of the National Lodge or the money of any member or candidate entrusted to him for payment of the same; or by divulging any of the proceedings of the lodge, or who has slandered any brother member, or advocated division of the funds or separation of lodge districts, or by action contrary to the established rules of this association or any question affecting the price of labor, or the system of working in the district, if opposed to the interest of his fellow-workmen in keeping with the rules of this association, shall, upon trial and conviction thereof, be punished by fine, suspension or expulsion as may be determined by two-thirds of the members present.

Sec. 2. Any member or members of this association having procured credit for groceries, board bill, provisions or clothing, and who refuses to pay or make arrangements to pay the same, he or they shall receive no protection from the Mill Committee or the lodge in case of discharge by the manager upon complaint of the person or persons to whom such debt or debts are owing.

Sec. 3. Members expelled from a subordinate lodge shall remain expelled for one month, when they may renew their connection with the association on application in writing to and on such conditions as may be agreed upon by the lodge to which they formerly belonged. But should the applicant for reinstatement consider the sum demanded exorbitant (or should the lodge refuse to reinstate him for any sum), and the lodge persistently refuse to reinstate him, the Executive Board of the National Lodge shall, upon application by the person or persons asking for reinstatement, have power to grant such applicant a card for an amount to be determined by said board, and should any sub-lodge, within thirty (30) days after receiving notice from the Executive Board of the amount determined upon by them to be charged for reinstatement, fail to reinstate such person or grant him or them a card, the President of the National Lodge shall issue such card to the person or persons asking reinstatement, collect the amount determined upon by the Executive Board and turn it over to the lodge, and no member shall refuse to work with such person or persons while their case is pending. In all cases, however, where a person applies to the Executive Board for a card, the sub-lodge refusing to grant the same shall be heard in evidence before the board.

ARTICLE XXXVI
CARDS

Section 1. The National Association shall issue a yearly working card, and also a withdrawal and an honorary card. Withdrawal cards shall be in possession of the Secretary of local lodge and shall bear the seal of said lodge. He shall distribute them per order of subordinate lodges for the use of any member in good standing and no subordinate lodge shall have authority to grant or receive any other card but those provided by the National Association.

Sec. 2. All members shall be provided with a working or due card, which will be issued at the end of each year, showing the member's standing in the lodge, said card to be produced at the request of the Mill Committee, and such members shall not be entitled to any benefits and privileges of the association, unless said card shows the member to be in good standing.

Sec. 3. Any person referred to or mentioned in Section 1, Article I, must, unless a reasonable excuse is given, produce a working card before they be allowed to work; and those not members, who have situations, shall be given four weeks' time to join, and the President of the sub-lodge will see that this section is enforced.

Sec. 4. Any member of this association going from one locality to another shall provide himself with a withdrawal card. Said card shall bear certificate of membership from subordinate lodge, with date of initiation, admission by card or reinstatement; and also a certificate of such lodge membership in the National Association; and any member obtaining such card must present the same for membership in any other lodge, except the holder of such card works by the day or hour in steel mills, in which case such card shall be deposited in the lodge composed of men working by the day or hour in said mill (if one be in existence) and no subordinate lodge shall have power to reject said card. No member shall be entitled to receive a withdrawal card unless he is in good standing and clear on the Secretary's books.

Sec. 5. Withdrawal cards shall not be dated for more than one month in advance, and any sub-lodge issuing cards for a longer period shall refund to the member to whom said card is granted all money paid in excess of one month's dues.

Sec. 6. Any member removing from one locality to another, and obtaining a situation, must deposit his card in the lodge which controls the mill wherein he works, and all cards not deposited within four weeks thereafter, shall be annulled.

Sec. 7. Where there are two or more lodges in one mill, the members must belong to the lodge governing the department in which said members are working.

Sec. 8. Members holding withdrawal cards and not depositing them as provided in Section 4 of this article (knowing the existence of a lodge in the locality where they reside or work), shall pay to the lodge in which said card is deposited such fine as said lodge may deem proper to inflict, also dues from the time said card became annulled until it was accepted by the lodge.

Sec. 9. The Secretary-Treasurer of the National Association shall attach the seal thereof to all cards before forwarding them to subordinate lodges; and all cards granted by any subordinate lodge shall be signed by the subordinate lodge President and Financial Secretary, and receive the seal of said lodge.

Sec. 10. Any member retiring permanently from this Association and desiring an Honorary Card must make application for it at the next stated meeting of his lodge, which card, upon the full payment of all obligations shall be granted him, failure on his part to make the application in the time specified shall forfeit his right to secure said Honorary Card, and no card shall be granted him unless he again resumes active membership in the Association in accordance with the provisions of Article I, Section 1.

Honorary Cards shall be in possession of National Secretary, and shall be issued by him, properly made out upon application of sub-lodge which must send name of applicant to National Lodge. Should the holder at any time desire to deposit said card in any subordinate lodge, the President thereof shall appoint a committee of three to investigate his conduct toward the order and its members during the time he held such card, if the committee report favorable, a ballot shall be taken, and by a majority vote the applicant shall be admitted to membership upon the payment of the sum of $5.00 admission fee, $2.00 of which shall be sent to National Lodge for Insurance Fund. This not to apply to silent members. But if the committee report unfavorable, then a ballot shall be taken, and unless two-thirds of the members vote in favor of his admission, the President shall reject his card.

ARTICLE XXXVII

BY-LAWS OF SUBORDINATE LODGES

Subordinate lodges shall have full power to make such by-laws for their government as they may deem necessary, providing they do not conflict with any of the laws, rules or regulations herein [con]tained.

ARTICLE XXXVIII

AMENDMENTS AND DISSOLUTION

Section 1. This Constitution shall not be altered or amended except by the National Convention a majority of the members present consenting thereto.

Sec. 2. No subordinate lodge can dissolve so long as there are ten members in good standing who are willing to continue it.

RULES FOR COMPOSITION AND METHOD OF HOLDING CONFERENCE

RULE 1. The President shall negotiate with manufacturers with a view of bringing about a conference between them and representatives of the Amalgamated Association, which conference is to discuss the scale adopted by convention and arrive at settlement of scale rates for the year succeeding.

RULE 2. To the end that thorough representation may be secured, there shall be appointed by the President a General Conference Committee, composed of forty members, who shall be selected with a view of their familiarity as to the trades that will be by them represented in conference. All Conference Committees shall be selected from the membership of Convention of that year in good standing in the organization.

RULE 3. This General Conference Committee, after having been appointed, shall be divided by the President into four divisions, constituted and operated as follows:

RULE 4. Division No. 1, composed of nine members from the Boiling department, which shall include Boiling, Scrapping, Busheling, Muck mill and Knobbling, and this division shall alone confer with manufacturers in the settlement of the rates for trades given.

RULE 5. Division No. 2, composed of eleven men from Bar, Guide, Plate, Structural and Jobbing mills working pipe iron. Any member of these trades having the necessary qualifications, as indicated above, shall be eligible to serve hereon, and this division shall confer and settle rates for the trades given.

RULE 6. Division No. 3, composed of nine members of the Sheet and Jobbing mills and the branches directly connected therewith, who shall confer and settle rates for trades given.

RULE 7. Division No. 4, composed of nine members from Tin and Black Plate mills, Tin houses and branches directly connected therewith, who shall confer and settle rates for their trade

RULE 8. The President and Secretary-Treasurer of the National Lodge shall be standing members of the General Conference Committee, and also of each division of the Conference Committee.

RULE 9. The President of the National Lodge shall, after consultation with manufacturers with whom conference is sought, arrange a method of procedure by which the scale may be taken up in conference in the order named, and the respective division shall be notified by the President of the readiness of the conference to proceed to the discussion of that class of trade in their charge.

RULES OF ORDER OF THE NATIONAL CONVENTION AND SUB-LODGES

RULE 1. The President having taken the chair, officers and members shall take their respective seats, and at the sound of the gavel there shall be general silence.

RULE 2. The President shall preserve order and pronounce the decision of the lodge on all subjects. He shall decide questions of order without debate, subject to an appeal to the lodge by three members; on which appeal no member shall speak but once, when the question before the lodge shall be: " Shall the decision of the President stand as the judgment of the lodge ?" Which question shall be taken up by the lodge.

RULE 3. During the reading of the minutes, communications and other papers, or when a member is addressing the chair, silence shall be observed in the lodge room.

RULE 4. Any member who shall misbehave himself in the meeting of the lodge, disturb the order or harmony thereof, either by abusive, disorderly or profane language, or shall refuse obedience to the presiding officer, shall be admonished of his offense by the President, and if he offends again he shall be excluded from the room for the session, and afterward dealt with as this Constitution provides.

RULE 5. No member shall be interrupted while speaking, except it shall be to call him to order, or for the purpose of explanation.

RULE 6. If a member, while speaking, be called to order, he shall at the request of the President, take his seat until the question of order is determined, when, if permitted, he may proceed.

RULE 7. Each member, when speaking, shall be standing, and respectfully address the President, confine himself to the question under debate and avoid all personalities or indecorous or sarcastic language.

RULE 8. If two or more members arise to speak at the same time, the President shall decide who is entitled to the floor.

RULE 9. No member shall speak more than once on the same subject or question until all who wish to speak shall have had an opportunity to do so, nor more than twice, without permission from the President.

RULE 10. No motion shall be subject to debate until it shall have been seconded and stated from the chair. It shall be reduced to writing at the request of two members.

RULE 11. When a question is before the lodge, no motion shall be in order except to adjourn, for the previous question, to postpone indefinitely, or for a certain time, to divide, commit or amend; which motions shall severally have precedence, in the order herein arranged.

RULE 12. On the call of five members, debate shall cease, and a vote shall be taken on the matter or subject under debate.

RULE 13. On the call of five members, a majority of the lodge may demand the previous question, which shall be put in this form: " Shall the main question be put?" and until it is decided shall preclude all amendments and all further debate.

RULE 14. When a blank is to be filled, the question shall be taken first upon the highest sum or number and the longest and latest time proposed.

RULE 15. Any member may call for a division of the question when the same will admit of it, but a motion to strike out and insert will be indivisible, except at the option of the mover.

RULE 16. Before putting the question the President shall ask: "Is the lodge ready for the question?" If no member rises to speak, he shall rise and put it, and after he has risen to put the question no member shall be permitted to speak upon it. When the President is addressing the lodge or putting a question silence shall be observed in the lodge room.

RULE 17. All questions, unless otherwise provided, shall be decided by majority of the vote given.

RULE 18. Communications, petitions and memorials shall be presented through a member of this lodge, or by the presiding officer; a brief statement of their contents shall be entered upon the minutes.

RULE 19. Any member may excuse himself from serving on a committee if at the time of his appointment he is a member of one other committee.

RULE 20. The person first named on a committee shall act as chairman until another is chosen by the members of the committee. The mover of a resolution referred to a special committee is usually the first named thereon.

RULE 21. No committee can be finally discharged until all the debts contracted by it shall have been paid.

RULE 22. A motion to adjourn is always in order after the regular order of business is gone through, which shall be decided without debate.

RULE 23. A motion to lay on the table shall be decided without debate.

RULE 24. When a motion is postponed indefinitely it shall not be acted on during that or the next succeeding stated meeting.

RULE 25. No motion for reconsideration shall be received if made by a member who voted in the minority in the first instance.

RULE 26. On the call of five members present the yeas and nays shall be ordered. When the question is decided by yeas and nays, each member shall vote and the names and manner of voting shall be recorded on the minutes.

RULE 27. All questions of order not provided for by these rules must be determined by Cushing's Manual or at the discretion of the lodge.

RULE 28. No scale question can be admitted into convention only through the program, unless such question has arisen after the program has been printed.

IV. COMPARATIVE TABLE OF THE NUMERICAL AND FINANCIAL GROWTH AND DECLINE OF THE AMALGAMATED ASSOCIATION SINCE ITS INSTITUTION, AUGUST 4, 1876, RUNNING BY YEARS FROM CONVENTION TO CONVENTION

Reported to Convention Held at:	Year	Delegates in Attendance	Number of Active Lodges	Total Membership	Average Membership	Total Receipts from all Sources	Total Disbursements for all Purposes	Balance in the Treasury
Columbus .	1877	77	111	3,755	34	$5065.49	$3162.83	$802.96
Wheeling .	1878	91	110	4,044	37	4913.81	3004.89	912.47
Youngstown	1879	104	104	5,500	52	15754.30	12423.71	1664.59
Pittsburgh .	1880	192	155	9,550	62	20963.84	13972.42	6991.20
Cleveland .	1881	173	166	10,359	62	39554.40	27150.98	12393.42
Chicago .	1882	213	197	16,003	81	91166.83	66239.98	24826.94
Philadelphia	1883	153	183	11,800	64	109711.31	96823.65	12877.66
Pittsburgh .	1884	149	160	9,242	58	50251.37	31959.84	18291.53
Wheeling .	1885	88	107	5,702	53	44324.82	16042.55	28282.27
Pittsburgh .	1886	121	106	7.219	68	45523.26	35601.98	9921.28
Pittsburgh .	1887	172	154	11,426	74	42522.78	11774.66	30748.11
Pittsburgh .	1888	194	172	14,946	87	81173.01	24206.21	56966.80
Pittsburgh .	1889	194	189	16,117	85	112338.19	40661.15	71677.04
Pittsburgh .	1890	253	234	20,781	88	138919.01	38460.16	100458.85
Pittsburgh .	1891	294	290	24,068	83	173231.27	26690.04	146541.23
Pittsburgh .	1892	254	291	20,975	72	226265.49	150549.33	75716.16
Pittsburgh .	1893	152	234	13,613	58	211347.13	178741.71	32605.42
Cleveland .	1894	96	150	10,000	66	57974.34	42404.71	15542.64
Cleveland .	1895	85	125	10,000	80	34539.57	21048.40	13491.17
Detroit . .	1896	115	132	11,000	83	35781.72	12525.76	23255.96
Detroit . .	1897	123	145	10,500	72	44426.65	15962.96	28463.69
Cincinnati .	1898	118	153	10,500	65	52663.62	25830.65	26832.97
Detroit . .	1899	140	145	11,050	76	57070.90	22202.62	34868.28
Indianapolis	1900	202	181	14,035	77	84307.81	27364.40	56943.41
Milwaukee .	1901	200	160	13,892	87	119659.07	44760.33	74898.74
Wheeling .	1902	211	174	14,467	83	273906.01	169710.50	104195.51
Columbus .	1903	200	185	15,198	82	183897.81	51172.16	132725.65
Cleveland .	1904	207	183	14,306	79	208065.67	83318.99	124746.68
Detroit . .	1905	166	157	10,904	69	203243.04	155730.75	47512.29
Cincinnati .	1906	170	144	11,410	79	129383.15	89758.60	39624.55
Toledo . .	1907	150	139	10,216	73	135321.56	85745.00	49576.56
Youngstown	1908	115	124	7,472	60	125710.53	67899.40	57811.13
Detroit . .	1909	95	114	6,295	55	125895.54	79546.14	46349.40
Ft. Wayne .	1910	116	103	8,257	80	247981.90	218634.62	29347.34

APPENDIX III

UNIONISM AT HOMESTEAD SINCE 1892

I

(From the *Pittsburgh Dispatch*, August 4, 1901. Page 6.)

The Amalgamated Association organization have tried every mill in the Carnegie system. A singular run of bad luck has followed them everywhere. Not a move could they make that was not instantly reported to the superintendent of the works. Every man in the employment of these establishments knows what will happen to him if he is discovered joining or aiding a labor organization and the system of that company for getting information was found to be so perfect, that in some instances the managers knew in advance what was contemplated. * * *

The story of their defeat is similar to that of former attempts to organize the Homestead works after the great strike of 1892. An open attempt was made by the skilled workmen to organize in 1895. Meetings were held in the opera house at Homestead, and the result was that the company broke up the lodge in short order and 35 of the most prominent members of the lodge were discharged.

Another attempt was made about a year ago. This time the men went about it secretly. They held their meetings in Pittsburgh. In a short time they had a good-sized organization. Then, like a bolt from the blue sky, the company let the newly made union men know that it was cognizant of every move that had been made. It was known just what men had attended the meeting once and names were given of workmen who had attended two and three times. As a result of this attempt to organize 14 men were discharged, and that is what caused the Amalgamated Association to fail in the present crisis.

II

Letter from T. J. Shaffer, President of Amalgamated Association of Iron, Steel and Tin Workers, to Samuel Gompers, President of the American Federation of Labor:*

Pittsburgh, Pa., March 19, 1900.

Dear Sir and Brother: In the early part of May, 1899, about twenty-three employees of the Homestead mill of the Carnegie Company came to the office of the Amalgamated Association of Iron, Steel, and Tin Workers, requesting that they be permitted to organize a lodge at Homestead. We consented, with the understanding that old conditions were to remain intact. No agreements were to be broken; no demands made, and all contracts fulfilled, and on no conditions was

* Page 400 of Report of hearings on eight-hour bill before Committee on Labor, House of Representatives, 56th Congress, 1st Session, 1900.

there to be a strike.   They organized a lodge that night, and every Saturday night for weeks thereafter others came until they numbered about three hundred.   In the meantime I was endeavoring to obtain an interview with Mr. Frick for the purpose of showing the advantages of dealing with us, because of the new régime of the Amalgamated Association of Iron, Steel, and Tin Workers, but I was never admitted to his presence.

About the close of July the company discovered the fact that the men were organizing, and an open, avowed, and expressed effort was made to destroy the work already done and prevent others from engaging in it.   Exactly how many were discharged I can not say, but all who were known to have joined us were told they were discharged, or would be if they refused to leave our organization.   We sent some of them to Newcastle, Pa., others to South Chicago, Ill., and made arrangements to send some to Endsley, Ala.

Some became frightened and, giving up their connection with us, were permitted to work.   I advised others, who thought the treatment of the company tyrannical, to take cards and go to work, agreeing to vouch for them at other organized mills in case they lost their jobs at Homestead.   These men, all of them, had been told plainly, and with no attempt at concealment of that motive, that they were discharged, or would be, for connecting themselves with a labor organization.   I had determined to institute legal proceedings against the Carnegie Company for violation of the "anti-discrimination law" of the State of Pennsylvania, but at this time Judge Gunster, I believe is his name, a judicial officer of an eastern county in Pennsylvania, decided that law to be unconstitutional, and consequently, the matter dropped.

I write this succinct history to show that Mr. Corey's statement regarding the attitude of the Carnegie Company toward labor organization is absolutely and unqualifiedly misleading and untrue, and request that you, as the president of the American Federation of Labor, take such steps to bring this before the Committee of Labor of the House of Representatives as shall convince that honorable and intelligent body of the unfairness and falsity of Mr. Corey's declaration as made before them.   All of the above can be substantiated, and if necessary affidavits can be obtained from the men who were not permitted or who refused to return, and if immunity from discharge and persecution can be procured for those still in the employ of the Carnegie Company, I assure you affidavits can be secured from many of them.

Yours fraternally,
(Signed)   T. J. SHAFFER, President

To Mr. SAMUEL GOMPERS,
       President of American Federation of Labor

APPENDIX IV

WAGE FIGURES

I. First Sliding Scale in Iron Industry

(From *National Labor Tribune*, February 7, 1874.)

MEMORANDUM OF AGREEMENT

Made the 13th day of February, 1865, between a committee of Boilers and a committee from the Iron Manufacturers, appointed to fix a scale of prices to be paid for boiling pig iron, based on the manufacturers' card of prices, it being understood either party shall have the right and privilege to terminate this agreement by giving ninety days' notice to the other party, and that there shall be no deviation without such notice.

When the manufacturers' card of prices are at the rate named below, the price for boiling shall be at the price opposite, per ton of 2,240 pounds.

SCALE OF PRICES

Manufacturer	Boiler
8½ cents per pound	$9.00
8¼ cents per pound	8.75
8 cents per pound	8.50
7¾ cents per pound	8.25
7½ and 7¼ cents per pound	8.00
7 and 6¾ cents per pound	7.50
6½ and 6¼ cents per pound	7.00
6 and 5¾ cents per pound	6.50
5½ and 5¼ cents per pound	6.00
5 and 4¾ cents per pound	5.75
4½ and 4¼ cents per pound	5.50
4 and 3¾ cents per pound	5.00
3½ and 3¼ cents per pound	4.75
3 and 2¾ cents per pound	4.50
2½ cents per pound	4.00

The scale was signed for the employes by

Miles S. Humphreys	Richard Thomas
Joseph Chiverton	Patrick Graham
Wm. Sheargold	B. A. McGinty
William Codrington	John D. Evans
John C. O'Donnell	Mathew Haddock

The manufacturers* signing the scale were

B. F. Jones	Barkley Preston
James I. Bennett	Jacob F. Slagle
Henry Loyd	

* B. F. Jones was of the firm of Jones and Laughlin; James I. Bennett, of

II. Wage Statistics of Representative Departments in a Typical Steel Company of Allegheny County, October 1, 1907

Blast Furnaces:

Total number of ten-hour men 625		
Average earnings per man per day		$2.01
Total number of twelve-hour men 804		
Average earnings per man per day		2.45
Rates per day for two most important positions:		
Blowers, per turn		3.70
Keepers, per turn		2.75

Steel Works—Open-hearth Department:

Total number of ten-hour men 93		
Average earnings per man per day		1.80
Total number of twelve-hour men 1517		
Average earnings per man per day		2.76

BESSEMER DEPARTMENT

Position	Number of Employes	Hours per Day	Rate	Earnings per Day
1. Superintendents, general foremen . .	3	12	$7.75	$7.75
2. Foremen	5	12	3.30	3.30
3. Clerks, timekeepers and weighers . .	5	12	2.43	2.43
4. Metal wheelers (per 100 tons) . . .	22	12	.64	2.28
5. Coke wheelers (per 100 tons) . . .	8	12	.56	1.99
6. Cupola foremen (per 100 tons) . .	2	12	1.00	3.56
7. Cupola foremen's assistants (per 100 tons)	16	12	.71	2.51
8. Bottom makers (per 100 tons) . .	4	12	.75	2.67
9. Blowers (per 100 tons)	2	12	1.20	4.27
10. Blowers' assistants (per 100 tons) . .	4	12	.68	2.42
11. Vessel foremen and assistants (per 100 tons)	9	8	1.23	2.94
12. Stopper setters, maker (per 100 tons) .	11	12	.66	2.43
13. Stripper men (per 100 tons) . . .	4	12	.65	2.31
14. Engineers, narrow gauge (per 100 tons) .	18	12	.77	2.76
15. Engineers, stationary	7	12	2.64	2.64
16. Ladle liners (per 100 tons) . . .	3	12	.85	3.03
Ladle liners.	4	12	2.35	2.35
17. Millwrights	6	12	2.65	2.65
18. Common labor, 16½ cents per hour. .	19	11	1.82	1.82
Common labor, unspecified positions .	9	12	2.04	2.04
Common labor, unspecified positions (100 tons)	20	12	.034	2.18

Graft, Bennett and Company; Henry Loyd, of Loyd and Black; Barkley Preston, of Everson, Preston and Company; and Jacob F. Slagle, of Schoenberg and Company; all of Pittsburgh, Pennsylvania. These firms were the representative iron manufacturers of the period. Of those signing the scale, workmen and manufacturers, only two are now living, Miles S. Humphreys and John D. O'Donnell.

IMPORTANT POSITIONS—OPEN-HEARTH DEPARTMENT

Position	Number of Hours per Turn	Number of Men, 24 Hours	Rate	Average Earnings per Day
Melter foremen . . .	12	2	{ $127.50 1.58	$8.14
" " . . .	12	2	{ 127.50 1.46	11.23
" " . . .	12	2	{ 108.00 1.80	7.46
" " . . .	12	2	{ 108.00 1.75	9.25
" " . . .	12	4	{ 108.00 1.46	9.61
" " . . .	12	8	{ 99.00 1.46	8.75
First helpers	12	2	15.00	3.83
" "	12	4	12.99	3.85
" "	12	14	9.08	5.63
" "	12	24	8.50	4.76
" "	12	8	7.41	4.82
" "	12	48	7.89	5.22
" "	12	20	8.10	5.34
Second helpers . . .	12	2	9.64	2.46
" " . . .	12	4	8.12	2.40
" " . . .	12	14	5.95	3.69
" " . . .	12	24	5.57	3.12
" " . . .	12	8	4.86	3.16
" " . . .	12	48	5.17	3.42
" " . . .	12	20	5.30	3.50
Cinder-pitmen . . .	12	10	5.74	2.37
" " . . .	12	10	5.03	2.32
" " . . .	12	16	4.33	2.57
" " . . .	12	16	3.83	2.39
" " . . .	12	48	.71	2.35
" " . . .	12	20	.82	2.50
Charging machine operators	12	2	2.14	3.04
" " "	12	2	1.71	3.11
" " "	12	6	.39	3.66
" " "	12	8	1.02	3.18
" " "	12	4	3.00	3.00
Steel pourers	12	2	1.41	2.99
" "	12	2	1.71	3.18
" "	12	4	.81	4.57
" "	12	8	1.06	4.12
" "	12	4	1.22	4.06
Stopper setters . . .	12	4	.99	3.42
" " . . .	12	2	1.30	3.39
" " . . .	12	8	.95	3.70
" " . . .	12	4	1.09	3.63

BLOOMING MILL

Positions	Number of Employes	Hours per Day	Rate	Earnings per Day
1. Superintendents, general foremen . .	1	12	$3.65	$3.65
2. Foremen	4	12	3.52	3.52
3. Clerks, timekeepers and weighers .	7	12	2.48	2.48
Clerks, timekeepers and weighers . .	4	12	.54	2.67
4. Heaters (per 100 tons)	2	12	1.32	6.47
5. Heaters' helpers (per 100 tons) . .	8	12	.77	3.77
6. Rollers (per 100 tons) . . .	2	12	1.32	6.47
7. Rollers' assistants (per 100 tons) . .	4	12	.62	3.06
8. Tongsmen	. .	. .	. .	. .
9. Shearmen (per 100 tons)	2	12	.77	3.77
10. Shear Helpers (per 100 tons) . . .	8	12	.53	2.58
11. Inspectors	2	12	2.70	2.70
12. Engineers, roll engine (per 100 tons) .	. .	. .	.25	1.23
Engineers, roll engine	4	12	3.04	3.04
13. Engineers, stationary	2	12	2.37	2.37
14. Crane and machine operators (per 100 tons)	4	12	.65	3.19
Crane and machine operators . . .	10	12	2.02	2.02
15. Engineers, narrow gauge (per 100 tons)	2	12	.60	2.94
16. Millwrights	6	12	2.66	2.66
17. Common labor, 16½ cents per hour, 28" and 38"	58	12	1.98	1.98
Common labor, unspecified positions .	13	12	1.90	1.90
Common labor, unspecified positions (per 100 tons)	2	12	.44	2.16

PLATE MILL

Positions	Number of Employes	Hours per Day	Rate	Earnings per Day
1. Superintendents, general foremen . .	2	12	$6.05	$6.05
2. Foremen	..	..	..	..
3. Clerks, timekeepers and weighers . .	18	12	2.63	2.63
4. Heaters (per 100 tons) . . .	4	12	2.52	7.21
5. Heaters' helpers (per 100 tons) . .	2	12	1.43	4.09
6. Rollers (per 100 tons)	2	12	2.95	8.44
7. Rollers' assistants (per 100 tons) .	10	12	1.54	4.40
Rollers' assistants	4	12	2.82	2.82
8. Markers (per 100 tons) . . .	12	12	1.22	3.50
Markers	3	10	2.17	2.17
9. Shearmen (per 100 tons) . . .	6	12	1.95	5.58
Shearmen	3	12	3.13	3.13
10. Shearmen helpers (per 100 tons) .	38	12	1.17	3.30
Shearmen helpers	4	12	2.07	2.07
11. Inspectors	7	12	2.70	2.70
12. Roll engineers	2	12	3.37	3.37
13. Crane and machine operators (per 100 tons)	6	12	1.63	4.18
Crane and machine operators . . .	10	12	2.33	2.33
14. Engineers, narrow gauge . . .	..	..	..	..
15. Millwrights	6	12	2.68	2.68
16. Shippers and checkers . . .	7	12	2.89	2.89
17. Common labor, 16½ cents per hour. .	49	11	1.82	1.82
Common labor, unspecified positions .	20	12	2.40	2.40

STRUCTURAL MILL

Positions	Number of Employes	Hours per Day	Rate	Earnings per Day
1. Superintendents, general foremen . .	1	12	$4.61	$4.61
2. Foremen	5	12	2.80	2.80
3. Clerks, timekeepers and weighers . .	4	12	2.33	2.33
Clerks, timekeepers and weighers (per 100 tons)	4	12	2.29	2.53
4. Heaters (per 100 tons)	6	12	12.50	4.98
5. Heaters' helpers (per 100 tons) . .	6	12	7.50	2.99
6. Rollers (per 100 tons)	2	12	6.67	7.38
7. Rollers' assistants (per 100 tons) . .	8	12	3.46	3.83
8. Hot sawyer and push over (per 100 tons)	2	12	2.50	2.77
9. Hot bed men (per 100 tons) . . .	4	12	2.23	2.47
10. Straighteners (per 100 tons) . . .	10	12	2.50	2.79
11. Cold sawyers (per 100 tons) . . .	8	12	2.41	2.70
12. Crane and machine operators (per 100 tons)	4	12	2.92	3.23
Crane and machine operators . . .	8	12	2.16	2.16
13. Engineers, stationary	4	12	2.76	2.76
14. Inspectors	2	12	2.70	2.70
15. Checkers	2	12	2.04	2.04
16. Common labor, 16½ cents per hour. .	50	12	1.98	1.98
Common labor, unspecified positions .	23	12	1.65	1.65

APPENDIX V

PROFIT-SHARING PLAN AND BONUS FUND OF THE UNITED STATES STEEL CORPORATION

[Memoranda furnished by the Office of the Chairman, E. H. Gary, New York.]

I. Memorandum Concerning United States Steel Corporation Profit-sharing Plan Through Employes' Subscriptions to Preferred and Common Stock of that Corporation

Attached hereto is a copy, marked "A," of the offer made under date of December 31, 1902, to employes permitting them to subscribe for preferred stock and the conditions attending such subscriptions which must be fulfilled to enable them to participate in the benefits (special compensation) which would be paid by the corporation in connection with such subscriptions. There are also attached hereto copies, marked "B" and "C," covering respectively the 1909 and 1910 offerings of stock. These latter circulars set forth the particulars of the plan somewhat more in detail than does the first circular. The conditions relating to the subscriptions as set forth in the 1909 and 1910 circulars are, with exception of the one hereinafter noted, those which have attached to the plan from the start. The one feature of importance in which a change was made is the following: Under the original plan if a subscriber withdrew before his subscription was fully paid up, he received back the installments he had paid in, the dividends which had been paid on his subscription stock and any of the special compensation items which may have accrued, and he was charged with interest at rate of 5 per cent per annum on the deferred balances due under his subscription. Beginning with the subscriptions for 1905, this was modified so that in case he withdrew or forfeited his subscription before it was fully paid up he received back only the installments he had paid in with interest thereon at 5 per cent per annum, and was not charged with interest on the deferred balances.

"A"

Circular of 1902

New York, December 31, 1902.

To the Officers and Employes of the United States Steel Corporation and of Its Subsidiary Companies:

Gentlemen: For several months the Finance Committee has been engaged in perfecting a plan which, in its opinion, would make it your common interest to become permanent holders of the preferred stock of the Corporation.

The Finance Committee has been endeavoring also to devise some comprehensive plan under which those of you who are charged with the responsibility of managing and directing the affairs of the Corporation, or of its several subsidiary companies, shall receive compensation partly on a profit-sharing basis.

The Committee has not been willing to adopt any system that shall not include every employe, from the President of the Corporation itself to the men working by the day in the several subsidiary companies.

A plan which, in the judgment of the Finance Committee, will accomplish these results, was submitted to the Board of Directors at its December meeting, and by unanimous vote the Finance Committee was authorized to proceed to perfect and to promulgate the plan. It is now submitted to you, in the hope and belief that it will receive from all of you the same hearty approval that was given to it by the Presidents of the several subsidiary companies, who were freely consulted while the plan was being thought out and put into shape.

The plan is divided into two parts.

Part One:

From the earnings of the Corporation during the year 1902 there will have been set aside at least Two Million dollars, and as much more as is necessary, for the purchase of at least 25,000 shares of the Corporation's Preferred Stock for the purpose of making the following offer to all the employes of the Steel Corporation and of its subsidiary companies:

At the present time there are in the service of the Corporation, and of its subsidiary companies, about 168,000 employees, whom we propose now to divide into six classes, as follows:

Class A will include all those who receive salaries of $20,000 a year or over.

Class B will include all those who receive salaries of from $10,000 to $20,000 a year.

Class C will include all those who receive salaries of from $5,000 to $10,000 a year.

Class D will include all those who receive salaries of from $2,500 to $5,000 a year.

Class E will include all those who receive salaries of from $800 to $2,500 a year.

Class F will include all those who receive salaries of $800 a year or less.

During the month of January, 1903, the above-mentioned stock will be offered to any and every man in the employ of the Corporation, or any of its subsidiary companies, at the price of $82.50 per share; subscriptions for this stock to be made on blanks obtainable at the office of the treasurer of any subsidiary company.

Every man can subscribe for as much stock as he chooses, not to exceed the sum represented by a certain percentage of his annual salary, as indicated in the following table:

Any man who belongs in class A, as indicated in the preceding classification, will be allowed to subscribe for an amount of stock represented by a sum not to exceed 5 per cent of his annual salary.

Class B, 8 per cent.
Class C, 10 per cent.
Class D, 12 per cent.
Class E, 15 per cent.
Class F, 20 per cent.

If, on this basis of subscription, more than 25,000 shares shall be subscribed for, 25,000 shares will be awarded to the several subscribers in the order of the classes beginning with the lowest or Class F, the upper classes to receive only in case any stock shall remain untaken by the Class below, and each class to receive ratably in the amount left for that class if there be not enough to satisfy the full subscription of that class, but each subscriber will be allotted at least one full share, even though this might make it necessary for the Finance Committee to purchase more than 25,000 shares.

Payment of the subscriptions for the stock must be made in monthly instalments, to be deducted from the salary or wages of the subscriber, in such amounts as he may desire, not to exceed 25 per cent of any one month's salary or wages.

A man may take as long as he chooses, not exceeding three years, to pay for his stock.

Dividends on the stock will go to the subscriber from the date on which he commences to make payments on account of his subscription.

Interest at 5 per cent will be charged on deferred payments on the stock.

In case a man shall discontinue payments before his stock shall have been fully paid for, he can withdraw the money he has paid on account of principal and may keep the difference between the 5 per cent interest he has paid and the 7 per cent dividend he has received on the stock; and thereupon his subscription and all interest on the stock to which the same relates shall cease and determine.

As soon as the stock shall have been fully paid for, it will be issued in the name of the original subscriber and the certificate will be given to him, and he can then sell it any time he chooses. But as an inducement for him to keep it and to remain continuously in the employ of the Corporation or of one or another of the subsidiary companies, and to have the same interest in the business that a stockholder or working partner would have, the following offer is made, viz.:

If he will not sell or part with the stock, but will keep it and in January of each year, for five years, commencing with January, 1904, will exhibit the certificate to the Treasurer of his company, together with a letter from a proper official, to the effect that he has been continuously in the employ of the Corporation or of one or another of its subsidiary companies during the preceding year, and has shown a proper interest in its welfare and progress, he will during each of such five years receive checks at the rate of $5.00 a share per year. For example: If a man buys one share of this stock in January, 1903, he will undertake to pay $82.50 for it. If after paying for it he keeps it for five years he will in each year have received dividends at the rate of 7 per cent on the par value of the stock, and also will have received each year an extra dividend, so to speak, of $5.00; this latter sum being paid him as special compensation for rendering continuous faithful service to the Corporation or to one or another of its subsidiary companies, as shown by the exhibition of his certificate together with a letter from a proper official showing that he has worked to promote the best interests of the company in which he has thus become practically a partner.

If he shall remain continuously in the service of the Corporation or of one or another of its subsidiary companies for five years, at the end of the fifth year the Corporation intends that he shall receive a still further dividend, which cannot now be ascertained or stated, but which will be derived from the following source, viz.:

All who subscribe for stock in January, 1903, and commence to pay for it, but who discontinue at any time during the five years, of course will not receive the $5.00 per share for such of the five years as remain after they discontinue. The corporation will, however, pay into a special fund each year the $5.00 payments that would have been made to such subscribers had they continued. This fund shall be credited with 5 per cent annual interest, and at the end of the five years' period the total amount thus accumulated will be divided into as many parts as shall be equal to the number of shares then remaining in the hands of men who shall have continued in such employ for the whole five years, and the Corporation will then by its own final determination award to each man whom it shall find deserving thereof as many parts of such accumulated fund as shall be equal to the number of shares then held by him under this plan:

Provided, however, that if a subscriber shall have died or shall have become disabled while faithfully serving the Corporation or one or another of its subsidiary companies, during such five years' period, the money theretofore paid by him on account of the stock he was purchasing, or, if he has fully paid for it, the certificate of stock may be turned over by the Corporation to his estate or to him, together with a sum equal to $5.00 per share for each of the five years not then expired.

If this plan shall be received favorably and shall meet with success, it is intended at the close of next year, to make a similar offer, excepting, of course, that the price at which the stock then will be offered cannot be guaranteed now; it is, however, the intention to offer it at about the then market price, and in all other respects to make the terms of the offer similar to those now submitted.

The continuation of this policy would make it possible for a man to buy one or more shares of the stock each year under a contract with the Corporation upon terms offering a safer and more profitable investment than he could possibly find for his savings anywhere else.

Part Two:

During the year we have been and are now engaged in making changes and adjustments in the salaries of the men who occupy official and semi-official positions and who are engaged in directing and managing the affairs of the Corporation and of its several subsidiary companies in all the various branches of the departments of mining, manufacturing and transportation.

We have been making these changes preparatory to inaugurating, on January 1, 1903, a plan by which all the men who are thus directly and indirectly charged with the responsibility of managing and operating these vast properties, will share with the stockholders in any profits made after a certain amount of annual net earnings shall have been reached, and to this end the following plan has been adopted.

In round figures it requires about $75,000,000 to pay the interest on the bonds of the Corporation and of its several subsidiary companies, the dividends on the preferred and common stock, at the rates now being declared, and to make sinking fund deposits.

The Board of Directors has approved the recommendation of the Finance Committee to the effect that

Whenever $80,000,000 and less than $90,000,000 is earned during 1903, 1 per cent shall be set aside;

Whenever $90,000,000 and less than $100,000,000 is earned during 1903, 1.2 per cent shall be set aside;

Whenever $100,000,000 and less than $110,000,000 is earned during 1903, 1.4 per cent shall be set aside;

Whenever $110,000,000 and less than $120,000,000 is earned during 1903, 1.6 per cent shall be set aside;

Whenever $120,000,000 and less than $130,000,000 is earned during 1903, 1.8 per cent shall be set aside;

Whenever $130,000,000 and less than $140,000,000 is earned during 1903, 2 per cent shall be set aside;

Whenever $140,000,000 and less than $150,000,000 is earned during 1903, $2\frac{1}{4}$ per cent shall be set aside;

Whenever $150,000,000 and less than $160,000,000 is earned during 1903, $2\frac{1}{2}$ per cent shall be set aside.

It is intended that not only the Presidents, Officers, Managers and Superintendents shall share in these profits, but they shall be shared in as well by all other men charged with responsibility in managing the affairs of the Corporation, and the final selection of the men who shall share is to be made by the Finance Committee of the Steel Corporation.

The question of what constitutes profits and all other questions shall be determined solely and finally by the Finance Committee, and as this Committee will have no interest whatsoever, directly or indirectly, in the profit-sharing plan, its rulings must be accepted by all as fair, impartial and conclusive.

We may not, in the first year, get an equitable apportionment, but it is not the intention to make permanent the above schedule or the apportionment of the same. The programme is hereby announced as the plan for the year 1903, and the Finance Committee reserves the right to modify any apportionment that is made at the end of each quarter during the year, and reserves the right to announce this or any other plan as a substitute for this, at the end of 1903 for the year 1904.

Any profits distributed under the above schedule and to the above classes of men will be paid out as follows, for example: If $80,000,000 be earned during the year 1903, then $800,000 would be the sum set aside for distribution. It is proposed to distribute one-half of this sum in cash quarterly during the year; reserve the other half until the end of the year; and then invest it in preferred stock; divide the amount of stock thus purchased, distributing one-half to the employes who are entitled to it, and holding the other half in the hands of the treasurer of the Corporation, giving each man a certificate for his interest, the certificate to recite among other things:

First. That if he remains continuously in the service of the Corporation or of one or another of its subsidiary companies for five years, the stock shall be delivered to him and he may do as he likes with it.

Second. That if he dies or becomes totally and permanently disabled while in the employ of the Corporation or of one or another of its subsidiary companies, the stock will be delivered to his estate or to him.

Third. That he can draw the dividends declared on the stock while it is held for his account and he remains in the employ of the Corporation or of one or another of its subsidiary companies.

Fourth. That if without previous consent voluntarily he shall have quitted the service of the Corporation or of its subsidiary companies, he shall forfeit all right to this stock, and in such case it will be held in a fund which at the end of five years will be divided among such employes as shall have complied with all the conditions.

Thus 25 per cent of all the money set aside in this profit-sharing plan will be held for five years and will be given to such only as at the end of that period shall be in the employ of the Corporation or of one or another of its subsidiary companies from and since January 1, 1903.

As the value of the interests of the United States Steel Corporation in the several subsidiary companies necessarily will be enhanced by everything that tends to increase their efficiency and earnings, this offer includes their employes as well as those of the Corporation itself.

By order of the Finance Committee.

UNITED STATES STEEL CORPORATION,
George W. Perkins,
Chairman.

"B"

CIRCULAR OF 1909

New York, January 5, 1909.

To the Officers and Employes of the United States Steel Corporation and of Its Subsidiary Companies:

Gentlemen: Annually for the past six years the Corporation has offered to its officers and employes and to the officers and employes of its subsidiary companies the privilege of subscribing for a specified number of shares of its Preferred stock under certain terms and conditions. The Corporation now offers to such officers and employes the opportunity to subscribe for an aggregate amount of 18,000 shares of its Preferred stock and 15,000 shares of its Common stock at the price of $110 per share for the former and $50 per share for the latter, subject to the following conditions:

First—All subscriptions shall be made with the express understanding that the decision of the Finance Committee of the United States Steel Corporation at all times shall be final with respect to the rights or interests of the subscribers or any question relating to the same.

Second—All subscriptions shall be for the value, at the subscription price, of one or more shares of Common or Preferred or both, *i. e.,*

$50 or multiples thereof,
$110 or multiples thereof,

or some combination of

$50 or multiples thereof, with
$110 or multiples thereof,

with the understanding that there may be allotted to the subscriber all or any part of his subscription in either Common or Preferred, or partly in Common and partly in Preferred, as such Finance Committee may determine.

Third—The following table shows the maximum amounts which may be subscribed for, in accordance with the preceding section, by employes whose salaries or wages are within the respective limits stated:

Employes receiving Annual Salaries of:	*May subscribe for a Maximum Stock Value, at Rate of $110 for Preferred and $50 for Common, of:*
$275.00 or less	$50
275.01 to $625.00 inclusive	110
625.01 to 799.99 "	150
800.00 to 1,100.00 "	160
1,100.01 to 1,500.00 "	220
1,500.01 to 1,833.33 "	250
1,833.34 to 2,166.66 "	330
2,166.67 to 3,125.00 "	350
3,125.01 to 3,208.33 "	400
3,208.34 to 3,541.66 "	440
3,541.67 to 3,958.33 "	450
3,958.34 to 4,125.00 "	500
4,125.01 to 4,791.66 "	550
4,791.67 to 6,050.00 "	600
6,050.01 to 6,750.00 "	660
6,750.01 to 7,150.00 "	700
7,150.01 to 7,750.00 "	770
7,750.01 to 8,250.00 "	800
8,250.01 to 8,750.00 "	880
8,750.01 to 9,250.00 "	900
9,250.01 to 9,350.00 "	950
9,350.01 to 9,750.00 "	990
9,750.01 to 12,812.50 "	1,000
12,812.51 to 13,062.50 "	1,050
13,062.51 to 14,062.50 "	1,100
14,062.51 to 14,437.50 "	1,150
14,437.51 to 15,312.50 "	1,210

Employes receiving Annual Salaries of:	May subscribe for a Maximum Stock Value, at Rate of $110 for Preferred and $50 for Common, of:
$15,312.51 to $15,812.50 inclusive	$1,250
15,812.51 to 16,562.50 "	1,320
16,562.51 to 17,187.50 "	1,350
17,187.51 to 17,812.50 "	1,430
17,812.51 to 18,437.50 "	1,450
18,437.51 to 18,562.50 "	1,500
18,562.51 to 19,062.50 "	1,540
19,062.51 to 19,687.50 "	1,550
19,687.51 to 19,937.50 "	1,600
19,937.51 to 33,500.00 "	1,650

An employe of any class is not obliged to subscribe for the full amount of stock value which he may be privileged to subscribe for, but if he so elects he may subscribe for a lesser amount.

Fourth—Payment of the subscriptions shall be made in monthly instalments, to be deducted from the salary or wages of the subscriber, in such amounts as he may desire, subject to the provision that the minimum amount of a monthly instalment shall be $2.50 per share for Preferred Stock and $1.25 per share for Common stock, and that no instalment shall exceed 25 per cent of any one month's salary or wages. It is hoped that subscribers will, whenever possible, pay their instalments in even dollars, but if more than the minimum is paid it must always be in even dollars. A subscriber may have as much time as he chooses, not exceeding three years, to pay for his stock. Interest at 5 per cent per annum will be charged on deferred payments on the stock.

Fifth—From the date on which payments begin and during the continuation of such payments, dividends on the stock will be credited to the account of the subscriber as part of his payments until the stock is fully paid and issued to him, after which dividends will be paid in the same manner as to other stockholders.

Sixth—In case a subscriber shall cancel his subscription before his stock shall have been fully paid for there will be returned to him the exact amount of his payments made on account, with interest at 5 per cent per annum on the same from time of payment, no credit being given him for dividends or for the special allowance referred to in third paragraph of Section Seventh, and no interest being charged on deferred payments; and thereupon his subscription and all interest in the stock to which the same relates shall cease and determine. Whenever such payments shall have been discontinued without the consent of the Corporation for the period of three months, his account will be closed forthwith as of a date thirty days subsequent to his last payment and his payments on account returned to him as above stated.

A subscriber who decides to cancel his subscription must cancel all of it, whether the allotment under his subscription has been in Common, Preferred, or both.

Seventh—As soon as the stock shall have been fully paid for, it will be issued in the name of the subscriber, it being understood and agreed that in case the allotment under any subscription includes both Preferred and Common stock, no certificate will be issued until the entire subscription is fully paid, when the certificates for both classes of stock will be issued and delivered. The subscriber may then sell his certificates whenever he chooses, but as an inducement for him to keep them and to remain continuously in the employ of the Corporation or of one or another of its subsidiary companies, and to have the same interest in the business that a stockholder or working partner would have, the following offer is made, viz.:

If he will not sell or part with the stock, but will keep it and in January of each year, for five years, commencing with January, 1910, will exhibit the certificates to the Treasurer of his company, together with a certificate from a proper official to the effect that he has been continuously in the employ of the Corporation or of one or another of its subsidiary companies during the preceding year, and has shown a proper interest in its welfare and progress, he will during each of such five years receive a cash payment at the rate of $5.00 a share for each share of Preferred stock, and $2.50 a share for each share of Common stock.

Subscribers who may not have fully paid their subscriptions by January in any year, will, if their subscriptions are still in force, and they have otherwise fulfilled all the conditions of continuous and faithful service as provided, be credited in their subscription account with the special allowance of $5.00 per share on their subscriptions for Preferred stock, and $2.50 per share on their subscriptions for Common stock.

Eighth—If the subscriber shall remain continuously in the service of the Corporation or of one or another of its subsidiary companies for five years, at the end of the fifth year the Corporation intends that he shall receive a still further dividend, which cannot now be ascertained or stated, but which will be derived from the following sources, viz.:

All who subscribe for stock in January, 1909, and commence to pay for it, but who discontinue at any time during the five years, of course will not receive the $5.00 or $2.50 per share for such of the five years as remain after they discontinue. The Corporation will, however, pay into a special fund at the end of each year the $5.00 or $2.50 payments that would have been made to such subscribers had they continued. This fund shall be credited with 5 per cent annual interest, and at the end of the five years' period the total amount thus accumulated will be divided into as many parts as shall be equal to the number of shares of Preferred stock plus one-half the number of shares of Common stock then remaining in the hands of subscribers who shall have continued in such employ for the whole five years. The Corporation will then by its own final determination award to each subscriber whom it shall find deserving thereof as many parts of such accumulated fund as he shall be entitled to on basis of the number of shares then held by him under this plan, i. e., one part for each share of Preferred and one part for each two shares of Common.

Ninth—If a subscriber dies or becomes disabled while faithfully serving the Corporation or one or another of its subsidiary companies, during such five years' period, the money theretofore paid by him on account of the stock he was purchasing, or, if he has fully paid for it, the certificate of stock may be turned over by the Corporation to his estate or to him, together with a sum equal to $5.00 or $2.50 per share for each of the five years not then expired, and also a pro rata amount of the special fund arising from forfeitures referred to in Section Eighth preceding, which may have accrued at the time of his death or disability.

Tenth—A subscriber may designate in his subscription the person to whom in the event of his death he desires the Corporation to pay all amounts in connection with his subscription which would otherwise be payable to his estate. When such designation has been made, the Corporation, upon satisfactory proof of death under the conditions of the subscription, will pay to the person designated, if then living, all amounts in connection with the subscription which would otherwise be payable to the estate of the subscriber. When such designation has been made the subscriber's estate shall have no claim to any such amounts, unless the person designated should die before the subscriber, and in that event payment will be made to the subscriber's estate. By written notice delivered to the treasurer of the company by which he is employed, a subscriber may change the person designated.

Eleventh—Subscribing employes whose employment has been or may be suspended by reason of the temporary closing of the plants and who shall continue ready and willing when required to resume their service, will not be deprived of the bonus of $5.00 or $2.50 per share per year during such suspension. This need not interfere with their accepting employment elsewhere during such suspension. As presumptive evidence of such willingness to resume their employment, the Corporation will accept (1) from the holders of fully-paid subscriptions, the presentation of the original certificate in January of each year, and (2) from the holders of partly-paid subscriptions, the retention by them of their subscription during the preceding year.

The above period of suspension will not be counted as part of the three years limited for the full payment of the subscriptions, and during such suspension monthly payments will not be required, though if so desired by the employe they may be continued.

Failure to present the original certificate as provided, or the withdrawal of a partly paid subscription or the failure to resume employment when requested, will constitute and be accepted as conclusive evidence of the termination of this employment by such employe and a relinquishment of all benefits referred to in this circular.

In case of the death during such suspension of any such subscribing and continuing employe, his estate or his designee as above, will be entitled to the same benefits accruing to his subscription as if he had died while under employment.

Twelfth—Subscriptions will be received until February 3, 1909, and allotment will be made a few days later. The first deductions will be made from February salary or wages.

By order of the Finance Committee,

UNITED STATES STEEL CORPORATION,
RICHARD TRIMBLE,
Secretary

"C"

CIRCULAR OF 1910

New York, January 7, 1910.

TO THE OFFICERS AND EMPLOYES OF THE UNITED STATES STEEL CORPORATION AND OF ITS SUBSIDIARY COMPANIES:

Gentlemen: Annually for the past seven years the Corporation has offered to its officers and employes and to the officers and employes of its subsidiary companies, the privilege of subscribing for a specified number of shares of its stock under certain terms and conditions. The Corporation now offers to such officers and employes the opportunity to subscribe for an aggregate amount of 25,000 shares of its Preferred stock at the price of $124 per share, subject to the following conditions:

First—All subscriptions shall be made with the express understanding that the decision of the Finance Committee of the United States Steel Corporation at all times shall be final with respect to the rights or interests of the subscribers, or any question relating to the same.

Second—All subscriptions shall be for an even number of shares with the understanding that there may be allotted to the subscriber all or any part of his subscription, as such Finance Committee may determine.

Third—The following table shows the maximum number of shares which may be subscribed for, in accordance with the preceding section, by employes whose salaries or wages are within the respective limits stated:

314

Employes receiving Annual Salaries of:		*May Subscribe for a Maximum Number of:*
$1,240.00 or less	.	1 Share
1,240.01 to $2,066.66 inclusive .	. . .	2 Shares
2,066.67 " 3,616.66 "	. . .	3 "
3,616.67 " 4,650.00 "	. . .	4 "
4,650.01 " 6,820.00 "	. . .	5 "
6,820.01 " 8,060.00 "	. . .	6 "
8,060.01 " 9,300.00 "	. . .	7 "
9,300.01 " 13,175.00 "	. . .	8 "
13,175.01 " 14,725.00 "	. . .	9 "
14,725.01 " 16,275.00 "	. . .	10 "
16,275.01 " 17,825.00 "	. . .	11 "
17,825.01 " 19,375.00 "	. . .	12 "
19,375.01 " 33,480.00 "	. . .	13 "

An employe of any class is not obliged to subscribe for the full number of shares which he may be privileged to subscribe for, but if he so elects he may subscribe for a lesser number.

Fourth—Payment of the subscriptions shall be made in monthly instalments, to be deducted from the salary or wages of the subscriber, in such amounts as he may desire, subject to the provision that the minimum amount of a monthly instalment shall be $3.00 per share, and that no instalment shall exceed 25 per cent of any one month's salary or wages. The monthly instalment, if more than the minimum is paid, must always be in even dollars. A subscriber may have as much time as he chooses, not exceeding three years, to pay for his stock. Interest at 5 per cent per annum will be charged on deferred payments on the stock.

Fifth—From the date on which payments begin and during the continuation of such payments, dividends on the stock will be credited to the account of the subscriber as part of his payments until the stock is fully paid and issued to him, after which dividends will be paid in the same manner as to other stockholders.

Sixth—In case a subscriber shall cancel his subscription before his stock shall have been fully paid for there will be returned to him the exact amount of his payments made on account, with interest at 5 per cent per annum on the same from time of payment, no credit being given him for dividends or for the special allowance referred to in third paragraph of Section Seventh, and no interest being charged on deferred payments; and thereupon his subscription and all interest in the stock to which the same relates shall cease and determine. Whenever such payments shall have been discontinued without the consent of the Corporation for the period of three months, his account will be closed forthwith as of a date thirty days subsequent to his last payment and his payments on account returned to him as above stated.

A subscriber who decides to cancel his subscription must cancel all of it.

Seventh—As soon as the stock shall have been fully paid for, it will be issued in the name of the subscriber. The subscriber may then sell his certificate whenever he chooses, but as an inducement for him to keep it and to remain continuously in the employ of the Corporation or of one or another of its subsidiary companies, the following offer is made, viz.:

If he will not sell or part with the stock, but will keep it and in January of each year, for five years, commencing with January, 1911, will exhibit the certificate to the Treasurer of his company, together with a certificate from a proper official to the effect that he has been continuously in the employ of the Corporation or of one or another of its subsidiary companies during the preceding year, and has shown a proper interest in its welfare and progress, he will during each of such five years receive a cash payment at the rate of $5.00 a share for each share of stock.

Subscribers who may not have fully paid their subscriptions by January in any year, will, if their subscriptions are still in force, and they have otherwise fulfilled all the conditions of continuous and faithful service as provided, be credited in their subscription account with the special allowance of $5.00 per share on their subscriptions.

Eighth—If the subscriber shall remain continuously in the service of the Corporation or of one or another of its subsidiary companies for five years, at the end of the fifth year the Corporation intends that he shall receive a still further compensation, which cannot now be ascertained or stated, but which will be derived from the following sources, viz.:

All who subscribe for stock in January, 1910, and commence to pay for it, but who discontinue at any time during the five years, of course will not receive the $5.00 per share for such of the five years as remain after they discontinue. The Corporation will, however, pay into a special fund at the end of each year the $5.00 payments that would have been made to such subscribers had they continued. This fund shall be credited with 5 per cent annual interest, and at the end of the five years' period the total amount thus accumulated will be divided into as many parts as shall be equal to the number of shares of stock then remaining in the hands of subscribers who shall have continued in such employ for the whole five years. The Corporation will then by its own final determination award to each subscriber whom it shall find deserving thereof as many parts of such accumulated fund as he shall be entitled to on the basis of the number of shares then held by him under this plan.

Ninth—If a subscriber dies or becomes disabled while faithfully serving the Corporation or one or another of its subsidiary companies, during such five years' period, the money theretofore paid by him on account of the stock he was purchasing, or, if he has fully paid for it, the certificate of stock may be turned over by the Corporation to his estate or to him, together with a sum equal to $5.00 per share for each of the five years not then expired, and also a pro rata amount of the special fund arising from forfeitures referred to in Section Eighth preceding, which may have accrued at the time of his death or disability.

No pensioner will be permitted to subscribe for stock under the offer herein made, but any employe who subscribes and is subsequently pensioned will at his request be permitted to continue his subscription on the same terms as if he had remained in the service.

Tenth—A subscriber may designate in his subscription the person to whom in the event of his death he desires the Corporation to pay all amounts in connection with his subscription which would otherwise be payable to his estate. When such designation has been made, the Corporation, upon satisfactory proof of death under the conditions of the subscription, will pay to the person designated, if then living, all amounts in connection with the subscription which would otherwise be payable to the estate of the subscriber. When such designation has been made the subscriber's estate shall have no claim to any such amounts, unless the person designated should die before the subscriber, and in that event payment will be made to the subscriber's estate. By written notice delivered to the treasurer of the company by which he is employed, a subscriber may change the person designated.

Eleventh—Subscribing employes whose employment has been or may be suspended by reason of the temporary closing of the plants and who shall continue ready and willing when required to resume their service, will not be deprived of the bonus of $5.00 per share per year during such suspension. This need not interfere with their accepting employment elsewhere during such suspension. As presumptive evidence of such willingness to resume their employment, the Corporation will accept (1) from the holders of fully paid subscriptions, the presentation of the original certificate in January of each year, and (2) from the holders of partly paid subscriptions, the retention by them of their subscription during the preceding year.

The above period of suspension will not be counted as part of the three years limited for the full payment of the subscriptions, and during such suspension monthly payments will not be required, though if so desired by the employe they may be continued.

Failure to present the original certificate as provided, or the withdrawal of a partly paid subscription or the failure to resume employment when requested, will constitute and be accepted as conclusive evidence of the termination of this employment by such employe and a relinquishment of all benefits referred to in this circular.

In case of the death during such suspension of any such subscribing and continuing employe, his estate or his designee as above, will be entitled to the same benefits accruing to his subscription as if he had died while under employment.

Twelfth—Subscriptions will be received until February 5, 1910, and allotment will be made a few days later. The first deductions will be made from February salary or wages.

By order of the Finance Committee,

UNITED STATES STEEL CORPORATION,
RICHARD TRIMBLE,
Secretary

The subscription price per share at which stock was offered in each year was as follows:

1903 . . . . $82.50	1907 . . $102.00
1904 . . . . 55.00	1908 . . 87.50
1905 . . . . 87.50	1909 . { Preferred, $110.00 Common, 50.00
1906 . . . . 100.00	1910 . . $124.00

Preferred stock was offered in each year, and in 1909 both preferred and common were offered.

The number of employes from whom subscriptions were received in each year, 1903 to 1910, by classes, was as follows:

Class	1903	1904	1905	1906	1907	1908	1909	1910
A	15	12	13	17	17	20	20	19
B	45	31	26	31	32	36	35	32
C	179	135	132	156	192	203	196	201
D	942	514	495	641	731	903	783	844
E	13,845	5,094	4,297	6,277	7,915	14,302	11,139	10,344
F	11,373	4,126	3,531	5,070	5,276	9,098	6,950	5,923
	26,399	9,912	8,494	12,192	14,163	24,562	19,123	17,363

The number of shares allotted to subscribers in each of the respective classes is shown in the subjoined table. In 1903, 1908 and 1909 the aggregate subscriptions received being considerably in excess of the number of shares offered, the amounts applied for by subscribers were reduced somewhat, those of the higher salaried employes being cut down relatively more than those of the lower salaried. Notwithstanding these reductions, however, a larger amount of stock was allotted

317

than was originally offered. In 1904 and 1907, although the total subscriptions received exceeded somewhat the amount of stock offered, no reduction was made in the number of shares applied for.

NUMBER OF SHARES ALLOTTED TO SUBSCRIBERS

(Stock allotted in each year was Preferred Stock, except in 1909, when both Preferred and Common was allotted as shown.)

Class	1903	1904	1905	1906	1907	1908	1909 Preferred	1909 Common	1910
A	188	472	257	344	338	220	124	376	301
B	396	735	372	352	365	251	154	358	323
C	1,232	1,982	890	1,170	1,312	922	474	1,258	1,196
D	4,688	4,045	2,228	2,884	3,026	2,296	783	3,444	2,715
E	28,203	15,709	9,921	13,641	16,051	17,392	11,161	7,377	14,122
F	12,844	8,701	4,512	5,610	6,058	9,369	5,264	2,574	5,923
	47,551	31,644	18,180	24,001	27,150	30,450	17,960	15,387	24,580

During the seven years, 1903 to 1909, the amount contributed by the Corporation for the special compensation or bonus paid and payable to employes in connection with their subscriptions to stock as above outlined, has been as follows: [See opposite.]

In 1908 the extra bonus was distributed to 5,409 employes, holding in all 12,339 shares of stock. Since in the subscription to which the above extra distribution applied, the total number of subscribers of the four higher salaried classes (A, B, C and D) numbered originally only 1181, it follows that about four-fifths of the employes participating in such extra bonus were in classes E and F. The amount of extra bonus per share of stock then held by subscribers was $65.04.

In 1909 the extra five-year bonus was distributed to 4,085 employes holding 16,019 shares, and the amount of such extra bonus was $19.10 per share of stock so held.

In 1910 the extra five-year bonus was distributed to 3731 employes holding 9624 shares, the amount per share being $16.80.

> The number of employes who have acquired stock under the plan and are now interested in the same through ownership of such stock, i. e., stockholders of record, is at present time (April, 1910) 17,835
> In addition there are employes to the number of 9,806
> who are interested in the plan through subscriptions made and who are now paying up, through installments, the amount of the subscription price.
> Total number of employes interested 27,641

On Account of Subscriptions for the Years Named

	Total	1903	1904	1905	1906	1907	1908	1909
1903	$240,035.00	$240,035.00						
1904	403,568.50	243,828.50	$159,740.00					
1905	500,204.50	249,634.25	160,875.25	$89,695.00				
1906	628,413.25	256,439.25	162,104.25	90,364.75	$119,595.00			
1907	776,359.00	264,026.50	164,539.00	91,028.25	121,465.25	$135,300.00		
1908	669,532.36		166,344.50	91,400.00	122,024.25	137,203.61	$152,560.00	
1909	665,726.75			104,157.25	129,561.50	144,172.30	157,575.70	$130,260.00
Total	$3,883,839.36	$1,253,963.50	$813,603.00	$466,645.25	$492,556.00	$416,675.91	$310,135.70	$130,260.00
Of the above totals there were paid to subscribers at close of the calendar years in which the plan was operative, but not including the extra five-year bonus	2,184,534.59	451,434.94	507,640.10	304,962.05	313,975.00	272,770.00	223,400.00	110,352.50
Balance distributed in the extra five-year fund	$1,270,174.66	$802,528.56	$305,962.90	$161,683.20				
Balance at Dec. 31, 1909, for distribution in extra five-year fund at end of such periods	429,130.11				$178,581.00	$143,905.91	$86,735.70	$19,907.50

II. MEMORANDUM CONCERNING UNITED STATES STEEL CORPORATION BONUS FUND PLAN

The original circular concerning the Bonus Fund was dated December 31, 1902, and is included in the circular of the same date covering the offer of preferred stock to employes for subscription. (See page 309.)

Attached hereto are copies of all the general circulars which have been issued bearing on the foregoing.

"D"

CIRCULAR OF 1906

New York, December 5th, 1906.

To THE OFFICERS OF THE UNITED STATES STEEL CORPORATION AND OF ITS SUBSIDIARY COMPANIES:

The Finance Committee of the United States Steel Corporation has decided that from the net earnings of 1906 as ascertained by such committee, there shall be set aside a certain sum as a Bonus Fund for the year 1906 for distribution to various officials and employes of said Corporation and its subsidiary companies, to be selected. About 70 per cent of the total Bonus Fund will be distributed forthwith in cash; and the remainder has been invested in Common Stock of the United States Steel Corporation. Non-assignable conditional certificates of interest in such Common Stock, on a basis of $45 per share, will be issued to participants in the Fund. In case 30 per cent of any allotment is less than $45 it will be paid in cash; and if the 30 per cent is more than multiples of $45 the excess will be paid in cash. The certificates of interest above referred to will provide, among other things, as follows:

First:—That if the participant remains continuously in the service of the Corporation or one or another of its subsidiary companies for three years and until January 1st, 1910, and shall during all of such time have rendered faithful and satisfactory service to such Corporation or one or another of its subsidiary companies, the stock called for by his certificate will be delivered to him as his property upon surrender of the conditional certificate of interest given him in such Common Stock.

Second:—That he will receive the dividends, if any, declared on the stock while it is held for his account, and while he remains in the employ of the Corporation or of one or another of its subsidiary companies.

Third:—That if he shall voluntarily quit the service of the Corporation, or of a subsidiary company, or shall be discharged or removed for cause by his employer, during such period, he shall forfeit all right to the stock; and in that case such stock will be held in a fund which at the end of the three years above named will be divided pro rata among such officers and employes as shall then be entitled to the delivery of the stock called for by the certificates of interest held by them.

Fourth:—That if, before January 1, 1910, he dies, or becomes totally and permanently disabled while in the employ of the Corporation, or of one or another of its subsidiary companies, the stock will be delivered to his estate (or to him if disabled) together with a pro rata amount of additions, if any, which have accrued up to the time of his death or disability by reason of any of the forfeitures above specified.

Fifth:—All questions relating to the rights or interests of any officer or employe in, or growing out of, the stock bonus fund above specified will be finally determined by the Finance Committee of the United States Steel Corporation; and the stock bonus above referred to is made on that condition.

By order of the Finance Committee,

UNITED STATES STEEL CORPORATION,

RICHARD TRIMBLE,
Secretary

" E "

CIRCULAR OF 1908

New York, December 22nd, 1908.

TO THE OFFICERS OF THE UNITED STATES STEEL CORPORATION AND OF ITS SUBSIDIARY COMPANIES:

The Finance Committee of the United States Steel Corporation has decided that from the net earnings for 1908 as ascertained by such committee, there shall be set aside a certain sum as a Bonus Fund for the year 1908 for distribution to various officials and employes of said Corporation and its subsidiary companies, to be selected. About 50 per cent of the total Bonus Fund will be distributed forthwith in cash; and the remainder in Common Stock of the United States Steel Corporation on the conditions hereinafter stated. Non-assignable conditional certificates of interest in such Common Stock, on a basis of $50 per share, will be issued to participants in the Fund. In case 50 per cent of any allotment is less than $50 it will be paid in cash; and if the 50 per cent is more than multiples of $50 the excess will be paid in cash. The certificates of interest above referred to will provide, among other things, as follows:

First:—That if the participant remains continuously in the service of the Corporation or one or another of its subsidiary companies for three years and until January 1st, 1912, and shall during all of such time have rendered faithful and satisfactory service to such Corporation or one or another of its subsidiary companies, the stock called for by his certificate will be delivered to him as his property upon surrender of the conditional certificate of interest given him in such Common stock.

Second:—That he will receive the dividends, if any, declared on the stock while it is held for his account, and while he remains in the employ of the Corporation or of one or another of its subsidiary companies.

Third:—That if he shall voluntarily quit the service of the Corporation, or of a subsidiary company, or shall be discharged or removed for cause by his employer, during such period, he shall forfeit all right to the stock; and in that case such stock will be held in a fund which at the end of the three years above named will be divided pro rata among such officers and employes as shall then be entitled to the delivery of the stock called for by the certificates of interest held by them.

Fourth:—That if, before January 1, 1912, he dies, or becomes totally and permanently disabled while in the employ of the Corporation, or of one or another of its subsidiary companies, the stock will be delivered to his estate (or to him if disabled) together with a pro rata amount of additions, if any, which have accrued up to the time of his death or disability by reason of any of the forfeitures above specified.

Fifth:—All questions relating to the rights or interests of any officer or employe in, or growing out of, the stock bonus fund above specified will be finally determined by the Finance Committee of the United States Steel Corporation; and the stock bonus above referred to is made on that condition.

By order of the Finance Committee,

UNITED STATES STEEL CORPORATION,

RICHARD TRIMBLE,
Secretary

" F "

Circular of 1909

New York, December 21st, 1909.

The Finance Committee of the United States Steel Corporation has decided that from the net earnings for 1909 as ascertained by such committee, there shall be set aside a certain sum as a Bonus Fund for the year 1909 for distribution to various officials and employes of said Corporation and its subsidiary companies, to be selected. About 60 per cent of the total Bonus Fund will be distributed forthwith in cash; and the remainder in Common Stock or Preferred Stock of the United States Steel Corporation on the conditions hereinafter stated. Each employe who is selected for participation in the distribution of the bonus fund is requested to state whether he prefers Common or Preferred stock for the 40 per cent of his allotment which is to be paid in either of such stocks; and so far as practicable and convenient the class of stock he elects to receive will probably be allotted him, although the Corporation reserves the right in every case to make allotments of stock as it may elect. No allotment will be made to any participant of part Common and part Preferred stock. Non-assignable conditional certificates of interest in such Common or Preferred Stock, on a basis of $90 per share for Common and $124 for Preferred, will be issued to participants in the Fund. If 40 per cent of any allotment is less than $90, in case the participant is allotted Common stock, or less than $124 if he is allotted Preferred stock, it will be paid in cash; and if the 40 per cent is more than multiples of $90 in the one case or more than multiples of $124 in the other, the excess will be paid in cash. The certificates of interest above referred to will provide among other things, as follows:

First:—That if the participant remains continuously in the service of the Corporation or one or another of its subsidiary companies for five years and until January 1st, 1915, and shall during all of such time have rendered faithful and satisfactory service to such Corporation or one or another of its subsidiary companies, the stock called for by his certificate will be delivered to him as his property upon surrender of the conditional certificate of interest given him in such stock.

Second:—That he will receive the dividends, if any, declared on the stock while it is held for his account, and while he remains in the employ of the Corporation or of one or another of its subsidiary companies.

Third:—That if he shall voluntarily quit the service of the Corporation, or of a subsidiary company (except that such voluntary retirement be made under any general pension scheme which may hereafter be adopted), or shall be discharged or removed for cause by his employer, during such period, he shall forfeit all right to the stock; and in that case such stock will be held in a fund which at the end of the five years above named will be divided pro rata, on basis of the price at which the respective classes of stock are issued, among such officers and employes as shall then be entitled to the delivery of the stock called for by the certificates of interest held by them.

Fourth:—That if, before January 1, 1915, he dies, or becomes totally and permanently disabled while in the employ of the Corporation, or of one or another of its subsidiary companies, the stock will be delivered to his estate (or to him if disabled) together with a pro rata amount of additions, if any, which have accrued up to the time of his death or disability by reason of any of the forfeitures above specified.

Fifth:—All questions relating to the rights or interests of any officer or employe in, or growing out of, the stock bonus fund above specified will be finally determined by the Finance Committee of the United States Steel Corporation and the stock bonus above referred to is made on that condition.

By order of the Finance Committee,

UNITED STATES STEEL CORPORATION,
RICHARD TRIMBLE,
Secretary

By reference to the circular of December 31, 1902, it will be noted the plan as therein set forth was to be effective for 1903 and that for subsequent years some modified plan might be announced: Accordingly in subsequent years the plan was somewhat modified, viz.:

1904.—On basis of minimum earnings necessary to permit of a bonus distribution, as provided in original plan, there would have been no distribution, but the amount below stated was notwithstanding appropriated. Moreover, the entire appropriation was paid forthwith in cash.

1905. The entire amount of the appropriation was distributed in cash.

1906.—Seventy per cent of the appropriation was distributed in cash and 30 per cent allotted in common stock at rate of $45 per share, which stock was in turn given to participants only at end of 1909.

1907.—The amount appropriated for bonus fund was only three-quarters of what the amount therefor would have calculated according to earnings and rates as named in original plan. In other words, a rate equal to only three-quarters of that specified in circular was used in calculating the amount for bonus. The entire appropriation was distributed in cash.

1908.—Fifty per cent of the bonus appropriation was distributed in cash and 50 per cent in common stock at rate of $50 per share, the stock being deliverable to participants at end of 1911. The total amount appropriated for the year was somewhat greater than what would have been provided per the rates named in original plan.

1909.—Sixty per cent of the bonus appropriation was distributed in cash and 40 per cent in common or preferred stock (at the option of the participant) at rates of $90 per share for common and $124 per share for preferred. Stock thus allotted is deliverable at end of 1914.

The aggregate amount appropriated each year, 1903 to 1909, for this Bonus Fund was as stated below, the same being paid to participants in the manner and at the times as above set forth.

1903.	$1,266,950
1904.	1,230,000
1905.	1,804,000
1906.	3,300,000
1907.	3,000,000
1908.	1,500,000
1909.	2,233,000

It is impossible to say what proportions of above amounts were distributed for "each of the leading purposes—to reward inventors, etc."* The basis of

* Quoted from letter of inquiry.

323

apportionment is not classes of service, but individuals, the amounts allotted to each individual being determined with reference to the service he rendered and the beneficial results to the organization obtaining therefrom.   Naturally such a basis nvolves many factors.

The distribution of the bonus fund is treated as a matter of confidence between the company and each employe.   No employe is supposed to know what amount any other one may receive or whether any is received at all.   This same privacy feature maintains as between aggregate amounts allotted to different plants.   For the aforesaid reason it would be inadvisable to give the aggregate sum allotted to any designated plant, or to specify the sum received by the employes in the respective departments of any plant which might not be designated by name. If the list of departments in any representative plant were given, it would enable any number of people to promptly locate which plant was covered by the figures, owing to the fact that no two representative plants contain all of the same kinds of departments.   In order to give a general idea of the classes of employes at plants who participate in the bonus distribution, the following figures are given for a representative plant.

	Number Participating
Superintendents, Assistant Superintendents, and Foremen	52
Mechanical, Civil and Electrical Engineers, and Assistants	9
Mechanical Department Employes and Laboratory Chiefs	6
Office Administrative Force	5
Total and average	72

APPENDIX VI

SEVEN-DAY LABOR

I. Orders Issued by United States Steel Corporation Officials Relative to Sunday Labor

Resolution with regard to Sunday labor passed by the Finance Committee of the United States Steel Corporation at a meeting held on April 23, 1907:

"On motion, it was voted to recommend to all subsidiary companies that Sunday labor be reduced to the minimum; that all work (excepting such repair work as cannot be done while operating) be suspended on Sunday at all steel works, rolling mills, shops, quarries and docks; that there shall be no construction work, loading or unloading of materials.

"It is understood that it is not at present practicable to apply the recommendation to all Departments, notably the Blast Furnaces, but it is desirable that the spirit of the recommendation be observed to the fullest extent within reason."

Copy of telegram sent to presidents of constituent companies of United States Steel Corporation, March 21, 1910:

"Mr. Corey, Mr. Dickson and I have lately given much serious thought to the subject-matter of resolution passed by Finance Committee April 23rd, 1907, concerning Sunday or Seventh Day Labor. Mr. Corey has written you on the subject within a day or two. The object of this telegram is to say that all of us expect and insist that hereafter the spirit of the resolution will be observed and carried into effect. There should and must be no unnecessary deviation without first taking up the question with our Finance Committee and asking for a change of the views of the Committee which probably will not under any circumstances be secured. I emphazise the fact that there should be at least twenty-four continuous hours interval during each week in the production of ingots.

"E. H. Gary."

II. Action of the American Iron and Steel Institute

At the first annual meeting of the American Iron and Steel Institute, May 27, 1910, a committee of five was appointed to investigate the question of seven-day labor in continuous processes. At this meeting William B. Dickson, First Vice-President of the United States Steel Corporation, made the following address:

I am quite aware of the difficulties surrounding a discussion of this subject; nevertheless, I believe it presents questions which must be faced, and that soon, and it is the American way to meet difficulties openly.

As you are aware, the United States Steel Corporation has recently taken

325

some advanced steps in matters vitally affecting the relations between our various companies and their employes; namely, the reduction of seven-day labor to a minimum, the establishment of a system of accident and accidental death relief and the establishment of a pension system.

In considering the first named, *i. e.*, the question of a seven-day week, we were, of course, met at the outset by the difficulty of adjusting a six-day week to the operations which are necessarily continuous and which are generally so recognized even by the most radical opponents of the seven-day week. This refers particularly to such departments as the blast furnaces. The corporation has not yet been able to devise a practical working system by which the men employed at these continuous operations can be given one day off in seven, and the purpose of this paper is to invite the co-operation of other companies operating blast furnaces with a view to devising some workable plan.

In this connection I may state that, as recently reported in the press, Mr. Schwab has very properly protested against the government officials singling out his company for criticism on this point, as the practices at Bethlehem which were criticized are common to all blast furnace plants.

The tendency of the times is plainly in the direction of some measure of regulation by the public authorities, both state and federal, of the conditions under which working-men are employed. The most striking evidences of this trend are the two employers' liability bills recently introduced in the New York Legislature, one of which has been passed and has been signed by the governor; the signing by Governor Harmon of Ohio, on May 12, of a drastic and far-reaching employers' liability law; the recent appointment by Governor Fort of New Jersey of a commission to recommend similar legislation to the next Legislature of New Jersey; and the amendment to the bill for the building of two battleships and other vessels, providing that all material used shall be the product of eight-hour labor. This amendment was introduced by Mr. Fitzgerald of New York, and has passed the House and Senate.

Shall we endeavor to pass through these troubled waters "under power," with sufficient headway to insure steerage way, or shall we be satisfied to drift, taking our chances of disaster on the sunken rocks of radical and ill-advised legislation? True conservatism consists not in standing still and attempting to ignore public sentiment, but rather in adjusting our methods of operating to meet the changing conditions of our times. We will thus take the place in the body politic to which our intelligence and experience entitle us, and give powerful aid in the difficult task of solving these pressing problems on a reasonable basis, which will be fair to all of the interests involved.

It is my own deliberate judgment, after a period of almost thirty years' continuous connection with the industry, the early part of which was passed in manual labor in the mills, that the present conditions, which necessitate the employment of the same individual workman twelve hours a day for seven days a week, are a reproach to our great industry and should not in this enlightened age be longer tolerated.

I therefore urge upon the directors of the institute the appointment of a committee to consider this question and devise a workable plan which can be recommended to all companies, whereby no individual shall be on duty for more than six consecutive days. I urge this because it is the right thing to do and is in line with the spirit of the age in which we live, and I am confident that these are sufficient reasons to insure its being done. If, however, any further reason should be necessary, in my judgment we have the conclusive one that if we do not do it voluntarily we will in the near future probably be compelled to do it by the passage of legislation by the various state legislatures, which may be so radical as to create a serious situation for the entire iron and steel industry.

III. Court Decisions Affecting the Validity of Sunday and Seven-Day Legislation

The New York State Department of Labor has published a report on Sunday and seven-day legislation, and court decisions affecting it, collated by the author of this book during the past year. In conclusion, the report states:*

Two important things have been revealed in this study of court decisions and laws. In the first place, it has been shown that it is possible to enact a law which affords real protection to workmen by forbidding employers to work them seven days a week, which protects the continuous industries from injury by permitting uninterrupted operation, and which, at the same time, preserves the day held sacred by a majority of the people by naming it as the day of rest for all workmen not employed in the continuous industries. The present Sunday laws do not protect the day as effectively as a one-day-in-seven law would do, for, as stated above, the latter would place a premium on Sunday rest by practically taxing the continuous industries. But it would do more than that; it would protect the thousands of workmen in the continuous industries as the Sunday laws have utterly failed to do.

The one-day-in-seven law would tax the continuous industries by compelling them to increase their working force, and hence presumably the pay-roll, by one-seventh. This tax would be largely shifted to the consumers, and hence to society, and it would be a very small tax in comparison to the one that society is paying now through the thousands of men in every large community who have no day of rest.

The second point revealed by the study is equally important and more surprising because unusual. Students of social legislation are frequently impressed with the difficulty of adapting European laws of tested merit, to American practice, owing to constitutional obstacles. No such difficulty prevents the adoption of one-day-in-seven laws. The court decisions sustaining the Sunday legislation would not more completely justify legislation establishing one rest day in seven if they had been made with reference to laws of that character instead of in the interpretation of the inadequate Sunday laws now upon our statute books.

This is plainly evident in the study of court decisions, above. Every decision which recognizes the police power as the basis for Sunday laws is a decision justifying the enactment of the laws embodying the newer ideas as described. These decisions declare the right of the legislatures to make laws insuring to employees a day of rest, because of the well known hygienic reasons demanding occasional cessation from toil. Obviously this end could be attained by the use of any day in the week, and under this reasoning the one-day-in-seven laws would be valid, even in the case of the continuous industries, where the rest day would not fall on Sunday. It was shown above that every important Sunday decision for forty years has been reasoned from the standpoint of police power, and these furnish a precedent too

* Bulletin, New York State Department of Labor, Sept., 1910.

well established to be overturned. But there are many decisions which go further than mere recognition of the police power as the basis of such legislation, and take pains to affirm that the legislature has authority to select the day of rest, or that the law would have had equal force if the legislature had chosen any other day.

In order to make clear how far the courts have gone in this direction, a few quotations from the court decisions, already cited, bearing directly on this point are again presented. The Ohio Supreme Court said in 1853, "Wisdom requires that men should refrain from labor at least one day in seven, and the advantages of having the day of rest fixed, and so fixed as to happen at regularly recurring intervals, are too obvious to be overlooked. It was within the constitutional competency of the General Assembly to require this cessation of labor and to name the day of rest."* Later, by nearly half a century, practically the same words were used by a Kansas Court. "It is clearly within the constitutional power of the Legislature to require this cessation of labor for one day in seven, and to designate the day of rest."† In 1895, the United States Supreme Court said, "The Legislature having . . . power to enact laws to secure comfort, happiness and health of the people, it was within its discretion to fix the day when all labor, within the limits of the State, works of necessity and charity excepted, should cease."‡

These statements are significant, but even more so is this one by the Illinois Supreme Court: "It is natural that the lawmaking power, as a matter of public policy, should specify Sunday as the day of rest." But "had any other day of the week been selected the enactment would have had the same binding force."§ And in Louisiana, in a decision sustaining the law, the court said, that a Sunday law was "to be judged precisely as if it had selected for the day of rest any day of the week other than Sunday."|| Following the precedents set by a long line of decisions an Ohio court in 1898 acknowledged the validity of Sunday laws in these words:

> The validity of Sunday laws has been repeatedly passed upon and in clear and vigorous language sustained by our Supreme Court, not on the ground that the day is holy, and by Christians observed as a day for religious thought and worship, but on the ground that it is the day set by the State for rest, quiet and peace, for the welfare, health and happiness of all people, Jew, Christian and unbeliever. * * * * In exercising the power to name a day of rest, the Legislature could have named any other day in the week, and required its observance. * * * It being admitted that the state has power to provide by legislation, for a day of rest, the question of selection is one of expediency. ¶

These decisions have been cited to show how much farther judicial opinion on this subject has gone than has legislation. In turning from the religious grounds

* Bloom v. Richards, 2 Warden 388.
† State v. Nesbit, 8 Kan. App. 104.
‡ Hennington v. Georgia, 163 U. S. 299.
§ Richmond v. Moore, 107 Ill. 429 (1883).
|| State v. Judge, 39 La. An. 136 (1887).
¶ State v. Goode, 5, Nisi Prius Rep. 179 (1898).

to the police power as the basis for rest-day legislation, the courts have gone decidedly forward. They have not retracted any of the older expressions of religious faith. They have even taken occasion to record their reverence for the Christian religion while declaring that the Sunday laws cannot be sustained on religious grounds. They have merely changed from the earlier reasoning which sustained the laws as religious measures for the protection of a religious institution, to the broader reasoning which sustains them as police measures for the protection of men who have no other defense against overwork and all its attendant evils.

The various state legislatures will eventually come to the same conclusion as that already reached by the courts, that the true principle in rest-day legislation is protection for the worker, rather than for the day. If the health and vigor of society is maintained through the aid of wise legislation, there need be no fear for institutions founded on morality and religion. But if there is still need of legislation to protect the Sabbath, it is afforded in the legislation that has been suggested, in equal measure with the Sunday laws now on the statute books. And when the legislatures do come to this point, and relief is afforded to the workers in the continuous industries, through the institution of a rest day, judicial precedents will be found waiting, as if made to order, that will sustain such legislation.

APPENDIX VII

ACCIDENT RELIEF PLAN OF THE UNITED STATES STEEL CORPORATION

I. Announcement Made by the United States Steel Corporation, on April 15, 1910, of the General Provisions of the Accident Relief Plan, Effective May 1, 1910

"Since December, 1908, officers of the United States Steel Corporation and subsidiary companies have been developing a plan for relief of men injured and the families of men killed in work-accidents. A plan has now been adopted, and will be put into operation at once. This is a purely voluntary provision for injured men and their families, made by the companies without any contribution whatsoever from the men. In principle it is similar to the German and other foreign laws and to recommendations which have been made by the Employers' Liability Commissions of New York and other States since our work upon this plan was begun.

"Under this plan relief will be paid for temporary disablement and for permanent injuries and for death. The relief is greater for married men than for single men, and increases according to the number of children and length of service. During temporary disablement single men receive 35 per cent of their wages and married men 50 per cent, with an additional 5 per cent for each child under sixteen and 2 per cent for each year of service above five years. Following the provisions of all foreign laws and all legislation suggested in this country, there is a period of ten days before payment of relief begins. For permanent injuries lump-sum payments are provided. These are based upon the extent to which each injury interferes with employment and upon the annual earnings of the men injured. In case men are killed in work-accidents, their widows and children will receive one and one-half years' wages, with an additional 10 per cent for each child under sixteen and 3 per cent for each year of service of the deceased above five years.

"For some years the subsidiary companies of the United States Steel Corporation have been making payments to men injured and families of men killed in practically all cases without regard to legal liability. These payments have amounted to more than $1,000,000 a year, but it is believed that the plan now adopted will result in additional benefits. It should be understood that these payments are for relief and not as compensation. There can be no real compensation for permanent injuries, and the notion of compensation is necessarily based on legal liability, which is entirely disregarded in this plan, as all men are to receive the relief, even though there be no legal liability to pay them anything, which is the case in at least 75 per cent of all work-accidents.

"Experience will perhaps lead to some modifications of this plan, but it will be in operation for one year from May 1, 1910, and if it meets with success and approval from the men and the public it is hoped that similar and possibly improved plans may be adopted in succeeding years.

"It is our purpose by this plan to treat employes fairly and generously even under the most enlightened view of an employer's responsibility.

"Also for the period first above referred to there has been under consideration a plan for the payment of pensions to disabled or superannuated employes and it is expected this will soon be put into practical effect."

II. ACCIDENT RELIEF OF THE UNITED STATES STEEL CORPORATION

Reprinted from *The Survey*, April 23, 1910.

The United States Steel Corporation has announced a plan for relief of men injured and the families of men killed in work-accidents. The plan is a distinct advance over any existing system of relief carried out under any of the constituent companies; it puts all the employes of the biggest payroll in America—225,000 men—on the same footing, and it establishes a system which can be adjusted to the new legislation that will probably be enacted in the next ten years in the different states in which the corporation operates.

In more ways than one, then, the new plan, which will go into effect May 1 for an experimental year, is a step in advance. The exact provisions are published below. While some of them do not measure up to the proposals made by the various state commissions which have been considering the subject, many of them are a radical departure from contemporary practice, and as a voluntary act show both foresight and liberality. The plan disregards the idea of negligence entirely and may be said to recognize that a share of the income loss due to work-accidents should be a charge on the industry; it covers hazardous and non-dangerous employments alike; it puts the entire cost of the plan on the business without any contribution whatsoever from the men. No relief will be paid if suit is brought. It naturally requires a release from legal liability upon payment of the relief, but it avoids the involved and questionable relationships created by such relief associations as, for instance, the Pennsylvania Railroad Relief Department to which, like a mutual insurance association, the employes pay dues, and from which they can receive no benefits from their dues until they sign a paper releasing the company from any legal liability.

The Steel Corporation makes a point in its announcement that the payments it proposes are "for relief and not as compensation." "There can be no real compensation for permanent injuries, and the notion of compensation is necessarily based on legal liability, which is entirely disregarded in this plan, as all men are to receive the relief, even though there be no legal liability to pay them anything.' In line with this position, there are no death benefits for single men and extremely low disability benefits for them. Large numbers of immigrant laborers fall in this class. Moreover, in death cases the wording of paragraph 24 specifies that relief will be granted "married men living with their families." This would exclude the non-resident families of aliens unless the manager of the relief sees fit to exercise his discretionary power in their favor. But it is understood that wide latitude has been left the company managers in cases where single men have old people or others demonstrably dependent upon them. The death benefit for a married man is eighteen months' wages and this is increased ten per cent for every child under sixteen; an adjustment of relief to need which is noteworthy. The plan includes medical and hospital treatment. It is a statement of a consistent policy which will give the man who goes to his work in the morning a fair knowledge as to what will happen in case he is killed. Much of the ill name of claim departments in all industries in years past has been due to the incentive to claim agents to "make a good showing" by keeping down awards. Here definite standards are set.

The most serious question raised by a first reading of the prospectus of the plan is as to the sufficiency of the benefits provided. In comparison with the three years' wages, which is the death benefit under the English system, and the four years' wages proposed by the New York State Commission, the Steel Corporation announces eighteen months' wages for a married man in case of death. By a sliding scale this is increased with an increased number of children and with length of service in the company. Yet the family of an employe of ten years' standing with five children would still get but two and one-half years' wages. If such a man were temporarily disabled, however, he would get eighty-five per cent of his weekly wages as against the flat rate of fifty per cent for all disabled men under the New York bill. The highest injury benefit specified in the Steel Corporation's announcement is for the loss of an arm—eighteen months' wages. The highest benefit for permanent disability under the proposed New York state law is half wages for eight years; that under the English law is half wages for life. But here again the discretion of the company managers enters in, and in the case of loss of both limbs or other more complete permanent disability, larger amounts would doubtless be paid. At several important points, therefore, the plan is flexible and results will be dependent upon the spirit in which the company managers carry out its provisions. It would be impossible to forecast these practical workings of the plan until after it has had at least the year's trial and until detailed statements are available as to the nature of injuries and actual benefits paid. The minimum provisions for death in the case of married men are in themselves higher than were the average benefits paid by any large employer in the steel district the year of the Pittsburgh Survey.

Nor is it likely that the Steel Corporation will know either the cost of the new policy or its acceptability to its employes earlier than after such a probationary year. The corporation has been able in the past to settle most cases out of court, yet the new plan may effect economies in gathering legal evidence, etc. Such a large plan of relief would scarcely have been attempted were it not for the energetic measures to lessen accidents which have been carried out in the plants of the constituent companies during the last two years. From the managers' standpoint, the plan has merit in its probable attraction to the men—a considerable point in keeping intact a non-union working force. From the public standpoint it is widely significant that the operating corporation, which has probably the largest accident experience in America upon which to base its plan, and which has spent a million dollars a year on accident payments in the past, should adopt a plan which it describes as "similar in principle to the German and other foreign laws and to recommendations which have been made by employers' liability commissions in New York and other states since our work upon this plan was begun (December, 1908)."

The plan was put into operation tentatively by the National Tube Company last December [1909]. A further plan for the payment of pensions to disabled and superannuated employes is under consideration.

III. Accident Relief Plan Effective in Subsidiary Companies of the United States Steel Corporation, May 1, 1910

ACCIDENT RELIEF

1. This plan of relief is a purely voluntary provision made by the company for the benefit of employes injured and the families of employes killed in the service of the company and constitutes no contract and confers no right of action. The entire amount of money required to carry out the plan will be provided by the company with no contribution whatsoever from the employes.

2. Where the word "manager" appears in this plan of relief it means that official of the company who has charge of this relief for his company.

3. The decision of the manager of this relief shall be final with respect to all questions arising under this plan of relief, and he shall have full discretionary power in paying relief to meet any conditions which may arise and may not be covered by this statement.

4. The privilege of this relief will take effect as soon as an employe enters the service of the company, will continue so long as the plan remains in operation during such service, and will terminate when he leaves the service.

5. Payment of this relief will be made only for disablement which has been caused solely by accidents to employes during and in direct and proper connection with the performance of duties to which the employes are assigned in the service of the company, or which they are directed to perform by proper authority, or from accidents which occur in voluntarily protecting the company's property or interests. Relief will not be paid unless investigation of the causes and circumstances of the injury show that it was accidentally inflicted and that it renders the employe unable to perform his duties in the service of the company or in any other occupation.

6. No relief will be paid for the first ten days of disablement nor for a period longer than fifty-two weeks.

7. No employe will be entitled to receive relief except for the time during which the surgeon certifies that he is unable to follow his usual or any other occupation.

8. Employes will not be entitled to receive disablement relief for any time for which wages are paid them.

9. The company will provide treatment by surgeons and hospitals of its selection.

10. The company will furnish artificial limbs and trusses in cases where these are needed.

11. All men injured in the service of the company must obey the surgeon's instructions in reporting for examination, using the remedies and following the treatment prescribed, and going to the hospital if directed. No relief will be paid unless these instructions are obeyed. All employes who are disabled but not confined to the house must report in person at the surgeon's office, from time to time,

as reasonably requested, and must keep any other appointments made by the surgeon.

12. All employes who wish, while disabled, to go away from their usual place of residence, must first arrange with their employing officer and with the surgeon in charge as to the absence and the evidence of continued disablement to be furnished. Such employes must report as often and in such manner as may be required of them.

13. No relief will be paid to any employe or his family if suit is brought against the company. In no case whatsoever will the company deal with an attorney or with anyone except the injured man or some member of his family in the matter of relief to be paid under this plan, because it is part of the plan that the whole amount paid shall be received by the employe and his family.

14. No relief will be paid for injuries caused or contributed to by the intoxication of the employe injured or his use of stimulants or narcotics or his taking part in any illegal or immoral acts.

15. All employes of the company who accept and receive any of this relief will be required to sign a release to the company.

TEMPORARY DISABLEMENT

16. Under the terms and conditions stated here, employes shall be entitled to the following temporary disablement relief (but no relief will be paid for the first ten days nor for longer than fifty-two weeks, as stated in paragraph six):

Single men: Single men who have been five years or less in the service of the company shall receive thirty-five per cent of the daily wages they were receiving at the time of the accident. Single men of more than five years' service shall receive an additional two per cent for each year of service over five years. But in no case shall single men receive more than $1.50 per day.

Married men: Married men living with their families who have been in the service of the company five years or less shall receive fifty per cent of the daily wages they were receiving at the time of the accident. For each additional year of service above five years two per cent shall be added to the relief. For each child under sixteen years five per cent shall be added to the relief. But in no case shall this relief exceed two dollars per day for married men.

PERMANENT DISABLEMENT

17. The amount of relief which will be paid to employes who have sustained some permanent disablement, such as the loss of an arm or leg, will depend upon the extent to which such disablement renders it difficult for them to obtain employment. The kinds of disablement that may occur and the extent to which each interferes with employment differ so greatly that it is impossible to provide any adequate schedule of relief which will be paid in all cases of permanent disablement. The amounts which will be paid in cases not specifically mentioned here must of necessity be left to the discretion of the manager; but it is the intention of the company that this discretion shall be so exercised in all cases as to afford substantial relief corresponding as far as possible with the amounts stated below, considering the special circumstances of each case and the character and extent of the injury.

(a) For the loss of a hand, twelve months' wages.
(b) For the loss of arm, eighteen months' wages.
(c) For the loss of a foot, nine months' wages.
(d) For the loss of a leg, twelve months' wages.
(e) For the loss of one eye, six months' wages.

DEATH

18. Relief for the families of employes killed in accidents which happen in the work of the company will be paid only where the death of the employe is shown to have resulted from an accident (or sunstroke or heat exhaustion) in the work of

the company during and in direct and proper connection with the performance of duties to which the employe had been assigned in the service of the company or which he had been directed to perform by proper authority, or from accidents which occur in voluntarily protecting the company's property or interests.

19. Death relief will be paid as soon as possible after the required proof of cause of death is obtained and a satisfactory release given.

20. The company will pay reasonable funeral expenses, not to exceed $100.

21. No relief will be paid for death caused or contributed to by the intoxication of the employe killed or his use of stimulants or narcotics or his taking part in any illegal or immoral acts.

22. No relief will be paid to the family of any employe if suit is brought against the company.

23. In no case will this relief be paid until the receipt by the company of a satisfactory release properly executed.

24. Under the terms and conditions stated here, the widows and children of the employes killed in accidents which happen in the work of the company shall be entitled to the following death relief:

In the case of married men living with their families, who have been in the service of the company five (5) years or less and leave widows or children under sixteen (16) years of age, the company will pay relief to an amount equal to eighteen months' wages of the deceased employe. For each additional year of service above five years, three per cent shall be added to this relief. For each child under sixteen (16) years, ten per cent shall be added to this relief.

But in no case shall this death relief exceed three thousand dollars ($3,000.00).

26. This plan of relief will be in operation for only one year from May 1, 1910. If the plan meets with success, it is hoped that some similar plan may be put in operation for succeeding years.

APPENDIX VIII

UNITED STATES STEEL AND CARNEGIE PENSION FUND

I. Announcement by E. H. Gary, Chairman United States Steel Corporation

Plans have now been consummated to begin on January 1, 1911, to pay pensions from the United States Steel and Carnegie Pension Fund, which was established last spring by the joint action of the United States Steel Corporation and Andrew Carnegie. This Fund was established for the purpose of paying old-age pensions from the income of the Fund to employees of the United States Steel Corporation and its subsidiary companies. For this purpose the United States Steel Corporation provided eight million dollars, which, with the Carnegie Relief Fund of four million dollars created by Andrew Carnegie on March 12, 1901, makes up a joint fund of twelve million dollars, This Pension Fund is administered by a Board of twelve Trustees, through a Manager appointed by the Board, with such powers and duties as may be given him by the Board.

The Board of Trustees has adopted Pension Rules for the administration of this Fund, to take effect on January 1, 1911, and apply to persons who are in the service of the United States Steel Corporation and its subsidiary companies on and after that date.

Under the Pension Rules three classes of pensions are provided:

First: Pensions by compulsory retirement, granted to employees who have been twenty years or longer in the service and have reached the age of seventy years for men and sixty years for women.

Second: Pensions by retirement at request, granted to employees who have been twenty years or longer in the service and have reached the age of sixty years for men and fifty years for women.

Third: Pensions for permanent incapacity, granted to employees who have been twenty years or longer in the service and have become permanently totally incapacitated through no fault of their own.

The monthly pensions to be paid from the income of the fund will be made up on the following basis: For each year of service one per cent of the average regular monthly pay received during the last ten years of service; provided, however, that no pension shall be more than one hundred dollars a month or less than twelve dollars a month. For example,—an employee who has been twenty-five years in the service and has received an average monthly pay of sixty dollars a month, will receive a pension allowance of fifteen dollars a month.

This Pension Fund provides for the support of faithful employees in their old age. It is entirely separate and distinct from the Voluntary Accident Relief Plan put into operation by the United States Steel Corporation on May 1, 1910, which provides for employees who may be injured and the families of employees who may be killed while at work in the service of the subsidiary companies of the United States Steel Corporation.

Neither the Voluntary Accident Relief Plan nor the United States Steel and Carnegie Pension Fund involves any contribution from the men themselves toward the accident relief or old age pensions.

II. United States Steel and Carnegie Pension Fund

The United States Steel and Carnegie Pension Fund was established in the year 1910 by the joint action of the United States Steel Corporation and Andrew Carnegie. Its purpose is the payment to employees of old age pensions from the income of the Fund. For this purpose the United States Steel Corporation provided $8,000,000, which, with the Carnegie Relief Fund of $4,000,000 created by Andrew Carnegie on March 12, 1901, makes up a joint fund of $12,000,000. This Pension Fund is administered by a Board of twelve Trustees, through a Manager appointed by the Board with such powers and duties as may be given him by the Board. The Pension Rules are established by resolution of the Board of Trustees.

PENSION RULES

Who May Obtain Pensions

1. Employees of the United States Steel Corporation or of any other corporation a majority of whose capital stock is owned or controlled by the United States Steel Corporation, or of the Board of Trustees of this Pension Fund, may obtain pensions under the following conditions:

First.—*Pensions by Compulsory Retirement.*

2. All men who have been twenty (20) years or longer in the service and have reached the age of seventy (70) years shall be retired and pensioned.

3. All women who have been twenty (20) years or longer in the service and have reached the age of sixty (60) years shall be retired and pensioned.

4. At the request of their employing officers persons employed in executive or administrative positions may be allowed to continue in active service after reaching the ages mentioned above.

Second.—*Pensions by Retirement at Request.*

5. Any man who has been twenty (20) years or longer in the service and has reached the age of sixty (60) years may be retired and pensioned either at his own request or at the request of his employing officer.

6. Any woman who has been twenty (20) years or longer in the service and has reached the age of fifty (50) years may be retired and pensioned either at her own request or at the request of her employing officer.

Third.—*Pensions for Permanent Incapacity.*

7. Any employee who has been twenty (20) years or longer in the service and has become permanently totally incapacitated through no fault of his or her

337

own as a result of sickness, or injuries received while not on duty, may be pensioned at the discretion of the Board of Trustees.

Amount of Pensions

8. The monthly pensions to be paid will be made up on the following basis subject to the provisions of section 27:

For each year of service one per cent (1%) of the average regular monthly pay received during the last ten years of service.

Illustration.—An employee who has been twenty-five (25) years in the service and has received an average regular monthly pay of sixty dollars ($60) a month will receive a pension allowance of twenty-five per cent (25%) of sixty dollars ($60) or fifteen dollars ($15) a month.

9. No pension granted shall be more than one hundred dollars ($100) a month or less than twelve dollars ($12) a month.

How to Obtain Pensions
Pensions by Compulsory Retirement

10. Employing officers will report to the Manager of the Fund the name of every man who has been twenty (20) years or longer in the service and has reached the age of seventy (70) years, and of every woman who has been twenty (20) years or longer in the service and has reached the age of sixty (60) years. These reports will be sent to the president of the company concerned for his approval.

Pensions by Retirement at Request

11. Any man who has been twenty (20) years or longer in the service and has reached the age of sixty (60) years, and any woman who has been twenty (20) years or longer in the service and has reached the age of fifty (50) years, who wishes to be retired and pensioned, should notify his or her employing officer.

12. Any employing officer who wishes to retire an employee who has reached the age and has had the length of service fixed for retirement by request must notify such employee and report to the Manager of the Fund the request that such employee be retired and pensioned. These requests whether from an employee or an employing officer will be sent to the president of the company concerned for his approval.

Pensions for Permanent Incapacity

13. Any employee who has served twenty (20) years and who is permanently totally incapacitated through no fault of his or her own as a result of sickness, or injuries received while not on duty, may notify his or her employing officer and apply for a pension. Every such application will be sent by the employing officer to the president of the company concerned for his approval. In every such case it must be shown to the satisfaction of the Board of Trustees by physical examination that the employee applying for a pension is permanently totally incapacitated to earn a livelihood

General Regulations

14. Pensions from the Fund will be paid only to those employees who have given their entire time to the service of corporations included under the provisions of the Fund.

15. The acceptance of a pension from the Fund shall not bar any former employee from engaging in other business so long as such other business is not of the same character as the former employment. No employee receiving a pension may re-enter the service.

16. Length of service shall be reckoned from the date since which the employee has been continuously in the service to the date when retired, and a part of a year if less than a half shall not be counted, if more than a half it shall be counted as a full year.

17. Leave of absence, suspension, temporary lay-off on account of reduction n force, or disability shall not be considered as breaks in the continuity of service, and time thus lost shall not be deducted in reckoning the length of service.

18. Dismissal or voluntarily leaving the service followed by reinstatement within two years shall not be considered as breaks in the continuity of service, but the time thus lost shall be deducted in reckoning the length of service.

19. The Board of Trustees shall fix the date, in each case, upon which the pensions shall begin.

20. Pensions shall be paid monthly at the close of each month, unless revoked by the Board, and shall terminate with payment for the month succeeding that in which the death of the employee occurs.

21. Whenever the terms "service" and "in the service" are used in these rules they mean employment by the United States Steel Corporation, by one or more corporations a majority of whose stock is owned or controlled by the United States Steel Corporation, by their predecessors, or by the Board of Trustees of this Fund.

22. Pensions may be withheld or terminated in case of misconduct on the part of the beneficiaries or for other cause sufficient in the judgment of the Board of Trustees to warrant such action.

23. In order that direct personal relations with retired employees may be preserved and that such employees may continue to enjoy the benefits of pensions granted them, no assignment of pensions will be permitted or recognized under any circumstances; neither shall pensions be subject to attachment or other legal process for debts of the beneficiaries.

24. This Pension Plan is a purely voluntary provision for the benefit of employees superannuated or totally incapacitated after long and faithful service and constitutes no contract and confers no legal rights upon any employee.

25. The Manager of the Fund shall decide all questions arising out of the administration of the Fund and relating to employees, subject to a right of appeal to the Board of Trustees within thirty (30) days after notice to the persons interested of the Manager's decision. The action of the Board of Trustees or of any committee designated by the Board to hear such appeals shall be final and conclusive.

26. Neither the creation of this Fund nor any other action at any time taken by any corporation included under the provisions of the Fund or by the Board of

Trustees shall give to any employee a right to be retained in the service, and all employees remain subject to discharge to the same extent as if this Pension Fund had never been created.

27. Whenever it may be found that the basis named for pensions shall create total demands in excess of the annual income increased by any surplus deemed applicable by the Board of Trustees, a new basis may be adopted reducing the pensions theretofore or thereafter granted so as to bring the total expenditures within the limitations fixed by the Board of Trustees. Notice of such new basis shall be given before the beginning of the year in which it may be decided to put the same into effect   These Pension Rules may be changed by the Board of Trustees at its discretion.

28. An annual report giving an account of the Fund and its administration will be made as soon after the first of each year as practicable, and copies of such report will be posted at all mills, mines, railroads, shops and other works and published in such newspapers as may be designated by the Board of Trustees.

By order of the Board of Trustees, these Rules for the administration of this Fund shall take effect on January 1, 1911, and shall apply to those who are in the service on and after that date.

III. Officers of the United States Steel and Carnegie Pension Fund

TRUSTEES

Frank D. Adams	Duluth, Minn.
Raynal C. Bolling	New York, N. Y.
William B. Dickson	New York, N. Y.
Robert A. Franks	New York, N. Y.
Elbert H. Gary	New York, N. Y.
James H. Hoyt	Cleveland, Ohio
Kemper K. Knapp	Chicago, Ill.
George W. Perkins	New York, N. Y.
James H. Reed	Pittsburgh, Penna.
Andrew Squire	Cleveland, Ohio
Charles L. Taylor	Pittsburgh, Penna.
Hampden E. Tener	New York, N. Y.

FINANCE COMMITTEE	PENSION COMMITTEE
Elbert H. Gary, *Chairman*	Raynal C. Bolling, *Chairman*
Robert A. Franks	Elbert H. Gary
George W. Perkins	James H. Reed
James H. Reed	Charles L. Taylor
Hampden E. Tener	

GENERAL EXECUTIVE OFFICERS

Elbert H. Gary, *Chairman*	New York, N. Y.
George W. Perkins, *Vice-Chairman*	New York, N. Y.
Robert A. Franks, *Treasurer*	New York, N. Y.
Raynal C. Bolling, *Secretary*	New York, N. Y.

MANAGER

J. B. Erskine..............Oliver Building, Pittsburgh, Penna.

APPENDIX IX

LABOR CONDITIONS IN THE MILLS OF THE BETHLEHEM STEEL COMPANY, AT SOUTH BETHLEHEM, PENNSYLVANIA

That conditions in the steel mills of the Pittsburgh District are duplicated in other steel producing centers, is indicated by a special report issued by the United States Bureau of Labor in May, 1910, on conditions at Bethlehem, Pennsylvania. A strike, begun on February 4, 1910, attracted so much attention that, in view of the government contracts that had been let to the Bethlehem Steel Company, a special inquiry into the strike and its causes was ordered by a resolution of Congress. This inquiry was carried out under Ethelbert Stewart, special agent of the U. S. Bureau of Labor, whose data as to wages and hours were drawn from the company books, and afford an exhaustive presentation of these labor conditions. A terse summary of the governmental findings was made by a committee of the Federal Council of Churches of Christ in America, in a special report to the churches, as follows:

DAILY HOURS OF LABOR

It appears from the Report on the Bethlehem Strike made by the United States Bureau of Labor, that 4,725—or 51 per cent. of all the employees—had, in January, 1910, before the strike, a 12-hour work day; 220 workmen had a 12-hour day except on Saturdays, when their hours were either 10 or 11; 4,203 employees had a work day of 10 5-12 to 11 hours in length generally, with a half day off on Saturday, and 47 worked on other schedules, unspecified.

These were the regular schedules, but those who had less than 12 hours were often called upon to work overtime. The 10-hour men frequently worked several hours additional at the end of the regular period, or on Saturday afternoons or Sundays.

This means that while 51 per cent. of the workmen had a 12-hour day, the tendency in other departments was to approach that schedule on account of overtime. Bad as such a schedule of hours must necessarily be under any circumstances, the situation in certain departments has been intensified by a system of speeding up that kept the men working at high pressure. A time bonus system has enabled a man to win a 20 per cent. bonus if he finished a job in standard time. There is said to have been no penalization for failure to do this and no employee has been paid less than his guaranteed daily rate; but these rates have apparently been fixed at points where it has been necessary for a man to earn the bonus in order to bring his earnings up to wages prevailing elsewhere for similar work. If he could cut down the standard time, he received in addition 50 per cent. of his hourly rate for the time saved. The normal speed rate developed under this system has made overtime work especially obnoxious. Apart from this, it is alleged that foremen received large additional bonuses for large outputs and that this led some of them to drive the men in their departments, hoping to beat the estimated output and win a share of the money saved.

SEVEN-DAY WEEK

Beyond, and intensifying, the evils of a 12-hour day is the existence in many departments of a 7-day week. The United States Labor Bureau showed 28 per cent. of all employees working regularly seven days in the week; in addition were those who worked on Sundays irregularly as overtime. The total number working on seven days in a week, both regularly and as overtime, in January, was 4,041, or 43 per cent.

With respect to both the 12-hour day and the 7-day week, the Bethlehem custom is very similar to that in the Pittsburgh mills. The proportion of regular 12-hour workmen is considerably greater among the employees of the steel companies in Pittsburgh, owing to the fact that the plants there are steel rolling mills, exclusively, where the work is continuous. At Bethlehem, there are very large machine shops, where the work is not necessarily continuous. The machinists were the regular 10-hour men at Bethlehem.

As to Sunday work, however, the Bethlehem situation is worse than that found in the Pittsburgh steel mills in 1907–8 by the Pittsburgh Survey. There 20 per cent. were estimated as 7-day workmen, but in Bethlehem the percentage runs rom 28 to 43.

It was claimed by the manager of the Bethlehem plant that practically only necessary work has been done on Sunday—that in January the excess of Sunday work over absolute necessity was about 2 per cent. But it appears from the Labor Bureau Report that rolling mills and open hearth furnaces were operated on seven days in every week in January in Bethlehem. In Pittsburgh in 1907–8, there was a full 24-hour stop for rolling mills each Sunday, and open hearth furnaces were not operated from Saturday night until Sunday morning, and then a full crew was not needed until Sunday noon or later.

But in Bethlehem these departments called out practically their full crews in January, seven days and seven nights a week. Nothing in the company's statements or payrolls, as furnished the Bureau of Labor, showed that there was any shut down or let up for 12 or 24 hours by the men in these departments. It is generally conceded that for technical reasons blast furnaces cannot be shut down on Sunday, but rolling mills and open hearth furnaces can be and generally are shut down.

It has been claimed by the management that Sunday and overtime work is,

in some departments at least, optional with the men. This is denied by the workmen, and it is obvious that in a great corporation where there cannot be the close
personal touch between management and men, details are in the hands of foremen.
With the necessity upon these foremen of getting the output desired by their
superiors and the lure of a bonus before them, they can hardly be expected to leave
the matter of overtime entirely optional. That it is not so left, and that men are
either discriminated against or discharged if they refuse to work overtime or on
Sundays, is commonly known in Bethlehem. As already pointed out, it was a case
of this kind that precipitated the strike.

At Bethlehem, as in Pittsburgh and throughout the country, the blast
furnaces are operated continuously—seven days and seven nights a week. Adjust
ment of the working schedule which would allow every man on such crews one day
off a week was recently advocated by W. B. Dickson, Vice-President of the United
States Steel Corporation, at a meeting of the Iron and Steel Institute in New York,
and, according to the newspaper reports, was supported by other practical steel
men, Mr. Schwab among them.

At present, every time the day and night shift turn about, these 7-day
workers are required to put in a long turn of 24 consecutive hours of labor.

WAGES

In January, 21 men out of the 9,184 employed earned 60 cents or more per
hour. This would be $7.20 or more for a 12-hour day. But, on the other hand, 61
per cent. earned less than 18 cents an hour, or $2.16 for a 12-hour day, and 31.9 per
cent. earned less than 14 cents an hour, or less than $1.68 for a 12-hour day. This
is a wage scale that leaves no option to the common laborers but the boarding boss
method of living, with many men to the room. When a man has a family with him
they take in lodgers or often the woman goes to work. It is reported that immigrant
parents send their little children back to the old country to be reared while the
mother goes to work. On such a wage basis, American standards are impossible.
The January pay-roll at Bethlehem showed, according to the Bureau of Labor,
large numbers of laborers working for 12½ cents an hour, 12 hours a day, seven days
a week.

These wage figures do not compare favorably with the wages paid by the
United States Steel Corporation in Pittsburgh, where the rate for common laborers
—the lowest rate paid to any workman, prior to the recent advance, was 16½ cents
an hour. It is now 17½ cents. Jones & Laughlin, the largest independent Pittsburgh mill, paid 15 cents in 1907–8. There has been a raise at Bethlehem since
January, and common labor now gets 13½ cents an hour. All of this mill labor is
paid lower than the rate for day labor in the bituminous mines of Pennsylvania,
where the unions enter into collective bargains with their employers, and common
labor benefits along with the skilled men. None of this common labor in any of
these steel mills is paid a living wage for an average sized family.

ACCIDENTS

There were 927 injuries in the Bethlehem plant in 1909, of which 754 involved
the loss of more than one week's time; 38 of these lost bodily members, and six

lost an arm or leg. Twenty-one lost their lives. There is a benefit association, composed of employees of the plant, who pay dues into its treasury. The company duplicates whatever the men pay in. This association pays $5 a week sick or accident benefit, and $100 to the family of a deceased member, or $50 in case of the death of the wife of a member. The company does not require the signature of a release when these payments are made. Accordingly its legal liability remains. But the only stated and regular compensation which a workman is sure of for his family in case of a catastrophe is through the benefit association. So large a corporation might well adopt a regular compensation policy as the United States Steel Corporation and the International Harvester Company have already done, and as provided for by laws passed this winter by the New York State Legislature.

SUGGESTED RECOMMENDATIONS BY THE INVESTIGATING COMMITTEE TO THE FEDERAL COUNCIL AND TO THE PUBLIC

1. A 12-hour day and a 7-day week are alike a disgrace to civilization. There is a way of avoiding each, but they will not be avoided until society requires the backward members of the community to conform to the standards recognized by decent men. The continuous industries—those necessarily operating on seven days a week—are numerous enough to require special regulation. They include today: railroads, street-cars, telegraph and telephone lines, heat, light and power plants, newspaper offices, blast furnaces, hotels and restaurants and other industries. There should be laws requiring three shifts in all industries operating 24 hours a day, and there should be laws requiring one day of rest in seven for all workmen in 7-day industries. Add one-seventh to the force and each could have a day of rest while the industry goes on. The New York State Department of Labor is about to publish a monograph on the general subject of Sunday legislation which throws much light on this point. The churches could do no more for the cause of human betterment than by working for such laws. They could well initiate a movement for 6-day legislation comparable with the old Sunday observance movement, which resulted in the placing of Sunday laws on the statute books of most States. Many of these laws prohibited all work except that of necessity and charity. With the development of industries and public service, many work operations have become continuous and the tendency has been to spread to other occupations; so much so that the Sunday laws in most States are in many respects dead letters. These Sunday laws are sustained by the Courts up to the Federal Supreme Court, not on the grounds of religious observance, but on the ground that unremitting toil debases man. Therefore the courts could be expected to sustain by similar reasoning 6-day legislation, providing that when an industrial operation is necessarily continuous, each man shall have one free day. Massachusetts and California already have such laws.

2. That the churches inaugurate a movement to place in the hands of the courts, or some similar appropriate body, the authority to determine when industrial operations are necessarily continuous, and must necessarily be performed on Sunday. As it is now, the decision is in the hands of managers who are pressed for haste by purchasers, for output by their directors, and for profits by their

stockholders, so that it is unfair to put the responsibility for drawing a line between what is necessary and what is unnecessary upon the shoulders of the managers. Those industrial operations which would be declared by such a tribunal to be unnecessary on Sunday would thus fall within the scope of the old Sunday laws; those declared to be necessary would fall within the scope of the proposed 6-day legislation.

3. That directly growing out of the Bethlehem situation the Federal Government be urged to include in its specifications for armor plate, war vessels, construction work and the like, that the work be done on a 6-day basis, and that where operations are necessarily continuous, the 24 hours be divided into three shifts of eight instead of two of 12. In letting its contracts for the great aqueducts now under construction, New York City has provided that, along with certain specifications as to tensile strength of steel, grade of cement, etc., the contractor in these outlying camps shall provide adequate water, sewage and shelter for his construction gang. This has been occasioned by the presence in some camps, which are temporary and peopled with transients, of conditions so unsanitary as to threaten the districts with epidemics. It would seem similarly that the United States Government could provide for certain minimum labor conditions in its contracts, as well as minimum specifications as to materials. As it is now, the progressive employer who wants to be fair to his men must compete for contracts at levels set by the least scrupulous. The tendency, therefore, is toward a lowering of standards, which the churches of America ought to be courageous enough to stand out against. The Government is rich enough to pay for vessels constructed under the best sanitary and economic conditions.

4. That the various churches making up the Federal Council be urged to set aside a day at their conferences, assemblies and conventions for the discussion of industrial conditions and the relation of the Church to the same; especially in line with the action of the Council in declaring against the 12-hour day, the 7-day week and for a living wage. Appropriate sources of information could be suggested in this connection—such as the Bethlehem Report of the Federal Government and the report to be issued by the New York State Department of Labor on "Sunday and 7-day Legislation."

5. That the attention of the churches in all parts of the country be called to the existence of the continuous processes in such industries as iron and steel, paper, railroads, street-railways, telephone, telegraph, mines, smelters and glass. That ministers be urged to visit the works and public service corporations of their localities and learn to what extent employees are obliged to work on seven days in the week.

6. That the Federal Bureau of Labor, the Russell Sage Foundation, or some other properly constituted body, be urged to take up an adequate study of the cost of living and wages in our different industrial districts, such as will inform the churches as to what is a living wage:—

a. One on which the immigrant laborer can safely undertake the responsibilities of home-making in each district without jeopardizing the health of his family and children.

b. The minimum upon which an ordinary American household may be maintained as a permanent proposition so as to provide not only for physical necessities, but for the education of the children, and for a fair degree of comfort, a fair share in the recreations, church support and other activities of the community, provision through insurance for death, injury and sickness, and a competence for old age. Less than this cannot be considered a living wage in America.

7. That the Federal and State Bureaus of Labor be urged further to investigate and report upon the extent of continuous industries in this country, and their working hours. We commend the Bethlehem Report for its incisive array of facts. Such reports should show us not only the extent to which the steel industry elsewhere is carried on along similar lines, but the practice in other trades and in public service corporations. Massachusetts, as well as New York State, has investigated the extent of Sunday work within its boundaries.

8. It is essential that there be some method whereby employees may approach their employers with their grievances without prejudice against those selected to represent them. The Committee would raise the question of the recognition of the right of all workmen to organize in such a manner as may seem best to them, provided that they keep within the limits of the law; and we recommend that employers of labor recognize such organizations when they speak in behalf of their members.

9. The Committee reaffirms, in the name of the Commission on the Church and Social Service, the three principles for which the Federal Council of the Churches of Christ in America asserts the Church must stand:

First. The gradual and reasonable reduction of the hours of labor to the lowest practicable point, and that degree of leisure for all which is a condition of the highest human life.

Second. A release from employment one day in seven.

Third. A living wage as a minimum in every industry, and the highest wage that each industry can afford.

SUGGESTIONS MADE BY THE COMMITTEE TO THE MINISTERS IN BETHLEHEM

1. That they collectively take a definite and pronounced stand against 7-day labor, so that the working people of the Bethlehems may know without question how they stand. If the present Ministerial Association, for constitutional limitations, cannot declare on such issues, it would seem that collective action could still be taken by those ministers so inclined through a committee or through a special meeting for this purpose.

2. In view of the statement made in the ministers' letter, that workmen have abused their holidays and Sundays by drunkenness, ball games, and the like, we recommend that the ministers appoint a committee to investigate what opportunities for clean recreation are open to the working people of the Bethlehems; what opportunities a 6-day, 12-hour man has for enjoying any outdoor amusements except on Sunday; what opportunities the 7-day, 12-hour man has at any time for enjoying them; what the mechanics and others who have Saturday half holiday do

with it; what public provision there is for adult recreation in Bethlehem other than that on a commercial basis—that is, enterprises depending on the admission tickets foods and drinks sold, in contrast to, for instance, the public recreation centers which serve many of the low-rent districts of Chicago.

3. That they organize an open forum for discussion, securing the co-opera-tion of the Catholic priests, at which workmen and merchants, non-churchmen and ministers could discuss industrial conditions and civic problems openly and without fear; so that there will not be the mistrust and misunderstanding which charac-terized this strike, between the strikers and the ethical forces of the community.

4. We would suggest that the Ministerial Association give over at least four meetings a year to a discussion of the Church's responsibility toward labor condi-tions in the Bethlehems. We were gratified at the specific and democratic testimony which was offered at the meeting we attended. For instance, when one of the general officers of the company was quoted as saying that Sunday work had been entirely optional with the men, there were ministers present who testified that reliable church members, church officers and others had been obliged to work, whether they wanted to or not.

5. That, inasmuch as the Bethlehem Steel Company has assured the ministers of Bethlehem that Sunday work will be cut down to what is inevitable and neces-sary, the ministers conceive of themselves as the Sunday guardians of the com-munity, and, taking the company's statement in good faith, request a weekly report as to the number of men employed on Sunday in each department. This suggestion is not offered in a spirit of espionage, but in a realization that in a large plant such as the Bethlehem works, where contracts must be turned out rapidly, where foremen and superintendents are rated on their output, the pressure is inevitably in the direction of overtime and extra work. Such a weekly report, published in the local paper or read in the churches, would automatically exert some pressure in the opposite direction.

6. That the Bethlehem Ministerial Association appoint a committee on ndustrial accidents to make inquiries as to the exact payments made during a given year to the families of workmen killed or disabled at work. The Bethlehem Steel Company has a relief association which provides weekly benefits in case of injury and funeral benefits in case of death; and in this the men co-operate. But it were well to go beyond this and find out the exact payments in case of death to take the place of the loss of income, so that when the question of amending the present employers' liability laws comes up at the next session of the Pennsylvania Legislature, the Bethlehem community as a whole will be awake and informed and a center of influence touching this problem, which has been engrossing the attention of state commissions in Minnesota, Wisconsin, New York, Illinois, Massachusetts and New Jersey. The recent action of the American Manufacturers' Association in declaring against existing liability laws and proposing an indemnity system which would put American practice somewhat on a par with that of England or of Germany, shows the moral obligation resting on a great industrial State such as Pennsylvania in getting abreast of the world movement in this field.

347

SUGGESTED QUESTIONS WHICH MIGHT BE DISCUSSED AT A MINIS-
TERIAL MEETING, BEARING ON 7-DAY WORK

a. What is the law in this State with respect to Sunday observance?

b. In what industrial operations is it not observed?

c. Do the men in these operations have to work seven days a week, or do they get one day off?

d. If it is stated that it is optional whether they work Sunday or not, are we sure that in practice it works out that way? If a foreman has to get out a piece of work requiring 50 men on Sunday and only 30 volunteer, what happens?

e. What is the effect of Sunday work on church attendance?

f. What sort of fathers can the men be who work seven days a week; when do they get a chance to be with their children? Do you consider it important, as a churchman, that a father should have time to spend with his children?

g. What sort of a householder can such a man be? What sort of a church member? What sort of a citizen?

h. Is a 7-day week a more exacting, strength-consuming, soul-shrivelling program than a 12-hour day?

i. What sort of recreational opportunities have men who work 12 hours a day?

j. What free time for refreshment and relaxation have they besides Sunday?

k. What do the men who have Saturday half holiday do with it? Has it any effect on their Sunday church attendance?

l. Have any steps been taken in your State to provide for one day of rest out of every seven in those industries where Sunday work is necessary? (Massachusetts and California are the only two States that have passed such laws.)

m. Is it the Church's part to support such 6-day legislation?

n. In continuous industries, 24 hours must be split up between two shifts of workers, or three. It is a choice between 12 hours or 8. Is the issue clear-cut enough so that the Church can favor legislation requiring three shifts of 8 hours each in continuous industries?

o. Is overtime paid in your locality, for extra work after hours or on Sunday?

p. What would be the effect if time and a half or double time were paid for such overtime? Would men prefer to work Sunday and lay off some other day? Or would such a tendency be rendered negligible by the management transferring all such work to week days, wherever possible, in order to save the extra-pay expense?

q. What sort of activities are commonly proceeded against under your Sunday laws? Saloons? Ball games? Candy shops? Manufacturing plants?

r. Aside from such repressive measures, what is your community doing concerning entertainment, outdoor recreation and relaxation that a workman may secure in his leisure hours? Is this provision left entirely to those who make money out of this natural desire for such things? Is it less important for the community to provide recreation centers than it is to provide a fire department or a jail?

348

APPENDIX X

MAKE-UP OF LABOR FORCE OF CARNEGIE STEEL COMPANY, ALLEGHENY COUNTY PLANTS

TABLE A.—EMPLOYES OF CARNEGIE STEEL COMPANY PLANTS IN ALLEGHENY COUNTY, PA., SHOWING RACE, SKILL, CONJUGAL CONDITION, ETC., MARCH, 1907.—BY RACIAL GROUP

	Total Number of Employes	Skilled		Semi-skilled		Un-skilled		Naturalized		Unnaturalized Foreigners		Married		Single		English Speaking		Non-English Speaking	
		Number	Per cent	Number	Per cent	Number	Per cent	Number	Per cent	Number	Per cent	Number	Per cent	Number	Per cent	Number	Per cent	Number	Per cent
American Born:																			
White......	5705	2316	40.6	1879	32.9	1510	26.5	5705*	100	..	..	2798	49	2907	51	5705	100	..	..
Colored......	331	66	20	76	23	189	57	331*	100	..	..	199	60	132	40	331	100	..	..
Foreign Born:																			
Teuton......	1820	714	39	585	32	521	29	1086	59	734	41	1323	73	497	27	1723	95	97	5
Celt......	1401	474	34	407	29	520	37	1013	72	388	28	1026	73	375	27	1399	99.86	2	0.14
Slav......	13003	359	3	1946	15	10698	82	914	7	12089	93	8349	64	4654	36	6172	47	6831	53
Other Races......	1077	59	5	96	9	922	86	265	25	812	75	575	53	512	47	528	49	549	51
Total......	23337	3988	17	4989	21	14360	62	9314	40	14022	60	14270	61	9067	39	15858	68	7479	32

* Native born citizens.

349

TABLE B.—EMPLOYES OF CARNEGIE STEEL COMPANY PLANTS IN ALLEGHENY COUNTY, PA., MARCH, 1907, CLASSIFIED ACCORDING TO AGE.—BY RACIAL GROUPS

	Under 16		16 to 19		20 to 29		30 to 39		40 and over		Total	Per cent of Grand Total
	Number	Per cent	Number	Per cent	Number	Per cent	Number	Per cent	Number	Per cent		
American Born:												
White....	221	3.9	942	16.5	2099	36.8	1354	23.7	1089	19.1	5705	24.5
Colored...	6	1.8	20	6.0	102	30.8	140	42.3	63	19.1	331	1.4
Foreign Born:												
Teuton ...	10	0.55	61	3.35	474	26.04	499	27.42	776	42.64	1820	7.8
Celt.......	2	0.14	21	1.50	273	19.49	417	29.76	688	49.11	1401	6.0
Slav.......	15	0.11	908	6.98	6229	47.91	4194	32.26	1657	12.74	13003	55.7
Other Races...	..	..	70	6.50	506	46.99	340	31.57	161	14.94	1077	4.6
Grand Total.	254	1.09	2022	8.66	9683	41.49	6944	29.76	4434	19.80	23337	100.00

TABLE C.—TOTAL ROSTER OF WORKMEN OF CARNEGIE STEEL CO. IN ALLEGHENY COUNTY, MARCH, 1907, SHOWING RACIAL MAKE-UP, AGE, CONJUGAL CONDITION, ETC.—BY COUNTRY AND NATIONALITY

Country and Nationality	Skilled		Semi-skilled		Un-skilled		Total		Naturalized		Un-naturalized		Married		Single		English-speaking		Non-English-speaking		Under 16 Years		16 to 19		20 to 29		30 to 39		40 or over	
	Number	Per cent	Number	Per cent	Number	Per cent	Number	Per cent	Number	Per cent	Number	Per cent	Number	Per cent	Number	Per cent	Number	Per cent	Number	Per cent	Number	Per cent	Number	Per cent	Number	Per cent	Number	Per cent	Number	Per cent
1. Austria-Hungary	275	3	1356	13	8789	84	10420	100	689	7	9731	93	6955	67	3465	33	5117	49	5303	51	7	0	781	8	4902	47	3361	32	1369	13
Slovak	137	2	946	15	5394	83	6477	62	484	7	5993	93	4573	71	1904	29	3532	55	2945	45	3	0	472	7	3053	47	2116	33	833	13
Polish	19	3	103	2	489	80	611	6	26	5	582	95	381	62	230	38	307	50	304	50	1	0	8	3	302	49	206	34	86	14
Austrian (other)	1	3	3	7	36	90	40	0	0	0	34	85	21	47	19	53	31	78	9	22	0	0	0	0	22	55	14	35	4	10
Bohemian	6	13	12	27	27	60	45	0	7	15	38	84	21	47	24	53	24	53	21	47	0	0	2	4	29	65	10	22	4	9
Croatian	18	2	82	10	748	88	848	8	37	4	811	96	497	59	351	41	348	41	500	59	2	0	89	10	427	50	221	26	109	13
German	37	27	33	24	65	49	135	1	23	17	112	83	100	74	35	26	166	79	29	21	1	0	0	0	45	33	42	31	39	29
Greek	0	0	0	0	2	100	2	0	0	0	2	100	1	50	3	0	0	0	2	100	0	0	0	0	1	50	1	50	3	50
Hebrew	5	42	4	33	382	25	391	0	1	50	384	50	9	75	207	25	12	100	195	53	0	0	28	7	238	61	7	7	3	25
Horvat	3	1	6	1	103	97	112	1	5	4	120	58	184	47	75	53	196	50	70	24	0	0	8	6	59	45	48	37	25	6
Hungarian	16	12	12	11	103	79	131	1	11	2	43	98	56	43	28	57	61	47	11	77	0	0	8	8	26	57	15	33	16	12
Krainer	0	0	5	12	41	89	46	0	0	0	1119	92	18	39	384	61	35	76	762	100	0	0	84	8	503	42	432	36	173	15
Magyar	32	3	142	12	1018	85	1192	11	73	8	1119	94	808	68	384	32	430	36	762	64	0	0	84	8	503	42	432	36	173	15
Russian	0	0	1	8	12	92	13	0	0	0	13	100	26	46	7	54	3	23	10	77	0	0	1	8	8	63	2	15	2	15
Bulgarian	0	0	2	6	34	94	36	0	0	0	36	100	26	72	10	28	0	0	36	100	0	0	1	3	25	69	19	52	7	20
Dalmatian	0	0	1	12	7	87	8	0	0	0	8	100	5	88	3	38	0	0	8	100	0	0	0	0	4	50	4	50	0	0
Ruthenian	0	0	1	9	10	91	11	0	2	0	11	100	3	18	18	0	0	0	0	82	0	0	0	0	0	27	19	64	0	16
Roumanian	1	0	2	0	407	100	410	4	0	0	408	100	230	56	180	44	24	6	386	94	0	0	65	16	168	41	113	29	64	16
Galician	0	0	1	33	2	67	3	0	0	0	3	100	6	67	1	33	1	33	2	67	0	0	1	33	2	50	2	67	2	25
Herzegovinian	0	0	0	0	8	100	8	0	0	0	8	100	6	75	2	25	3	37	5	63	0	0	0	0	4	50	1	25	0	25
Prussian	0	0	0	0	0	100	0	0	0	0	1	100	1	100	1	100	1	100	1	100	1	100	1	100	1	100			2	
2. England	577	39	441	30	468	31	1486	100	1025	69	461	31	1100	74	386	26	1484	100	0	0	1	0	32	2	344	23	426	29	683	46
Irish	147	24	170	28	291	48	608	41	465	76	143	24	442	73	166	27	606	100	2	0	0	0	4	1	106	17	180	30	318	52
Scotch	105	57	45	24	33	18	183	12	108	59	75	41	139	73	44	24	183	100	0	0	0	0	5	3	52	28	52	28	73	40
English	279	40	204	34	119	20	602	40	381	63	221	37	440	73	162	27	502	100	0	0	0	0	21	3	175	29	168	28	238	40
Welsh	41	50	18	22	23	28	82	6	66	80	16	20	72	88	10	12	82	100	0	0	0	0	2	3	78	10	23	28	51	62
Canadian	46	46	4	4	6	28	11	100	5	45	6	55	33	64	4	36	11	100	0	0	0	0	2	19	2	10	3	27	3	27
3. France	13	25	18	35	21	40	50	100	25	50	25	50	33	50	19	36	47	90	5	10	0	0	4	8	11	21	12	23	25	48
French	13	26	17	34	20	40	50	96	25	50	25	50	32	64	18	36	45	90	5	10	0	0	3	8	11	21	11	23	25	50
German	0	0	1	100	0	0	1	2	1	100	0	0	1	100	0	0	1	100	0	0	0	0	0	0	0	0	1	100	0	0
Slovak	0	0	0	0	1	100	1	100	0	100	0	0	1	100	0	0	1	100	0	0	0	0	0	0	0	0	0	0	0	0
4. Germany	273	32	272	32	313	36	855	100	564	66	291	39	659	77	196	23	792	93	63	7	11	1	31	4	163	19	213	25	437	51
German	246	34	232	32	238	33	716	84	489	68	227	32	558	78	158	22	675	94	41	6	9	1	25	3	128	18	170	24	384	54

(Continued on next page.)

351

TABLE C.—(Continued)

Country and Nationality	Skilled Number	Skilled Per cent	Semi-skilled Number	Semi-skilled Per cent	Un-skilled Number	Un-skilled Per cent	Total Number	Total Per cent	Naturalized Number	Naturalized Per cent	Un-naturalized Number	Un-naturalized Per cent	Married Number	Married Per cent	Single Number	Single Per cent	English-speaking Number	English-speaking Per cent	Non-English-speaking Number	Non-English-speaking Per cent	Under 16 Years Number	Under 16 Years Per cent	16 to 19 Number	16 to 19 Per cent	20 to 29 Number	20 to 29 Per cent	30 to 39 Number	30 to 39 Per cent	40 or over Number	40 or over Per cent
Polish	25	20	38	30	63	50	126	15	71	56	55	44	90	71	36	29	106	84	20	16	2	2	6	5	32	25	38	30	48	38
Slovak	0	0	0	0	2	100	2	0	0	0	2	100	1	50	1	50	1	50	1	50	0	0	0	0	1	50	1	50	0	0
Prussian	1	14	1	34	5	71	7	1	3	33	4	57	7	100	0	0	6	86	1	14	0	0	0	0	1	14	2	29	4	57
Roumanian	0	0	1	30	2	67	3	0	1	33	2	67	2	67	1	33	3	100	0	0	0	0	0	0	1	33	1	33	1	33
Hebrew	0	100	0	0	0	0	1	0	0	0	1	100	0	0	1	100	0	0	0	0	0	0	0	0	0	0	1	100	0	0
5. Italy	24	3	43	5	829	93	896	100	210	24	686	76	470	53	426	47	384	43	512	57	0	0	63	7	431	48	288	33	114	12
Italian (South)	11	3	25	6	379	91	415	46	51	12	364	88	234	56	181	44	196	47	219	53	0	0	33	8	197	48	130	31	55	13
Italian (North)	7	3	17	6	246	91	270	30	28	10	242	90	118	44	152	56	146	54	124	46	0	0	16	6	127	47	101	37	26	10
English	0	100	0	0	0	0	1	0	0	0	1	100	0	0	1	100	1	100	0	0	0	0	0	0	0	0	1	100	0	0
Slovak	0	0	0	0	1	100	1	0	0	0	1	100	1	100	0	0	1	100	0	0	0	0	0	0	1	100	0	0	0	0
Other Italian	5	2	0	0	203	97	209	23	131	63	78	37	117	56	92	44	40	19	169	81	0	0	13	6	107	51	56	27	35	17
6. Russian Empire	106	4	600	23	1871	72	2577	100	195	8	2382	92	1394	54	1183	46	1105	43	1472	57	0	0	121	5	1334	52	835	32	280	11
Slovak	0	0	3	30	7	70	10	0	0	0	10	100	8	80	2	20	3	30	7	70	0	0	0	0	2	20	5	50	1	10
Polish	72	4	400	24	1172	71	1644	64	133	8	1511	92	872	53	772	47	724	44	920	56	0	0	82	5	839	51	513	31	203	12
Hebrew	1	25	2	50	1	25	4	0	0	0	4	100	3	75	1	25	2	50	2	50	0	0	0	0	1	50	1	25	1	25
Lithuanian	20	4	103	22	353	74	476	18	47	10	429	90	215	45	261	55	212	45	264	55	0	0	18	3	238	50	169	36	51	11
Scandinavian	0	0	0	0	0	0	2	0	0	0	2	100	1	50	1	50	1	100	0	0	0	0	0	0	1	50	0	0	0	0
Bulgarian	1	50	0	0	3	43	7	0	2	50	5	71	6	86	1	14	2	100	3	43	0	0	1	50	1	50	5	71	0	0
Finnish	2	29	2	29	13	48	27	1	2	29	5	71	19	70	8	30	4	57	3	11	0	0	1	5	12	44	9	33	0	0
German	4	15	10	37	19	95	20	1	6	22	19	95	10	70	10	30	24	89	3	25	0	0	1	5	14	70	9	25	6	22
Servian	0	0	0	0	0	0	1	0	0	0	1	100	1	100	0	0	1	100	0	0	0	0	0	0	1	100	0	0	0	0
Greek	0	0	78	20	301	78	385	15	5	1	380	99	260	68	125	32	117	30	268	70	0	0	19	5	218	57	130	34	18	4
Russian (other)	6	0	0	0	6	100	6	0	0	0	6	100	2	33	5	67	4	67	2	33	0	0	0	0	6	100	3	16	0	0
7. Servia	0	0	0	0	1	100	1	100	0	0	2	100	4	74	5	26	19	100	2	33	0	0	0	0	7	37	6	33	8	0
8. Switzerland	5	47	4	21	6	32	19	100	14	74	5	26	8	33	1	26	19	100	0	0	0	0	0	0	7	37	3	16	9	47
German	5	45	4	36	2	18	11	100	9	82	2	18	8	73	3	27	11	100	0	0	0	0	0	0	6	55	1	9	4	36
Swiss	3	43	0	0	4	57	7	37	5	71	2	29	6	86	1	14	7	100	0	0	0	0	0	0	1	14	1	14	5	72
French	1	100	0	0	0	0	1	5	0	100	0	0	0	0	0	0	0	100	0	0	0	0	0	0	0	0	0	0	0	0
9. Sweden	125	44	94	33	64	23	283	100	155	55	128	45	164	57	119	23	263	93	20	7	0	0	5	2	99	35	93	33	86	30
Scandinavian	108	44	80	32	59	24	247	87	127	51	120	49	139	55	108	45	227	92	20	8	0	0	5	2	95	38	79	32	68	28
Swede	17	47	14	39	5	14	36	13	28	77	8	22	25	69	3	11	36	100	0	0	0	0	0	0	4	11	14	39	18	50
10. Australian	3	50	1	17	1	33	6	100	1	17	5	83	3	50	3	50	5	83	1	17	0	0	0	0	3	50	1	17	2	33
German	1	50	0	0	1	50	2	33	1	50	2	50	0	0	2	100	2	100	1	100	0	0	0	0	0	0	0	0	0	0
Slovak	0	0	0	0	1	100	2	17	0	0	2	100	2	100	0	0	1	100	1	100	0	0	0	0	1	50	0	0	1	100
English	1	50	1	50	0	0	1	33	0	0	1	100	1	100	0	0	2	100	0	0	0	0	0	0	1	50	0	0	1	50
Scotch	1	100	0	0	0	0	1	17	0	0	2	100	0	0	1	100	1	100	0	0	0	0	0	0	1	100	0	0	0	0

11. British North America																	
English .																	
French .																	
German .																	
Scotch ..																	
Irish .																	
Magyar .																	
Canadian (other) .																	
African .																	
12. Montenegro																	
13. Roumania .																	
14. Bulgaria .																	
15. Brazil—Irish																	
16. Denmark .																	
17. Galicia—Polish.																	
18. Greece .																	
19. Spain .																	
20. Turkey in Europe																	
Greek .																	
Bulgarian .																	
Syrian .																	
Turkish .																	
21. Belgium .																	
French .																	
Flemish .																	
Hebrew .																	
22. Ireland .																	
Irish .																	
English .																	
Scotch .																	
23. The Netherlands																	
24. Norway—Scandinavian .																	
25. Scotland .																	
Scotch .																	
Irish .																	
English .																	
26. Wales .																	
English .																	
Irish .																	
Welsh .																	
U. S. White .																	
U. S. Colored .																	
Grand total .	3988	4990	14359	23337	9318	14019	14270	9067	15858	7479	254	2022	9683	6945	4433

353

INDEX

INDEX

depression of 1907–08, 160; sliding scale of wages proposed by Andrew Carnegie, 115; speed record attained in, at Braddock, 186; speeding up, 186; strike of 1886, 114, 167; Sunday work at, 168; sympathetic strike at, avoided by settlement of Homestead strike of 1889, 121, 122; temporary settlement with, urged by National Amalgamated Association of Iron and Steel Workers, 116; terms of, in 1884–85 controversy accepted by men, 113; twelve-hour day reinstated in, in 1888, 167; two short-lived unions at, 88; wage scale presented by Knights of Labor to, 115; wages and labor cost in, compared with Chicago, 116, 117, 118; work-accidents at, 66; working day, 112, 113, 114, 115, 167. See also *Braddock; Carnegie Steel Company*

Eight-hour day. See *Working day*

Employers—
Attitude of, toward independent activity on part of workingmen, 218; certain policies of, not affected by non-unionism, 200; motive of, in destroying unionism, 205–206; organized, 110; responsibility assumed by, 205, 206; responsibility of, for work-accidents, 67

Employers' control—
Autocratic, 192, 204, 206, 232, 233, 234; automatic processes reinforce, 139; bitterness among workingmen engendered by unjust, 232, 233; co-ordination of labor force under, 199; cost of defiance of, 217, 218, 219; destructive policies introduced under, 205; determination to achieve, 6; effect of exploitation under, on home life, 201, 202, 203, 204, 205; effect of exploitation under, on morality and mentality of workers, 201, 202, 203, 204, 205; effect of exploitation under, on society, 201, 202, 203, 204, 223; grouping of races strengthens, 148; hostility to unionism under, 217, 218, 219; in politics, 229, 230, 231; motives of present labor policies under, 204, 205; of labor situation, 139, 140, 141; pension system strengthens, 197, 198; policy of reducing cost by increasing tonnage

under, 139; profit-sharing system strengthens, 198; reasons for workingmen's acquiescence to, 207–220; repression safeguards, 206; repression underlying policy in, 6; secured, 139; speeding-up system, 199, 200; spy system of, 217, 218, 219, 220; twelve-hour day schedule for majority, 199; wages decreased, 152, 153, 199; working-day lengthened, 199. See also *Labor policies of employers; Repression; United States Steel Corporation*

Employers in the Saddle, The, 137–220

Employes—
Control sought by, 5

Employes' negligence—
Cause of work-accidents, 66

England—
Eight-hour day in, 177, 178, 179

English iron and steel workers—
Percentage of mortality among, 62

English Workman's Compensation Act, 197

Espionage—
By United States Steel Corporation, 214, 215, 216, 217, 218, 219, 220

European working day—
Compared with American, 177, 178, 179

Factory law—
Probable effect of enforcement of, on work-accidents, 71; Pennsylvania, non-compliance with, 67, 71

Fatalities—
In steel plants of the Pittsburgh District, July 1, 1906–June 30, 1907, classified by causes. (Table I) 64. See also *Work-accidents*

Federal Bureau of Labor—
Compilation of wages made by, 164; directed to investigate industrial conditions in the iron and steel industry, 136

McKees Rocks. See *Pressed Steel Car Company*

McKeesport—
Saloons in, 228, 229; socialism in, 216; United States Steel Corporation and brewing interests dominant force in, 229

McLaughlin, President, 78

Men and the Tools, The, 7–71

Metallurgy of Iron and Steel—
By Bradley Stoughton, 32

Mills visited in making study, 9

Milwaukee—
Sympathetic strike of men in, 134

"Mixer"—
Used in steel making, 39, 40

Moorhead, McCleane and Company—
And the eight-hour day, 93, 94

Morality and mentality—
Effect of exploitation under employers' control, 201, 202, 203, 204

Morgan, Senator, 108, 109

Mortality—
Causes of, among steel workers, 62; English iron and steel workers, percentage, 62

Muck mill—
Description of, 35. See also *Iron industry*

Munhall—
Socialism in, 216

National Amalgamated Association of Iron and Steel Workers—
Abuse of power by subordinate lodges of, 102, 103, 104, 123; advantage of, modified by existence of large companies, 192; agreement not to become members of, required of employes, 118; amicable period between Association and employers, 87, 88; and the closed shop, 90; and the contract labor system, 99, 100, 101, 103; and the keeping of con-

tracts, 104, 105; and various labor issues, 97; and wages, 90, 91, 97, 104; and the working-day, 91, 92, 93, 94, 95, 96, 97, 104, 168; Associated Brotherhood of Iron and Steel Heaters, Rollers and Roughers join, 85; attempt of, to force "heat" system in steel mills, 104; attempt to re-establish unionism by, 217; automatic processes not opposed by, 140; beginnings of, 84, 85, 86; cause of decline in membership and strength of, 101, 105, 106; collective bargaining carefully guarded by, 90; constitution, 99, 100; constitutional amendment passed in 1900, 134; definition of a "job" under contract labor system by, 100; demand general scale agreement from American Tin Plate Company, 133; development of, 86; difficulties confronted by, in securing better terms for men, 106; driven from important steel mills, 5; eight-hour day controversy, 93, 94, 95, 96, 97, 104, 179, 180; employers' hostility to, engendered by union tactics, 101, 102, 103, 123; employers' tactics used to weaken, 106; failure of, to abolish system of single payment for crew's work, 100, 101, 103; former officers of, 106, 107; fight lockout and discharge, 218; Frick's antagonism to, 124, 125, 126, 127, 131; Homestead strike of 1892 most disastrous in history of, 86; Homestead strike of 1892 not well controlled by, 101; internal dissension and secessions, 98, 99, 100, 101; internal policies of, 97, 98; Iron and Steel Roll Hands of the United States join, 85; iron workers suggest withdrawal of, from American Federation of Labor, 96; jealousy among different trades and races in, 97, 98, 99, 100, 101; lack of control by, 99, 100, 101, 103; legitimate demands of, contested, 102; limitation of membership of, 97, 101; lodges of, organized, 89, 109, 111, 114; membership of, 86, 101, 111, 132, 133, 136; no large steel mill in jurisdiction of, 135; officers of, 86, 87; organization formed, 5, 85, 86; outcome of Homestead strike of 1892 a blow to, 5, 88, 89, 132; panic of 1893 a blow to, 132; per cent of steel workers members of, in 1891,

future for, 44; Homestead furnaces, 44; Jones and Laughlin Company's, furnaces at Aliquippa, Pennsylvania, 44; plants making, 38; United States Steel Corporation, furnaces at Gary, Indiana, 44

Open-hearth steel workers—
Duties of "assistant superintendent," 43; duties and positions, 43, 44. See also general topics.

Operating days—
Definition of, 171, 172; number of, in blast furnace department, 173, 174; number of, in open-hearth furnace department, 172, 173; number of, in rolling mills, 172; number of, in Talbot open-hearth furnace department at Jones and Laughlin plant, 172, 173; number of, in week, 172

"Outlook," 229

Output. See *Tonnage*

Overstrain—
Caused by working conditions, 6

Overwork—
Workmen should not be required to injure health by, 76

Painter's Mill, Pittsburgh—
Increase in tonnage at, 182

Painter's Row, 193

Pennsylvania Bureau of Industrial Statistics, 82, 83, 85, 105

Pennsylvania Factory Law—
Non-compliance with, 67, 71

Pennsylvania law—
Liability under, 196

Penrose, Boies, 230, 231

Pension Fund—
United States Steel and Carnegie, Appen. VIII, 336

Pension system—
Age limit in, of American Steel and Wire Company, 184; Carnegie Relief Fund provides for, 195; developed by United States Steel Cor-

poration, 196, 197; effect of, on membership of unions, 198; mobility of labor force hampered by, 198; of American Steel and Wire Company, 194; of United States Steel Corporation, 194, 195; strengthens employers' control, 197, 198

Pig iron—
Method employed in manufacturing, 23, 24, 25. See also *Blast furnace*

Pinkertons. See *Homestead Strike of 1892*

Pittsburgh—
Proximity of bituminous coal fields, 22; transportation facilities of, 22

Pittsburgh Bessemer Steel Company, 89, 109

Pittsburgh Central Lodge Number 10—
Membership of, 83; organized in 1875, 83

"Pittsburgh Chronicle-Telegraph," 112, 113

"Pittsburgh Commercial Gazette," 77, 99, 109, 110, 115, 118, 121, 122

"Pittsburgh Dispatch," 184

Pittsburgh District, The, (Pittsburgh Survey volume), 193

"Pittsburgh Post," 125, 186

Pittsburgh puddlers strike, 1849–50, 77, 108; 1865, 79, 108

Pittsburgh steel workers—
Political activity of, increasing, 243

Plant, David A., 83, 84, 86

Pneumonia—
Result of conditions among steel workers, 62

Policies of the Amalgamated Association, 90–107

Political unrest—
Among workingmen, 235, 236

INDEX

Politics—
Activity of American Federation of Labor in, 243; common action in, by union labor, 243; employers' control in, 229, 230, 231; increasing activity of Pittsburgh steel workers in, 243; possibility of opposing present industrial conditions by, 242; relation of liquor situation to, 229; United States Steel Corporation dominant force in, 229, 230, 231

Popular sovereignty. See *Democracy*

Potter, Superintendent, 103

Pressed Steel Car Company—
Compensation for work-accidents, 196; strike at McKees Rocks in 1909, activity of Slavs in, 237, 238; grafting chief grievance in, 144

Prevention of Work-accidents. See *Work-accidents*

Profit sharing—
Repression result of, 213, 214; scheme of United States Steel Corporation obstacle to unionism, 207, 211, 212, 213; system of United States Steel Corporation, 207–213; system strengthens employers' control, 198. See also *Bonus system*

Profit-sharing and bonus fund—
United States Steel Corporation, Appen. V, 306

Promotion—
Line of, in steel industry, 141, 142; prospect of, for Slavs, 148, 149; typical worker's experience in, 13, 14, 15, 16, 18

Puddlers—
Health of, 37; single payment system of, for crew's work, 100, 101; and iron rollers, 32–37

Puddling furnace—
Conditions of labor at, 34; description of, 33, 34; description of "squeezer," 34

Race problem, 4, 9, 29, 30, 31, 140, 142–149

Races—
Effect on steel industry of grouping, 142; grouping of, favorable to employers' control, 148

Racial divisions—
In steel industry, 147, 148

Radicalism—
Among workingmen, 235

Rate per 100 tons —
On 84-inch mill at Homestead, (Table) 159

Recreation—
Steel workers', 226

Reed, Joe, 19, 20

Reheating furnaces, 49, 50

Relief plan—
Developed by United States Steel Corporation, 196, 197

Religious differences—
Among workers in steel industry, 147, 148

Rent—
Advance in cost of, 151; congestion result of high, 152; effect of high, on housing conditions, 151, 152

Repression, 207–220; effect on civic life, 6; result of profit-sharing scheme of United States Steel Corporation, 213, 214; safeguards employers' control, 206; self, and apprehension among employes of United States Steel Corporation, 215, 216, 217, 219; underlying labor policy, 6

Responsibility—
Assumed by employers, 6, 205, 206

Revolution—
Group of workingmen looking to, as a solution of the labor question, 236; possibility of opposing present industrial conditions by, 242, 243

"Right-to-quit" theory—
Present industrial conditions defended by, 238, 239, 240, 241

Risks—
Wages not adjusted to individual, 241

371

of 1892, 169; opposition to, 199; prevails in Pittsburgh steel mills, 170, 171; schedules for majority under employers' control, 199

Working day and the working week, The, 166–181

Working days—
Number of, for construction force, 174, 175; number of, in Bessemer department, 176; number of, in blast furnace department, 173, 174, 176; number of, in open-hearth furnace department, 172, 173, 176; number of, in rolling mills, 172, 176; number of, in Talbot open-hearth furnace department at Jones and Laughlin plant, 172, 173; number of, in week, 171, 172; summary of, a week in Allegheny County in 1907–08, 176; workers having eight a week, 175, 176; workers having seven a week, 173, 174, 175, 176, 180, 181, 199; workers having six a week, 175, 176, 181

"Workingman's Advocate," 78, 79, 82

Workingmen—
Attitude of employers toward independent activity on part of, 218; attitude of foreign, toward industrial conditions, 237, 238; attitude of, toward church, 224, 225; attitude of, toward industrial conditions, 232, 233, 234; bitterness among, engendered by unjust control, 232, 233; classification of, according to attitude toward industrial conditions, 233, 234, 235, 237; common feeling among, in a crisis, 232; effectual disfranchisement of, by United States Steel

Corporation, 229, 230, 231; group of financially successful, individually hopeful, 234; group of hopeless, 233, 234; group looking to revolution as a solution of the labor question, 236; group looking to socialism as a solution of labor problem, 235; group looking to unionism as a solution of labor problem, 235; group socially hopeful, 234, 235; influence of Slavic, on industrial conditions, 238; personal contact necessary to understand, 10; personal experience of typical, 12–20; political unrest among, 235, 236; protection of, legitimate purpose of unionism, 204, 205; radicalism among, 235; reasons for acquiescence of, to employers' control, 207–220; recreation of, 226; self-repression and apprehension among, under United States Steel Corporation, 215, 216, 217, 219; socialism among, 216, 232, 235; strategic position occupied by foreign, 237, 238

Workmen, The, 9–21

Wrought iron—
Definition of, 32; method employed in manufacture, 33, 34, 35, 36, 37

Wyandotte, Michigan—
Bessemer steel first made in United States at, 39

Youngstown, Ohio, strike—
Caused by disagreement between rollers and roughers, 99